HELPING STUDENTS
MAKE SENSE OF THE WORLD
USING
NEXT GENERATION SCIENCE AND ENGINEERING PRACTICES

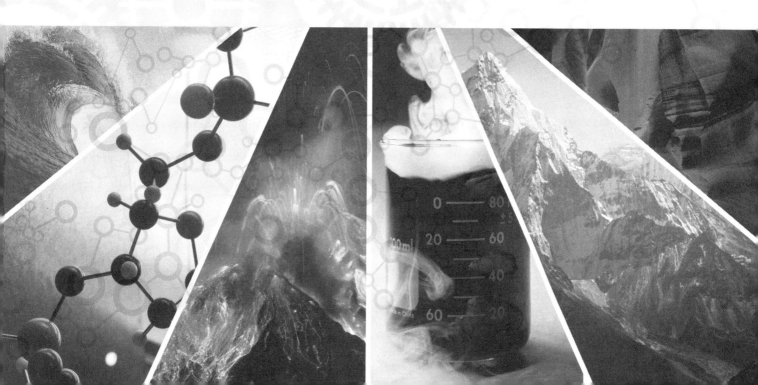

HELPING STUDENTS
MAKE SENSE OF THE WORLD
USING
NEXT GENERATION SCIENCE AND ENGINEERING PRACTICES

CHRISTINA V. SCHWARZ • CYNTHIA PASSMORE • BRIAN J. REISER

National Science Teachers Association

Arlington, Virginia

National Science Teachers Association

Claire Reinburg, Director
Wendy Rubin, Managing Editor
Rachel Ledbetter, Associate Editor
Amanda Van Beuren, Associate Editor
Donna Yudkin, Book Acquisitions Coordinator

ART AND DESIGN
Will Thomas Jr., Director
Himabindu Bichali, Graphic Designer, cover and
    interior design

PRINTING AND PRODUCTION
Catherine Lorrain, Director

NATIONAL SCIENCE TEACHERS ASSOCIATION
David L. Evans, Executive Director
David Beacom, Publisher

1840 Wilson Blvd., Arlington, VA 22201
www.nsta.org/store
For customer service inquiries, please call 800-277-5300.

Library of Congress Cataloging-in-Publication Data
Names: Schwarz, Christina. | Passmore, Cindy, 1969- | Reiser, Brian J., 1955-
Title: Helping students make sense of the world using next generation science and engineering practices /
    [edited] by Christina Schwarz, Cindy Passmore, and Brian Reiser.
Description: Arlington, VA : National Science Teachers Association, [2016] | Includes bibliographical references.
Identifiers: LCCN 2016034298 (print) | LCCN 2016045530 (ebook) | ISBN 9781938946042 (print) | ISBN
    9781941316955 (e-book)
Subjects: LCSH: Mathematics--Study and teaching. | Science--Study and teaching. | Logic, Symbolic and
    mathematical--Study and teaching. | Curriculum-based assessment. | Curriculum evaluation.
Classification: LCC QA9 .H41155 2016 (print) | LCC QA9 (ebook) | DDC 507.1/2--dc23
LC record available at *https://lccn.loc.gov/2016034298*

SUSTAINABLE FORESTRY INITIATIVE
Certified Sourcing
www.sfiprogram.org
SFI-00756

CONTENTS

ABOUT THE EDITORS
vii

CONTRIBUTORS
ix

SECTION 1

The Big Picture

Why Science and Engineering Practices, and
What Do They Mean for Us in the Classroom?

1

Chapter 1

Moving Beyond "Knowing About" Science to Making Sense of the World

CHRISTINA V. SCHWARZ, CYNTHIA PASSMORE, AND
BRIAN J. REISER

3

Chapter 2

The *Framework*, the *NGSS*, and the Practices of Science

JONATHAN OSBORNE AND HELEN QUINN

23

Chapter 3

Toward More Equitable Learning in Science

Expanding Relationships Among Students, Teachers, and
Science Practices

MEGAN BANG, BRYAN BROWN, ANGELA CALABRESE
BARTON, ANN ROSEBERY, AND BETH WARREN

33

Chapter 4

The Role of Practices in Scientific Literacy

BETH A. COVITT, JENNY M. DAUER, AND
CHARLES W. ANDERSON

59

SECTION 2

What Do the Practices Look Like in Classrooms?

Unpacking Each Practice

85

Chapter 5

Asking Questions

BRIAN J. REISER, LISA BRODY, MICHAEL NOVAK,
KEETRA TIPTON, AND LEEANN (SUTHERLAND) ADAMS

87

Chapter 6

Developing and Using Models

CYNTHIA PASSMORE, CHRISTINA V. SCHWARZ,
AND JOCELYN MANKOWSKI

109

Chapter 7

Planning and Carrying Out Investigations

MARK WINDSCHITL

135

Chapter 8

Analyzing and Interpreting Data

ANN E. RIVET AND JENNY INGBER

159

Chapter 9

Using Mathematics and Computational Thinking

MICHELLE HODA WILKERSON AND MICHELLE FENWICK

181

SECTION 2
(CONTINUED)

Chapter 10
Constructing Explanations
KATHERINE L. MCNEILL, LEEMA K. BERLAND, AND PAMELA PELLETIER

205

Chapter 11
Engaging in Argument From Evidence
LEEMA K. BERLAND, KATHERINE L. MCNEILL, PAMELA PELLETIER, AND JOSEPH KRAJCIK

229

Chapter 12
Obtaining, Evaluating, and Communicating Information
LEAH A. BRICKER, PHILIP BELL, KATIE VAN HORNE, AND TIFFANY L. CLARK

259

Chapter 13
Engineering Practices
CHRISTINE M. CUNNINGHAM

283

SECTION 3
How Can We Teach Using the Practices?
309

Chapter 14
From Recitation to Reasoning
Supporting Scientific and Engineering Practices Through Talk
SARAH MICHAELS AND CATHERINE O'CONNOR

311

Chapter 15
Putting It All Together
Two Examples of Teaching With the *NGSS*
MARK WINDSCHITL, CAROLYN COLLEY, AND BETHANY SJOBERG

337

Chapter 16
Summary and Conclusions
CHRISTINA V. SCHWARZ, CYNTHIA PASSMORE, AND BRIAN J. REISER

355

. . . .

INDEX
367

ABOUT THE EDITORS

Christina V. Schwarz is an associate professor of teacher education at Michigan State University (MSU). She teaches undergraduate and graduate courses in science and science education and has been the elementary science subject area leader for MSU's teacher preparation program for the past decade. She received her PhD in science, math, and technology education from the University of California at Berkeley and her undergraduate degree in Earth, atmospheric, and planetary science from the Massachusetts Institute of Technology. Her background includes conducting research in astronomy, designing curriculum materials for science learners, and working in classrooms with students and teachers. Her research primarily focuses on enabling students and teachers (preK–16) to understand and engage in scientific practices, particularly model-based scientific inquiry. She also works with beginning teachers to support and enhance their practices such as noticing and responding to scientific sense-making. She is the principal investigator for the National Science Foundation (NSF) grant Studying How Beginning Elementary Teachers Notice and Respond to Students' Scientific Sense-Making, the co-principal investigator for the NSF-funded project Supporting Scientific Practices in Elementary and Middle School Classrooms, and the principal investigator for the former Learning Progression for Scientific Modeling project. She is also co-principal investigator of the NSF-funded Head Start on Science preschool science project and was co-principal investigator for the Modeling Hydrological Systems in Elementary Science project. She has been an associate editor for the *Journal of Research in Science Teaching* and has published articles in journals such as *Cognition and Instruction, Journal of Research in Science Teaching, Journal for Science Teacher Education, Science and Children,* and *Science Education.* She has facilitated several National Science Teacher Association professional development webinars about the *Next Generation Science Standards* (*NGSS*) practices over the past few years.

Cynthia Passmore is a professor specializing in science education at the University of California, Davis, School of Education, where she instructs future science educators in the teacher education program. She completed her doctoral work at the University of Wisconsin, Madison. Before that, she was a high school science teacher in southern California and Wisconsin and served as a Peace Corps Volunteer in Malawi. Her research focuses on the role of models and modeling in student learning, curriculum design, and teacher professional development. She investigates model-based reasoning in a range of contexts and is particularly interested in understanding how the design of learning environments interacts with students' reasoning practices. In recent years, she has collaborated with groups of teachers to interpret and implement the vision of science education described in the *NGSS*. She has been the principal investigator of several large grants from the NSF and other agencies and foundations. Currently, she is working with collaborators to develop a year-long high school biology instructional resource package supporting the *NGSS*. She has coauthored papers on modeling in science education that have been published in journals such as the *International Journal of Science Education, Journal of Research in Science Teaching, School Science and Mathematics,* and *Science and Education.*

Brian J. Reiser is a professor of learning sciences at Northwestern University. He earned his PhD in cognitive science from Yale University. His current research examines how to make the scientific practices of argumentation, explanation, and modeling meaningful and effective for classroom teachers and students. He co-led the development of IQWST (Investigating and Questioning Our World Through Science and Technology), a three-year middle school curriculum that supports students in science practices to develop disciplinary core ideas. He is a member of the National Research Council's Board on Science Education. He has served on the National Research Council committees that authored *A Framework for K–12 Science Education* (which guided the development of the *NGSS*), *Developing Assessments for the Next Generation Science Standards,* and *Guide to Implementing the Next Generation Science Standards.* He has also worked with Achieve on tools to support implementation of the *NGSS*. He is currently collaborating with several state initiatives to design and provide professional development and create curriculum materials for K–12 teachers to support them in implementing in their classrooms the reforms in the *NGSS*.

CONTRIBUTORS

LeeAnn (Sutherland) Adams
University of Michigan
Ann Arbor, Michigan

Charles W. Anderson
Michigan State University
East Lansing, Michigan

Megan Bang
University of Washington
Seattle, Washington

Angela Calabrese Barton
Michigan State University
East Lansing, Michigan

Philip Bell
University of Washington
Seattle, Washington

Leema K. Berland
University of Wisconsin
Madison, Wisconsin

Leah A. Bricker
University of Michigan
Ann Arbor, Michigan

Lisa Brody
Park View School
Morton Grove, Illinois

Bryan Brown
Stanford University
Stanford, California

Tiffany L. Clark
University of Colorado Boulder
Boulder, Colorado

Carolyn Colley
University of Washington
Seattle, Washington

Beth A. Covitt
University of Montana
Missoula, Montana

Christine M. Cunningham
Museum of Science
Boston, Massachusetts

Jenny M. Dauer
University of Nebraska
Lincoln, Nebraska

Michelle Fenwick
Cajon Valley Union School District
El Cajon, California

Jenny Ingber
Bank Street College of Education
New York, New York

Joseph Krajcik
Michigan State University
East Lansing, Michigan

Jocelyn Mankowski
Okemos Public Schools
Okemos, Michigan

CONTRIBUTORS

Katherine L. McNeill
Boston College
Chestnut Hill, Massachusetts

Sarah Michaels
Clark University
Worcester, Massachusetts

Michael Novak
Park View School
Morton Grove, Illinois

Catherine O'Connor
Boston University
Boston, Massachusetts

Jonathan Osborne
Stanford University
Stanford, California

Cynthia Passmore
University of California, Davis
Davis, California

Pamela Pelletier
Boston Public Schools
Boston, Massachusetts

Helen Quinn
SLAC National Accelerator Laboratory
Menlo Park, California

Brian J. Reiser
Northwestern University
Evanston, Illinois

Ann E. Rivet
Teachers College Columbia University
New York, New York

Ann Rosebery
TERC
Cambridge, Massachusetts

Christina V. Schwarz
Michigan State University
East Lansing, Michigan

Bethany Sjoberg
Highline School District
Burien, Washington

Keetra Tipton
Park View School
Morton Grove, Illinois

Katie Van Horne
University of Colorado Boulder
Boulder, Colorado

Beth Warren
TERC
Cambridge, Massachusetts

Michelle Hoda Wilkerson
University of California, Berkeley
Berkeley, California

Mark Windschitl
University of Washington
Seattle, Washington

SECTION 1

THE BIG PICTURE

Why Science and Engineering Practices,
and What Do They Mean for Us in the Classroom?

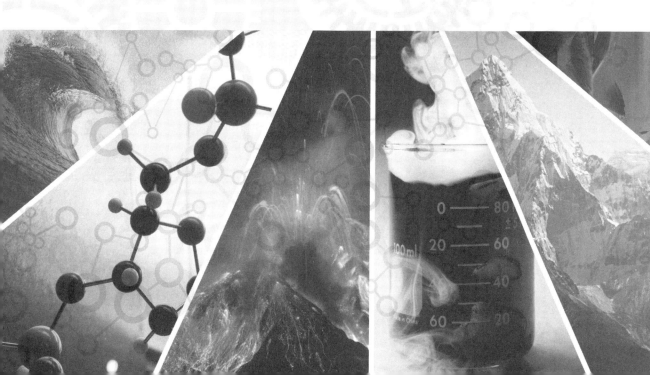

1

MOVING BEYOND "KNOWING ABOUT" SCIENCE TO MAKING SENSE OF THE WORLD

CHRISTINA V. SCHWARZ, CYNTHIA PASSMORE, AND BRIAN J. REISER

An Introduction to Scientific and Engineering Practices

Sarah is a conscientious teacher. She has been teaching science to middle school students for eight years. During that time, she's gone from being a tentative novice teacher to being a competent veteran. Throughout her career, she's been alternatively frustrated and pleased with her teaching. Sometimes things seem to be going well, and other times she feels she should be able to get more from her students; she wants them to think more deeply and wishes that she had more "Aha!" moments in her class. Sarah uses the district-wide pacing guide and follows the textbook that was adopted by her school several years ago. Of course, she supplements the district materials with things she's found online, gotten from teaching colleagues, and picked up at conferences, but for the most part, she does many of the same activities from one year to the next. Recently, she has begun to hear about changes that may be coming to the science standards in her state. She is at once excited and intimidated by the big changes in science education. The more she hears about these reforms, the more questions she has about what this means for her as a teacher of science.

As Sarah looks over *A Framework for K–12 Science Education* (*Framework*; NRC 2012) and the *Next Generation Science Standards* (*NGSS*; NGSS Lead States 2013) documents, she has a lot of specific questions about what she is reading. She wonders:

- "What is this focus on practices all about?"

- "Is this just a new name for inquiry?"

- "How should my class look different if I am "doing" the *NGSS*?"

- "If I'm pretty happy with what I've been doing, why would I want to take this on?"

In another school district, Carlos has been teaching third and fourth grades for many years and loves working with his students. He tells great stories, and the students enjoy doing hands-on activities, such as exploring different rocks and taking field trips to the local children's garden. Carlos's state has recently adopted the *NGSS*, and he is wondering what these new standards mean for him:

- "What will I have to do differently?"

- "How is this different from the hands-on inquiry I do now?"

- "How will I have time for the *NGSS?* There is already so much to cover with the literacy and math curricula."

Perhaps you can see yourself in Sarah's or Carlos's situation. You may have some of the same questions about the goals of this reform and what it means for you as a teacher of science. This is an exciting time in science education. We have many opportunities before us to make significant and lasting change in the ways we teach science at the K–12 level. But with major change comes some anxiety. We hope this book can begin to answer some of your questions about the reforms found in the *Framework* and the *NGSS*. Even if your state is not adopting the *NGSS*, you and your colleagues can take advantage of the research-based recommendations in the *Framework* for making science learning more meaningful and effective for all students.

The title of this book expresses a major goal of the current science education reform effort: that students make sense of the natural and designed world by engaging in science and engineering practices. To some educators, this may seem like nothing new. For many years, it has been a goal of science reforms to move from students as passive recipients of knowledge to classrooms in which students are active participants in generating knowledge. Since the 1990s, attempts to incorporate inquiry into science classrooms have been a step forward in efforts to accomplish this. Yet, while these efforts have made some inroads, studies of today's U.S. classrooms and curriculum materials show that many of our classrooms do *not* involve students in very sophisticated versions of scientific practice (Banilower et al. 2013). Instead, in many classrooms, students are primarily studying and recounting factual information and definitions provided by textbooks and teachers and reinforced through hands-on activities that may not be linked to advancing students' conceptual ideas and practices.

As a science education community, let's embrace an opportunity to do more. The reform agenda articulated in the *Framework* and the *NGSS* provides a vision and way forward toward making science education inspiring and meaningful. While the *Framework* and standards do not tell us exactly *how* we should teach, they do provide clear direction for what we should be aiming for in our science instruction. They help us see that there are productive ways to integrate the processes of science with the learning of science and help clarify that we should be pushing for outcomes related to what students should be able to do with the knowledge they have developed over time. The *Framework* states that

> *K–12 science and engineering education should focus on a limited number of disciplinary core ideas and crosscutting concepts, be designed so that students continually build on and revise their knowledge and abilities over multiple years, and support the integration of such knowledge and abilities with the practices needed to engage in scientific inquiry and engineering design. (p. 2)*

Even though some of the themes in the *Framework* and the *NGSS* around engaging students in science and engineering may sound familiar, the documents offer new ways to talk about and organize instruction to meet these goals. In this book, we concentrate on one of the key innovations of the *Framework*: a focus on the practices of science and engineering. The editors and contributors to this book have a great deal of experience in working on how to focus our science classrooms on making sense of the world through engaging in the practices of science and engineering. The contributors include science education researchers and teachers who have explored these ideas in their own classrooms. We, along with many other science educators and researchers, have been collectively working on these problems for years preceding the publication of the *Framework* and the *NGSS*. The work of many of the authors within this volume contributed to the vision put forth in the *Framework*. What you read about in these pages are not ivory tower, experimental ideas or the latest fad that some hope will make all the difference. Instead, these are ideas that have been tested and refined in real science classrooms over many years. This book represents a true collaboration between practicing teachers, those in science education, and learning sciences researchers.

From Scientific Inquiry to Practices

The emphasis on science and engineering practices attempts to build on prior reforms and take advantage of what research has revealed about the successes and limitations of inquiry classrooms. We like to think of the focus on practices as a kind of Inquiry 2.0—not a replacement for inquiry but rather a second wave that articulates more clearly what successful inquiry looks like when it results in building scientific knowledge. The configuration of inquiry classrooms typically allows students to explore the relationship between two variables (e.g., how the mass of a toy car affect its velocity going down a ramp), but often this empirical exploration is not taking place in an ongoing process of questioning, developing, and refining explanatory knowledge about the world. Testing and confirming or disconfirming hypotheses is part of science, but these actions become meaningful by being a part of the broader work of building explanatory models and theories.

This attempt to take our ideas of inquiry in science beyond designing investigations and testing hypotheses has led to the fuller articulation of inquiry as the scientific and engineering practices that enable us to investigate and make sense of phenomena in the world by building and applying explanatory models, and by designing solutions for problems. Making sense of the world, or *sense-making* for short, is the fundamental goal of science and should be at the core of what happens in science classrooms.

What is involved in this sense-making? Sense-making, as we are using it here, is the conceptual process in which a learner actively engages with the natural or designed world; wonders about it; and develops, tests, and refines ideas with peers and the teacher. Sense-making is the proactive engagement in understanding the world by generating, using, and extending scientific knowledge within communities. In other words, sense-making is about actively trying to figure out the way the world works (for scientific questions) and exploring how to create or alter things to achieve design goals (for engineering questions).

When student sense-making is the focus of the classroom goals and purposes, it becomes critical to use science and engineering practices to make sense of the world. Science and engineering practices are the way we build, test, refine, and use knowledge either to investigate questions or to solve problems. As defined in the *Framework*, the science and engineering practices are the different parts of the sense-making process. Here are the eight practices identified in the *Framework* and used in the *NGSS:*

1. Asking questions (for science) and defining problems (for engineering)
2. Developing and using models
3. Planning and carrying out investigations
4. Analyzing and interpreting data
5. Using mathematics and computational thinking
6. Constructing explanations (for science) and designing solutions (for engineering)
7. Engaging in argument from evidence
8. Obtaining, evaluating, and communicating information

Now that we have listed these practices, we can be a little more specific about how they are designed to flesh out scientific inquiry. The list includes some familiar ideas that are often present in classes attempting inquiry. We usually think of Planning and

Carrying Out Investigations and Analyzing and Interpreting Data as ways to involve students in an inquiry investigation. But the *NGSS* practices move beyond these two practices to include others such as Constructing Explanations (practice 6). As we will see later (in Chapter 10, p. 205), using the practice of explanation requires more than what sometimes happens with hypothesis testing, in which students figure out how two variables are related. The goal of Constructing Explanations is to be able to say *why* something happens. In the process of figuring out why something in the world happens the way it does, students will often have different ideas and will need to evaluate one another's ideas against evidence (practice 7). As students reach consensus through this argumentation, they represent their general account for why something happens as a general model (practice 2). And, of course, this should all be sparked in the classroom from explanatory questions (practice 1) that arise from an attempt to make sense of some data or patterns in the world. We will get to specifics about these practices and consider the engineering aspects in Section 2 of this book. For now, notice that the mix of these practices leads students to develop explanations and models and interact with one another to compare ideas and reach a consensus.

One critical feature of a sense-making classroom is that students are genuinely engaged in science and engineering practices. An observer should be able to walk into a science class on any day and ask a student, "What are you trying to figure out right now?" The intellectual aim of any work in the science class should be clear to everyone. Rather than stating, "We are learning about photosynthesis or plate tectonics," students should be able to say (and believe!), "We're trying to figure out how the tiny seed becomes this huge oak tree" or "We're trying to better understand why volcanoes and earthquakes happen more often in some parts of the world." These examples illustrate how the students are figuring out the world and illustrate a sense-making goal in the classroom.

In addition to these sense-making goals, another critical aspect of engaging successfully in science and engineering practices is related to the classroom. These practices create a need for designing our classrooms as places in which students are working together to share ideas, evaluate competing ideas, critique one another's ideas, and reach consensus as a classroom community. This shift to practices highlights the importance of working with one another to build and debate knowledge, adding social interaction and classroom discourse to what students need to learn as they participate in scientific sense-making. In this way, the practices extend prior visions of inquiry to define processes for building and refining scientific knowledge as a community.

Exploring the Difference in Vision in Two Classroom Cases

One way to begin exploring the implications of a focus on student sense-making with practices is to examine two contrasting learning environments. Below we explore vignettes of two science classrooms. Both vignettes involve middle school students learning about the phases of the Moon, but they differ in some important respects. As you read these vignettes, look for several critical parts of the science learning environment. Ask yourself the following questions:

- Where do the questions come from?

- Who is involved in figuring out how to investigate the question?

- How do students get to an explanation?

- What is the role of agreement, disagreement, and consensus?

Case 1: Moon Phases in Ms. Sheridan's Class

The students come into Ms. Sheridan's class and find that the topic for the day is Moon phases. The day before this class, students had reviewed the order of the planets from the Sun. They had also made a chart of key characteristics of each planet.

After she introduces the topic of the day, Ms. Sheridan asks the students to raise their hands and when called on tell the class one thing they know about the Moon. Students offer ideas such as "I know we've sent rockets to the Moon" and "Isn't the Moon involved in tides?"

After three or four students have shared, Ms. Sheridan asks them if they have ever noticed that the Moon has different shapes at different times. She explains that the different shapes are called the "phases of the Moon" and puts up a list naming eight phases of the Moon. Next, she explains that today they are going to learn why the Moon's shape appears to change. She starts with the main facts about Moon phases: The phases occur in a cycle. The cycle is one revolution of the Moon around the Earth, about 28 days. She explains that the Sun is relatively far away from the Earth and the Moon. She shows the class how light from the Sun falls on the Moon, always lighting up exactly half of it.

Then she explains that the part of the lit Moon you can see varies depending on where the Moon is in its orbit around the Earth. She shows the class a diagram on the smart board, walks them through the different steps in the Moon's orbit, and describes the phase that can be seen at that point in the orbit, along with telling students the name of each Moon phase that she expects them to learn.

Ms. Sheridan then tells the class that they can now try it out for themselves to see each phase of the Moon. She divides the class into eight groups and gives each group a small Styrofoam ball to represent the Moon and a larger blue ball to represent the Earth. Each group also gets a flashlight to represent the shining Sun. Ms. Sheridan gives each group one of the eight phases to prepare to demonstrate. Each group gets the name of a phase and a diagram showing the positions of the Moon, Earth, and Sun for that phase. The teacher gives each group five minutes to match the position of the Moon (the small Styrofoam ball), the Sun (flashlight), and the Earth (larger blue ball) to the diagram for its phase. She turns out the classroom lights, and students excitedly position the Moon and Sun to match their diagrams.

Then, each group shows the rest of the class its model of the positions of the Sun, Earth, and Moon for its phase. For homework, Ms. Sheridan asks students to make eight flashcards with a picture of a Moon phase on one side of the card and the name of that phase on the other. She lets them know that they will have a quiz the following day on this material and on the planets they learned about the previous day.

Ms. Sheridan has shared this lesson with some of her colleagues. They all like how hands-on the lesson is. They really like having students demonstrate the phases with a flashlight and Styrofoam balls and feel that this activity helps make the ideas more concrete and understandable to students. One of her colleagues wonders whether using a flashlight and Styrofoam ball to represent the Sun and Moon is what the *NGSS* means by Developing and Using Models.

There is much to like in Ms. Sheridan's lesson. Let's come back to it after we look at how Ms. Lee's classroom works on similar ideas.

Case 2: Moon Phases in Ms. Lee's Class

The students in Ms. Lee's class have been working on near-Earth astronomy for a few weeks. They have been pursuing the overarching question "Why do the Sun, Moon, and stars move in our sky and change in appearance over time?" Recently, the students have been investigating the appearance of the Moon. They wonder why it is visible in the sky at different times of day and appears some nights and not others. For over a month they have been spending a few minutes each day recording the appearance of the Moon on that day in a data table in their notebooks. As the Moon goes through the cycle of phases, the students learn the technical name of each phase. Prior to this lesson, they used moonrise time data to figure out that the Moon orbits the Earth in the same direction as the Earth spins, and it takes about a month to complete one orbit.

Ms. Lee begins class on this day with a discussion to help the students summarize what they have figured out so far and what questions remain about their observations. Ms. Lee draws their attention to the main question about the Moon that started them off on their investigation: "Why does the Moon change shape during the month?" The students have collected data about the Moon's appearance with the observations made throughout the month. They know that it takes the Moon 28 days to complete a cycle as it orbits the Earth, but they still haven't figured out why the shape changes during that time.

Based on what they have discovered so far, the class refines its original question to "Why does the appearance of the Moon change as it orbits the Earth?" The students brainstorm their initial ideas about why the apparent shape of the Moon might change, using what they have figured out about the orbit of the Moon around the Earth as a starting point. In the discussion, Ms. Lee raises the question of how it is even possible to see the Moon from Earth. Students draw on what they know about light sources and how light allows us to see and generally agree that it must be the light from the Sun reflecting off the Moon that makes part of the Moon visible from the Earth (since the Moon is not a light source). But students are not in agreement about why this would change as the Moon revolves around the Earth.

Ms. Lee suggests they try to picture what is happening as the Moon goes around the Earth and recommends they use physical props to see for themselves why the shape might appear to change. Students like the idea and are eager to see what would happen to light from the Sun as the Moon orbits the Earth. As in earlier modeling activities in their classroom, Ms. Lee has the class agree on the question the model needs to explain and then brainstorm what needs to be represented in the model. In discussion, students decide they need to represent the Earth, the Moon, and the Sun. Ms. Lee gives each group of students a Styrofoam ball and says that they can use the ball to represent the Moon. She suggests using a lamp she has without the shade to represent the Sun and places it in the center of the room so all the kids can use its light in their investigation (she also covers the windows so that the lamp "Sun" is the only light in the room). Since the goal of the activity is to see what the Moon looks like from Earth, Ms. Lee helps the students come up with the idea of using the ball and their own bodies to simulate the Moon's orbit around Earth (recalling what they had already figured out about that from the moonrise times). Before they begin, Ms. Lee asks students to state what they are trying to figure out and how they will use the props to test their ideas. The students agree that they need to figure out what parts of the Moon they can see in each part of the orbit.

The students talk actively as they engage and make notes about what they can see from each position. Once they have collected all their evidence and reported on it, the students are ready to try explaining the phenomenon. Ms. Lee asks them to discuss in their groups and draw a representation on their poster paper that shows why the Moon's appearance changes over the course of the month. Once each group has finished, she has the students put up their diagrams around the room. They do a gallery walk so they can all see what the other groups have created. Then the students spend time in their groups talking about what they have seen, trying to identify where they have agreed or disagreed with other groups and what makes for a good representation. As a whole class they then discuss the differences among the various explanations and how they have represented them. The teacher guides a discussion to help the students decide on a consensus explanation and a way to represent that explanation in a diagram. Ms. Lee tells students that their homework for the day is to write a short paragraph that they could use to explain to a friend from a different class why we see phases of the Moon from Earth. The next day in class they apply their ideas by finding pictures in children's books that should be drawn differently based on their knowledge of the Moon and its phases.

Comparing the Cases

There are some similarities between these classrooms, as well as a number of important differences. In both classrooms, students are engaged in hands-on science using physical materials and active learning strategies. In both classrooms, they are trying to generate an explanation about why the shape of the Moon appears to change. In both classrooms, students are challenged to think through the ideas. But there is an important difference in the work the teachers and students are doing in these two classrooms and in how that work is divided. We could characterize Ms. Sheridan's classroom as one in which students are *learning about* lunar phases, while Ms. Lee's classroom is one in which students are *figuring out* lunar phases.

In Ms. Sheridan's class, her job is to provide the explanation, and the students' job is to work with the explanation and try to learn it. The hands-on activities allow students to see and understand the teacher's explanation. The role of the students is to follow the directions, do the activity, try to apply the ideas provided by the teacher, and to learn material for assessments. Although students are working hard to understand the explanation provided by the teacher, it is Ms. Sheridan who has the authority and has done the "heavy lifting" of building the knowledge, not the students. And while the explanation was stated as the goal, the teacher's assessment in fact ended up focusing mostly on the names of the phases and their order rather than assessing whether students could use that explanation and reason with it.

In contrast, Ms. Lee's lesson engages students in the science and engineering practices that are targeted in the *NGSS*. Students are positioned as the ones doing the figuring out, though they are guided by the teacher and given appropriate props. If you were to walk over to a group of students during the activity, you could ask them, "What are you trying to figure out?" and they would say something such as "We know that the Moon is lit up by the Sun, but we are trying to figure out why the sunlit part of the Moon changes in shape as it goes around the Earth." They are manipulating the objects or analyzing data not because they are simply following directions but because they are trying to figure out and construct an explanation in response to a question. Ms. Lee didn't just give them the challenge and let them "discover," "explore," or "do inquiry." She gave them a lot of probing questions and guidance to get them to realize what needed to be investigated and helped them converge on a good starting point. But throughout, students were taking on the responsibility of making sense of phenomena, developing explanations, comparing them as a class, and reaching a consensus. Ms. Lee's students were *investigating* why the Moon appears to change shape. They were engaged in science practices such as questioning, analyzing data, and modeling to make sense of the phenomenon. The students and their ideas are at the center in this classroom. (See Barton 2001 and *http://ncisla.wceruw.org/muse/Earth-Moon-sun/index.html* for more information on the instructional sequence described here.)

To go a bit deeper into the differences between these two lessons, we will ask a series of questions about the sense-making process that help us see how the practices played out in these classrooms.

Where Do the Questions Come From?

In both cases, students are working on a similar idea: The apparent shape of the Moon changes over time. But in Ms. Sheridan's class, the question originally came from the teacher. She told the students they were going to learn about the phases of the Moon, introducing it as the next topic in their unit. Meanwhile, in Ms. Lee's classroom the question emerged from the students' own observations. As part of a larger investigation of why things change in the sky, they noticed patterns in the shapes of the Moon and uncovered the fact that these occur in cycles. In both cases, "lunar phases" is the name of the scientific idea they are investigating, but in Ms. Lee's classroom the question was identified and phrased in terms of the phenomena they experienced: Why does the shape of the Moon change over time? Students were involved in co-constructing this question with the teacher. In Ms. Sheridan's class, a question was not at the center of their work at all. Although Ms. Sheridan made an attempt to motivate the work on Moon phases by pointing out that the shape of the Moon changes during the month, the students did not frame their exploration of Moon phases in terms of a question. (You will read more about the importance of the Asking Questions practice in Chapter 5, p. 87.)

Who Is Involved in Figuring Out How to Investigate the Question?

In both cases, students were exploring how sunlight falls on the Moon and how that influenced what could be seen from Earth. Notice, however, that in Ms. Sheridan's class, the design of the investigation came directly from the teacher, and it wasn't really an investigation at all. The students were given directions about how to demonstrate something they had already been shown. In contrast, in Ms. Lee's classroom, the activity was co-constructed. Certainly, the teacher played a critical role, but the students were also involved in thinking through how they would investigate their question and why particular aspects of the setup might relate to their ongoing work. The teacher proposed using physical props to explore light falling on the Moon but asked the students which objects they would need to represent in the model. After agreeing with the students on what the model needed to contain and providing the objects they needed, Ms. Lee asked the class how it would manipulate the objects to explore the question. In both classrooms, the students ended up doing similar activities—interacting with balls and light sources—but in Ms. Lee's classroom, the students were part of thinking through the logic of what they were doing. (You will read more about the Planning and Carrying Out Investigations practice in Chapter 7.)

How Do Students Get to an Explanation?

This is perhaps the biggest difference between our two scenarios. In Ms. Sheridan's classroom, the teacher walked the students through the explanation up front. She then gave them the opportunity to see the ideas in action by exploring the different lunar phases. As the students worked with the props, they attempted to match the diagrams they had been given. They already knew that they should be seeing different amounts of the Moon's illuminated surface. Doing the activity helped them visualize that idea and see that it worked, but they already knew that what they were doing was correct. In contrast, in Ms. Lee's classroom the students were more involved in building and using the explanation. They didn't start from scratch, of course. Ms. Lee helped the class arrive at a good starting point so that all students were starting their investigation constrained by the ideas that what we see is sunlight reflecting off the Moon and reaching the Earth. But, it was up to the students to figure out why different positions in the orbit of the Moon around the Earth led to the different apparent shapes and why a host of other possible explanations (such as that the Moon phases are caused by a shadow from the Earth) would be inaccurate. In Ms. Sheridan's classroom, students had to understand and replicate the teacher's explanation; in Ms. Lee's classroom, students were guided by the teacher in constructing that explanation. (You will read more about the Developing and Using Models and Constructing Explanations practices in Chapters 6 and 10, respectively.)

What Are the Roles of Agreement, Disagreement, and Consensus?

In Ms. Sheridan's classroom, the teacher was the authority, providing the explanation. The students' job was to try to understand and use it. In Ms. Lee's classroom, the authority was more distributed. In their groups, students grappled with trying to explain why the shape of the Moon changed. In the gallery walk, they shared their group's ideas and compared them with other groups' ideas. In the discussion, they figured out where all the groups agreed, identified disagreements, and talked through the disagreements to reach a class consensus about the phenomenon. The decision for the final model involved all the students, guided by the teacher. (You will read more about Engaging in Argument From Evidence in Chapter 11.)

Coordinating Practices to Achieve Sense-Making

Now that we have seen an example of a class engaged in using science practices to make sense of scientific phenomena, we turn toward thinking about how this happens in general and how you can think about using practices to help your students make sense of the world.

How do we use the science and engineering practices to work toward sense-making? It may be tempting to think of the practices as a sequence, perhaps like "the scientific method" or as an instructional sequence like the 5Es. As we will see in Section 2 of this book, there are many different paths to take through the practices, depending on the specific investigation or design problem. And practices may need to be brought in at multiple points as students build and refine an explanation, model, or design. But regardless of the path, there are four guiding questions that can help organize the work of the practices as part of sense-making.

1. WHAT ARE WE TRYING TO FIGURE OUT?

What is the observable phenomenon, object, or system we are trying to figure out or the problem we are trying to define? Investigations and engineering problems are built around phenomena and the questions connected with them. Engaging in practices means that we are always trying to figure something out or solve a problem connected with some phenomenon in the world rather than defining terminology (such as "What is gravity/energy/an ecosystem?"). While the word *phenomenon* is not explicitly part of the names of any of the eight practices, phenomena are central to what the practices are all about. One goal of the *NGSS* is connecting the science that students learn with the application of these ideas in the world. What can we explain with this idea? What problems do these ideas help us understand and solve? When engaging in practices, there must be something about the world we are trying to figure out. In other words, there is some event (such as an earthquake, a storm, movement of objects in a collision, change of materials in a chemical reaction) or a pattern (resemblances of offspring to prior generations, changes in atmospheric conditions before a storm, changing shapes of the Moon) that we are trying to figure out or problems connected with events or patterns that we are trying to understand to design a solution (e.g., early warning system for tsunamis, less polluting sources of energy). In science, once we recognize the phenomenon we need to ask about the what, how, and why. For engineering, once we have a problem we ask what factors are influencing this problem and how we can intervene to alter these factors.

The most obvious practice involved in making sense of the world is Asking Questions and Defining Problems. But it's important to stress that sense-making is an incremental process. Questions will arise not only in the beginning of an investigation or design but also throughout the process of sense-making. In our attempts to explain phenomena, we may uncover new questions or realize that our models work for some parts of the phenomenon but not others. We may end up in the Asking Questions and Defining Problems practice as we are in the midst of trying to design solutions, construct explanations, or develop models, as well as when we are starting an investigation or design. Furthermore, we may need to compare alternative questions or framing of the design problem in principled ways, drawing on the practice of argumentation. So part of refining what we are trying to figure out needs to build on the next three questions.

2. HOW WILL WE FIGURE IT OUT?

How will we develop, explore, and test the model and associated explanation or solution? When we have phenomena that motivate questions to investigate and problems to address, another collection of practices comes into play to make progress on the work: Planning and Carrying Out Investigations. Typically, this may also involve clarifying what is known to inform the investigation or design, which draws on the practice of Obtaining and Evaluating Information. Again, because of the incremental nature of sense-making, constructing explanations and developing solutions will be ongoing, perhaps with initial ideas informing the planning of subsequent investigations or design explorations. Argumentation may be needed to make principled decisions between competing investigation plans and design ideas.

3. HOW DO WE KEEP TRACK OF WHAT WE ARE FIGURING OUT?

Making sense of what we are seeing goes hand in hand with planning and conducting the investigation or design work. Key questions related to this aspect of sense-making include "What happened?," "Is this what we expected?," "What worked?," "What didn't work?," and, most important, "*Why* did this happen the way that it did?" Rather than viewing investigation or design as a sequential process, proceeding stepwise from questioning to planning to solution, it is often more accurate and productive to view sense-making as incrementally building understanding or solutions, engaging in cycles of questioning, gathering data through investigations or tests of part of a design, making sense by developing or revising models, constructing explanations or solutions, and then evaluating progress and determining where to go next. For this to be effective, we have to have a way to keep track of what we are figuring out along the way. There are many effective strategies for this kind of work (see Windschitl and Thompson 2013 for a nice summary of some tools). The practices central here are Analyzing Data and Using Mathematics and Computational Thinking, which feed into the processes of Developing and Using Models, Constructing Explanations and Designing Solutions, and Obtaining, Evaluating, and Communicating Information. Argumentation is especially important in a classroom since there are often many different emerging student ideas, which the class will need to compare, evaluate, and eventually reach consensus about.

4. HOW DOES IT ALL FIT TOGETHER? WHAT DOES IT MEAN?

How does what we have figured out answer the questions or solve the problems we identified? How do we decide? Ultimately, our goal is to develop deep understanding of the disciplinary core ideas that help us account for how the world works the way it does. We have to continually check our developing ideas against the phenomena that inspired our work to begin with. Two practices that are central in this process are Developing and Using Models and Constructing Explanations and Designing Solutions. In other words, we have to see if what we have figured out so far is helpful in answering the questions that drove us at the beginning of our inquiry. This cycle of wondering, working to figure out, and checking whether our emerging ideas are actually useful to satisfy our initial wondering is at the core of deep engagement in the practices. As has been necessary throughout the process, we also need to engage in principled evaluation of competing ideas through argumentation and reaching consensus as well as the processes of communicating information.

As this quick overview has shown, scientific and engineering practices need to be used together to work toward making sense of the world. This idea is summarized in Figure 1.1 (p. 18).

We saw a number of these connections in the scenario from Ms. Lee's classroom. In her scenario, we saw the practice of Asking Questions as students brainstormed questions about why objects appear to move in the sky. The students conducted an investigation of rising and setting times for the Moon, analyzed data (their own and secondary data), and constructed an initial model that included the explanatory idea that the Moon orbits the Earth. This led to another question about why the shape changes in patterns, which then led to the main investigation using a physical depiction of the Moon, Sun, and Earth system. Students worked together to construct an explanatory model of why the Moon's shape changes, shared their models, and engaged in argumentation from evidence to reach consensus on a shared explanation.

The idea that practices work together for making sense of the world is one of the most important themes in this book. The goals of the *Framework* and the *NGSS* will not be met if lessons are taught by focusing on one practice at a time. The practices work with one another to help us understand how and why the world works and for engineering how to design solutions to problems. Focusing on the larger investigation context

Figure 1.1
Sense-making and the science practices

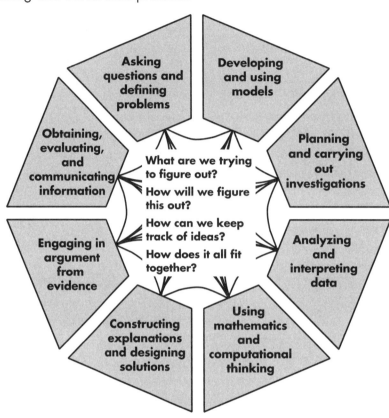

The science and engineering practices work together to achieve four parts of sense-making. This diagram illustrates how the practices always operate in conjunction with each other.

leads to authentic and purposeful reasoning and connected practices. Looking back at our questions informing the sense-making process, we can see how thoughtful work can happen in many places: during initial attempts to understand phenomena, during efforts to make sense of patterns in empirically related phenomena and related scientific theories, and in applying the revised theories and models to explain and predict other phenomena in the world.

The Structure of This Book

We compiled this book to help teachers of science grasp three sets of questions related to the *NGSS* practices, and we suggest that you use the question that each section asks to guide you as you read.

- **Section 1: What is the vision put forth in the *Framework* and the *NGSS*, and how will engaging students in science and engineering practices help us improve our science classrooms?** The chapters in Section 1, including this one, take a big-picture view and show how a focus on practices has the potential to reshape our classrooms. This chapter introduces the book and explores the fundamental shifts implied by engaging students in science and engineering practices. Chapter 2, written by two of the authors of the *Framework,* explicates the rationale for focusing on science and engineering practices and traces the development of this idea from earlier notions of inquiry in science. Chapter 3 examines some important questions about equity in the science classroom and explores how a focus on practices is in line with goals we have to make science accessible, intelligible, and meaningful for all learners. Chapter 4 takes up the question of our broader societal goals for science literacy and explains the connections between these goals and the focus on engaging students in science and engineering practices.

- **Section 2: What are the practices, and what does it look like to engage students in the practices in the classroom?** Chapters 5–12 each take on one of the practices and provide rich descriptions and rationales for each as well as detailed accounts of what is involved in engaging students in them. Chapter 13 discusses aspects of the eight practices that focus on engineering design. Although Chapters 5–12 focus on a single practice, an important section in each chapter highlights the connections between and among the practices.

- **Section 3: How do I get started? What are some ways to begin?** The individual practices chapters in Section 2 contain some ideas about how to begin to involving students in the practices. Building on this, Section 3 provides some guidance for planning *NGSS*-aligned instruction and for creating classroom discourse environments that create opportunities for students to engage in the practices. The concluding chapter highlights some key ways to get started.

This book is intended to help teachers of science develop a strong understanding of what the practices strand of the *Framework* and the *NGSS* is all about. Engaging students in practices helps motivate them, builds their curiosity, helps them understand how science is connected with their lives, and is more consistent with how science and engineering are practiced in the real world.

Conclusion

Despite past reforms and our best intentions as educators, there are many ways in which our typical science instruction continues to send the message to students that all they need to do is know some information, use the right vocabulary, and follow the right procedures to learn science. But, this is not what science learning should be about. People do need to know some information to make sense of the world, but simply learning a set of facts will not guarantee that one will come to understand or make sense of anything. Likewise, engaging students in a hands-on discovery with little conceptual guidance or grounding will not lead students to robust and accurate understanding of the science ideas because the data don't speak for themselves about what is the most scientifically accurate and explanatory idea.

The emphasis on science and engineering practices in the *NGSS* attempts to continue key themes from past efforts to reform science classrooms, integrating inquiry and the doing of science, and pushing toward conceptual understanding rather than focusing solely on facts, definitions, and formulas. The sense-making emphasis in the *NGSS* focuses on incrementally building and testing explanatory models and working together with argumentation to compare ideas and reach consensus. The practices reflect the different ways that we need to be able to develop and use knowledge to make sense of the natural and designed world: explaining phenomena, critiquing arguments, and evaluating explanations or trade-offs in an engineering argument. Three-dimensional learning in the *Framework* and the *NGSS* is about using the practices to develop and use the disciplinary and crosscutting ideas of science. If we define science in this way, preparing literate adults requires that we give students experience engaging in the practices of science and engineering to build and gain facility with science and engineering ideas.

In this chapter, we have introduced the theme of the book: the contrast between merely knowing about scientific ideas and figuring out how the natural and designed world works by formalizing, sharing, and refining those idea within a community. We call this figuring out aspect sense-making. The *NGSS* reflect the contrast between asking students to know and recall scientific information that has been given to them and viewing scientific ideas and practices as useful tools for reasoning and making sense of the world. This is a radical shift in framing what learning science is about. This book is intended to give you ideas about how to engage students in practices for the purpose of making sense of the world by sharing thoughts and strategies about how to get started using practices in the *Framework* and the *NGSS* in your own teaching. We hope that you are inspired by this radical shift and that this book is helpful to you as you explore ideas and methods for moving this vision forward so that all learners can participate in science and engineering practices to make sense of the world.

Acknowledgments

We wish to acknowledge the contributions of many teachers, students, and colleagues with whom we collaborated and thank them for opening their classrooms to us. This material is based, in part, on work supported by the National Science Foundation under Grant No. DRL-1020316 to the Scientific Practices Project at Northwestern University, Grant No. ESI-0628199 to the MoDeLS Project at Northwestern University, Grant No. DRL-0554652 and Grant No. DRL-13489900 to the University of California at Davis, grants from the Gordon and Betty Moore Foundation and the Michigan Department of Education to Northwestern University, and with support from a Math Science Partnership grant to the Connecticut Department of Education. The opinions expressed herein are those of the authors and not necessarily those of the foundations and other agencies that helped fund this work.

References

Banilower, E., P. S. Smith, I. R. Weiss, K. A. Malzahn, K. M. Campbell, and A. M. Weiss. 2013. *Report of the 2012 national survey of science and mathematics education.* Chapel Hill, NC: Horizon Research.

Barton, A. M. 2001. The Moon also rises: Investigating celestial motion models. *The Science Teacher* 68 (6): 34–39.

National Research Council (NRC). 2012. *A framework for K–12 science education: Practices, crosscutting concepts, and core ideas.* Washington, DC: National Academies Press.

NGSS Lead States. 2013. *Next Generation Science Standards: For states, by states.* Washington, DC: National Academies Press. *www.nextgenscience.org/next-generation-science-standards.*

Windschitl, M., and J. J. Thompson. 2013. The modeling toolkit: Making student thinking visible with public representations. *The Science Teacher* 80 (6): 63.

2

THE *FRAMEWORK*, THE *NGSS*, AND THE PRACTICES OF SCIENCE

JONATHAN OSBORNE AND HELEN QUINN

Background on the Work of the *Framework* Committee

In 2012, the National Research Council (NRC) released *A Framework for K–12 Science Education: Practices, Crosscutting Concepts, and Core Ideas (Framework)*, which was the first step in a process intended to lead to a common set of standards for science. The work of formulating standards was divided into two steps: First, an agreement on the big picture of what students should learn needed to be reached; second, there was a need to develop an explicit set of standards based on that vision. The first step required a considered articulation of the core knowledge of science every student needs to know. The wisdom of dividing the development into two parts was that it provided an opportunity to convene scientists as well as science educators to form a committee charged with developing the *Framework* (referred to hereinafter as the *Framework* committee); together they could bring to bear both expert knowledge of science and expert knowledge of science education. Thus scientists, who in general have little knowledge of the challenges of K–12 education, could contribute to the vision of what mattered without being required to write the specific standards that schools should address. The second step, the writing of the *Next Generation Science Standards (NGSS)*, was then carried out by a group assembled by Achieve involving teams from 26 states that signed on as "lead states" for the development of the new standards.

In creating the *Framework,* the committee drew on its vision of what is important for students to learn, what the committee viewed as successes or failures of past standards, and what other national and international documents had articulated as visions of what matters in science education. The *Framework* committee decided to divide its description of what is to be learned into three "dimensions": science and engineering practices, crosscutting concepts, and disciplinary core ideas.

The idea of specifying a set of science and engineering practices as part of the *Framework* and standards was not only to define what scientists do when they engage in scientific inquiry—and what engineers do when they engage in engineering design—but also to define *what students need to do* to support the development of their own conceptual understanding of science and their engagement with science. After all, science is clearly something that is done. It involves some kind of activity on the part of people (scientists) and the product of that activity is knowledge. Any good education in science, therefore, must offer an account of not only what we know but also how we know it and why it matters.

Telling a story about the knowledge that is a product of science practices is the common stock-in-trade of the science teacher. However, telling a story about how that knowledge was produced, and the common practices that led to that knowledge, has suffered from 150 years of confusion. Indeed, as the *Framework* states, "because the term 'inquiry,' extensively referred to in previous standards documents, has been interpreted over time in many different ways throughout the science education community, part of our intent in articulating the practices in Dimension 1 [of the *Framework*] is to better specify what is meant by inquiry in science and the range of cognitive, social, and physical practices that it requires" (NRC 2012, p. 30). Both we as authors and our colleagues on the *Framework* committee felt that a shift to talking about practices rather than inquiry was necessary for two main reasons.

First, there was a need to better define what is meant when talking about "inquiry" in the science classroom. A long-standing problem in all educational discourse is the use of ambiguous terms. The definition found in the 1996 *National Science Education Standards (NSES)* offered a vision of teaching science through inquiry in which

> *students describe objects and events, ask questions, construct explanations, test those explanations against current scientific knowledge, and communicate their ideas to others. They identify their assumptions, use critical and logical thinking, and consider alternative explanations. In this way, students actively develop their understanding of science by combining scientific knowledge with reasoning and thinking skills. (p. 23)*

The *Framework* committee found that the problem with this definition was that although it encompasses a wide range of practices, it was too often ignored or interpreted to mean that engaging in any one of them would justify an argument that the teaching of science had fulfilled the requirement of engaging in inquiry. A bigger problem, however, was that inquiry was listed separately from the *NSES* content standards and thus was not well attended to in the development of the multiple state standards that followed the *NSES*. Our concern is that it is important for students to experience *all* of these practices, and that that needed to be clear not only in the *Framework* but also, explicitly, in the standards themselves.

What resulted from these discussions was the notion of three-dimensional learning, in which participating in the practices would be completely and inextricably intertwined with learning the disciplinary core ideas and crosscutting concepts. The recommendation in the *Framework* to the writers of the *NGSS* was that every standard should attend to all three dimensions.

The second reason the *Framework* committee placed an emphasis on the practices is that a persistent myth, often conveyed in the teaching of science, is that there is a singular "scientific method." More than 70 years after the Harvard Committee argued that "nothing could be more stultifying, and … nothing is further from the procedure of the scientist than a rigorous tabular progression through the supposed 'steps' of the scientific method" (COGEFS 1945, p. 158), the need to replace the myth of a unitary scientific method with a broader and more authentic view of the way scientists work to reach their conclusions is more urgent than ever. This myth is repeated in the opening chapter of many textbooks and has a mantra-like status, yet no card-carrying philosophers or even scientists have any faith in such an account. The eminent American zoologist Marston Bates wrote to a colleague that he wondered "if the fellows who teach biology in our country really believe the crap about the 'scientific method' with which they uniformly start their textbooks" (Bates and Fuller 1954). The *Framework* committee felt there was an urgent need to ensure that all students meet a fuller version of scientific inquiry, at a level appropriate for their grade, rather than the previously foreshortened view that overemphasized the hands-on aspect of science and failed to include the analytic and discourse practices of scientists or show a more diverse range of scientific methods.

What Does It Mean to Participate in the Practices of Science?

The *Framework* committee began with an underlying assumption that "science is not just a body of knowledge that reflects current understanding of the world; it is also a set of practices used to establish, extend, and refine that knowledge. Both elements—knowledge and practice—are essential" (NRC 2012, p. 26). In deciding which aspects of science practice to highlight, the *Framework* committee was guided by a consideration of "how science works," which divides the activity of scientists into three spheres.

Figure 2.1 (p. 26) appears in the *Framework* and serves as one way to illustrate and consider the different elements of what it means to engage in scientific practice. The sphere of investigating phenomena in the real world, depicted on the left of the diagram, uses the practices of Asking Questions (practice 1), Planning and Carrying Out Investigations (practice 3), and Analyzing and Interpreting Data (practice 4). Analyzing and Interpreting Data often requires Using Mathematics and Computational Thinking (practice 5). Investigating, the area most stressed in many inquiry-based classrooms, however, is just one of the three spheres of activity.

Figure 2.1

The three spheres of activity for scientists and engineers

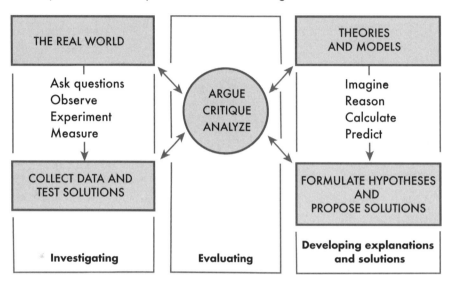

Equally important, on the right of the diagram, is the complementary activity of developing explanations and solutions. Important practices highlighted on this side of the diagram include Developing and Using Models (practice 2) and Constructing Explanations (or explanatory hypotheses; practice 6)—both of which often require Using Mathematics and Computational Thinking (practice 5) and Obtaining and Evaluating Information (practice 8). When we focus on this sphere, we notice that scientists construct models, theories, and explanations of systems and phenomena. It is this theory and explanation building that is the goal of science. It forms a large part of the activity of scientists as they imagine, reason, calculate, and predict what their model or theory says will happen, or how it explains what did happen.

In the central part of the diagram, linking the other two spheres of activity, is the critical intellectual activity of analyzing, critiquing, and Engaging in Argument From Evidence (practice 7). This analytic and evaluative practice is key to doing science. For instance, it helps to establish what to measure, how to measure any variable, how many measurements to take, and with what accuracy. Likewise, argument is essential for evaluating the implications and predictions of any theories and how well these predictions do, or do not, match the evidence. If the predictions do not match, then the theory has to be rethought. Thus, the interpretive and analytic work of the scientist is highlighted in the center sphere labeled "evaluating." Argument—in the sense of deliberate reasoned and critical dialogue—is then an essential process by which scientists identify flaws in their reasoning and gradually build consensus for the ideas they develop about the material world. Indeed, the process is so central to establishing new claims to knowledge that it has been institutionalized through the process of peer review in scientific journals.

New ideas in science have to be communicated. They are either presented at conferences or written in the form of articles for publication. At conferences, the ideas are communicated using a mix of oral discourse and visual presentations. In writing, they are communicated using a mix of words, graphs, charts, photographs, mathematics, and diagrams. Both of these methods require scientists to engage in communicating information (as in practice 8). Other scientists then review and evaluate this work—either publicly at a conference—or anonymously when, as expert peers, they consider the rigor and value of the work for the editors of journals. They consider carefully the theoretical premises of the work, the methods used to collect the data, and whether the findings and conclusions are justified. Only when others approve is the work deemed a valuable contribution to knowledge.

The search for the Higgs boson is an archetypal example of this process. Work by theoretical physicists led to the establishment of a common view that this type of particle should exist within a certain range of mass values—an idea established after much deliberation, argument, and interpretation of prior experiments. Further, theory predicted the particle would have particular and characteristic modes of decay. Work by experimental physicists and engineers then led to the construction of a machine that would enable the detection of such a particle through its decay products. Designing and building the machine took an enormous amount of thought, deliberation, and the elimination of flawed designs. Comparing the predictions with the observations has enabled physicists to argue that sufficient evidence has accumulated to support the claim that the Higgs boson does indeed exist. Detection required detailed prior argument to determine what signals to look for and what other processes could produce similar signals, and detailed data analysis and argument were needed to support claims that evidence for the particle had been established. This example shows the interconnected work in all three spheres highlighted in Figure 2.1. It was the interaction and the back and forth between the investigating sphere and the explanations and solutions sphere through the evaluation sphere that resulted in a major advance in the field of physics.

Focus on Practices as a Step Forward

The vision that all these practices are part of scientific inquiry was indeed in prior standards documents such as the *NSES, Benchmarks for Science Literacy,* and *Science for All Americans.* However, when the *Framework* committee looked at classrooms or science methods courses preparing teachers to teach science, it saw that inquiry-based science learning had, for many, come to mean a stress on the doing part of inquiry (the left-hand side of Figure 2.1). The outcome was a misrepresentation of science, which failed to show that such empirical work serves the goal of developing a set of explanatory ideas about the world and the way it is. At higher grades, the opposite flaw often occurs, with stress only on the right side of the diagram, as students learn established theories and models. Only once students have been told about the established scientific ideas do they move to laboratory exercises that follow prescriptive procedures to demonstrate the phenomena.

In both modes of teaching, opportunities for model building, interpretation, argumentation, and communication were not well developed. Thus, to ensure that students experience and are taught the importance of the multiple facets of what a scientist or engineer does to engage in inquiry, the *Framework* committee decided that a set of practices comprehensive enough to ensure the inclusion of all the major aspects of scientific inquiry in the classroom was needed. This became the list of eight practices that are specified in the *Framework* and carried through into the *NGSS* document. The list is designed to be sufficiently explicit to make clear the range of different practices that students need to experience. For students, engaging in these practices should be a means of both developing a deeper understanding of the content of science and building a better understanding of the nature of the discipline and how it functions.

However, students are unlikely to come to this understanding of science just by engaging in these practices. Teachers need to step back and have discussions with their students about the nature of the activity they have undertaken—be it developing a model or evaluating competing claims—and talk about why the activity is central to science or engineering. Students need the opportunity, for instance, to discuss why uncertainty is an inherent feature of measurement in science, why the mechanism of peer review is so essential to maintaining our faith in science, and why scientists find it essential to build models of the world. For example, the Bohr model of the atom is a useful picture, but it is important to point out that when it comes to representing things we cannot see, such models are just maps. Further, while certain aspects of such a model are quite faithful to our knowledge, such as the idea that electrons surround the nucleus, other aspects are totally misrepresented, such as the size of the electrons compared with the protons and neutrons as well as their distance from the nucleus. Students will develop this kind of knowledge only if science teachers engage in a process of reflecting on the practices as well as asking students to undertake the practices themselves. It is important that students be given an opportunity to understand how theory and data are related, how the process of science goes back and forth between investigating and explaining, and that this is all done in a social context.

Note that we do not intend to imply that students should develop new scientific theories or even rediscover existing ones through their engagement in the practices. Rather, engagement in the practice of science is part of the process of learning existing theories, models, and explanations and coming to understand their value. We do, however, expect that students will attempt to develop models based on their understanding of the system in question and of the relevant scientific theories—models that should then be used to interpret phenomena occurring in a system. In other words, students should develop models and explanations of the phenomena and support or refute claims about them.

Attention to Engineering Practices

How are the practices specific to engineering included? The practice of Asking Questions is critical in science because it begins the cycle that leads to the practice of Constructing Explanations to answer the questions. Likewise, the practice of Defining Problems begins the cycle for engineers, who are in the business of developing solutions for human problems, whether it is designing for a new bridge, making a building earthquake resistant, or making a better magnetic resonance imaging machine. Solving these problems requires clarity about the nature of the problem and the *scientific knowledge* that might help solve it. The engineer's challenge is not so much to construct an explanation but to design a solution (practice 6). Like scientists, engineers too develop and use models (practice 2), and plan and carry out investigations (practice 3) into their proposed solutions that often require the use of mathematics and computational thinking (practice 5). Designing Solutions (practice 6) often requires obtaining information from other sources, and engineers build models (practice 2) for their solutions along with collecting data that must then be analyzed and interpreted (practice 4). They too must engage in argument from evidence (practice 7), but in their case the evidence may be broader and involve considerations of aesthetics, costs, and environmental consequences.

Some may ask the more fundamental question of why engineering practices are included at all. After all, are the *NGSS* not a set of standards for science? Engineering practices are included for three primary reasons. First, engaging in design projects as a way to apply emerging scientific knowledge helps students refine and deepen that knowledge. Only two practices, practice 1 (Defining Problems, which happens at the start) and practice 6 (Designing Solutions), distinguish engineering from science. All other practices are common to both engineers and scientists, though used with somewhat different ends. The second reason for including the engineering practice is the close relationship between science and engineering. Not only can engaging in engineering projects help students learn science, it can also help them understand the practical value of scientific knowledge. A third reason is that participating in engineering practices may open a window on the world of engineering as a possible career path, helping students gain a richer experience of engineering at a young age. Even at the high school level, where a deeper exposure to engineering may be available through career and technical education courses, only a small percentage of students take such courses. The inclusion of engineering within the required science courses guarantees that all students get at least some exposure to this rich discipline at all ages—especially at the K–8 level, which is when students begin to develop their interest in science, technology, engineering, and mathematics (Tai et al. 2006).

Connections Between Practices and Crosscutting Concepts

Another issue that the *Framework* committee considered important was that there is, and should be, cross-link between certain practices and crosscutting ideas. While the science disciplines do differ from each other in obvious ways (e.g., physics is interested in the inanimate world while biology is interested in living things), they do share common features that help define the discipline. For instance, the practice of Developing and Using Models requires that students develop the concept of a system and models of a system; the practice of Using Mathematics and Computational Thinking requires students to develop the concept of scale, proportion, and quantity; and the concepts of cause and effect and of patterns are important guides to questioning, planning investigations, and analyzing data. Taken together, the practices and the crosscutting concepts provide a vision of what unifies the various science disciplines into a single area of study. If students are to understand what it is that makes science distinctive, then there is considerable value in acknowledging and discussing these commonalities and in developing a universal language within science education. What the crosscutting concepts and the practices offer, then, is a way of talking about the different science areas that helps build student understanding of what the sciences share. Hopefully, it offers that vision—an answer to the question of what is this thing called science. Even as long ago as 1952, it was argued that formal science education leaves its students with a knowledge of miscellaneous facts but little understanding of how science has been so successful in developing our understanding of the material world (Cohen 1952). Evidence suggests that this is still the dominant way in which science is taught (Banilower et al. 2013).

Concluding Comments on the Goals of the *Framework* With Regard to the Practices

The fundamental issue in developing any framework and associated standards is whether they are an effective guide to science instruction. To be effective they must offer a vision of what it means to do and learn science. Moreover, that vision should suggest a form of science education that is both challenging and engaging. The attempts in earlier standards documents to focus in on inquiry in science were a step toward this vision, but they have fallen short. It was the intention of the *Framework* committee to take earlier standards one step further and place greater emphasis on the practices of science. Over time, the overemphasis on content has led to a form of instruction that is reliant on textbooks, with too few opportunities to engage in critical thinking, evaluate competing explanations, or design experiments and solutions to practical problems (Banilower et al. 2013). The foregrounding of practices does not mean that they are a replacement for content. It is impossible to engage in any of these practices without at the same time addressing some domain of science and building an understanding of some science knowledge. What it does mean is that, in going from the *Framework* to the *NGSS*, the expectations of what students might achieve will not be framed solely in terms of what students should know but also what students should be *able to do*. This we see as potentially a major transformation in the teaching of science.

No longer can we treat our students as sponges for the knowledge that we provide. No longer is it the responsibility of the teacher to provide the explanations, design the experiments, and draw the conclusions. Rather, students must have the opportunity to do some of this work themselves. Whether it is analyzing a set of data about the different types of organisms that they can identify in the school yard, or testing hypotheses about the difference in reaction times between individuals as measured with a smartphone, students will be doing science. And by doing science, we do not just mean collecting data—we mean designing the experiment, deciding how much data to collect, developing models and constructing explanations, and communicating their findings to others. It is this activity that so grips and inspires scientists themselves. And it is only this kind of activity that can really show what a creative and imaginative endeavor science is and lead to truly deep understanding of the science ideas themselves.

Our hope is that the vision of science offered by the *Framework* and the *NGSS* will be a means to offer more students more of these kinds of experiences and to give them the thrill and liberation that comes from the understanding that science is a means of creating new knowledge.

References

Banilower, E., P. S. Smith, I. R. Weiss, K. A. Malzahn, K. M. Campbell, and A. M. Weiss. 2013. *Report of the 2012 national survey of science and mathematics education.* Chapel Hill, NC: Horizon Research.

Bates, M., and H. Fuller, eds. 1954. *Marston Bates Papers.* Ann Arbor: University of Michigan, Bentley Historical Library.

Cohen, I. B. 1952. The education of the public in science. *Impact of Science on Society* 3: 67–101.

Committee on the Objectives of a General Education in a Free Society (COGEFS). 1945. *General education in a free society: Report of the Harvard Committee.* Cambridge, MA: Harvard University Press.

National Research Council (NRC). 2012. *A framework for K–12 science education: Practices, crosscutting concepts, and core ideas.* Washington, DC: National Academies Press.

Tai, R. H., C. Q. Liu, A. V. Maltese, and X. Fan. 2006. Planning early for careers in science. *Science* 312 (5777): 1143–1145.

3

TOWARD MORE EQUITABLE LEARNING IN SCIENCE

Expanding Relationships Among Students, Teachers, and Science Practices

MEGAN BANG, BRYAN BROWN, ANGELA CALABRESE BARTON,

ANN ROSEBERY, AND BETH WARREN[1]

The emphasis on practices in the *Next Generation Science Standards* (*NGSS*) has the potential to shift science education toward more equitable, active, and engaged learning for all students. Realizing this potential is particularly important in relation to students of color, students who speak first languages other than English, and students from low-income communities who, despite numerous waves of reform, have had limited access to high-quality, meaningful opportunities to learn in science.

What is the potential of the emphasis on science practices? It expands the territory of sense-making in science to include more wide-ranging, intellectually powerful practices than what has conventionally been highlighted in school science (e.g., *the* scientific method). Practices such as argumentation, modeling, interpreting data, and communicating represent fundamental ways in which children and adults, across diverse communities, make sense of the world. In this sense, a focus on science practices invites teachers to attend closely to the varied ways in which students argue from evidence or interpret data as a foundation of learning in science, and to build on students' ideas, experiences, and perspectives as a core part of teaching. By attending closely to what students actually say and do in science, teachers can expand the relationships that are possible among themselves, their students, and science. In this way, they can begin to create more equitable opportunities to learn in science for historically underserved students. This chapter describes and illustrates three principles for teachers to consider as they seek to create such opportunities in their science classrooms.

As a society, we have historically failed to provide meaningful, challenging, and engaging science education for students from historically underserved communities. For the most part, students from these communities experience science instruction as disconnected from their experiences in life, their questions about the world, and the concerns of their communities. Not surprisingly, they disengage from science in large numbers.

---

1. Authors are listed alphabetically.

As recently as 2008, African American, Latino/Latina, and Native American students earned only 17.5% of bachelor's degrees, 14% of master's degrees, and 7% of doctoral degrees awarded in science fields (NSF 2011). These patterns are troubling because they indicate that STEM (science, technology, engineering, and mathematics) career paths and their associated benefits are not available to these students, their families, or their communities. Of equal importance, these patterns show that neither our schools nor our society is benefiting from the voices and participation of these students in critically shaping classroom learning and responses to our increasingly vulnerable social-ecological world.

Inside the science classroom, teachers can play a uniquely powerful role in addressing issues of equity, in particular, by valuing the insights, perspectives, and experiences of students from historically underserved communities as they make sense of scientific phenomena and making the intellectual value of these contributions visible to the students and the class as a whole. Without question, orienting one's science teaching toward equitable practice is an ongoing project of professional learning that takes time and effort. There are actions that one can take immediately, however, to begin making a difference for students. For example, if a student says something you don't understand, ask her to elaborate, to tell you more. Stick with her and her thinking rather than moving quickly on to another student. Moves of this kind are illustrated in action in this chapter. The bottom line is, the more you show genuine intellectual and scientific interest in your students' sense-making, the more you expand the space of possible relations among you, your students, and science. You may be surprised to find that the principles described in this chapter not only deepen your understanding of your students' sense-making and your relationship with your students but also heighten your students' interest in one another's ideas and their engagement with science.

Science Instruction in Historically Underserved Communities

Before moving to the principles and illustrations, we take a step back to explore briefly how it is that students in historically underserved communities have had limited access to high-quality science instruction. The story behind this problem is multifaceted. One contributing factor is that schools in underserved communities do not benefit from the same resources as schools in middle-income, affluent, and often European American communities. Resource inequalities range from differences in the number of well-prepared science teachers to the number of rigorous, exciting science courses offered to the state of facilities and quality of computers, laboratories, and textbooks.

Another, less obvious factor has to do with the rather narrow range (or repertoire) of ways of speaking, knowing, acting, and valuing that are privileged in our public schools.

These include, for example, known-answer questions, taxonomic thinking, and strict turn-taking. Often identified with aspects of European American, middle-class cultural practice, the more these ways of thinking, talking, and acting are privileged in the classroom, the more they limit the participation and sense of belonging of students from underserved communities, all of whom command ways of talking and thinking that are more wide-ranging and equally intellectually powerful as those privileged in school. The lack of connection between students' diverse repertoires and what teachers expect often becomes a ground of misunderstanding and misinterpretation.

For example, students from European American middle-class families learn at an early age to name and organize objects according to observable characteristics (e.g., color, shape). This way of thinking prepares students for the kinds of classification systems prevalent in school science, such as hierarchical taxonomies that define groups of biological organisms based on shared characteristics. Such systems are both useful and powerful but, like any system, are also limited. Biological knowledge may also be organized in other powerful ways. One is according to the relative roles and relationships of organisms to each other and within larger systems of life and living. Research in some Indigenous communities has demonstrated that, in fact, children and adults organize their knowledge of organisms relationally, developing focus on ecological systems instead of taxonomical categories and focusing on properties of kinds, and they apprentice their children into these systems at an early age (e.g., Medin and Bang 2014). Therefore, if a child is asked a question that requires classifying something as one thing or another, she may answer with a more nuanced, relational response. But because relational knowledge systems are not privileged in school science, she may be heard by her teacher as confused, off topic, or even wrong. Importantly, this perspective increasingly stands in tension with ecologically oriented scientific disciplines concerned with urgent issues of climate change and its intersection with social and economic justice.

The privileging in school of European American middle-class culture and ways of knowing extends to students' sense-making practices as well. For example, schools tend to accord higher status to explanations that are expository or definitional in nature. These modes of explaining are common in European American middle-class communities. Explanatory modes commonly used in other communities, such as forms of storytelling and uses of metaphor, are not accorded the same intellectual status in the classroom, despite the deep connections between these modes and scientific theorizing, explanation, and modeling (Warren et al. 2001).

Human beings, no matter who we are, where we live, or what language we speak at home, develop our ways of knowing, talking, valuing, and acting as we live our day-to-day lives inside family and community. These ways of living are what is now understood as *culture.* Indeed, across communities, human beings make sense of the world in ways that are both similar and different. In other words, the cultural practices of communities are both overlapping and varied. One implication of this is that in school, as in all other spheres of life, learning and teaching are cultural processes in which the diverse experiences, ideas, perspectives, histories, and values of teachers, students, and disciplines (e.g., science) interact with one another in complex ways (Gutiérrez, Baquedano-López, and Tejeda 1999; Nasir et al. 2014). Understanding that learning and teaching are cultural processes, wherein certain ways of thinking, talking, acting, and valuing may be privileged over others, is powerful for teachers in creating more equitable opportunities for science learning.

We are suggesting that the diversity of ways that all students make sense of the world—that is, their sense-making repertoires—affords teachers powerful opportunities to create expansive science instruction (Tan and Calabrese Barton 2012). By *expansive,* we mean, first, that teachers and students together approach scientific phenomena from varied perspectives, expanding the conventional school repertoire. Second, we mean that teachers and students together narrate deep connections between phenomena and their experience, raise and explore unexpected questions, and engage routinely with unspoken aspects of phenomena (e.g., Is water alive?). Creating equitable learning opportunities depends critically on teachers' skill in seeing and hearing students' ideas and reasoning as *connected* to science (as opposed to being off topic or, worse, disruptive). When teachers see these connections, they can then expand the range of scientific practices and ideas traditionally valued in school (Calabrese Barton and Tan 2010).

Making the Shift in Practice

What does shifting toward equitable, culturally expansive sense-making mean for teacher practice? To illustrate the kinds of opportunities and challenges that arise in routine classroom interactions, we present an actual classroom event (Warren and Rosebery 2011). The event occurred in a combined first- and second-grade classroom of students from diverse linguistic, socioeconomic, and ethnic communities (African American, European American, and various immigrant communities from Brazil, Cape Verde, Ethiopia, Eritrea, and Haiti). Ms. T is a European American teacher who was a participant in a professional learning community with other teachers. She was investigating her practice, in particular, how she was interpreting and responding to her students' varied ways of talking and participating in science.

The class was investigating plant growth and development. As part of their study, the class visited a pumpkin farm, planted pumpkin seeds, and created a visual representation of the pumpkin plant's life cycle that they revised throughout their study. They also germinated pumpkin seeds in petri dishes using moist paper towels, *without soil.* One morning, Ms. T planned to introduce her students to a root chamber, a glass-sided container that makes root growth visible *in soil.* To set the stage, she reviewed the work they had done to germinate seeds in paper towels. As she talked, she showed the class a petri dish containing a sprouting seed. Simon, an African American student, called out a question: "Did you put magic beans in there or something?"

When another teacher asked Ms. T about this moment, she said she was initially "irritated" by Simon's question. Her reaction was shaped in part by the way Simon spoke—without raising his hand and with an affect that sounded "provocative" to her. She heard his question as a challenge, at the very least as taking her plan off course. In short, when Simon *first* spoke, Ms. T interpreted his participation from what might be called a social-behavioral rather than a sense-making frame; she did not initially recognize the scientific and intellectual substance of his question.

However, to someone familiar with patterns of African American language use, Simon's ways with words were neither random nor mysterious. He spoke from a powerful intellectual and expressive tradition of African American discourse practices, making use of incisive argumentation, keen wit, and language play (Lee 2007; Mitchell-Kernan 1982; Smitherman 1977, 2000). His question, rather than signaling disrespect, showed attentive intellectual engagement. However, because it was different in form, tone, timing, and content from what is conventionally expected and valued in school, Ms. T was initially unsettled and unsure of his meaning and purpose (Heath 1983, 1989; Lee 2001, 2007; Warren, Ogonowski, and Pothier 2005).

This kind of moment is not unique to Ms. T's classroom, to schooling, or to science education more broadly. Teachers make rapid, consequential interpretations of children's meanings and intentions as a routine part of teaching. Their sensibilities and perspectives with respect to students' sense-making repertoires shape how they interpret these meanings and intentions. Because teachers are trained to expect students' language and ways of making sense to map to those of middle-class European American communities, their skill in recognizing and interpreting other ways is limited (Brown 2004, 2006; Warren and Rosebery 2008). A consequence of this is that the sense-making repertoires of students from historically underserved communities can be misread as signs of disrespect, confusion, digression, lack of knowledge, or disengagement (Nasir 2011).

Fortunately, however, Ms. T had been learning to attune herself to her students' diverse sense-making repertoires and how these related to science. If this had not been the case, let's imagine how Simon might have experienced this interaction. Given her initial feeling of irritation, Ms. T could have easily ignored, deflected, or dismissed his question, or reprimanded him for calling it out. Now, imagine such responses as typical, daily experiences in science. How would Simon, or any student, develop as a scientific thinker or learn a sense of belonging in science? In asking this question, we do not mean to minimize Simon's or other students' resiliency or agency in adverse circumstances (Nasir et al. 2014; Nasir and Saxe 2003; Spencer 2008). However, we also do not want to minimize the cumulative effects involved in these struggles, which is why recognizing and altering their course is, from our perspective, at the heart of creating equitable opportunities to learn in science. The more students are misinterpreted as to their meaning and intention, the more likely they are to be viewed as "disruptive," "inattentive," "unskilled," or "underachieving," reflecting well-worn stereotypes of students from underserved communities. These labels can dramatically shape their experience in schools, relationship with science, and sense of belonging and identity in both (Lee, Spencer, and Harpalani 2003; Martin 2009; Nasir 2011; Sue et al. 2007).

However, because of Ms. T's ongoing examination of her own teaching, her interaction with Simon took a different path. Her immediate reaction of irritation served as a signal to her that *she* was misinterpreting him. She realized that she was not hearing him from a sense-making perspective and did not fully understand him or his concern. What did she do? Rather than dismissing him, *she asked him to say more*—a remarkably simple move with large effects. Her move invited Simon to explain that he was wondering how seeds could germinate *without* soil. This elaboration helped Ms. T see his question in the light of the class's work up to that point, which had foregrounded the importance of soil in plant growth, as had her introduction of the root chamber. As Simon elaborated, she understood that his question was marking a *contradiction* between the class's experience germinating seeds in petri dishes *without* soil and the work they had done to establish soil as a condition *necessary* for plant growth. This allowed Ms. T to recognize and comment on Simon's detailed insight, connect it more fully to the class's past work and her plan for the day, and return later to the contradiction he had raised.

By inviting Simon to elaborate his thinking, she gave him the opportunity to identify an important asymmetry in representations of plant growth used in the classroom. Ms. T's response opened a space of new possible relationships to science and science practices, a space in which Simon was positioned as a powerful, engaged, and critical scientific thinker. In this way, Ms. T, by constructing meaning *with* Simon, transformed a potential site of struggle—in this case, located inside a core practice of question asking about scientific representations—into an expansive learning opportunity in science for Simon and the class as a whole.

Our goal in this chapter is to share three principles that teachers can experiment with as they work to create more equitable learning opportunities in science. These principles can help position teachers and students to engage in expansive science learning. In the next section, we present the principles and illustrate the ways that students' everyday sense-making practices resonate and connect with the broad outline of science practices highlighted in *A Framework for K–12 Science Education* (*Framework*; NRC 2012) and the *NGSS* (NGSS Lead States 2013). The vignettes show how science practices and students' sense-making repertoires can be brought together to create scientifically meaningful learning. Each illustrates students engaging in science practices in ways that broaden valued relationships among teachers, students, and scientific phenomena.

Expanding Meaningful Opportunities to Learn in Science: Three Principles

- **Principle 1: Notice sense-making repertoires.** Attend to, listen to, and think about students' diverse sense-making as connecting to science practices.

- **Principle 2: Support sense-making.** Actively support students in using their sense-making repertoires and experiences as critical tools in engaging with science practices.

- **Principle 3: Engage diverse sense-making.** Engage students in understanding how scientific practices and knowledge are always developing and how their own community histories, values, and practices have contributed to scientific understanding and problem solving and will continue to do so.

In our partnerships with teachers, we have found that through attention to these principles, teachers learn to see and hear the deep connections between their students' sense-making and scientific practices and ideas. Seeing these connections allows teachers to recognize and create rich opportunities to engage with science practices and students' sense-making as a core part of science learning and teaching.

Science Practices in Culturally Expansive Learning

In this section, we share three vignettes focused on science practices identified in the *Framework* and the *NGSS*. The vignettes vary in type of learning environment, student community and age, conceptual domain, and science practice focus. Each illustrates one or more of the principles in action, highlighting ways in which they can be used to foster expansive learning in science.

The first vignette, "There Was a Bullfrog!" focuses on a group of Native American middle school–aged students and their teachers as they transformed a conventional macro-invertebrate indicator task (water sampling to determine water health) to reflect Indigenous community histories, values, and systems of knowing. The second vignette, "But What Would Granny Say?" tells the story of how a group of lower-income and African American youth participating in an after-school program for middle school students used their community-based sense-making repertoires to develop and present an evidence-based solution to a real-life engineering design problem: recommending the placements of three skylights in the roof of their community center. The third vignette, "Pause: Without Me Nothing Matters …," describes how a group of African American high school students integrated scientific explanation with formal aspects of lyricism—a sense-making repertoire integral to language use in hip-hop—to produce videos of the human urinary and digestive systems for a fifth-grade audience.

Introduction to Vignette 1: "There Was a Bullfrog! Investigating the Oxbow"

In this vignette, a group of Native American middle school–aged students and their teachers investigated biodiversity and ecological health at a local forest preserve in a large city in the Midwest (aligned with LS2.A: Interdependent Relationships in Ecosystems, LS2.C: Ecosystems Dynamics, Functioning, and Resilience, and LS4.D: Biodiversity and Humans). This narrative explores how the teachers' ongoing close attention to their students' thinking (principle 1) created learning opportunities that actively supported the students in using their own experiences to engage in scientific practice (principle 2) and at the same time connected meaningfully to the students' community histories, values, and practices (principle 3).

The episode is part of a larger designed unit in which the students were investigating the biodiversity and health of an oxbow. An oxbow is a place where a river used to flow but, over geologic time, the course of the river changed, sometimes forming lakes and other times creating unique ecological niches in the former river beds. This vignette is in a place where an ecological niche has formed, and the still-flowing river is nearby. The river sometimes floods and makes its old course visible. During the investigation, the teachers and students engaged with several science practices from the *NGSS*, including Asking Questions and Defining Problems (practice 1), Planning and Carrying Out Investigations (practice 3), Constructing Explanations and Designing Solutions (practice 6), and, to an extent, Engaging in Argument From Evidence (practice 7). The oxbow was also a place where the students, their families, and other community members harvested culturally salient plants for medicinal and culinary purposes. This explicit connection to students' lives was designed into instruction intentionally to engage principle 3, which is often not part of science learning environments. Importantly, the teachers recognized that students are often given messages that science originated with Western Europe, reinforcing the stereotyped perception that science is something only white males do. Similarly to the case with Ms. T and Simon, the teachers worked to uncover how this positioning occurs in moment-to-moment interactions in science teaching and learning. This vignette illustrates how close attention to and support of students' sense-making can at times be planned and straightforward but at other times must be emergent and nuanced in the way it lives in the stances, language uses, and classroom practices in which teachers and students engage.

The teachers, in partnership with parents and other community members, created lessons that built on family-based and community-based practices (e.g., harvesting plants for a variety of purposes) and on science practices and core ideas within life sciences and Earth and space sciences (reflective of principle 3). A key aspect of this work developed around the kinds of values and relationships that are constructed during science teaching and learning and, more specifically, around the place of human beings and their relations with the rest of the natural world (LS4.D: Biodiversity and Humans). The teachers came to see how science classrooms implicitly and explicitly define relationships among entities (e.g., animals, plants, and natural elements such as water) and position human relations with the natural world in ways that are often culturally and historically inflected by European American norms and values, and that in some cases may not reflect contemporary scientific understanding. They referred to this positioning of human beings in relation to the natural world as "part of," which reflects Indigenous perspectives, or "apart from," which reflects European American perspectives. (To learn more about what the teachers did that led them to this realization, see Medin and Bang 2014. To learn more about the positioning of human beings as part of or apart from the natural world, see Kawagley and Barnhardt 1999.)

Not unlike the future we imagined for Simon if his experiences in science were consistently misunderstood, what would a history of experience being apart from versus a part of nature mean for these students? A singular example of this relational dynamic may seem unremarkable, but the teachers recognized that the cumulative effect of this positioning would narrow the possible space for Native students' learning in science. In particular, doing so made Native students feel and think that doing science reflected European American values and perspectives, not those of their communities. In this vignette, we explore a specific event to exemplify these dynamics and how these relations shaped engagement with science practices.

Vignette 1: "There Was a Bullfrog! Investigating the Oxbow"

As part of their field investigation of biodiversity and ecological health at the forest preserve, the students and teachers wanted to assess the health of the river at the oxbow. In particular, they wanted to know what about the oxbow made it possible for both wetland plants and prairie plants, whose needs for water and soil are quite different, to grow in relative proximity to one another. In earlier lessons at the site, the students and teachers had learned about indicator species and indicators of ecosystem health primarily focused on wetland and prairie plants. They wanted to use this knowledge as part of their assessment of the health of the oxbow and to help them answer their question about wetland and prairie plants. To do this, they planned an on-site investigation that included collecting and analyzing water samples for the presence or absence of indicator macro-invertebrates to construct an explanation about water quality.

As part of their instructional design work, the teachers adapted a relatively canonical macro-invertebrate indicator task and transformed it in two important ways. The first reflected their attention to relationships and human positioning. The teachers felt that the standard protocol typically used in this activity (standing at the edge of a river and collecting samples using a dipping method) implicitly reflected an "apart from" stance because it separated the students from the river. They decided that their students needed to feel the river and develop a sense of being a part of the river. Thus, the plan was to have the students put on waist-high waders and immerse themselves in the river to collect their data.

During their walk to the river's edge, the teachers and students broke into small groups and made informal observations of health indicators. They talked about and looked for frogs because frogs are especially sensitive to water quality. At the river's edge, the teachers incorporated a community-based story that reinforced the students' community values and positioned the activity and the students as a part of a longer history of Indigenous peoples, thereby creating an expansive space for student learning (principle 3).

Importantly, this move also increased the teachers' attunement to their students' sense-making repertoires (principle 1). We now take a close look at how the teachers and students co-constructed the beginning of this adapted macro-invertebrate activity. This event involved three teachers, Allan, Ashley, and Rick, and five students, Eric, Sarah, Ellen, Greg, and Rachel. Allan started to explain the activity and its learning objectives by highlighting the data collection protocol they would use and the relationship between pollution and the presence or absence of organisms. Without realizing it, his explanation left unspoken and invisible the relationships among humans, pollution, and the organisms that students would be looking for, implicitly supporting a view of humans as apart from nature.

Ashley, a second teacher, recognized this and elaborated on Allan's explanation, connecting the students' cultural practices to the river and its health. She offered a view of humans as a part of the ecosystem they were investigating and connected to plants and other animals, thus motivating the activity as directly meaningful to students' lives: "One of the reasons that this is important is that we've harvested medicine from this place, right? And this river feeds the plants and animal life that's here. We want to make sure that we're harvesting medicine when it's ready to be harvested. In addition to finding out just basic health indicators, we also want to know the health of the system here."

Ashley's expanded framing gave explicit voice to an "a part of" stance and repositioned students' community-based practices as connected to their learning objectives. Further, she expanded the intellectual space of the conversation by articulating how the plants and animals are affected by the health of the river, thus reinforcing an "a part of" view of possible relations. Finally, she reconnected the relationship between macro-invertebrates and water quality introduced by Allan but in a broader space of relations.

As he listened to Ashley, Allan recognized the reframing she was doing and extended it to make visible to the students the plants' active relationships with the local habitat: "All right, so Ashley is right on. The plants that we use to heal ourselves are going to heal the Earth before they're ready for us. So if we find out that this place is unhealthy, we're not going to want to use the plants here because they're not ready to be used for us; they still have to work on the Earth first."

Allan has implied that the data they are collecting are going to help them assess whether the ecosystem is healthy. Significantly, he positioned humans in direct and deferential relationships to both plants and habitat, reflecting the values of students' communities. In this way, Allan expanded views of human–nature relations often defined hierarchically by European American cultural values to reflect students' community-based sense-making repertoires and connect with the purpose of the scientific investigation.

A student, Eric, then asked, "If it's nasty, why are we going in?"

Not unlike Ms. T's initial reaction to Simon's question, Allan was caught off guard and interpreted Eric's question as a challenge to him and the activity. However, unlike Ms. T, he didn't pause to reflect on whether he might be misinterpreting Eric. He responded, "The water isn't *that* unhealthy so there isn't anything to worry about."

In the moment, he was more concerned with moving the activity forward than with connecting Eric's thinking with the learning goals at hand. As a result, he positioned Eric as disruptive rather than as deeply engaged with the science, in effect, narrowing the opportunity to learn for Eric and the other students.

Another student, Sarah, dissatisfied with Allan's response to Eric, commented sarcastically, "Well, I guess we'll gain special powers [if we fall in]."

Sarah seems to have understood Eric's question as relevant to their activity and recognized Allan's response as a dismissal of its importance. Crosstalk among the students erupted, reflecting both concern and laughter about the exchange and Allan's response to Eric's question. Again, Ashley stepped in to reframe the interaction, propelling the students and teachers into a conversation that connected Eric's question to the intellectual agenda of the class. She prompted them to reflect on the relevance of their observations of indicator species during their walk to the river as a way to reconsider Eric's question. In this seemingly simple reframing, Ashley opened the space for students to connect their observations and construct evidence-based claims to a question driven by a student. The students' engagement transformed instantly:

Ashley: "But we did see some health indicators. When my group was walking along the river—"

Sarah: "There was a bullfrog, no?"

Ashley: "There was a—"

Greg: "There was a bullfrog!"

Allan: "Did our group find—"

Ellen: "Tadpoles!"

Sarah: "Tadpoles! We seen them."

Allan: "They were actually little frogs."

Rick: "And somebody found a big clamshell? So that big clamshell that you guys found …"

In this Aha moment, bullfrogs and clamshells came alive as "a part of" the oxbow ecosystem rather than as individual species the students had observed. This reflects the disciplinary core idea in the *NGSS* of understanding interdependent relationships in ecosystems. Based on this, the students also immediately realized that the water quality was probably not "nasty," addressing Eric's and Sarah's expressed concerns.

We want to pause to step through some of the implications in this interaction as the students' excitement and insights erupted. First, notice the immediate shift in Sarah's participation. Her first comment expressed sarcasm toward Allan's response. Her second comment, however, took up Ashley's redirection; she was so excited she even interrupted Ashley to connect to it. Sarah's excitement reflected her emerging understanding of interdependent relationships in ecosystems as well as her ability to connect their frog observation data to the kind of explanation about the water's health that Ashley was prompting them to explore.

Greg, another student, also interrupted Ashley to confirm Sarah's observation. Then Allan, who recognized the power of Ashley's reframing, invited other students to make similar connections from their observations. Ellen and Sarah excitedly shared their observations: "Tadpoles!" Rick, another teacher, then connected the students' observations to another indicator species, freshwater clams. At this point there was an explosion of talk as the students shared their observations of health indicators during their walk to the river.

Excited by this brief interaction, a group of girls then led the way *into* the river to begin data collection. The students spent an hour sampling the water, matching their samples to a macro-invertebrate identification sheet, and recording their data. Then they got together in their small groups and developed a claim about the health of the river based on their evidence. Eventually they reconvened as a large group to share claims and explore their evidence.

In this episode, we see the teachers grappling with and continually working with the three principles identified above, from noticing students' sense-making (principle 1), to designing activities that support students' sense-making and engagement with science practices (principle 2), to engaging students in understanding how their own community histories, values, and practices are deeply relevant to scientific understanding and problem solving (principle 3). By engaging in creative and principled instructional work, they created new relations among themselves, their students, and scientific phenomena. They wove into the students' learning experience serious attention to different ways of understanding the place of human beings and their relations with the rest of the natural world reflective of different values and knowledge systems. Finally, the in-the-moment exchange between teachers and students highlights both the complexities and opportunities possible in learning environments where intersections among science practices and students' ideas and sense-making repertoires are nurtured.

We do not underestimate the challenges faced by teachers in creating more equitable, culturally expansive learning in science, especially in light of the many pressures they face, including those associated with high-stakes achievement tests and the need to move activities and curricula forward. However, this vignette demonstrates that it is both possible and effective to strategically adapt conventional curricular materials guided by the three principles and to create meaningful learning experiences in science for students from historically underserved communities. The design work described here moves beyond static views of culture that, when applied to curriculum and instruction, often result in simplified and stereotyped cultural connections that are typically added on to preexisting curricula, without thoughtful reflection and analysis informed by the teaching principles offered in this chapter. Indeed, while a "culture-added" approach has been widely advocated and used, it has not achieved the desired results (Hermes 2000; Yazzie-Mintz 2007). In this example, had the adaptation stopped with the addition of the opening story, it seems unlikely that expansive learning would have occurred. The teachers in the river study worked actively to see how students' community-based sense-making repertoires could be built on to create a culturally expansive space of science learning at various levels of practice. Importantly, this occurred in the small and regular interactions in classrooms (e.g., introducing lessons and responding to questions) and in the field. Working to hear students in different ways in routine classroom interactions does not require significant additional time; rather, it requires a shift in the stances and ways of noticing and interpreting students' talk and activity—especially those of students from historically underserved communities.

Introduction to Vignette 2: "But What Would Granny Say? The Skylight Investigation"

In the summer of 2009, the Great Lakes City Youth Club, a neighborhood youth organization serving a predominantly lower-income and African American population, had a new energy-efficient roof installed that included skylights. The club leaders requested that the youths involved in GET City, a year-round green energy science and engineering program, determine the locations for the skylights based on their knowledge of energy-efficient building design (e.g., LEED certification).

We felt this was an excellent opportunity to engage youths in at least two core engineering practices: (1) defining problems and (2) designing solutions. In particular, we felt this would be a good opportunity to help the youths in more precisely understanding a design task's boundaries, including its criteria and constraints from this integrated vantage point. We were concerned with how to support the youths in seeking out, analyzing, and integrating both scientific and community knowledge as they sought to make the problem space clearer and more finely constrained while also taking on layers of complexity. At the same time, we wanted to support the youths in systematically refining design constraints and in evaluating possible solutions toward optimization. This practice includes cycles of prototyping solutions, designing and conducting tests toward optimizing solutions, gathering and analyzing data from multiple perspectives, and engaging in dialogue on complicated conflicts in perspective and design trade-offs. We view ongoing communication among design partners and with stakeholders as elemental to this practice.

Vignette 2: "But What Would Granny Say? The Skylight Investigation"

To develop recommendations for the best placement for the skylights, the teacher began by eliciting students' prior knowledge and understanding about skylights. A student, Tami, drawing from previous learning experiences in GET City around engineering, suggested they conduct a community needs assessment. The group talked briefly about the assessment done previously and then focused on what they needed to learn and what kinds of data would help them to learn it through the community needs assessment. The youths began to define the design problem posed by "Where should the skylights go?" through a set of criteria that mattered to them. Their ideas for the community needs assessment reflected their experiences at the club—playing basketball, finding something to do in stormy weather, socializing, and doing homework, among other things. The youths and teacher collaboratively began to more precisely define the design task's criteria and constraints.

Later, in explaining their findings to the club leaders, Chantelle, one of the students, captured part of the problem's design complexity when she said, "First, we decided on the criteria that we thought would add most in the placement of the skylight. We thought about how the room was used, including the number of hours the room is used, who uses the room, and for what reason. How many people use the room? Then we thought about how a skylight might impact the room, including amount of natural light, light intensity, reliability, safety, and beauty—sweetness—how it might affect work performance in varying conditions."

Here, we see Chantelle summarizing the criteria the youths settled on, including physical conditions (the amount of natural lighting a room receives), environmental issues (saving electricity), social concerns (sweetness), and, as we will see, equal access. That they felt they could include a sweetness factor was particularly salient to them. They initially worried that others might not view sweetness as scientific, despite the fact that this was critically important to them. Figuring out that their experiences mattered in establishing criteria helped the youths develop a sense of belonging in this design problem.

The youths surveyed 12 rooms, and each room was scored on a scale of 1 to 3 for each of their criteria (e.g., the need for natural lighting, light intensity, light reliability, safety, sweetness, and performance) and was assigned a "priority" rating based on a scale of 1 to 10 determined by the youths. The data were compiled into charts, and then they began to analyze it and interpret their findings (Figure 3.1). They noticed some contradictions in the data around needs and priority scores. A conversation ensued about the asymmetries in their scores.

After some deliberation, Patricia offered a solution: "The criteria that rated high in the club room were different from the criteria that rated high in the conference room or the gym. The club room does not have any natural lighting and is used by lots of kids, but the conference room does have some natural lighting, but it is used for a lot more hours. … I think we should talk to Granny."

Granny is a community elder. Everyone, adults included, calls her Granny. She is not in charge at the club, but her opinion matters. As one of the youths explained, "You have to run everything by Granny or it might not work out."

The youths took their questions and data analysis to Granny. They showed her their survey, their charts, and the differences in scores. Granny carefully looked at these documents and offered critical feedback. She suggested that they might want to look at the actual ceilings in the rooms. Did the ceilings look as if they could be modified to fit a skylight? She also suggested that the youths might look more closely at their last stated criterion: What would be fair to the different members of the club? Lastly, she suggested that the youths ask around to see if other people at the club had other ideas about their data.

In this part of the investigation, the youths were engaged in an aspect of practice 6, Constructing Explanations and Designing Solutions, because they were constructing and revising explanations based on evidence obtained from a variety of sources and peer review. They went to Granny with a question of how to deal with the asymmetries as they attempted to resolve a dilemma in the interpretation of their data. They needed to consider how to revise their initial approach and interpretation of data for determining the

Figure 3.1
Data collected about the various rooms at the club

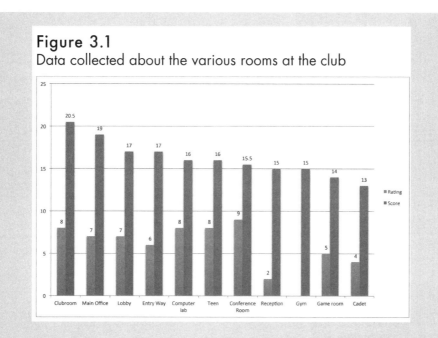

location of the skylights, and they needed to seek out peer review and critique to do so. In other words, the youths began to see that their needs assessment was only one form of data. While important, it was not enough. They decided they needed to show their results to people at the club and get their take on what they thought of the criteria they listed and how they rated the rooms for these criteria.

While critique and iterative refinement are central to engaging deeply in science practices, the youths approached this practice in a socially meaningful way that also reflected a view of science as "a larger ensemble of activities that includes networks of participants and institutions" (NGSS Lead States 2013, p. 43). Granny ultimately took the youths back to the intersection of the design problem and the human, social element involved in their investigation. The youths' design solutions had to take account of the evidence they had collected *and* had to take account of—that is, respect—the forms of life of the people who work and play at the club. This recognition led the youths to revisit each room and engage more community members in the process. Ultimately, Granny's comments caused the youths to embrace the complexity of their data and to situate the data in a broader ecology of concerns that mattered in the lives of people at the club.

In their final report, Tami and Bethany wrote about the placement of one skylight in the club room: "The club room should get one of the skylights because it has no natural light; it got a high rating of 28.5 (the highest rating of all). It also often has kids in it during activities such as healthy habits and gogirlsgo; it also is used for lunch. … The club room should get a skylight because compared to the other candidates, the clubroom has absolutely no natural light and natural light is proven to make people happier, healthier, and save more energy. When you are eating and participating in activities, you need energy. … The cool factor would be that the club room would be much cooler in many ways, such as, we wouldn't have to waste as much electricity and that we could look out of it. lol. And, Granny said that it was a great idea!"

The youths formally presented their recommendations for three skylight locations to club leaders and the roof contractor using data from their needs assessment and follow-up investigation. Their recommendations were accepted, and the skylights were installed in the summer of 2010.

The real-world, real-time design work encouraged by the *Framework* (NRC 2012) and the *NGSS* (NGSS Lead States 2013) emphasizes creating authentic contexts for youths to develop their abilities to design an investigation, analyze and interpret data, and design solutions. The teacher noted that she worried that the eight-week investigation, findings, and design solution would not be accepted by the club leaders or the engineering firm for reasons outside of her control. However, she believed that the youths' careful work in incorporating a range of design concerns and clearly explaining the rationale behind their design solutions made their efforts persuasive and effective. They positioned themselves as experts at the same time that they explicitly broadened the participation of members of their community.

Returning to our three principles for transformative science education, in this vignette example, the attention to student sense-making repertoires (principle 1) meant valuing the intellectual contribution and language of "sweetness" in the investigation. Importantly, while this term may sit outside what is normatively expected as part of scientific language, this example shows how using this term expanded the scope of the investigation and deepened science learning. The investigation also reflected principle 2, incorporating students' *experiences of 21st-century life as critical tools in engaging with science practices* by incorporating *why* the youths attended the club and *what* they cared about to shape *how they sought to design solutions.* It mattered to the investigation that the youths wanted the teen and club rooms to be "sweet spaces." It also mattered that these skylights were equitably distributed across the club. These culturally enacted design features did not outweigh—nor were they outweighed by—other criteria, such as the presence of natural lighting or room location. The students' and community's experiences and values infiltrated the way the students framed the questions they asked about skylight placements, the criteria they developed, how they sought and interpreted their data, and how each of these informed their final design solutions. These values opened up powerful spaces to *expand* the scope of the problem and possible solutions beyond prescriptive procedures and answers.

How teachers interpret, assess, and value the meanings and sense-making repertoires of students like Simon, Eric, or Chantelle is connected to how they understand the practices of science and how they imagine children and youths participating in these practices. Constructing explanatory accounts of phenomena is central to the scientific endeavor. Contrary to the ways scientific explanations are presented in the media and schools, scientific explanations are diverse in nature (Gilbert 1984; Latour and Woolgar 1986). In lab settings, scientists engage in discourse practices that vary from the vernacular to the explicitly scientific. Scientific communications are communal in nature and can occur as scientists share data and ideas in research meetings, conferences, and working groups. Although scientists' explanations of phenomena are commonly portrayed as noncreative and monolithic, they are more diverse than most imagine. Ultimately, authentic scientific explanations oscillate between informal and canonical (Gilbert 1984; Latour and Woolgar 1986). In our final vignette, we consider how an orientation toward expert practices can expand learning opportunities in classrooms.

Introduction to Vignette 3: "Pause: Without Me Nothing Matters ... : Lyricism and Science Explanation"

The *Framework* suggests that the goal of science is to explain phenomena. As a practice, students are expected to construct their own explanations as well as apply standard explanations that they learn (NRC 2012). To do this, teachers encourage students to "construct their own explanations" to compare and reconcile with the standard explanations valued in canonical science. Adopting a culturally relevant lens on this explanation process and fostering all students' explanation practices means that teachers need to intentionally integrate students' sense-making repertoires with scientific ways of explaining. This vignette explores one way of expanding students' repertoires of scientific explanation by integrating aspects of the explanation practice and scientific ideas with the culturally rich language of lyricism. This approach is another example of rejecting deficit perspectives of students' sense-making repertoires; it works to integrate multiple discourses into classroom learning in ways that help students understand the value of their own discourse and scaffolds them into using scientific explanations.

Vignette 3: "Pause: Without Me Nothing Matters ... : Lyricism and Science Explanation"

The Mural and Music Arts Project (MMAP) is a nonprofit group that seeks to help impoverished youths learn to value art and its impact on the world. MMAP provides children with free courses in graphic arts, painting, music, dance, and poetry, and then engages them to use their art to empower the larger community. Recently, MMAP commissioned the production of hip-hop music videos as a way to assist with community education. Youths produced science videos for fifth graders that explored standards-based lessons on the urinary system and the digestive system and were communicated through lyricism, a component of hip-hop.

Lyricism represents a unique variation of literary text that involves detailed, metered, and clever forms of language. To shape their project, students were taught the basic mechanisms of lyricism, which include analogy, simile, personification, and polysemy. The students produced two songs and two music videos that were about 5 minutes long and released them via YouTube (see *www.youtube.com/watch?v=Fab7JRibvMw and www.youtube.com/watch?v=5jRbKtwNKeQ*). The fundamental principle guiding this work involved an assumed relationship between lyricism and the production of scientific explanations. The assumption was that producing complex, lyrically rich explanations would first require students to generate canonical scientific explanations. For example, one student, Bonde, created lyrics to explain how water travels through and is processed in the body. To do this, he had to learn what the kidneys look like and the function they play in the human body. And because his audience was fifth graders, he had to synthesize this information and transform it into an explanatory form that would resonate with young students. Producing contrastive modes of language, a canonical scientific mode and a lyrical mode, helped him develop skill in and understanding of the value of both modes.

Throughout the project, students used different literary forms to produce lyrics that explored and explained scientific phenomena. In some of the lyrics they generated, students put themselves in the role of the phenomenon—or imagined that they were a part of it—offering examples of the anatomical nature and physiological role of the urinary and digestive systems. For example, using lyrical principles of personification, Akil described himself as the urinary system. "I'm your urinary system, just in case you didn't know. I filter good and bad blood to start your urine flow." In this excerpt, Akil provided a description of the physiological function of the urinary system. His explanation of how the system filters the blood and "starts the urine flow" is one that he did not come to by chance. Akil continued his explanatory narrative, here using polysemy: "But instead of the water, this is where the urine falls. Pause: Without me nothing matters, 'cause I'm the middle man to the kidney and the bladder."

In this line, he used the pause sign to mark a common cultural practice in which speakers say, "Pause," to make sure the listener does not misinterpret their statement. He was also suggesting that the physiological structure of the ureters looks like the symbol for pausing: two vertical lines (see Figure 3.2, p. 54). This is scientifically significant because Akil is not only describing what the organs are and the sequence of the filtering process, but how the organs are positioned in the body as they do their filtering work. This incisive double meaning is a striking example of the students' use of polysemy for explanatory purposes.

During their study, students generated short scientific explanations of phenomena as a precursor to their lyric writing. This process was fruitful for Akil because it allowed him to assess his science knowledge at various points as he created his explanatory account and still retain some of the essential elements of his description of the function of the kidneys in the urinary system.

These examples highlight the potential of creating expansive learning spaces in which students can use their sense-making repertoires to develop, refine, and effectively communicate explanations of human biological systems. Pairing the use of lyrical and canonical scientific modes of expression provided students with a rich understanding of the value of multiple forms of language and thus with access to powerful scientific literacies.

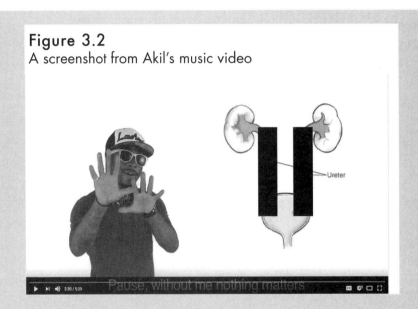

Figure 3.2
A screenshot from Akil's music video

What did the students think about their learning process? In interviews, they shared their perceptions of their learning and experiences constructing explanations of scientific phenomena.

One student, Imani, explained, "Obviously, me transferring that information into a more interactive and a more engaging way to where it was like, 'Okay, yeah, I know I'm just basically regurgitating this information, but I'm [making it interesting] so that they can learn better.'"

The program's goals for students' learning clearly went beyond "regurgitating information" and extended to making sense of scientific processes and mechanisms. Imani recognized that the writing process in which he engaged, in which he transformed information from canonical science language into a lyrical version, helped him learn about the biological systems in ways he may not have otherwise: "So yeah, I think that's what drove me to [learning science]. And I don't think I really really retained the information until after I finished the song, which was the most interactive part of the learning."

His reflections suggest that his understanding deepened as he worked on developing his song, and that it wasn't until the song was completed that he felt he'd really learned the science.

Writing lyrics may seem far from generating scientific explanations. However, as the work and words of Akil and Imani demonstrate, inviting students to use their sense-making repertoires to support engagement in scientific practices can be powerful (principle 2). These students engaged in serious intellectual work as they translated canonical scientific explanations into their own voices to create meaningful artifacts for their peers and communities. In this way, they created an alternative, expansive space for learning science.

Concluding Thoughts

As we hope we have shown, in the hands of determined teachers, the practices focus of the *NGSS* and the *Framework* offers the potential to push against prescriptive views of knowing and doing science. In this chapter, we have framed the eight science practices as a wide-ranging repertoire with potential to create more equitable, active, and engaged learning in science for all students. Science practices, taken up in expansive contexts of meaningful engagement with scientific phenomena and with attention to students' diverse sense-making repertoires, concerns, and passions, encompass a rich variety of forms and purposes.

The investigations in the vignettes shared certain design features reflecting the three principles outlined in this chapter. They were extended, rooted in students' and communities' local interests and needs, and developed in response to students' unfolding ideas and work, and they afforded students considerable authority for their learning and aimed at co-constructing understanding. These features were in evidence in students' efforts to explore the biodiversity and health of a local river through an ecological lens integrating Western and Indigenous scientific knowledge systems, solve a green design problem in a local community center, and explain human body systems to elementary students.

The vignettes also illustrated how a culturally expansive perspective on science practices in action can create new opportunities for students from diverse communities to engage meaningfully with science. This perspective allows for more fluid relations between science practices and the sense-making practices in which students engage in their everyday lives. It allows for broader recognition and understanding of students' language use and thinking practices than are typically valued in school. It encourages connections that cut across ideas, phenomena, perspectives, and disciplines in ways that reflect emerging shifts in 21st-century science. In short, it allows for expanded relationships to develop among teachers, their students, and science.

The work that scientists do reflects who they are, what they care about, and how they experience the world. It should be no different for students. It is in recognizing who our students are as cultural beings—the ideas, perspectives, and sense-making resources they bring, the issues they care about, the reasons they have for wanting to do science—that we can expand our efforts to engage them deeply. As students develop their sense-making repertoires within and across multiple domains of cultural activity (including those of science), they also develop critical insight into the relationships among them. For students from historically underserved communities, meaningful participation in science *depends on* engagement with the intersections and tensions in ways of making sense of the world.

Without question, teachers hold considerable power to legitimize students' ideas and sense-making in ways that give meaning to science practices and scientific ideas. We wrote this chapter in the hopes that teachers will feel encouraged to experiment with the principles described as they respond to challenges in taking up a practices focus in their science teaching. The principles are intended as reminders of the importance of recognizing and incorporating students' ideas, sense-making repertoires, and experiences as integral to intellectually powerful meaning-making in science. Working from them, teachers will be in a strong position to create equitable, culturally expansive learning that can transform conventional relationships among themselves, their students, science, and the world.

Acknowledgments

This material is based on work supported by the National Science Foundation under Grant No. 1348462 and Grant No. 1205758. Any opinions, findings, and conclusions, or recommendations expressed in this material are those of the authors and do not necessarily reflect the views of the National Science Foundation.

References

Brown, B. 2004. Discursive identity: Assimilation into the culture of science and its implications for minority students. *Journal of Research in Science Teaching* 41 (8): 810–834.

Brown, B. 2006. "It isn't no slang that can be said about this stuff": Language, identity, and appropriating science discourse. *Journal of Research in Science Teaching* 43 (1): 96–126.

Calabrese Barton, A., and E. Tan. 2010. We be burnin'! Agency, identity and learning in a green energy program. *Journal of the Learning Sciences.* 19 (2): 187–229

Gilbert, G. N. 1984. *Opening Pandora's box: A sociological analysis of scientists' discourse.* Cambridge, UK: Cambridge University Press.

Gutiérrez, K. D., P. Baquedano-López, and C. Tejeda. 1999. Rethinking diversity: Hybridity and hybrid language practices in the third space. *Mind, Culture, and Activity* 6 (4): 286–303.

Heath, S. B. 1983. *Ways with words: Language, life and work in communities and classrooms.* Cambridge, UK: Cambridge University Press.

Heath, S. B. 1989. Oral and literate traditions among Black Americans living in poverty. *American Psychologist* 44 (2): 367–373.

Hermes, M. 2000. The scientific method, Nintendo, and eagle feathers: Rethinking the meaning of "culture-based" curriculum at an Ojibwe tribal school. *International Journal of Qualitative Studies in Education* 13 (4): 387–400.

Kawagley, A. O., and R. Barnhardt. 1999. Education indigenous to place: Western science meets Native reality. In *Ecological education in action: On weaving education, culture, and the environment,* ed. G. A. Smith and D. R. Williams, 117–140. Albany, NY: State University of New York Press.

Latour, B., and S. Woolgar. 1986. *Laboratory life: The construction of scientific facts.* Princeton, NJ: Princeton University Press.

Lee, C. D. 2001. Is October Brown Chinese? A cultural modeling activity system for underachieving students. *American Educational Research Journal* 38 (1): 97–141.

Lee, C. D. 2007. *Culture, literacy, and learning: Taking bloom in the midst of the whirlwind.* New York: Teachers College Press.

Lee, C. D., M. B. Spencer, and V. Harpalani. 2003. "Every shut eye ain't sleep": Studying how people live culturally. *Educational Researcher* 32 (5): 6–13.

Martin, D. B. 2009. Researching race in mathematics education. *Teachers College Record* 111 (2): 295–338.

Medin, D. L., and M. Bang. 2014. *Who's asking? Native science, Western science, and science education.* Cambridge, MA: MIT Press.

Mitchell-Kernan, C. 1982. Linguistic diversity in the service delivery setting: The case of Black English. In *The Afro-American family: Assessment, treatment, and research issues,* ed. B. A. Bass, G. E. Wyatt, and G. J. Powell, 85–98. Philadelphia: Grune & Stratton.

Nasir, N. I. 2011. *Racialized identities: Race and achievement among African American youth.* Palo Alto, CA: Stanford University Press.

Nasir, N. S., A. S. Rosebery, B. Warren, and C. D. Lee. 2014. Learning as a cultural process: Achieving equity through diversity. In *The Cambridge handbook of the learning sciences,* 2nd ed., ed. R. K. Sawyer, 489–504. New York: Cambridge University Press.

Nasir, N., and G. Saxe. 2003. Ethnic and academic identities: A cultural practice perspective on emerging tensions and their management in the lives of minority students. *Educational Researcher* 32 (5): 14–18.

National Research Council (NRC). 2012. *A framework for K–12 science education: Practices, crosscutting concepts, and core ideas.* Washington, DC: National Academies Press.

National Science Foundation (NSF). 2011. *Women, minorities, and persons with disabilities in science and engineering: 2011.* Arlington, VA: NSF.

NGSS Lead States. 2013. *Next Generation Science Standards: For states, by states.* Washington, DC: National Academies Press. *www.nextgenscience.org/next-generation-science-standards.*

Smitherman, G. 1977. *Talkin and testifyin: The language of Black America.* Vol. 51. Detroit, MI: Wayne State University Press.

Smitherman, G. 2000. *Talkin that talk: Language, culture, and education in African America.* New York: Routledge.

Spencer, M. B. 2008. Lessons learned and opportunities ignored since *Brown v. Board of Education*: Youth development and the myth of a color-blind society. *Educational Researcher* 37 (5): 253–266.

Sue, D. W., C. M. Capodilupo, G. C. Torino, J. M. Bucceri, A. Holder, K. L. Nadal, and M. Esquilin. 2007. Racial microaggressions in everyday life: Implications for clinical practice. *American Psychologist* 62 (4): 271–286.

Tan, E., and A. Calabrese Barton. 2012. *Teaching science and mathematics for empowerment in urban settings.* Chicago: University of Chicago Press.

Warren, B., C. Ballenger, M. Ogonowski, A. S. Rosebery, and J. Hudicourt-Barnes. 2001. Rethinking diversity in learning science: The logic of everyday sense-making. *Journal of Research in Science Teaching* 38 (5): 529–552.

Warren, B., M. Ogonowski, and S. Pothier. 2005. "Everyday" and "scientific": Re-thinking dichotomies in modes of thinking in science learning. In *Everyday matters in science and mathematics: Studies of complex classroom events*, ed. R. Nemirovsky, A. Rosebery, J. Solomon, and B. Warren, 119–148. Mahwah, NJ: Erlbaum.

Warren, B., and A. Rosebery. 2008. Using everyday experience to teach science. In *Teaching science to English language learners*, ed. A. Rosebery and B. Warren, 39–50. Arlington, VA: NSTA Press.

Warren, B., and A. Rosebery. 2011. Navigating interculturality: African American male students and the science classroom. *Journal of African American Males in Education* 2 (1): 98–115.

Yazzie-Mintz, T. 2007. From a place deep inside: Culturally appropriate curriculum as the embodiment of Navajo-ness in classroom pedagogy. *Journal of American Indian Education* 46 (3): 72–93.

4

THE ROLE OF PRACTICES IN SCIENTIFIC LITERACY

BETH A. COVITT, JENNY M. DAUER, AND CHARLES W. ANDERSON

Scientists and engineers account for only about 5% of the U.S. workforce (Mather and Lavery 2012). Thus, the vast majority of students in K–12 science classrooms are not learning science in preparation for science and engineering careers. Given this, why is there so much emphasis on science practices in the *Next Generation Science Standards* (*NGSS*; NGSS Lead States 2013)? In other words, why do the majority of U.S. students who aren't going to be scientists still need to learn how to *practice* science?

There are multiple reasons that becoming proficient in both the content and practice of science is important. Oft-cited arguments for teaching science to all students (including the majority who will not pursue a science or engineering career) include fostering a sense of wonder about and appreciation for the material world and developing a citizenry that is capable of using science to inform personal and societal decisions about issues for which science is relevant (i.e., socioscientific issues). In this chapter, we focus on the second reason, discussing how individuals who are scientifically literate can use science as a tool for understanding and for making informed decisions about socioscientific issues they encounter in their lives.

Though science educators frequently talk about scientific literacy as a goal for students, succinctly defining *scientific literacy* has proven to be an elusive task (DeBoer 2000; Feinstein, Allen, and Jenkins 2013). Without presuming to offer a comprehensive definition, we suggest that a person who is scientifically literate is able to understand, judge, and use science in productive and scientifically aligned ways in his or her life. Leveraging this idea of scientific literacy, we use this chapter as an opportunity to discuss the role of science practices in a context based on a traditional meaning of "literacy"—namely, making sense of scientific information encountered in print and other media sources. All citizens need to be able to make sense of information in the media about myriad personal and societal issues such as food, medicine, climate, technology, and so on.

This definition has important implications for K–12 science teaching. Let's begin the discussion of these implications by considering *when* and *how* the students in school today are going to need to be scientifically literate.

When: Preparation for Future Learning

Bransford and Schwartz (1999) suggest that "preparation for future learning" is a key goal for education. This phrase captures an important characteristic of scientific literacy. Something educators have to do for students is *prepare* them for their lives after school, when they will need to learn new scientific knowledge to inform their decisions about socioscientific issues (Zeidler and Kahn 2014; Zeidler et al. 2009). All of the scientific knowledge that students will need in their future lives cannot be taught while they are in school both because of curricular time limitations and because the boundaries of scientific knowledge will continue to change and expand after students graduate.

How: Dealing With Varied and Sometimes Unreliable Sources of Information

In K–12 science classrooms, teachers generally control the sources of information available to students and try to make sure that the texts students read are accurate, informative, and written at an appropriate level for their understanding. Outside of the classroom, though, individuals encounter scientific information in a wide variety of media sources. Some of these sources compromise scientific accuracy because they are designed to persuade or entertain. Other sources oversimplify complex data or models. The most carefully verified texts (i.e., peer-reviewed scientific articles) are often written for specialized audiences and can be difficult to understand. Thus, the sources of information citizens are likely to encounter in their daily lives present challenges that K–12 students rarely have opportunities to grapple with in science classrooms.

DEFINING THE WORK OF SCIENTIFIC LITERACY

To continue the theme developed in Chapter 1 (p. 3), scientific literacy may be thought of as *preparation for future sense-making*, and this requires the capacity to engage in science and engineering practices. These practices involve both physical and intellectual work. In this chapter, we focus on the careful intellectual work that nonscientists need to do to make sense of information in the media about socioscientific issues, including information that may be oversimplified, intended to persuade, or even intentionally deceptive in nature.

Scientifically literate people can use science practices and knowledge to make sense of and make informed decisions about socioscientific issues. In the first section of this chapter, we examine how research on human thinking and the relationships between scientific knowledge and practice shed light on what it means to be scientifically literate, and importantly, why it's so challenging to teach for scientific literacy. In the second section, we develop two examples (diet and climate change) to illustrate some ways in which the use of science practices can enable people to make sense of, and consequently make better decisions about, issues and questions they encounter in their lives.

Why and How Scientifically Literate People Use Science Practices

So how can science education prepare students for future scientific sense-making in places and contexts that cannot be predicted today? In this section, we use research on learning and the relationships between scientific knowledge and practice to discuss challenges involved in teaching for scientific literacy:

- **Why do people need science practices?** First, we discuss and contrast two ways that humans have evolved for thinking and making decisions: fast, intuitive thinking versus slow, effortful thinking (Kahneman 2011). While fast, intuitive thinking makes day-to-day life feasible, it is slow and effortful thinking that can help people use science to evaluate sources of information they encounter. We need science practices to counteract some of the problems and limitations associated with the fast and intuitive way we often perceive and make sense of the world.

- **How can people use science practices?** Second, we discuss how individuals can use science practices to understand the world, and in particular, complex socioscientific issues that they need to make decisions about. People can use science practices and knowledge to further build their scientific knowledge and to help them design solutions.

WHY DO PEOPLE NEED SCIENCE PRACTICES?

Why can't scientific literacy just be quick and easy? Couldn't we simply find sources of scientific information that are accurate and easy to understand and rely on those? Aside from the difficulty of finding those sources, there are reasons embedded in the nature of human perception and learning that make engagement in slow and intellectually demanding practices a necessary part of scientific sense-making.

One reason for this has to do with how humans—over millions of years—have evolved to think and make decisions (Evans 2008; Mithen 2002). Humans can't be deliberative about every decision they make, so we have developed abilities to perceive the world and to make most decisions very rapidly. People rely on quick, intuitive thinking for most day-to-day decisions, and in general that's a good thing. Fast thinking enables us to take quick and decisive action using incomplete information, and there are many times when quick action is better than slow or no action.

However, there are problems inherent in quick and intuitive thinking. Fortunately, humans have also evolved a parallel way of thinking that is slow and requires conscious effort. Figure 4.1 provides an interesting example of the contrast between fast, intuitive and slow, effortful thinking. First, you perceive immediately that the woman on the left is angry, and you can be glad your fast intuitive thinking alerts you to this possibility quickly. But you also perceive immediately that the three silhouettes on the right are different sizes—except they aren't.

Figure 4.1
Uses of fast and slow thinking

(a) You need fast, intuitive thinking to be ready when this woman speaks.

(b) But you need slow, effortful thinking to figure out that the three silhouettes are actually the same size.

How can you tell that the three silhouettes are actually the same size? Well, you can't tell by just looking at the picture. No matter how long you stare, the right-hand silhouette still looks bigger. To confirm that this is an illusion, you need a different, slower strategy, such as getting out a ruler and measuring the three silhouettes. And as soon as you measure the silhouettes, you are engaging in science practices. You are generating data to interpret and analyze, and you are using mathematics and computational thinking.

Some other characteristics of the measurement strategy are also worth noting. In addition to being slower than our initial perceptions, it is also a product of conscious decision making and effort. We have to decide to measure rather than just seeing the picture—we have to do work to arrive at our conclusions. And we can remember and consciously keep track of the steps of our process. In contrast, the automatic processing done by our eyes and brains to produce visual perceptions happens immediately, without conscious thought or effort.

It would be nice to say that the reward for the effort we put into slow and effortful thinking is that we discover the "real truth" about the world. Unfortunately, the real truth is still elusive even after engaging in science practices. You still can't be sure that the silhouettes are the same size because you might have made a mistake measuring, or a more accurate ruler might show that the silhouettes really are a little bit different. The best we can do is to recognize and manage the multiple sources of uncertainty in our lives. While it falls short of knowing the real truth, managing sources of uncertainty by using slow and effortful thinking is still a very important aspect of scientific literacy. Table 4.1 summarizes and generalizes this discussion about fast, intuitive and slow, effortful thinking.

Table 4.1
Features of fast and slow thinking

Fast, intuitive thinking	Slow, effortful thinking
Unintentional, runs automatically	Intentional and controllable
Process inaccessible, only aware of results	Process consciously accessible
Does not demand attentional resources	Demands attentional resources, which are limited
Perceives stories and visual patterns	Analyzes patterns in data
Perceptions feel certain	Analyses acknowledge uncertainty

Source: Adapted from Haidt 2001.

So how are these features of fast and slow thinking connected to science and engineering practices? In many ways, as it turns out. Science practices are valuable for a lot of reasons, but one key reason is that they help people *slow down*—to recognize when and how we need to question our perceptions and intuitions and analyze them more carefully.

As Table 4.2 (p. 64) shows, the science practices are inherently strategies for slowing down thinking. Perceptions and informal ways of thinking provide people with quick and easy answers that are often wrong. It is possible to use science practices to slow down, verify data, check sources, and consider alternatives. Table 4.2 contrasts characteristics of fast perception with science practices from *A Framework for K–12 Science Education (Framework;* NRC 2012) and the *NGSS.*

These contrasts are not just coincidence. Scientific communities have spent many generations developing practices that help their members avoid the pitfalls of too-hasty thinking and develop well-reasoned alternatives. These practices are an important cultural legacy—a gift from generations of scientists to our children today, a gift that they can use to employ slow thinking when they need it. We show how this gift can work in the real world in our diet and climate change examples below.

Table 4.2
Comparing fast-thinking practices with science practices

Issue	Fast, intuitive thinking practices (from Kahneman 2011)	Slow, scientific thinking practices (from NRC 2012)
Answering questions	*Substituting an easier question:* When confronted with a complex, difficult question, fast thinking supplies an answer to an easier, related question.	*1. Asking questions (for science) and defining problems (for engineering):* Science practice defines specific questions that are answerable with arguments from evidence.
Validating models and patterns in data	*Confirmation bias:* Fast thinking gives greater credence to sources, information, and arguments that agree with our personal perceptions and narratives.	*2. Developing and using models:* Science practice searches out ways to falsify or test models.
Sources of evidence	*Seeing is believing:* Fast thinking makes use of information at hand to construct perceptions and stories, without asking whether critical information might be flawed or missing.	*4. Analyzing and interpreting data:* Science practice accepts only replicable data and constantly seeks out new data.
Patterns in data	*Stories, not statistics:* Fast thinking fits patterns we see around us into storylines that make sense but may not account systematically for all the data.	*5. Using mathematics and computational thinking:* Science practice involves using statistical methods to find and verify patterns in data.
Explaining events	*Simple cause and effect:* Fast thinking finds single, simple causes for events.	*6. Constructing explanations and designing solutions:* Science explanations use models and recognize complex causes.
Recognizing uncertainty	*False certainty:* Fast thinking produces instant conclusions that seem wholly true based on available information without evaluating the quality of the information.	*7. Engaging in argument from evidence:* Science practice relies on careful use of evidence and reasoning to reduce, but not eliminate or ignore, uncertainty.
Communicating results	*Source amnesia:* Fast thinking makes use of available information without questioning whether the source it came from is reliable, and quickly forgets the source entirely.	*8. Obtaining, evaluating, and communicating information:* Science practice documents and verifies sources of knowledge claims.

Note: NGSS science practice 3, Planning and Carrying Out Investigations, is not included in this table because it is a slow-thinking practice that does not have a fast-thinking analogue.

HOW CAN PEOPLE USE SCIENCE PRACTICES?

Sometimes people need science practices to help them make sense of information they find in various media sources, but how should they go about using the practices? What does this work of scientific sense-making actually entail? Current views suggest that science practices need to be both learned and used in concert with scientific knowledge (Millar and Driver 1987; NRC 2007). Thus, the *Framework* and the *NGSS* forward a notion of "intertwined knowledge and practice" (see Figure 4.2 and Chapters 1 and 2, pp. 3 and 23, respectively).

But how can people use scientific knowledge and practice together to make sense of socioscientific issues? Key relationships among scientific knowledge and practices are depicted in Figure 4.3 (p. 66). Some kinds of scientific knowledge are represented by the segments of the triangle:

Figure 4.2
Strands of scientific literacy

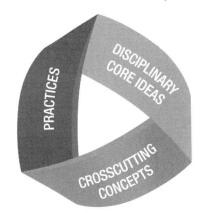

- **Data:** Scientific data are observations, but observations that are carefully made and selected to be precise, accurate, and replicable.

- **Patterns in evidence:** Analysis of data can lead to the identification of patterns in evidence that extend across space and time. Patterns in evidence are verified and validated using statistical approaches.

- **Models:** Models are conceived to explain patterns in evidence and tested through predictions they make about future observations. The small top of the triangle in Figure 4.3 indicates that the power of scientific models lies in their parsimony—a few models can explain many different patterns, each of which is based on thousands of observations that extend across space and time.

The arrows around the triangle describe actions people take to develop and use scientific knowledge. Thus, the three arrows represent the practices of scientific sense-making as a cycle of developing and using knowledge. The arrows are important because they connect scientific knowledge and practice together. *Data* alone is not useful as *evidence* unless one can find and verify *patterns* in the data and explain those patterns using scientific *models*.

Figure 4.3
Key relationships among science practices and scientific knowledge

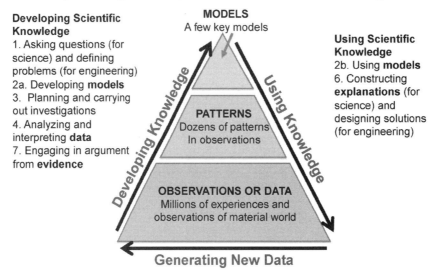

Developing Scientific Knowledge
1. Asking questions (for science) and defining problems (for engineering)
2a. Developing **models**
3. Planning and carrying out investigations
4. Analyzing and interpreting **data**
7. Engaging in argument from **evidence**

MODELS
A few key models

Using Scientific Knowledge
2b. Using **models**
6. Constructing **explanations** (for science) and designing solutions (for engineering)

Developing Knowledge

Using Knowledge

PATTERNS
Dozens of patterns
In observations

OBSERVATIONS OR DATA
Millions of experiences and observations of material world

Generating New Data

General Practices Associated With the Three Arrows
5. Using mathematics and computational thinking
8. Obtaining, evaluating, and communicating information

Thus, scientific sense-making involves using sources of information to build and use scientific knowledge. Scientifically literate people engage in practices to *evaluate and connect data, patterns, and models.* This enables them both to be critical users (i.e., evaluating the quality of data, patterns, and models in the sources they encounter) and to know what they are looking for (i.e., finding sources that they can use to "fill in gaps" in their own understanding).

What Does This Mean for Science Education?

Clearly, the challenge of helping students become scientifically literate is daunting. Science education has to prepare students to learn about new scientific findings that can't be anticipated and to make decisions about socioscientific issues that will be different from the issues of today. In their future lives, students will often have to rely on media sources that are designed to entertain, persuade, or oversimplify, rather than to educate, or they will have to search for more reliable sources that can be difficult to obtain and understand. What can be done in science classrooms to prepare today's students for these future challenges?

In this section, we have argued that research about how people learn and about the nature of scientific understanding suggests two important ways that educators can prepare students to use science practices:

1. First, educators can prepare students to use science practices to *slow down and critically evaluate the sources of information* they encounter. Human minds reach some kinds of conclusions quickly and effortlessly, and writers who develop media to persuade and entertain know this; they provide instantly believable stories that ignore conflicting data and alternative interpretations. Science practices provide well-established ways to be critical of the stories that the media tells and consider the alternatives.

2. Second, educators can prepare students to *build scientific understanding* by connecting verified data, robust patterns (often statistical) that extend across time and space, and validated scientific models. Scientifically literate individuals can identify the gaps in the information sources they encounter and in their own understanding, then pose questions and seek out additional sources that enable them to develop more complete and robust scientific accounts.

In combination, these practices can help prepare students to d*esign solutions to problems* that simultaneously consider and respect their personal goals and values and use scientific sense-making to better understand the nature of the problems and the possible consequences of their actions.

Examples of Science Practices and Scientific Literacy

We now turn to two examples of how these ideas apply to citizenship and day-to-day life. Our examples focus on issues that affect everyone: diet and climate change. There is important science related to these issues that can be taught now, but the science is still evolving. Thus, it's not possible to teach today everything that students will need to know in the future. For each issue, we discuss how science practices can help individuals live healthier lives and be more responsible citizens.

EXAMPLE 1: DIET

As Figure 4.4 (p. 68) shows, people are routinely inundated with claims about diet and its relationship to health and weight. These claims reflect the importance of diet and weight to all kinds of people. More than two-thirds of U.S. adults are overweight or obese, and obesity continues to be a leading public health problem in the United States (Ogden et al. 2014). Let's consider how science education can prepare students to use science practices as they learn and make decisions about diet in their own lives.

Figure 4.4

Popular media messages about diet and weight loss

How Can Science Practices Help?

Fast thinking provides humans with guidance about diet in the form of tastes and appetites, and this guidance, like what helped us quickly understand the first image in Figure 4.1, worked pretty well for our ancestors. Taste helps people identify safer and more nutritious foods, hunger motivates people to search for food, and satiety tells people when to stop eating. Overall, fast thinking worked pretty well in times when food was scarce and hunger was the main dietary threat to well-being.

But times have changed in countries like the United States, where for many people food is always as close as the nearest refrigerator or fast-food restaurant. Now, as we found in the second image of Figure 4.1, perceptions can lead one astray. Food and restaurant advertising is designed to appeal to fast thinking, providing tempting images of tasty food that spur people to eat without stopping to think about alternatives or consequences. Humans don't necessarily benefit from their appetites for sweet and fatty foods or from our bodies' ability to store fat in case there is a future famine. Today, people need slow thinking to reason about and regulate diets and body weight (see Diamond 2012, Chapter 11, and Pollan 2006, Chapter 1).

Many of us care about our own weight and health, worry about our children's nutrition, or have to teach about diet and health to students. So what should we do when confronted with thousands of media messages about food and diet, the majority of which likely purvey information of dubious scientific value? How can we decide which claims and whose advice are worthy of our attention? As with other issues involving scientific literacy, this isn't just a scientific question. People legitimately use personal feelings, cultural traditions, and past experience to make judgments about what and how to eat. But in addition, people can use science practices to recognize when and how science may be relevant to choices and actions. In particular, using science practices can help people (1) slow down and critically evaluate sources of information and (2) build scientific knowledge to design solutions.

Slowing Down and Critically Evaluating Sources of Information

Figure 4.4 immediately makes one problem clear: There is a lot of useful information available that can help in designing an appropriate diet, but there's a lot of junk out there, too. As of 2001, the Federal Trade Commission (2002) found that more than half of all weight-loss ads contain one or more deceptive claims. How can people tell the difference? Science practices are not the only way to judge claims; it is also important to consider journalistic standards of publications and legal restrictions on advertising claims. However, science practices, including Engaging in Argument From Evidence (practice 7) and Developing and Using Models (practice 2), are still fundamentally important for making informed judgments.

Let's consider one claim from Figure 4.4: "The vitamin D discovery that *shrinks female fat cells* and boosts weight loss up to 70%." We know from our research about how students understand metabolism (Jin and Anderson 2012; Mohan, Chen, and Anderson 2009) that many students will find this claim believable. Students often think of weight gain and weight loss as actions that our bodies take, with the help of enablers such as food for weight gain and exercise for weight loss. So if exercise enables bodies to shrink fat cells, why couldn't there be a pill that does the same thing?

Evaluating this claim using science practices requires a more thorough analysis and consideration of relevant evidence and models. Let's start with models. Bodies basically have one way to get rid of excess fat: using it as an energy source for cellular respiration. Exercise increases a body's energy use, and it makes sense that exercise could change fat cells. The claim that vitamin D shrinks fat cells suggests a mechanism (supplements shrinking fat cells without bodies expending energy) that contradicts current scientific models. At best, the vitamin D advertisement glosses over an important detail about energy use; at worst, it deceptively implies that weight loss can be easily achieved simply by taking a dietary supplement.

What about evidence? Well, some evidence in recent scientific literature has suggested that vitamin D supports mitochondrial function, thus decreasing fatigue and supporting exercise (Sinha et al. 2013). But how does this evidence cohere with both scientific models and the claims made in the advertisement? A careful read shows that the fine print in the advertisement says weight loss did not require exercise. This suggests a claim about vitamin D that does not align with scientific evidence or models of metabolism. Thus, using science practices to carefully examine evidence and models can help people be productively skeptical about the many potentially dubious media messages they will encounter in their lives.

Building Scientific Knowledge to Design Solutions

Fortunately, there is also plenty of valid scientific information about nutrition available. For example, the U.S. government has long been aware that nutrition is important, both because healthier people have higher quality of life and because healthier people are more productive citizens. Given its interest in public health, the government has sought to provide guidance to people who want to make good nutritional choices. Scientifically literate individuals can use this information to plan and to change diets.

PLANNING DIETS

Figure 4.5 shows two different approaches to designing solutions (practice 6) by planning a diet that meets nutritional needs. The Choose My Plate *(www.choosemyplate.gov)* approach begins with an image that appeals to fast thinking—an image of a balanced meal that probably provides sufficient guidance for many healthy people. It does leave important questions unanswered, though:

- Just how big are the servings supposed to be?

- What about foods that mix ingredients from different food groups?

- What about the diversity of foods within each group? Are they actually equivalent from a health and diet perspective?

Figure 4.5

Choosemyplate.gov (a) and nutrition labels (b) offering two different approaches to communicating nutrition information

(a)

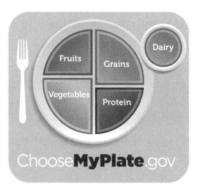

(b)

The nutrition label, in contrast, can be used as the basis for a slower approach to designing a diet that makes use of science practices—the equivalent of getting out a ruler to measure the silhouettes in Figure 4.1. Nutrition labels provide opportunities for slow thinking that use both scientific knowledge and practices to plan a diet. A scientifically literate person can use the information on nutrition labels as evidence, look at patterns across different food types, and rely on a scientific model that explains how eating protein versus sugars or fats can affect body function.

Thus, designing a diet using nutrition labels involves science practices, including the following:

- **Asking Questions:** Reference to a nutrition label allows one to pose and consider the more difficult question "What's the chemical composition of this food?" rather than the easier but potentially superficial question "What kind of food is this?"

- **Engaging in Argument From Evidence:** Nutrition labels offer valid and pertinent evidence that readers can use to recognize trade-offs associated with different foods.

- **Developing and Using Models:** Food labels connect ingredients with theoretical models of metabolism and nutrition. People can trace how different molecules in food are used in the body.

- **Using Mathematics and Computational Thinking:** Food labels allow readers to reason quantitatively about the nutrition they are getting from the food they eat.

As you can see, nutrition labels provide an opportunity for scientifically literate citizens to develop deeper knowledge about food and investigate the possible consequences of dietary decisions. Taking advantage of this opportunity requires some slow thinking that is inherent in the use of science practice and knowledge. Unfortunately, the average consumer often has difficulty understanding which types of molecules are in the foods they eat and how consuming different types of molecules can impact weight and health (Cowburn and Stockley 2005). Many consumers also have difficulty engaging in computational practices such as interpreting serving size information and converting from numbers on the labels to conclusions about the servings they actually eat (Cowburn and Stockley 2005). Thus, science education has an important role to play in helping students develop facility with practices needed to make better choices about diet.

CHANGING DIETS

Scientifically literate people also *interpret and analyze data* to monitor health and modify diets. No matter how carefully we plan our diets, there are still plenty of uncertainties involved. Studies reveal new information every day about how individuals process food differently and about subtle effects of dietary choices on health and fitness. It is impossible to predict in advance exactly how any person will respond to a diet—or how well our actual eating habits will reflect our conscious dietary choices. We all know that fast thinking can take over when we are hungry and the food is tempting!

Wise people will monitor the effects of diet solutions they have designed and interpret the data they collect (practice 4). Some information about the effects of our diets is instantly available through fast thinking—how energetic we feel, how hungry we feel, and how fat or thin we look in the mirror. We can also get out our "rulers" and measure the results of our diets using slow thinking by, for example, measuring our weight, blood pressure, blood sugar, cholesterol level, and endurance. There may also be new data that come from studies about other people: evidence about how individuals with different personal histories or body types respond to diet and exercise; evidence about risks associated with particular foods or dietary supplements; and evidence about how sleep, exercise, and other activities affect health and fitness.

The practice of interpreting and analyzing data plays an essential role for scientifically literate people who want to plan their diets and maintain their health, and this practice is connected in turn with other practices, such as constructing and analyzing arguments from evidence (practice 7) and designing new solutions (practice 6) based on those arguments. Science practices cannot tell us the right thing to do, but they can help us evaluate claims, plan solutions, and respond to new evidence as it becomes available.

EXAMPLE 2: CLIMATE CHANGE

The first example in this chapter focused on how using science and engineering practices can help individuals make *personal* decisions about diet and health. The second example shifts to the large-scale *public* issue of climate change. We first discuss how science and engineering practices can help people learn about the issue. We then focus on how specific practices can help people evaluate the merits of claims, design solutions, and interpret and analyze data to inform decisions about policies and actions.

How Can Science Practices Help?

Unlike diet, where fast thinking in the form of taste and appetite provides people with hardwired evolutionary guidance, human understanding of climate change comes solely as the product of scientific data collection and analysis. Knowledge of climate change relies on the slow-thinking efforts of scientists from as early as 1827, when Fourier calculated that the Earth would be colder without an atmosphere (Jones and Henderson-Sellers 1990).

Humans' fast-thinking perceptions, experiences, and impressions of the material world are limited in scope, and therefore are not sufficient for observing something as large in magnitude and as slowly changing as climate. People must engage in slow, scientific thinking to scrutinize evidence and explanations for climate change. Climate change is best understood through consideration of patterns in data across time and space (i.e., long-term atmospheric data collected in locations around the world) and through reference to complex scientific models of Earth's systems.

However, given the human proclivity for fast, intuitive thinking, weather rather than climate tends to be more persuasive to many Americans. For example, the number of Americans who believe that global warming is real dropped between September 2012 and April 2013, likely influenced by a relatively cold winter of 2012–2013 compared with the prior year (Leiserowitz et al. 2013). Being persuaded about climate change by short-term weather or extreme events is an intuitive thinking way of both substituting an easier question (e.g., "What's happening with the weather this year?" rather than "What do climate data reveal?") and relying on confirmation bias (i.e., thinking that a cold winter provides persuasive evidence supporting a climate change–denier argument). A key challenge, therefore, is to prepare fast-thinking minds to comprehend a slow-developing process.

We next discuss how science practices can help people use scientific knowledge, develop new knowledge, and make decisions about global climate change. As in our discussion of nutrition and diet, we discuss how people can use practices to (a) slow down and critically evaluate sources of information and (b) build scientific knowledge to design solutions.

Slowing Down and Critically Evaluating Sources of Information

These days, Americans encounter many conflicting messages about climate change (see Figure 4.6). Mixed messages may be presented by journalists who give undeserving weight to deniers' arguments in an attempt to sound balanced and present both sides of the issue (Antilla 2010; Moser 2010). Climate change deniers use media to describe nonexistent controversies within the scientific community and to promote discredited evidence, patterns, or models (Moser 2010). Sometimes environmental advocates who think more should be done to mitigate future climate change also use arguments that are not adequately supported by current evidence (e.g., blaming all kinds of extreme weather events on climate change). The result is that climate change is a confusing, if not confounding, topic to make sense of.

Figure 4.6
News articles about climate change

Figure 4.7

Two views of patterns in data about global temperature change, one from (a) realists and one from (b) skeptics

(a)

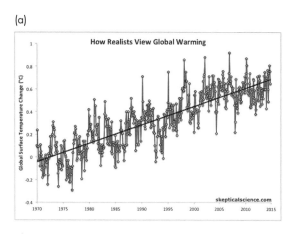

(b)

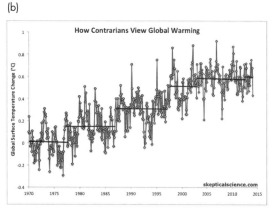

Sources: Panel (a) *http://static.skepticalscience.com/pics/Real-Trend.jpg*; panel (b) *http://static.skepticalscience.com/pics/Step6.jpg*.

Many Americans aren't sure what to believe about climate change. A gap in science literacy is illustrated by how many fewer Americans (63%) believe that anthropogenic climate change is occurring compared with the consensus among scientists (97–99%) (Anderegg et al. 2010; Leiserowitz et al. 2013). Recently, the Intergovernmental Panel on Climate Change (IPCC 2013) reported that it is "extremely likely" that human activities are driving warming. This high level of confidence, however, is not always emphasized in media reports (see Figure 4.6). News articles like those shown in Figure 4.6 pose a challenging dissonance. How should a person make sense of claims about how Earth's climate is (or isn't) changing?

Science practices can play a useful role. To use scientific knowledge to evaluate a claim, a scientifically literate person will pay attention to different kinds of knowledge, including data, patterns, and models (segments of the triangle in Figure 4.3). All three components of the triangle are important. The data must be relevant and connect to the claim. The patterns must be robust and hold up to statistical testing. Also, there needs to be a principled reason (i.e., a model) that explains patterns in the data.

Let's use scientific knowledge and practices to evaluate the claim in the Fox News headline above: Global warming has experienced a slowdown in recent years. This example demonstrates the importance of multiple science practices, notably Using Models (practice 2) that explain and do not just represent patterns, Analyzing and Interpreting Data (practice 4), Using Mathematics and Computational Thinking (practice 5), and Engaging in Argument From Evidence (practice 7).

Analyzing and Interpreting Data

The World Meteorological Organization defines climate using observational averages from the previous 30 years (Arguez and Vose 2011). Thus, relevant evidence needed to evaluate a claim about a pause in warming must include at least several decades of data. Climate deniers can choose periods of short-term noise in data that look like cooling. This is called cherry picking. The two graphs in Figure 4.7 illustrate how climate deniers can misrepresent patterns in temperature data (e.g., by identifying short decreasing temperature time segments within a larger increasing temperature pattern).

Using Models

Many debates about cutting-edge science focus on procedures (i.e., experimental design and the peer review process) and statistics (or pattern finding, as in Figure 4.7). While these are important issues, understanding models and mechanisms is also critical to making informed judgments. Scientific arguments require a principle-based reason or model to explain a pattern in the data. Thus, a pattern by itself is not necessarily meaningful unless it can be explained in terms of how the material world works (practice 2, Developing and Using Models).

Figure 4.8

Estimate of Earth's annual and global mean energy balance as referenced in IPCC's *Fourth Assessment Report*

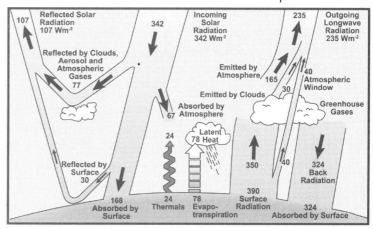

Source: Kiehl and Trenberth 1997.

Even climate deniers generally do not dispute that concentrations of greenhouse gases in the atmosphere are increasing. Statistical arguments by climate deniers (Figures 4.6 and 4.7) typically ignore this inconvenient fact. But this fact is at the core of scientists' arguments. Models focusing on heat exchange between the Earth and space (Figure 4.8) demonstrate that thermal energy *must* be building up in the Earth's atmosphere and oceans. Atmospheric temperature data are just one (particularly noisy) indicator of this underlying trend.

Building Scientific Knowledge to Design Solutions

Many people accept that climate change is real and believe we should do something about it. Unfortunately, wanting to do the right thing is not the same as knowing what to do. For example, while many people believe correctly that humans can address climate change by using less gasoline or burning less coal, these same people may also indicate that climate change can be mitigated by cleaning up toxic waste, fixing the hole in the ozone layer, and decreasing use of nuclear power (Bostrom et al. 1994; Kempton, Boster, and Hartley 1995; Leiserowitz and Smith 2010). These latter actions will not reduce emissions of greenhouse gases or mitigate climate change. Clearly, many people need some support in using scientific models (practice 2) to consider what options may comprise reasonable solutions (practice 6) for mitigating human-caused climate change

Using Mathematical Reasoning

Designing solutions that will stabilize greenhouse gas emissions also requires knowledge of the magnitude of carbon emissions associated with different human actions. How many trees offset the emissions from one coal-fired power plant? Is it more important to improve the fuel efficiency of our cars or the insulation in our homes? A scientist and an engineer at Princeton University together came up with an approach to answering these kinds of questions. Their idea was to compare different strategies for increasing efficiency and conservation, decarbonizing electricity and fuels, or amplifying natural sinks for carbon dioxide (Pacala and Socolow 2004). They defined strategies that produced comparable reductions in greenhouse gases as "stabilization wedges" that, when implemented now, take a large bite out of future carbon dioxide emissions (Figure 4.9).

The wedges idea can be used as the basis for a slow-thinking approach to designing solutions for climate change that makes use of science practices. Individuals can use scientific models to evaluate different approaches for reducing greenhouse gases. To understand what makes a wedge a wedge, it is necessary to use science practices such as Constructing Explanations and Engaging in Argument From Evidence (practices 6 and 7; see the "Stabilization Wedges Game" at *http://cmi.princeton.edu/wedges*). Choosing which wedges to enact also requires players to draw on a combination of knowledge, values, and priorities to compare the costs and benefits of different strategies.

Interpreting and Analyzing Data

The best ideas for mitigation strategies today may not be the same as the best ideas tomorrow. There are many unknowns in global climate change: How fast will ice caps melt? How will the occurrence of extreme weather events be affected? How much carbon dioxide will the oceans absorb? There are many different potential future scenarios, as illustrated by the IPCC (Figure 4.10, p. 78), with different projections that depend, to a large extent, on future

Figure 4.9
Stabilization wedges

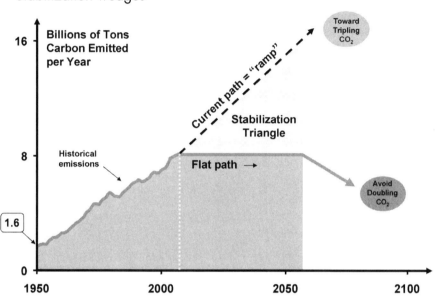

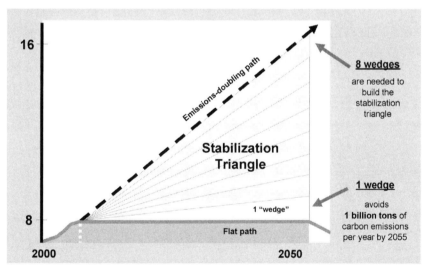

Source: Pacala and Socolow 2004.

Figure 4.10

Future scenarios for global temperature in IPCC's
Fifth Assessment Report

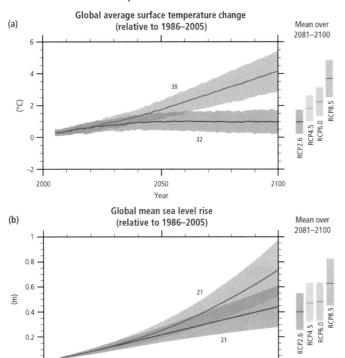

human actions. Science can predict what will happen in the future only in broad terms.

The National Research Council report *America's Climate Choices* recommends a strategy for responding to inherent uncertainties associated with a changing climate on its first page:

> *A valuable framework for making decisions about America's Climate Choices is **iterative risk management** [emphasis in original]. This refers to an ongoing process of identifying risks and response options, advancing a portfolio of actions that emphasize risk reduction and are robust across a range of possible futures, and revising responses over time to take advantage of new knowledge. (NRC 2011, pp. 1–2)*

How can science education help prepare students for a world in which iterative risk management is necessary? *America's Climate Choices* makes it clear that responses to climate change and other environmental issues cannot simply be left to the experts. These are choices that will affect all aspects of everybody's lives—what kinds of houses we live in, whether and how much we drive, how much electricity will cost—so experts and ordinary citizens need to be engaged in a deliberative process that includes interpreting and analyzing continually evolving data and responding in ways that adapt over time.

Thus, our nation's response to climate change requires an essential role for scientifically literate citizens. Science practices cannot tell us the right thing to do, but they can help us with iterative risk management, which involves responding to new evidence as it becomes available and using that evidence to inform plans and decisions about possible solutions.

Conclusion: Scientific Literacy in the Science Classroom

The examples above focused on what people know today about nutrition and climate change. We have tried to show how scientifically literate individuals can critically evaluate varied sources of information and use those sources to build scientific knowledge and design solutions.

We have located our examples outside of science classrooms because that's where the practices of scientific literacy are enacted—in the public and private domains of day-to-day life. We close, though, with some thoughts on practices in science classrooms that can prepare young people for scientifically literate reasoning and action. The discussion in this chapter has implications for both the kinds of issues science education should address and the information sources that should be used in science classrooms.

The examples above illustrate that topics students encounter in their daily lives and in the news—such as nutrition and climate change—provide multiple opportunities for engaging in practices to develop and use scientific knowledge. These are also topics that will capture the interest of many students, so they are prime candidates for what Engle and Conant (2002) refer to as "productive disciplinary engagement." Such topics deserve to be included in the required science curriculum because as they engage these topics, students can use science practices to (1) slow down and critically evaluate sources of information and (2) build scientific knowledge to design solutions.

SLOWING DOWN AND CRITICALLY EVALUATING SOURCES OF INFORMATION

Issues that arise in students' lives provide rich opportunities to explore the nature and limits of scientific knowledge and practice. When addressing these issues in science classrooms, though, it has often been assumed that the information provided to students should be authoritative and scientifically correct. We suggest in this chapter that maybe that's not always such a good idea. Science teachers are understandably reluctant to include incorrect claims in their curricula, but the popular media have no such limitations. Outside of school, students are barraged with information of dubious scientific merit, mixed in with ideas and data that have strong scientific support. Given the largely uncontrolled body of science information in popular media, preparing students for life as scientifically literate citizens requires them to learn how to sort out claims of differing scientific merit.

There are a variety of strategies students can use to evaluate the credibility of claims, including judgments about the editorial standards of different media sources, an understanding of the scientific peer review process, evaluations of the quality of data supporting an argument, and strategies for spotting self-interest in the claims that people make (see Covitt, Harris, and Anderson 2013; Kolstø 2001, 2006; Nicolaidou et al. 2011;

Zeidler and Kahn 2014). In this chapter, we have focused on one strategy that makes use of the practice of model-based reasoning. Students can learn to judge the quality of arguments from evidence supporting claims that they read and determine whether those claims are supported by credible evidence and are consistent with accepted scientific models. None of these strategies leads inevitably to the "right answer," but effective science education can help students make better-informed judgments about the validity of information they encounter.

BUILDING SCIENTIFIC KNOWLEDGE TO DESIGN SOLUTIONS

Media sources also provide multiple examples of scientific information that students can interpret and use. Nutrition labels, for example, provide chemical analyses of every kind of food found in the grocery store, and they are readily available online (e.g., *www.nutritiondata.com*). As discussed above, interpreting these labels involves several different science practices. Our discussion focused on how nutrition labels can be practically useful for making nutrition decisions, but we have found that nutrition labels can also be used in other important ways in science classrooms. The labels provide detailed analyses of the chemical content of foods and (since foods are made from the bodies of plants and animals) of plant and animal tissues. Thus, the labels can be used to help students trace matter and energy through living systems—addressing both an important crosscutting concept and a key disciplinary core idea.

There are many other kinds of data readily available on the internet that students can use in their science practices: weather data, geographic information, data about plants and animals in local ecosystems, and so on. These data can be used in classrooms to make science teaching more place-based, more relevant to students' lives, and more interesting. Students will learn important science content in ways that extend their scientific literacy—their ability to find and use the information they need for personal understanding and action.

Public and personal issues also afford multiple opportunities for students to develop new knowledge through experience and to discuss and evaluate recent scientific findings. For example, students could monitor their own weight and health data or weather and climate data. Students could also monitor energy use in their homes and schools. There are also many programs that engage students in citizen science—contributing to databases that are created by thousands of people sharing observations of similar phenomena from around the country or the world. One example is Project BudBurst *(www.budburst.org)*, which engages students in collecting phenomenological data that can be used to study how plant species are responding to changes in climate.

All of these activities afford students opportunities to participate actively in the scientific enterprise on a personal, regional, national, or global scale. Such activities can support students in learning about ways that all citizens can participate in science and about how scientific knowledge is developed. Thus, by teaching for scientific literacy it is possible to engage students in science practices in ways that are interesting, relevant, and scientifically valid. We see a great deal to gain and little to lose in using teaching materials and strategies like those suggested above. It is not necessary to compromise the rigor of scientific content to teach for scientific literacy, thus preparing all students to use science in meaningful ways in their future lives.

Acknowledgments

This research is supported, in part, by grants from the National Science Foundation under Grant No. 0815993, Grant No. DRL-0832173, and Grant No. DRL-1020187. Any opinions, findings, and conclusions or recommendations expressed in this material are those of the authors and do not necessarily reflect the views of the National Science Foundation.

References

Anderegg, W. R. L., J. W. Prall, J. Harold, and S. H. Schneider. 2010. Expert credibility in climate change. *Proceedings of the National Academy of Sciences USA* 107: 12107–12109.

Antilla, L. 2010. Self-censorship and science: A geographical review of media coverage of climate tipping points. *Public Understanding of Science* 19 (2): 240–256.

Arguez, A., and R. S. Vose. 2011. The definition of the standard WMO climate normal: The key to deriving alternative climate normals. *Bulletin of the American Meteorological Society* 92 (6): 699–704.

Bostrom, A., M. G. Morgan, B. Fischhoff, and D. Read. 1994. What do people know about global climate change? 1. Mental models. *Risk Analysis* 14 (6): 959–970.

Bransford, J. D., and D. L. Schwartz. 1999. Rethinking transfer: A simple proposal with multiple implications. *Review of Research in Education* 24: 61–100.

Covitt, B. A., C. B. Harris, and C. W. Anderson. 2013. Evaluating scientific arguments with slow thinking. *Science Scope* 37 (3): 44–52.

Cowburn, G., and L. Stockley. 2005. Consumer understanding and use of nutrition labelling: A systematic review. *Public Health Nutrition* 8 (1): 21–28.

DeBoer, G. E. 2000. Scientific literacy: Another look at its historical and contemporary meanings and its relationship to science education reform. *Journal of Research in Science Teaching* 37 (6): 582–601.

Diamond, J. 2012. *The world until yesterday: What can we learn from traditional societies?* New York: Viking.

Engle, R. A., and F. R. Conant. 2002. Guiding principles for fostering productive disciplinary engagement: Explaining an emergent argument in a community of learners classroom. *Cognition and Instruction* 20 (4): 399–483.

Evans, J. S. 2008. Dual-processing accounts of reasoning, judgment, and social cognition. *Annual Review of Psychology* 59: 255–278.

Federal Trade Commission. 2002. Weight-loss advertising: An analysis of current trends. *www.ftc. gov/reports/weight-loss-advertisingan-analysis-current-trends.*

Feinstein, N. W., S. Allen, and E. Jenkins. 2013. Outside the pipeline: Reimagining science education for nonscientists. *Science* 340: 314–317.

Haidt, J. 2001. The emotional dog and its rational tail: A social intuitionist approach to moral judgment. *Psychological Review* 108 (4): 814.

Intergovernmental Panel on Climate Change (IPCC). 2013. Summary for policymakers. In *Climate change 2013: The physical science basis contribution of Working Group I to the Fifth Assessment Report of the Intergovernmental Panel on Climate Change,* ed. T. F. Stocker, D. Qin, G.-K. Plattner, M. Tignor, S. K. Allen, J. Boschung, A. Nauels, Y. Xia, V. Bex, and P. M. Midgley, 3–30. New York: Cambridge University Press.

Jin, H., and C. W. Anderson. 2012. A learning progression for energy in socio-ecological systems. *Journal of Research in Science Teaching* 49 (9): 1149–1180.

Jones, M. D. H., and A. Henderson-Sellers. 1990. History of the greenhouse effect. *Progress in Physical Geography* 14 (1): 1–18

Kahneman, D. 2011. *Thinking, fast and slow.* New York: Farrar, Straus and Giroux.

Kempton, W., J. S. Boster, and J. A. Hartley. 1995. *Environmental values in American culture.* Cambridge, MA: MIT Press.

Kiehl, J. T., and K. E. Trenberth. 1997. Earth's annual global mean energy budget. *Bulletin of the American Meteorological Society* 78 (2): 197–208.

Kolstø, S. D. 2001. Scientific literacy for citizenship: Tools for dealing with the science dimension of controversial socioscientific issues. *Science Education* 85 (3): 291–310.

Kolstø, S. D. 2006. Patterns in students' argumentation confronted with a risk-focused socio-scientific issue. *International Journal of Science Education* 28 (14): 1689–1716.

Leiserowitz, A., E. Maibach, C. Roser-Renouf, G. Feinberg, and P. Howe. 2013. *Climate change in the American mind: Americans' global warming beliefs and attitudes in April 2013.* New Haven, CT: Yale School of Forestry and Environmental Studies.

Leiserowitz, A., and N. Smith. 2010. *Knowledge of climate change across global warming's six Americas.* New Haven, CT: Yale School of Forestry and Environmental Studies.

Mather, M., and D. Lavery. 2012. U.S. science and engineering labor force stalls, but trends vary across states. Washington, DC: Population Reference Bureau. *www.prb.org/Publications/ Articles/2012/scientists-engineers.aspx.*

Millar, R., and R. Driver. 1987. Beyond processes. *Studies in Science Education* 14: 33–62.

Mithen, S. 2002. *Human evolution and the cognitive basis of science*. In *The cognitive basis of science*, ed. P. Carruthers, S. Stich, and M. Siegel, 23–40. Cambridge, UK: Cambridge University Press.

Mohan, L., J. Chen, and C. Anderson. 2009. Developing a multi-year learning progression for carbon cycling in socio-ecological systems. *Journal of Research in Science Teaching* 46 (6): 675–698.

Moser, S. C. 2010. Communicating climate change: History, challenges, process and future directions. *Wiley Interdisciplinary Reviews: Climate Change* 1: 31–53.

National Research Council (NRC). 2007. *Taking science to school: Learning and teaching science in grades K–8.* Washington, DC: National Academies Press.

National Research Council (NRC). 2011. *America's climate choices.* Washington, DC: National Academies Press.

National Research Council (NRC). 2012. *A framework for K–12 science education: Practices, crosscutting concepts, and core ideas.* Washington, DC: National Academies Press.

NGSS Lead States. 2013. *Next Generation Science Standards: For states, by states.* Washington, DC: National Academies Press. *www.nextgenscience.org/next-generation-science-standards.*

Nicolaidou, I., E. A. Kyza, F. Terzian, A. Hadjichambis, and D. Kafouris. 2011. A framework for scaffolding students' assessment of the credibility of evidence. *Journal of Research in Science Teaching* 48 (7): 711–744.

Ogden C. L., M. D. Carroll, B. K. Kit, and K. M. Flegal. 2014. Prevalence of childhood and adult obesity in the United States, 2011–2012. *Journal of the American Medical Association* 311 (8): 806–814.

Pacala, S., and R. Socolow. 2004. Stabilization wedges: Solving the climate problem for the next 50 years with current technologies. *Science* 305: 968–972.

Pollan, M. 2006. *The omnivore's dilemma: A natural history of four meals.* New York: Penguin.

Sinha, A., K. Hollingsworth, S. Ball, and T. Cheetham. 2013. Improving the vitamin D status of vitamin D deficient adults is associated with improved mitochondrial oxidative function in skeletal muscle. *Journal of Clinical Endocrinology and Metabolism* 98 (3): E509–E513.

Zeidler, D., and S. Kahn. 2014. *It's debatable! Using socioscientific issues to develop scientific literacy, K–12.* Arlington, VA: NSTA Press.

Zeidler, D. L., T. D. Sadler, S. Applebaum, and B. E. Callahan. 2009. Advancing reflective judgment through socioscientific issues. *Journal of Research in Science Teaching* 46 (1): 74–101.

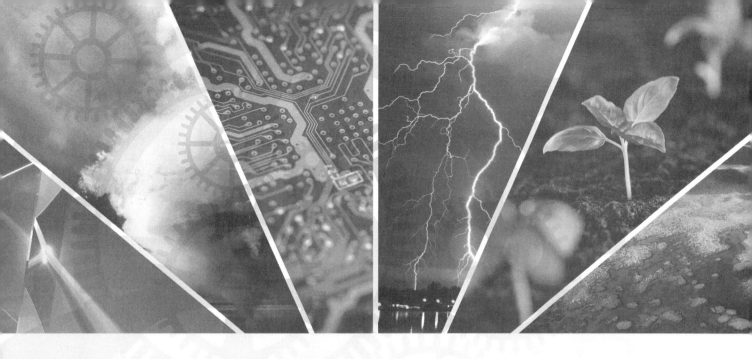

SECTION 2

WHAT DO THE PRACTICES LOOK LIKE IN CLASSROOMS?

Unpacking Each Practice

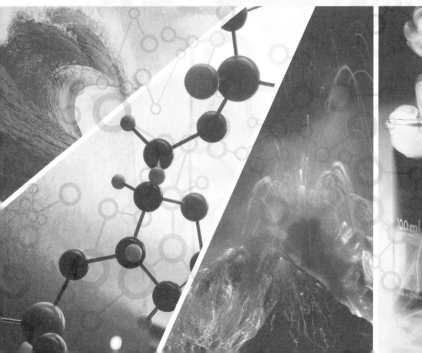
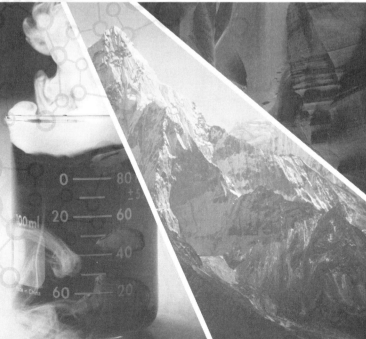

5

ASKING QUESTIONS

BRIAN J. REISER, LISA BRODY, MICHAEL NOVAK, KEETRA TIPTON, AND LEEANN (SUTHERLAND) ADAMS

The Importance of Asking Questions in Science

At first glance, Asking Questions might seem like a practice that is already in widespread use in today's science classrooms. Teachers ask questions throughout a class period for both formative and summative purposes. Teacher-posed questions elicit prior knowledge and check students' developing understanding. Students ask questions when they do not understand a concept or are unsure about what they are supposed to do. They sometimes ask questions that interest them, but those may or may not be related to learning goals. These kinds of questions are, indeed, common. But the practice of Asking Questions as envisioned in the *Next Generation Science Standards* (*NGSS*; NGSS Lead States 2013) is not at all common. Although teachers may pose questions to prompt discussion and probe thinking, the *NGSS* focus on the *students'* role in the work of asking questions that become the center of knowledge building in the classroom learning community. From teachers' own self-reports, involving students in questioning and in reflection to evaluate where more work is needed is less common (Banilower et al. 2013). In this chapter, we examine student engagement in the science practice of Asking Questions. (The associated engineering practice of Defining Problems is described in Chapter 13, p. 283.)

Questioning, like the other science and engineering practices, requires collaborative work between teachers and students. Students' questions should be a key part of figuring out what the classroom community needs to do. Before students can build a model or explanation, they need to raise questions about phenomena. Teachers also play a critical role in the knowledge-building work of classroom discussions. Teacher questioning can help students figure out where the gaps lie in their preliminary ideas. Teacher questioning can help uncover ideas that students take for granted (e.g., "How do we know this?"). It can spark students' realization that their current explanations are not yet sufficient (e.g., "How does this explain *this* part of the phenomenon?"). In this way, teacher questioning can help students construct new questions to push the investigation forward.

If we can create an environment in our classrooms that supports students being comfortable in sharing their questions, it becomes apparent that students indeed have many questions and are capable of constructing questions worth investigating. They wonder and can be curious about many things (e.g., "Why did I get sick when my friend did not?" "Why can I run faster now than I did last week?" "Why did the rain flood part of the school yard when the rest of the school area drained?"). Because science and engineering involve making sense of our world, Asking Questions and Defining Problems are critical for learners to be able to engage and focus their curiosity and creativity. Once we begin to honor students' questions as central to learning, and students realize that we are going to deliver on a promise to make progress on answering their original questions, students will begin to generate many more questions.

As teachers, we can help them develop thoughtful questions worth investigating. Teachers' questions are often needed to help students figure out and refine their own questions. Students' questions are a key part of science and engineering practices. When students can ask and refine their own questions, they are more motivated to engage in the hard work of figuring out phenomena, step by step. Even more important, learning is more effective when teachers ask questions to drive sense-making rather than sim-

Making sense of the world begins with questions that identify what needs to be explained about the phenomena.

ply presenting ideas. Learners process things more deeply when they encounter ideas or data that are relevant to questions they have raised. Asking these types of sense-making questions, exploring alternatives, and then planning investigations leads to deeper learning than simply being presented with an investigation to do or a problem to solve. Just as we don't want to simply spoon-feed students full-blown explanations in a classroom environment based on figuring out answers, we also don't want to just hand them questions and tell them what they need to investigate. We have to work with students to develop both questions and answers if we are building science knowledge together.

What Does Questioning Look Like in the Classroom?

Let's begin by considering two extended classroom examples of the collaborative process of *NGSS*-like questioning in action.

SCENARIO 1: HOW AND WHY DOES ODOR TRAVEL?

The unit in this scenario builds toward the performance expectation 5-PS1-1, "Develop a model to describe that matter is made of particles too small to be seen"; helps build the disciplinary core idea PS1.A: Structure and Properties of Matter, which explains that "matter of any type can be subdivided into particles that are too small to see, but even then the matter still exists and can be detected by other means"; and addresses the aspect of PS1.A that deals with conservation of matter (NGSS Lead States 2013, p. 43). But from the students' perspective, they are questioning, investigating, and modeling phenomena about the behavior of air, beginning with the puzzling phenomena of odor. This scenario is based on our experience with fifth- and sixth-grade classrooms working with the unit "How Can I Smell Things From a Distance?" from the Investigating and Questioning Our World Through Science and Technology curriculum series (IQWST; Krajcik et al. 2013).

Students enter the classroom on the first day of a new eight-week unit. The teacher says to the students, "Think of a time when you smelled an odor and knew what it was even before you could see it." Students eagerly share their experiences and quickly provide many examples. A common example is smelling something cooking in the kitchen as soon as they walk in the door at home. The teacher uses this and other examples to then ask, "How can this happen? How can you smell something you can't even see? How can you smell something when you aren't anywhere near it?" Students talk about their ideas with a partner and then share as a whole class.

As this discussion continues, and without mentioning what she is doing, the teacher opens an opaque jar in front of her. A student calls out, "Hey, I smell something." The teacher responds, "Does anybody else smell something? What do you smell?" A few students say they do. The teacher asks students to raise their hands if they smell something different from when they walked in the room. A few hands go up, all from students sitting near the teacher. Students guess that they are smelling mint or peppermint. The teacher confirms, "You're right. The odor actually is from peppermint oil. Why do you think these people," she points to those near her, "can smell it, but the rest of you can't? Talk to your partner about why that could be."

While students are doing this, the teacher walks slowly around the room with the jar in hand so that all students get a chance to detect the odor themselves. She waves her hand over the open jar as if trying to push the odor toward students as she walks around the room.

Students then share ideas about how they think the odor gets to their noses. Some students say that it starts by leaving the jar. The teacher asks, "But why didn't you smell it when you first came into the room?"

Students agree that the lid had to be removed for the odor to "get out." One student suggests, "It goes from the jar to our noses." Other students question this: "Wait—doesn't it have to go into the air first?"

The teacher then says, "Interesting. Why does it need to go into the air first?" Students agree that they weren't right next to the jar, so the peppermint odor had to go into the air to get to them.

The teacher asks, "Does it go into all of the air at the same time? What evidence do we have?"

Students point out that their hands were going up at different times as the teacher moved around the room, so people smelled the peppermint at different times. The teacher raises another question: "We agree that we have evidence that we don't all smell the odor at the same time, and it matters where you are compared with the odor. So how does that work?"

Students generate a lot of ideas—the smell is in the air, odors spread out, the air carries odors—all of which the teacher encourages without critique, sometimes asking more questions to push students to go further: "What does it mean to spread out? What causes it to spread out?" (See Chapter 14, p. 311, for a discussion of discourse strategies to draw out students' thinking.)

At the end of this lesson, students leave with a shared experience of a common phenomenon that we often take for granted, but there are central aspects of this phenomenon that they cannot yet explain scientifically. They have identified some starting points for how the phenomenon works: There is an odor source; the odor travels in the air and is then detected by people's noses. The class has agreed on some starting questions about what the odor is made of, how it gets from the source to the nose, and why people closer smelled it before those who are farther away. A homework reading supports the class in thinking about odors they like and don't like, so that their own experiences can be referenced throughout the unit. Students read about carbon monoxide, an odorless gas to which a rotten egg odor is added to make it detectable to human noses.

The next day, the teacher suggests that students try to flesh out yesterday's questions and new questions prompted by the reading so that the class can agree on what it is trying to figure out. The teacher sets up an organizer called a Driving Question Board (DQB; Nordine and Torres 2013; Weizman, Shwartz, and Fortus 2010). Students write on sticky notes their questions that have arisen in the activity, discussion, and the reading thus far. They are encouraged to think of *how* or *why* questions that they might be able to investigate (see Chapter 10, p. 205, for a discussion of explanatory questions). Here are a few of the starting questions developed in two different classrooms:

Fifth-grade student questions:

- Why do we open windows when we cook?

- What are odors made out of?

- Why is natural gas odorless?

- Why do odors disperse?

- Why does it take a long time for skunk smell to go away?

Sixth-grade student questions:

- Why do some people smell odors better than others?

- Why do smells eventually go away?

- How does an odor actually get out of the food?

- Why can I smell brownies baking over the other odors in the room?

- Why do some odors smell good to some people but not to other people?

The students discuss how to organize their questions. In the sixth-grade classroom, they decide to organize questions into three clusters: (1) How does the odor get from its source to my nose? (2) What makes one odor different from another? (3) How can a material change so we can smell it? The teacher suggests that many of their questions could be clustered into these categories and asks students to share one question they would like to be able to answer. Students share and post their questions to the DQB by listening carefully and linking their own to another student's question. For example, one student begins with "My question is, why doesn't a banana smell like an orange even though they're both fruits?" and suggests this is related to the category "What makes one odor different from another?"

Another student then adds the question "Why can you smell hot pizza better than cold pizza?" and indicates, "Mine is related to his because I want to know why the smell is different." The sharing continues until all students have shared at least one original question.

The teacher ends the lesson by saying, "Throughout this unit, you will think of more questions. Whenever you have a question, write it on a sticky note and add it to the DQB." The teacher explains that now that the class has a group of questions linked to each other, making progress on one of these groups might allow students to answer a lot of questions at once. The teacher explains that, while every question might not get answered in detail, as a class, students should aim to gather evidence to be able to explain the answers to many questions in this unit.

Figure 5.1
Sample of fifth-grade questions

Figure 5.1 shows a sample of fifth-grade student questions. Figure 5.2 (p. 92) shows the full DQB after that fifth-grade class has organized it (these students have developed more categories for their questions than the sixth-grade classroom). Figure 5.3 (p. 92) shows a close-up of one of the sections of the board for "What do odors look like?"

Figure 5.2
The DQB for "How can I smell things from a distance?" from a fifth-grade classroom organized into subquestions

Figure 5.3
The DQB for "What do odors look like?" from a fifth-grade classroom

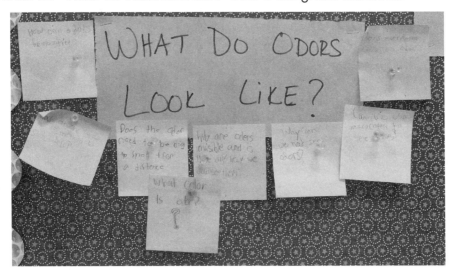

What Are the Key Aspects of the Asking Questions Practice?

As students progress through the investigations that follow, they begin to figure out partial answers to these questions and to generate new questions. This classroom scenario, "How and why does odor travel?" demonstrates a number of aspects of the practice of Asking Questions. First, notice *the nature and role of questioning* in the scenario. Many of us think of students raising questions when they are confused or want help. In contrast, the *NGSS* questioning practice emphasizes that students ask questions to help them identify what they need to figure out to help explain phenomena. This process is motivating and engaging and helps students focus on what needs to be explained.

Second, consider *how the questions get started*. The teacher did not simply prompt the students with "What questions do you have about odors?" A more effective way to prompt questions from students is to solicit them as contextualized in a shared phenomenon. Students observed something happen (an odor traveled through the air) and made observations about that event (the odor took time to travel; it traveled in all directions; the odor allowed them to identify the source of the odor). The teacher asked about and clarified students' initial ideas until they realized there were interesting questions to be figured out and explained.

Third, notice that *both the students and the teacher are critical players in asking questions that are productive for investigations.* Students bring in prior, out-of-class experiences that connect to the in-class phenomenon under investigation, and those experiences enable students to expand on their own initial ideas and focus on what needs to be explained. One student pointed out that it is hard to smell things when he has a cold, which suggests that a working odor detector is needed. The hot and cold pizza question led to the idea that temperature may be a relevant factor.

Teachers may need to probe and help students refine their questions to expand on things they take for granted and to help them see that there is something there that they can't explain. By actively attempting to explain the phenomena and connecting to their own experiences, students engage in thinking through and uncovering gaps in their explanations that can lead to productive questions to investigate. Notice also that these need to be explanatory questions—questions that get at how and why phenomena happen—if they are going to help the class get at the targeted disciplinary core ideas. Learning to ask how and why questions is part of the process that teachers model and that students come to understand quite quickly as central to asking the kinds of questions that can be answered scientifically. "Why does …?" is a common starter for young students that is easily turned into a question worthy of pursuit.

We return to these points after first considering our second example.

Key Features of the Asking Questions Practice

- Questioning involves developing and revising explanatory questions about how and why phenomena happen.

- Both teachers and students are critical players in asking productive questions.

- Questioning helps identify what about the phenomena needs to be investigated.

SCENARIO 2: WHAT IS GOING ON IN MY BODY SO I GET THE ENERGY TO DO THINGS?

This scenario shows the key role that teachers play in pushing students to go deeper than their intuitive explanations and how this can help uncover rich explanatory questions. It is from a middle school classroom investigating how the human body does the things it is capable of doing. The seventh-grade classroom is working with the IQWST unit "What Is Going On Inside of Me?" (Krajcik et al. 2013). Students are trying to figure out how our body manages to perform physical activities such as playing a piano, swimming, or throwing a basketball. A secondary question is how we can improve our performance in these activities with practice. A third related question that emerges is how the body can recover from injury. These questions provide a context in which students address a bundle of two performance expectations: MS-LS1-3, "Use argument supported by evidence for how the body is a system of interacting subsystems composed of groups of cells" (NGSS Lead States 2013, p. 67), and MS-LS1-7, "Develop a model to describe how food is rearranged through chemical reactions forming new molecules that support growth and/or release energy as this matter moves through an organism" (NGSS Lead States 2013, p. 67). Students' investigations and models help them build central parts of the disciplinary core idea LS1: From Molecules to Organisms: Structures and Processes.

The unit begins with students discussing a series of videos that show a range of physical activity, including athletic activities (swimming, shooting a basketball, a handstand, and one-arm pushups) and skilled motor performances (playing the piano). Some interesting consequences of these activities are evident, such as a swimmer gasping for breath after swimming two lengths of an Olympic-sized swimming pool underwater. The videos also show a range of performance, comparing a two-year-old's wobbly attempts to shoot a basketball with that of a skilled teenager shooting a three-pointer.

The teacher pushes students to try to explain what is going on inside our bodies that allows us to do these kinds of activities. In this discussion, the teacher also brings up questions about what happens when something goes wrong and a person becomes injured and asks students how the body manages to "fix itself." Students have a lot of prior knowledge they share, but they also discover important gaps in what they can explain.

For example, students know that they need energy to do things. They take for granted that their bodies respond in particular ways when they exercise. They have experienced sweating, increased heart rates, and increased breathing rates while exercising many times in their lives. They know of course that breathing and a pumping heart are needed to keep them alive. But when pushed, they are not able to explain very much about *why* these internal actions of the body are needed. Here are some of the ways that the teacher responds to students and pushes with how and why questions to help them become unsatisfied with their simple answers:

- *"How* do our bodies use energy? Where does that happen? What do you mean by 'use energy'? Does the energy disappear? What do we mean by burning calories? Where do calories come from? How are they related to energy?"

- *"How* does food provide us with energy? Where does that happen inside the body? How does that work? Where did the energy in food come from to begin with?"

- *"Why* do we need blood to live? How does it keep us alive? Why do our hearts beat faster after exercise than before?"

- *"Why* do we need to breathe to stay alive? How does it keep us alive? Why do we breathe harder after exercise than before?"

- "If oxygen is what we breathe in and carbon dioxide is what we breathe out, where is the oxygen going? Where is the carbon dioxide coming from?"

- "A lot of you said exercising makes your muscles stronger and increases your stamina. But how does that work? What is different when the muscle is stronger?"

These lines of questioning from the teacher support students in recognizing that explanations based on prior knowledge may fall short of providing a causal set of mechanisms that describe how and why these phenomena occur. Note that although the goal of the practice is for students to generate questions about the explanatory stories behind phenomena, the teacher's role is key in asking the kinds of probing questions that support students in thinking more deeply and wondering about things they take for granted. In the scenario, notice that choosing this particular set of phenomena helps raise questions about patterns in the data that (1) motivate curiosity, (2) connect to prior experiences, (3) help students recognize that their prior knowledge cannot explain how or why the phenomena occur, and (4) set up the need for the future investigations the teacher has anticipated.

As a result of this discussion, the class realizes there are many questions about how the body works to accomplish all the things it can do. The teacher introduces a driving question that captures all the questions students realized they must answer to explain how the body performs, grows, and repairs itself: "What is going on inside of me?" After the teacher introduces this, students are asked to develop more specific question that will help them address it. Figure 5.4 shows the regions of the DQB, and Figure 5.5 shows a close-up of some students' questions about injuries.

Figure 5.4
The DQB for "What is going on inside of me?"

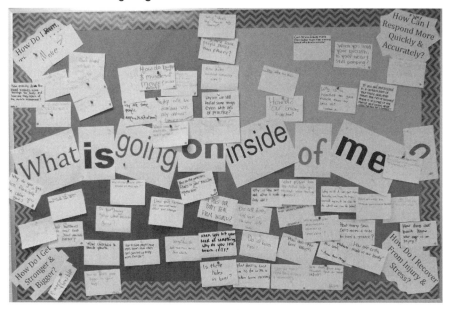

Here is a sample of the range of questions these seventh-grade students generated:

- Why does the heart beat faster when you do physical activity?

- What makes your muscles grow?

- What does blood do for your body?

- Why are some people faster than others?

Figure 5.5
A close-up of DQB for "What is going on inside of me?"

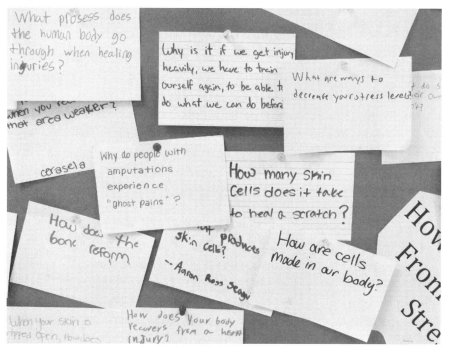

- How does your brain help your body do physical movements?

- What happens inside your body as you recover from injuries?

- Why do heavier weights make you stronger?

- How are cells made in your body?

- How does the bone reform?

- How is new skin made?

In discussing these questions, the goals become to explore how the body gets the materials and energy it needs to perform activity, to grow, and to repair itself. So as the unit progresses, rather than simply going though body systems one by one, examining the components and their functions, there is a cluster of explanatory questions that motivate following paths through the body to uncover a matter and energy transformation story.

In the next sections, we draw on these two scenarios to characterize the question-asking practice and explore its relation to the other science and engineering practices.

The Role of Questioning in the Science and Engineering Practices

WHY IS THE PRACTICE OF QUESTIONING IMPORTANT?

The key focus in *A Framework for K–12 Science Education* (NRC 2012) and the *NGSS* is developing systems of explanatory ideas rather than isolated facts. The disciplinary core ideas in the *NGSS* are defined as generative ideas that students can use to make sense of the natural world. Questions and problems play a critical role in the practices that develop and use this knowledge. Questions articulate what it is about a phenomenon that needs to be explained. It is explanatory questions that push teachers and students to go beyond merely knowing the names of things (e.g., the parts of a cell) or the definition of a process (e.g., photosynthesis is how plants make food). Explanatory questions such as "How does a cell get what it needs?" or "Why does the weather vary across the year?" require more than identifying the name of something or the definition of a scientific term. They require an explanation, a step-by-step account (as described in Chapter 10, p. 205), often drawing on general explanatory models (as described in Chapter 6, p. 109). Addressing questions may require argumentation that uses data as evidence to tease apart and decide between possible accounts (as described in Chapter 11, p. 229).

Throughout this book, we talk about engaging in practices as a way to shift classrooms from *learning about* to *figuring out* how the world works. The goal of the *NGSS* is not to "explain photosynthesis" in the sense of giving students the science topic and asking them to describe what they know about it. The goal is to explain something in the world that occurs—a phenomenon—and to *figure out* and reach consensus on how and why it works the way that it does. Students ask questions about how plants actually grow and then work to explain how plants get the mass they need to get bigger or how they get the energy they need to survive. Eventually, we apply the label of "photosynthesis" to this process. Questioning plays a critical role in this shift by helping the class figure out what the important aspects of the phenomena that need to be explained are and then evaluating candidate explanations to see whether they account for these important aspects. The classroom's ongoing questions are the articulation of the gap between what the class has figured out so far and what they are still trying to make sense of. Examining phenomena and using models help students uncover gaps in their understanding, gaps that lead to asking new questions, engaging in new investigations, revising models, and developing explanations. In that process, the class generates new questions to guide the next steps of the investigation.

In this way, constructing questions is not an act of idle curiosity. Instead, it is an integral part of figuring out what needs to be explained and where the class needs to go next in figuring out how and why something works the way it does in the world. By building on prior knowledge and articulating the gaps in what can be explained, questions enable students to dig more deeply when interpreting the data and observations they analyze. The questions provide a lens that guides sense-making and pushes sense-making and learning deeper than if students were merely encountering the data without this preparation.

QUESTIONS BOTH LEAD INTO THE OTHER PRACTICES AND ARE SPARKED BY PROGRESS IN THE OTHER PRACTICES

In the work of the classroom, questions are a starting point, but their importance does not stop there. We have already described how questions can help the class figure out what they need to explain and therefore are a key step of beginning to investigate a new phenomenon, such as a drop in a population of organisms or patterns across generations in traits. But questions also arise throughout the process of investigating and making sense of phenomena. Here we consider how questions both lead into the other practices of investigating and explaining, and how progress in developing our explanations and models can lead to further questions.

Questions arise throughout the process of sense-making when we realize the explanation we are building is only part of the story we need. For example, in the human body scenario described earlier, students' work in following food through the body eventually leads to the detection of broken-down food (in the form of glucose) in the bloodstream, which is shipped around the body through the circulatory system and then reaches all the cells of the body. This leads immediately to students questioning whether anything in the blood can actually get into cells or out of cells. This becomes a context to investigate what materials can get into and out of cells, leading to the discovery of the cell's semipermeable membrane. Identifying that glucose can get into cells then leads to questions about what cells are actually doing with that glucose. Investigating this question eventually leads students to put together an argument that a chemical reaction involving glucose and oxygen is going on inside of all our cells, and that this uses the energy in food to perform the functions the cell needs.

As students build pieces of the puzzle to explain phenomena, this leads to new questions (with teachers' guidance) that then uncover new phenomena that need to be investigated. Then, new data sets or experiments become something that students ask for to solve questions they have raised, rather than doing a sequence of labs driven by a logic known only to the teacher or the textbook. Learning goals such as the role of cells in processing food become part of a coherent storyline students pursue, rather than labs provided to students to do without motivation (Reiser et al. 2016).

WHO ASKS QUESTIONS?

Questioning is collaborative work. Questions are not just built into phenomena. Often, there are a lot of different things one could choose to wonder about. The teachers' role is central in helping students see what is important, confusing, surprising, or relevant about some phenomenon. In some cases, phenomena are exciting and surprising (e.g., a strong combustion reaction or an exciting case of predation), but in many cases, a phenomenon worth explaining may be something we take for granted, such as being able to smell something from across a room or breathing hard after sprinting. As we saw in these scenarios, the teacher's role is central in helping students uncover something in everyday phenomena that is nevertheless difficult to explain.

We also see that students can piggyback on each other's questions. Often when students hear another student's question, they want to change their earlier questions. Another student's idea spurs their own thinking, causing them to want to refine their question or generate a new one. Having students explicitly link their questions to a previous question someone has posed is one strategy to support this type of coherence in knowledge building.

WHAT MAKES A GOOD QUESTION?

To understand what makes a good question, we need to consider the goal of science practices. The goal is to figure out how and why something happens the way it does in the natural world. Questions then need to connect to phenomena that need to be explained. To help students understand what we are targeting in science, we need to move beyond some simple factual questions. If a question can simply be looked up in a book or typed into Google to find the answer, it is not a good research question.

First, we need to go beyond yes/no questions such as "Do fish breathe underwater?" and ask questions that get at explanation and mechanism, such as "How do fish get the resources they need to survive?" Second, we need to do more than accept answers that simply name or categorize the phenomenon. Knowing that we inherit our traits through DNA or that plants make food through photosynthesis is not an explanation. We need to go beyond just knowing the name to explaining how and why the phenomenon works as it does. Third, we need to go past questions that simply get at empirical evidence. Even some questions that call for an investigation are not really explanatory. Consider the common task in chemistry labs in which students are given a mystery substance and have to do various tests to determine what kind of substance it is. While such a task may be useful for familiarizing students with important chemical tests, students aren't *explaining* anything or building knowledge of disciplinary core ideas if they are simply using the tests to provide empirical support for the claim of the identity of the mystery substance. Good questions need to not only demand empirical evidence from an investigation but also require building explanations and models that advance our knowledge and apply to new situations. In this way, helping students understand what makes good questions involves helping students understand and buy into what counts as an answer in science. Table 5.1 shows examples of explanatory questions that reflect the Asking Questions practice and examples of questions that are not what the practice is targeting.

Table 5.1
Example explanatory questions and problematic questions

Questions	Comments
Examples of students using the Asking Questions science practice	
• Why do we sweat when we exercise? • Why do we need oxygen?	These questions ask *why* something happens. They link phenomena students are familiar with and ask how and why they happen. These types of questions make explicit that we know this happens, and we may know some of the characteristics of situations in which this happens. But *why* does this happen? This is the core of explaining.
• How long can something store energy? • Do different foods give different kinds of energy?	While these are phrased as factual or yes/no questions, teachers can work with questions like this and help students revise them to be more explanatory: What happens when something stores energy? Why do foods differ in the way they provide energy to the body?
What we do *not* mean by students asking questions	
• I don't understand what you meant when you said that "plants make their own food." • What does "symbiotic" mean?	Of course, it makes sense for students to ask for clarification, but to contribute to the process of developing scientific knowledge, the practice needs to involve students posing questions that push thinking and investigating further. Rather than asking about what teachers have explained to students, these questions should move the class forward to the next steps in the investigation.
• Where do camels live? • What else is in air besides oxygen?	These may be interesting questions, and they ask about things students haven't figured out yet, but these questions, as posed, are all about factual information. There is nothing to explain in investigating these questions. You might want to try pushing students to expand these questions to get at something that needs to be explained. For example, we might ask the following: *Why* do camels live where they do? *How* did the stuff in the air get there?

What the Questioning Practice Is Not

- The questioning practice is not about teachers asking students vocabulary definitions of science terms; it is not about asking factual or yes/no questions.

- The questioning practice it is not about students asking the teacher to clarify when they misunderstand ideas or directions.

- The questioning practice is not just the first step in the science unit. It goes beyond only asking, "What do you want to know about X?"—though this could be incorporated successfully in the unit.

- The questioning practice is not a form of a trivia game. If students can simply search online for the answer, then it's not an interesting question for investigation.

Supporting Questioning in the Classroom
DELIVERING ON THE PROMISE OF ASKING QUESTIONS

Generating questions is an important first step, but then those questions need to be used for knowledge-building purposes. The DQB is one approach for representing questions in a shared, public way: for tracking questions, for enabling anyone in the class to refer back to them, to periodically revisit them to acknowledge what has been figured out thus far, and to determine what still has to be learned. However, any approach that allows you to publicly represent, organize, and track student questions could support this practice.

Science practices are an interrelated set of activities that are meaningful because they work together to help people investigate and make sense of the natural world. Thus, the meaning of asking questions comes, in part, from how it connects to the other practices. There is no point in generating questions if it is just to have questions. The point is to articulate something that the class is going to try to figure out. By establishing and recording questions, the class commits to attempting to address the questions. Therefore, it is important to return to these questions as the students start building explanations and see what they can answer. Progress may also be made prior to having satisfactory answers; in some cases, the class now knows more about the situation and can ask a more precise question.

As mentioned earlier, we have to deliver on these promises. This means going back to the questions to figure out if we have answered them yet, or if we have new questions that spring from our earlier questions. This helps students see that their questions really matter. Posing questions has consequences for the rest of the unit. By involving students in generating these questions, evaluating progress on them, and determining when we have a sufficient model or explanation that addresses the question, students develop ownership over the ideas they are building and refining in their science classrooms.

Once the class has sufficient information to answer questions raised and posted earlier, there are several different strategies to use. One critical step is to acknowledge those questions—acknowledge by saying, "Today, we're going to look more closely at these ideas and see what we can figure out." The teacher might read one or more questions aloud that he or she suggests the class should work on that day. This process makes it clear to students that their questions are part of the knowledge-building work of the class. Their questions have value beyond writing them on sticky notes and putting them on the classroom wall.

Another strategy for using answerable questions is to turn them into bellwork questions. The teacher can take a question off of the board, say to the class, "I think we can answer this one now," and use the question for formative or summative purposes. Different questions can be taken down from the DQB and given to different groups of students to answer collaboratively. These questions can be posed to the class, and students can choose one to answer, writing an explanation that uses evidence from class activities, readings, and what they have figured out thus far. Students can be invited or assigned to pursue questions independently and to present them to peers or to create a booklet to teach a younger student about a topic. What is important is that questions are shared publicly, become part of the knowledge-building experience, and are used in ways that show they "count" for something in the classroom.

SCAFFOLDING QUESTIONING

One useful approach is to develop categories for types of questions related to the overarching or driving question guiding the investigation. The anchoring phenomena in the scenarios in this chapter led to many specific questions for investigation. The teacher can also use the brainstorming discussion to map out the main questions for the investigation, co-constructing categories with students. Once categories are established, teachers can support students in reasoning about the phenomena to uncover questions by prompting, "Where would that question go?" or "Which section is it most related to?" This can help focus questions on productive avenues for investigation; it supports students in thinking about the key aspects of the phenomena to be explained. It can help students' questions connect to the explanatory models that are the target of the investigation.

Teachers can also model the types of explanatory questions that will be useful in developing explanations and models. Teacher modeling of how to extract questions from observations of phenomena can be very helpful in supporting students in developing the kinds of questions for engaging in other science and engineering practices, such as building explanatory models. Here are some examples of teacher modeling of how phenomena can provoke questions for explanation: "I don't know! How does that happen? How is it possible that some objects let lots of light through and others do not?" or "How is it possible that you smell warmer stuff sooner?" In general, it is helpful when teachers wonder along with students by asking questions such as "That's so weird—I wonder how this works?" and "How can we extend our model to explain this?"

An important part of what teachers can do is to help students become dissatisfied with their current explanations. As we saw in the scenarios, begin with a phenomenon so students become interested in wanting to figure out the explanation. Then help students become dissatisfied with their current ideas about the phenomenon they thought they already knew. When students realize they can't really explain it even though they thought they could, they can begin to formulate high-quality questions that lead to investigations and other practices.

USING QUESTIONS TO MOVE THE INVESTIGATION FORWARD OR REVISE MODELS

Students' questions can also be used to lead to the next steps in an investigation, helping guide the storyline of the curriculum. For example, in the first scenario, a teacher might say, "I was reviewing our questions last night and found one that we haven't really talked about yet: 'Why can I smell hot pizza better than cold pizza?' Our model doesn't really have anything in it that would explain whether temperature affects how odors behave. What do you think about investigating this question next? Let's take a few minutes to brainstorm some ideas."

Using students' questions can lead to revising or elaborating models or explanations further. For example, a teacher working on a unit about light (disciplinary core idea PS4: Waves and Their Applications in Technologies for Information Transfer) with her students might say the following:

> I noticed that one of you had asked, "Why does light go through glass and not wood?" That made me realize that our model doesn't say anything about light going through an object. So far, our model says that light travels in straight lines and bounces off objects and to our eyes, and that's how we see objects. So now I am not sure: How can we explain how can light can go through some

*objects rather than bounce off? Take a moment to write down some ideas about
what you think we should investigate next related to our question "Can light
go through some objects and not others?"*

Another strategy for supporting students in questioning and moving toward investigations is to help them create testable questions from their ideas about phenomena. When students have ideas about how and why something happens, asking "How could we test that?" is often a very useful strategy in getting students to be more precise about exactly what they are expecting and how they might figure it out. For example, when the teacher asked, "So how can we figure out whether temperature affects odors?" students had many suggestions: "We could see how long it takes for us to smell just-popped hot popcorn and cold popcorn." "We could try that with hot chocolate that has been sitting out for a while so it's cooled down and a cup of hot chocolate that is fresh." "We could time it." "We could see if it smells different, if the odors smell differently."

TAKING STOCK OF PROGRESS ANSWERING THE QUESTIONS

It is useful to revisit questions and take stock of which questions can be answered and which require more investigation. Revisiting questions allows teachers to ask, "Can we come to consensus on that idea? What have we agreed on? What have we figured out?"

Another way to take stock on progress toward answering the classroom's questions is to periodically ask students to summarize: "What do we know about our big question?" For example, a teacher might ask, "What do we now know air can do?" (It can be compressed, expanded, added to, or taken out. It has mass and takes up volume.) "What do we now know light must do for us to see it?" (There must be a light source. Light travels in a straight line and bounces off an object. There must be an eye or detector.) It is also important to recap with students what evidence we have that supports the answers to those questions: "How do we know light travels in a straight line? What did we do in class that gave us evidence for this?" "Wait, can we add air to a container that already has some air in it? Did we test that idea? What did we do to help us figure that out?"

These strategies depend on student questions being public. Keeping students' questions in a visible place in the classroom (or in a digital space that can be accessed by the class) enables teachers to revisit these questions and for students to add new questions as they arise. Revising questions helps students keep track of what we have figured out so far—for example, by grouping answered questions together and adding important punchlines to answered questions.

How Can We Create an Equitable Classroom That Supports Questioning and Other Science Practices?

In this book, we have focused on how the science and engineering practices work together, as a system. These practices require a shift in the culture of the classroom, in which students, guided by the teacher, form a learning community that is building, evaluating, and refining knowledge (see Chapter 1, p. 3). This requires classroom norms in which classrooms are "a safe intellectual space for students to offer, tinker with, and produce ideas that everyone eventually owns" (Krist et al. 2016, p. 8). Establishing these may require a shift from traditional classroom norms, requiring students to take more responsibility for making decisions about the scientific ideas they build. In the case of the Asking Questions practice, this may pose particular challenges in creating a safe intellectual space for all students.

For example, if a student says, "I don't understand how X happens," this usually indicates confusion or a failure on the part of the student to grasp the concept. Yet the science practices require and celebrate even the most basic questions. Developing science knowledge requires being willing to consider an idea we may take for granted, such as "food gives us energy," and take another look at that "fact" and ask, "But how does that actually happen?" It takes us beyond thinking of questions as having simple answers that we either know or don't know and causes us to recognize that science is about building more sophisticated answers to questions for which we may already have partial answers.

In the image of school held by many students, we might imagine that it is usually not the "successful students" who have to ask questions admitting a lack of understanding. Asking this type of question may be seen as a sign of failure, or at least a struggle. To fully embrace knowledge building and the central role of questions will mean getting students comfortable with admitting that they don't know something and seeing the process of asking a question as a positive action, rather than as admitting a lack of knowledge.

In Chapter 14 (p. 311), the authors discuss particular strategies you can use to help create a classroom climate in which all students expect to take responsibility for the knowledge we are building in the classroom. In addition to these more general talk moves, we consider a number of specific ideas here related to the question-asking part of science practices, building on the suggestions about creating classroom climate made by Krist et al. (2016).

Celebrate questions. Throughout this chapter, we have discussed several types of activities that make the posing of questions an explicit goal. As teachers, we need to create the expectation that all of us in the class (both the teacher and students) are responsible for building scientific knowledge. This means that we all have the opportunity, and the responsibility, to raise additional questions related to main question we are pursuing.

We need to help students see that developing questions is a central part of learning. We can't develop an important scientific idea unless we first identify what it is about phenomena that we need to figure out. So every question we generate is potentially valuable. We need everybody to contribute and raise questions. We need everybody to work on trying to connect what we figure out each class to the questions that motivated our investigation. It may be necessary to reassure students so that they are not worried that theirs will not be the "right" questions. We may need to keep reassuring students that all questions related to our main question are useful and welcome in the classroom.

Encourage participation. Culture takes time to build. While you will eventually need to probe students and push them to go deeper, to first get students comfortable, you may want to focus more on encouraging somebody who has not shared yet to share and not put students on the spot by pushing for elaboration on their ideas. Another strategy is to hand the control of turn-taking over to the students. Let the student who has just shared be responsible for calling on the next student.

Krist and colleagues also suggest that teachers can encourage participation if they "police behavior—not ideas." They provide some strategies for adjusting a grading scheme so that "it reflects the importance of productive participation in class discussions" (Krist et al. 2016, pp. 11–12). Occurrences of nonproductive participation, such as being disrespectful of other students' comments, can be penalized. Krist and colleagues suggest having students fill out discussion reflection sheets on major discussion-focused days in which students are asked to record whether they raised their hands to share, how they tried to connect to the discussion if they were called on, and what they had hoped to contribute if they were not called on. A key part is asking students to write down "one new idea or question that someone else shared" to encourage students to listen to one another and build on each other's ideas.

In general, building the culture in which students are willing to take responsibility for offering questions, sharing incomplete ideas, and receiving critiques requires ongoing attention to ensuring that the classroom is a safe place for sharing ideas, in which we are willing to critique ideas, but not one another, so that we can accomplish something as a community.

Conclusion

Questioning is a central part of the science and engineering practices. The commitment to making "figuring out" be the work of science classrooms means that we always need a focus for what we are trying to figure out. Our questions will evolve and change as we learn more about what we are investigating. But articulating, revisiting, and evaluating progress toward questions is a central part of sharing the responsibility for knowledge building with our students.

Acknowledgments

Brian J. Reiser's research was funded by the National Science Foundation under Grant No. ESI-1020316 to the Scientific Practices Project at Northwestern University, by grants from the Gordon and Betty Moore Foundation to Northwestern University, and with support from a Math Science Partnership grant to the Connecticut Department of Education. The opinions expressed herein are those of the authors and not necessarily those of the foundations and other agencies that helped fund this work.

References

Banilower, E., P. S. Smith, I. R. Weiss, K. A. Malzahn, K. M. Campbell, and A. M. Weiss. 2013. *Report of the 2012 national survey of science and mathematics education.* Chapel Hill, NC: Horizon Research.

Krajcik, J., B. J. Reiser, L. M. Sutherland, and D. Fortus. 2013. *Investigating and questioning our world through science and technology (IQWST).* 2nd ed. Greenwich, CT: Sangari Active Science.

Krist, C., L. Brody, M. Novak, and K. Tipton. 2016. Cultivating a next-generation classroom culture. *Science Scope* 39 (5): 8–14.

National Research Council (NRC). 2012. *A framework for K–12 science education: Practices, crosscutting concepts, and core ideas.* Washington, DC: National Academies Press.

NGSS Lead States. 2013. *Next Generation Science Standards: For states, by states.* Washington, DC: National Academies Press. *www.nextgenscience.org/next-generation-science-standards.*

Nordine, J., and R. Torres. 2013. Enhancing science kits with the driving question board. *Science and Children* 50 (8): 57–61.

Reiser, B. J., M. Fumagalli, M. Novak, and T. Shelton. 2016. Using storylines to design or adapt curriculum and instruction to make it three-dimensional. Paper presented at the NSTA National Conference on Science Education, Nashville, TN. *www.academia.edu/24083676/Using_Storylines_to_Design_or_Adapt_Curriculum_and_Instruction_to_Make_It_Three-Dimensional.*

Weizman, A., Y. Shwartz, and D. Fortus. 2010. Developing students' sense of purpose with a driving question board. In *Exemplary science for resolving societal challenges,* ed. R. E. Yager, 110–130. Arlington, VA: NSTA Press.

DEVELOPING AND USING MODELS

CYNTHIA PASSMORE, CHRISTINA V. SCHWARZ, AND JOCELYN MANKOWSKI

Fifth-grade students are busy working in small groups deciding how to show others in their class what they have figured out about how and why water evaporates. During their science lessons, these students have been trying to determine how a solar still works to clean dirty water. This phenomenon has led them to wonder about how water seems to move from one place in the apparatus to another. They've considered other cases of water seeming to "disappear," like when the water dries up on the playground after a rainstorm. They have spent the first part of the unit doing investigations around evaporation and modeling their ideas about how and why evaporation occurs.

The students talk to each other to decide what they want to include in their model diagram. Melanie suggests showing "before, during, and after"—or change over time—to illustrate the liquid disappearing. She also suggests showing "hot and cold," and Andrew agrees, saying that "hot water is more humid" and wants "to show that hot water evaporates fast and stuff." Andrew and Melanie argue about whether they should include the exact humidity measures in the air for the different temperatures of liquid, or whether they should use a general term like "slower" or "faster." They don't agree, so they compromise and do both. Finally, they decide that they need to include water vapor, as Melanie says, by "drawing dots in the air for water vapor in 'during' and 'after.' More in the 'after.'" Figure 6.1 (p. 110) shows student drawings of evaporation.

Each group in the class shares its consensus model, and the other students and the teacher offer ideas about strengths and weaknesses about each group's model. During this exchange, one student suggests that he likes that they have the exact percentage of humidity. The teacher reiterates that this is important because it "directly comes from the humidity detector investigations." So students are learning to use ideas and evidence from their investigations to inform their ideas about

Figure 6.1
Student drawings of water evaporating under different conditions

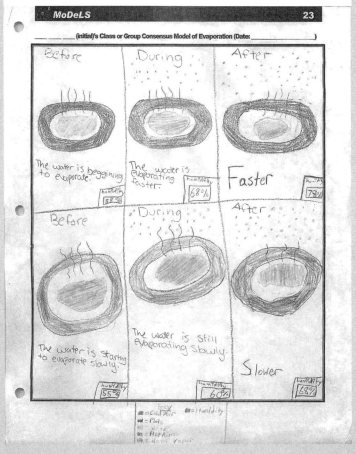

the process of how evaporation is occurring. They are still working through their ideas about why this is happening by building on some key elements of the model, such as water particles spreading out into the air in different amounts when there is hot water evaporating.

The students and teacher continue this work until they have come to some satisfactory ideas about how and why evaporation happens and how to represent that, and they continue their progress in the second part of the unit to figure out what else might be happening in the solar still, such as condensation, that helps them account for how water moves around in the solar still.

This vignette comes from a real fifth-grade classroom and helps illustrate one of several important activities involved in Developing and Using Models to make sense of the world. It addresses the performance expectation from 5-PS1-1, "Develop a model to describe that matter is made of particles too small to be seen," because students are developing and revising models to address the general phenomena of evaporation and condensation to explain why water disappears from the blacktop of their playground or appears on the outside of their cold drink (NGSS Lead States 2013, p. 43). In this case, they are figuring out the components of the model (what's important to include about the phenomena), the conditions under which the phenomena occur (the role of temperature and air), and how the components are related and interact over time (water particles moving and spreading out or clumping together under different temperature conditions) to help them account for how and why the phenomena occur in the world. The students and teacher are engaged in a process of model development and revision—making their ideas visible and testable to themselves and each other. They are evaluating and revising those models against data they have collected, against strategically introduced scientific ideas (from simulations), and against other students' ideas about what is going on and why to figure out how to best explain and predict similar phenomena. These are some of the essential aspects of engaging in the practice of scientific modeling.

Why Is the Modeling Practice Important?

> *Models serve the purpose of being a tool for thinking with, making predictions and making sense of experience. (NRC 2012, p. 56)*

From birth, humans are concerned with figuring out how the world around us works. Doing this helps us better predict what might happen to us in the future and gives us a better sense for how we are part of the world. As humans, we wonder about things; we conjure up ideas about how they work from a range of sources; we test those ideas; and we wonder, construct, and test some more. From the baby figuring out how adults react to certain facial movements, to the small child working out the rules of an imaginary game with his siblings, to the elementary student working out where the water comes from on the outside of her soda bottle, to the young adult coming to understand the ways force and motion are related to each other, we never stop trying to figure out how the world ticks. Sometimes we're happy that we can reliably predict the actions of our world, but often we want to know *why* something behaves the way it does. Knowing why can help us become even better at figuring out what will happen in the future. As we do this, we are searching for underlying reasons and mechanisms that help us make sense of our experience and of the world around us.

This innate drive to figure out and make sense of the world is at the core of the practice of modeling and forms the basis of the scientific enterprise. Like the baby working out some basic rules for physical objects by repeatedly dropping them from her high chair, the scientist is concerned with explaining and generalizing ideas about how and why the world operates the way it does. There is an important connection between the innate sense-making drive we all share and the formal scientific enterprise (Gopnik, Meltzoff, and Kuhl 1999) because both are harnessing the powerful learning mechanisms of the human mind.

To make progress on understanding how and why something happens, one has to consider the parts of the system and figure out how those parts are interconnected and related, and then develop ideas about how those relationships interact and lead to the initial observation or phenomenon. *A Framework for K–12 Science Education* (NRC 2012, pp. 56–57) reminds us that "scientists use models … to represent their current understanding of a system under study, to aid in the development of questions and explanations, and to communicate ideas to others."

In science, modeling forms the core of the intellectual work of scientists helping to organize and integrate theoretical and empirical work toward a fundamental goal of sense-making about phenomena. *In school,* modeling can function the same way and bring students into scientific practice in productive ways. It can lead to deep content understanding, and by participating in science, students may come to a more robust understanding of the scientific enterprise. Models as tools and modeling as a practice can help externalize and refine our ideas and thinking, which can bring students into the practice of *doing* science, not just hearing about it.

Because modeling is at the core of the intellectual work of science *and* it is intimately connected to our innate sense-making drive, it should lie at the core of the intellectual life of the science classroom. We like to think that modeling, or figuring out how certain aspects of the world work, is the action that brings coherence to the intellectual work in the classroom. When our goals as teachers center on working with our students to figure out and agree on a small set of ideas that can be used to explain a phenomenon in the world, then our classroom becomes a scientific community with the goal of advancing our knowledge about the world, and our students are put in the role of active knowledge builders in the learning environment.

What Is the Modeling Practice All About?

Why do we need a bridge between wondering about how something works and explaining how that thing works? It turns out that when we explain how something works, we are using, often implicitly, a set of ideas we have about the system or problem. Modeling is the process of making those ideas explicit. Recall the short vignette (pp. 10–12) about students learning near-Earth astronomy from Chapter 1. In this modeling unit (*http://ncisla.wceruw.org/muse*), students work through a series of phenomena like day and night, the direction of sunrise and sunset, moonrise, and phases. Through each cycle where they examine and wonder about a phenomenon, they work with props and each other to figure out what motions of the Earth and Moon cause that phenomenon. Students develop parts of the larger model by illustrating their ideas using words and diagrams. For example, in considering what causes the Sun to rise in the east and set in the west, the students must use the idea that the Earth rotates on its axis (established already by wondering about day and night) and add a particular direction of Earth spin. So, the ideas about what objects are relevant and what those objects are doing make up the model. In other words, the model, in this case, is the set of ideas about the Earth, Moon, and Sun, including their positions relative to each other, their motions, the relative distances between them, and so on, that can be used to explain why we see, for example, the Sun rising in the east and setting in the west. Thus, the model sits between the observed world (the phenomenon) and the explanation for what we see.

Models, as we are defining them here, are simply sets of ideas for how or why something in the world works the way it does. This definition focuses on a small set of ideas and the relationships between and among those ideas that allow us to explain what is happening in the world. From this simple definition, we can get at the full range of the modeling practice when we consider where those ideas come from, how they are shared and modified by a group working on a common problem, and how they are used to explain the problem at hand. **The essence of the Developing and Using Models practice is to figure out and use specific ideas about theoretical and actual objects and the relationships between them to account for the behavior of systems in the natural and designed world.**

What Are Models?

In science and in science education, the word *model* is used in a variety of ways. Sometimes a model is thought of as a typical or exceptional example of something (e.g., a model airplane that represents the features of the larger object) or something that can stand for something else (e.g., mouse models of humans for testing medicines). Sometimes, a model is thought of as an illustration of a phenomenon or a smaller copy of the phenomenon (e.g., stream table models). It is no wonder that the inclusion of Developing and Using Models among the list of eight practices in the *Framework* has caused a lot of confusion and some consternation among teachers.

To help clarify this practice, we introduce two big ideas about what a model is that may help you understand this practice a bit more deeply:

1. **Models are defined by how they are used.** Again, scientific models are sense-making tools that help us predict and explain the world. In engineering, models are used for analyzing, testing, and designing.

2. **Models are distinct from the representational forms they take.** They can take the form of diagrams, words, equations, or computer programs, as long as they embody ideas about how and why the phenomenon occurs or about components and relationships of the system being studied.

Okay, so what do we mean by that first point? Why is the *use* of models so important? Let's begin by making a distinction between two kinds of knowledge goals in the classroom. One kind of goal in the science classroom might be that students know *about* some scientific facts. Take, for example, the idea that the world is made up of tiny particles. As a teacher, I might have that "fact" as my learning target. Another way to think about this, though, is to consider what I want my students to be able to do with that fact. Do I merely want them to know *about* particles, or do I want my students to *reason with* the idea of particles to account for various phenomena in the world? Similarly, do I just want my students to know that the Moon orbits the Earth, or do I want them to be able to use that idea to reason through why we see phases of the Moon from Earth? This distinction between a fact-focused science class and a reasoning-focused science class is at the core of the first point about models being defined by how they are used.

We take the position that models are not merely depictions of science facts, but are tools for reasoning. This first point means that *we cannot really decide if something is or is not a model without also attending to how it is being used.* A model is used *in service of* making sense about an observable phenomenon in the world. Often, models are referred to as being of a system or phenomenon. For example, we sometimes talk about a model *of* the solar system. It is a convenient shorthand, but one that sometimes focuses us on the wrong relationship. Models in science are not merely *of* things in the world; rather, they are best thought of as tools *for* making sense of something in the world. So, the model, if it is truly a reasoning tool, is not *of* the solar system but something that can be used *for* explaining why, for example, we can only see Venus from Earth low in the sky just before and after sunrise and sunset. To be used as a reasoning tool, the model needs to be constructed *for* some sense-making purpose; it needs to be linked to a phenomenon. If something is merely shown to students or constructed for the purpose of depicting the parts of the system, but not how they interact in ways that help us understand why we see particular things in the world, then it is not truly operating as a model in the scientific sense. This is the distinction between learning science as sets of facts versus learning science as models that can be used to understand and explain our world. This is what the focus on Developing and Using Models in the *Framework* and the *NGSS* is all about (Figure 6.2).

Figure 6.2

The difference between models *of* and models *for*

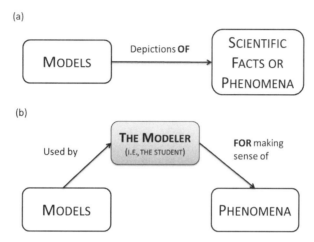

In the science classroom, we want students to go beyond merely knowing about science facts. In diagram (a), the model is positioned as a depiction *of* something. In diagram (b), we keep the modeler in mind and consider what the model is being used *for*.

We want students to develop flexible and useful knowledge; knowledge that is a tool for understanding and interpreting the world, not just inert facts. Figure 6.2b shows how taking the modeler (the reasoner) into account helps us focus our attention on the purpose of the model and not just the relationship between the model and the phenomenon. This idea is developed more fully by Passmore, Gouvea, and Giere (2014).

The second point about models being distinct from their representational forms follows from the point about models as tools *for* reasoning. It is quite common to call a picture, drawing, physical replica, or mathematical equation *the model*. Take something like the foam ball representing the Moon in the near-Earth astronomy vignette (pp. 10–12). The ball itself is just a ball until it is used in the service of figuring out how the Moon moves around the Earth. Thus, it is not the ball that is the model here, but the *ideas* about what that thing is showing and how it helps us understand what the Moon looks like from Earth that makes it into a part of a model. We could just as easily represent that thing (the Moon) with a wadded-up piece of paper, a student's own body, or a circle drawn on the board. Each of these depictions could be representing the same underlying idea that this spherical object is moving around the Earth in a particular way. Thus, the representational form should not be confused with the model.

To make this distinction is not to underplay the importance of the representational aspects of the modeling practice. The format we use to share our ideas is very important, but in our work, we've found that sometimes if we don't make clear to students that the drawing or object is distinct from the underlying idea, then students can get distracted by representational concerns at the expense of the scientific ideas. To illustrate this point, imagine the group of students in the opening vignette (pp. 109–110) spending 10 minutes arguing about whether to use a green pen or a blue pen to draw their dots of water vapor. In this case, most likely the color of the depiction of water droplets would not be central to the model ideas, given that the key feature they are trying to represent with those dots has nothing to do with color. On the other hand, an extended conversation about which situation should have more dots would help them focus on the central ideas that they are working with in terms of relative abundance of water vapor under different conditions.

The key point here is not to get too concerned about what is or is not a model or what the best representation may be, although the representation can be an important instructional consideration. As educators, we must always ask ourselves about the purpose of any material activity in the classroom: What is the depiction, representation, or other item being used *for* in our classroom? If it is merely to show students the parts of a system and have them learn those parts as inert, declarative knowledge, then we are missing the point of the modeling practice. If, however, the objects are being used to represent sets of ideas for how a system is put together for the purpose of understanding how those parts and relationships interact to account for the phenomena we see in the world, then we are indeed modeling.

What Is *Not* Intended by the Modeling Practice

- Art projects that merely translate a two-dimensional image into a three-dimensional depiction or words into a drawing.

- Representations that only ask students to identify the parts of a system. These are not models unless they also depict relationships between the parts and can be used in an explanatory context.

- Students using a computer simulation to gather information without paying attention to underlying mechanisms—for example, tracking what conditions plants need to grow (light vs. no light, soil vs. no soil) or using a food web simulation that just shows who eats whom. Finding these kinds of patterns is important, but without attention to how and why the patterns exist, this kind of work falls short of the modeling practice.

What Is Modeling?

So, if a model is something used for making sense of phenomena and something that can be represented in a variety of ways, then what is the modeling practice? There are a number of ways to engage in modeling. We find it useful to distinguish two types of modeling. Broadly, we think about two main ways we use models in science: We think *about* models, and we think *with* models.

To think *about* the model is to do the intellectual work of deciding what goes into it and what doesn't, and how to portray those ideas to others. There are some fairly useful ways to think about models in the classroom. To help students think about models, students engaging in the modeling practice should be developing and revising scientific ideas in an effort to understand how or why something happens in the world. Overall, the practice of modeling should involve students in *developing* a model that embodies aspects of a theory and evidence, *evaluating* that model against empirical evidence and theory, and *revising* that model to better meet the goals of explaining and predicting. When students are doing these things, we see them wondering about what goes into their model. They must examine the component parts of a system and figure out what the key parts are and how they are related to each other. To come back to the near-Earth astronomy example, students were thinking *about* the model when they were deciding what objects were relevant and how to describe what those objects were doing (spinning, orbiting, or staying still with regard to another object). In the opening vignette in this chapter (pp. 109–110), students are thinking *about* the model when they are deciding on the importance of the humidity data.

A goal of science education should also be to help students "think with" models. To do that, students need to *use or apply* models to predict and explain phenomena in particular ways. This is sometimes called "model-based reasoning." So, for example, the students developing and revising their models of the Earth–Moon–Sun system were using their models when they were predicting and explaining what causes the Moon phases. By the time they wondered about that phenomenon, they had all the necessary pieces in their model. Their model stipulated that the Moon orbited the Earth about one time per month. To explain phases, they had to use that idea in their model. In this chapter's opening vignette, the goal was for students to *use* their models about evaporation and condensation to explain the functioning of the solar still. They began by wondering about that apparatus and how it worked, they spent several days in class modeling the underlying processes that govern it, and ultimately they used the resulting models to fully account for how the water moves around in the solar still.

The practice of scientific modeling and engineering modeling involves these iterative cycles of development, testing, and use—guided by the goals of sense-making. These cycles of developing, testing, and revising are very important for learners to better understand how the practice can help them develop and refine their own understanding of the world.

In addition to the iterative cycles of model development and revision, there are important criteria for models and modeling. Science typically aims to develop a model that is accurate with respect to predicting and explaining phenomena and that can provide some insights into how and *why* the phenomenon happens—by giving some sort of mechanism for why the phenomenon happens. It is also important that models be general enough to be applicable to other phenomena and useful for the modelers. In engineering, the model needs to help the developers test and refine their systems, to solve the problem they aim to solve. (For more on the practices as they play out in engineering contexts, see Chapter 13, p. 283.)

Each class can develop its own knowledge and norms about modeling. There is research showing that these are very important for helping students move beyond producing pretty pictures or three-dimensional representations toward using the models as sense-making tools. It is also helpful to talk with the class explicitly about goals and how we are going to meet them as we engage in modeling. This helps some students better understand what they need to do and why.

It is essential that students be given the opportunity to do both kinds of reasoning we have described here. They need to be engaged in thinking *about* the model—what goes into it and why. Having the teacher tell them about the model, or show it to them and then have them use it, only gets them so far. They need to have a chance to think in generative ways about what the model is meant to do and how it might be constructed to do those things. So, although model use (or thinking *with* the model) is important, it is not the only aspect of the modeling practice. Thinking *about* the model by developing it and revising it can help students gain more ownership of the ideas and can help them see clearly how the theoretical ideas being developed in class connect to the phenomenon under study. It might feel more efficient to just skip the model-generation part of the lesson, but doing so diminishes the power of this practice and makes it less likely to be linked to sense-making.

How Does the Modeling Practice Relate to the Other Practices?

Modeling can be an anchor practice that motivates, guides, and informs the other practices and brings them into a broader approach to productive sense-making. As we work to develop models for what is happening in the world on a mechanistic or causal level, we will seamlessly engage in the full range of other scientific practices highlighted in the *Framework* and the *NGSS*. Any modeling endeavor is inherently linked to some phenomenon in the natural world and therefore can and should be connected to a question or set of questions. In our work with teachers, we often help them make this link by asking them to work with kids to clarify exactly what it is they are trying to figure out. In the opening vignette, the students are presented with the phenomenon of the solar still and are led to wonder about how the water moves from one place in the apparatus to another. This wondering is best made explicit through asking questions such as these: Where did the water in the upper receptacle come from? Is it pure water, or did some of the dirt from the lower receptacle come with it? How did the water move? Why does it need to be in the Sun to work? These questions then imply a range of investigations that will generate data that need to be analyzed. As we plan investigations, we use our beginning models to guide us and help us interpret our results. Likewise, the results of the investigations may lead us to add to or modify our models. Throughout this process we must engage with other learners or investigators to check in about what we think we are figuring out and why we think those ideas are useful. These comparisons, elaborations, and justifications are at the heart of the argumentation practice. Often in science one way to depict the relationships within a model leads us to use some mathematics. This happens in physics a lot but can be salient in other disciplines as well. Consider how we might model relationships among the number of gas particles, the space in which they are contained, and the frequency of hits on the side of the container (i.e., the idea of pressure). Using a mathematical relationship might be a powerful way to depict these ideas. The aim of all of this work is to account for how something works in the world, and thus if we are truly engaged in Developing and Using Models, then we must attend to explanations. An explanation is the ultimate use of a model (more on this below). Throughout every aspect of this work, students must be engaged in the communication practice. Science is a social process, and to engage in it requires communication as we present and work through different ideas as a community.

Thus, we see the practice of Developing and Using Models as inexorably entwined with the other practices. You cannot be modeling without asking questions, investigating, arguing, communicating, and explaining. To summarize, we see some of the central connections as depicted in Figure 6.3 (p. 120).

One particular connection we've made earlier probably deserves some extra attention, and that is the relationship between models and explanations. This can get a bit sticky. Indeed, you might hear the phrase "explanatory model" or "model-based explanation" in science. So, are explanations and models really just the same thing? We think models are different from explanations. The distinction might seem a bit theoretical to some, but we think it is important to understand. The model is the set of ideas that are used in an explanation for some phenomenon, and the explanation is the product of playing out the model in a particular situation to account for that phenomenon. For example, to return to the Earth–Moon–Sun astronomy example, we would say that the ideas in the model are about the relative positions of the celestial bodies. In other words, the model contains

Figure 6.3
The relationship between modeling and other *NGSS* practices

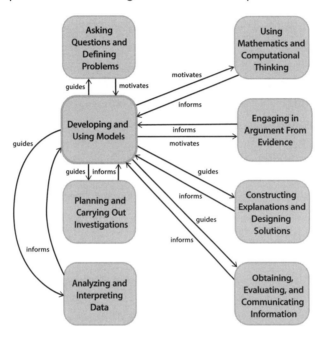

- Models help identify questions and predict answers.

- Models help point to empirical investigations.

- Models are the filter through which data are interpreted.

- Models are revised and applied to "answer" or explain, predict, and solve.

- We use mathematics to formulate some models and mathematical reasoning to evaluate models.

- Argumentation is involved in both developing and evaluating models.

- Models hold and organize relevant information and become the focus of communicating ideas.

theoretical ideas, such as that the Earth is spinning on its axis once every 24 hours, or the Moon orbits the Earth in the same direction that Earth spins. Depending on the phenomenon we are trying to explain, we will draw on elements of the model and specific features of the phenomenon. If we are trying to account for the phenomenon of Moon phases, simply stating the relevant model feature (the Moon orbits the Earth approximately one time per 28 days) is not enough. On its own, this does not actually explain anything. Instead, to craft an explanation for this phenomenon, one would have to *coordinate* the model with the phenomenon itself to generate the explanation. An explanation would be something like the following:

> When we look at the Moon from Earth, *we only see half of it and at any given time* only half of the Moon is illuminated by the Sun. Because the Moon orbits the Earth once every 28 days, the position of the Moon with respect to the Sun and Earth changes throughout the month, and therefore the *part of the illuminated half that we can see from Earth changes.* Sometimes *we can see the entire illuminated part, which we call a full Moon, and sometimes the entire illuminated half is facing away from us, which we call a new Moon.* Throughout the month, the portion of the lit half of the Moon that we can see from Earth gradually changes from one day to the next as the Moon orbits the Earth, and thus we see *the Moon go through phases* from our perspective on Earth.

In this explanation, you can see that there is text that refers to the specifics of the phenomenon and text that refers to the model woven together. In the explanation above, we have italicized the parts specific to the phenomenon and underlined those that state the model ideas. Text that is neither italicized nor underlined is the "glue" that holds it all together to form a coherent explanation.

Another way to think of this is to think of the model as the underlying rules of a system and an explanation as a description of how those rules play out in particular ways. Let's use a nonscience example to illustrate. I might know the rules of baseball, but to explain to someone what happens during a particular play in the game, I would have to coordinate the ideas about the rules with descriptions of what actually happened. Imagine that there is a player on second base and the batter hits a pop fly, which is caught by the center fielder. The runner on second took off for third right when the batter made contact; after catching the ball, the center fielder then throws it to the second baseman; and the runner is called out. If I don't know the rules of baseball, this play would mystify me. If my companion watching the game with me merely stated the rule that "a fly ball caught in the air is an out, and the runner cannot advance," I would be no less confused. This is like telling me only the relevant piece of the model. To actually *explain* why the runner was out, my companion would have to help me see why that rule was relevant to the situation. So, knowing the rule is critically important in this scenario, but having the rule as inert knowledge would do a baseball fan little good if she could not think through how that rule applied in particular situations. Likewise, in the science classroom students must come to understand the models, but they must also be given opportunities to apply those models to account for phenomena in the world. Ultimately, both models and explanations are critical for sense-making in science, which is why they play such important roles in the *Framework* and the *NGSS*.

> ## Relationship Between Modeling and Mathematics and Computational Thinking
>
> There is a special connection between the Using Mathematics and Computational Thinking practice and the Developing and Using Models practice. As illustrated in this chapter and in Chapter 9 (p. 181), there can be a great deal of overlap in the intellectual work of students (and scientists!) when they engage in these two practices. The essence of the modeling practice is to develop and use specific ideas about theoretical and actual objects and the relationships between and among them to account for the behavior of systems in the natural and designed world. Very often, those relationships can be specified in mathematical or computational terms, so the two practices can become completely intertwined. Mathematical relationships and computational processes are often powerful ways to represent, share, and test our ideas about how and why a phenomenon happens. It is important to note, however, that not all models can be expressed mathematically or computationally, and not all mathematical expressions or simulations are necessarily models. To reiterate a point in this chapter, it depends very much on how the student thinks about and uses mathematical or computational representations.

What Does the Developing and Using Models Practice Look Like When It Happens in the Classroom?

What can modeling can look like in the classroom? We will share two cases of classroom modeling—one from the upper elementary or middle school level in physical science and the other from the secondary level in biology. Both illustrate ways in which students are positioned as knowledge developers trying to make sense of the world—by thinking about and thinking with models.

FIFTH-GRADE EVAPORATION AND CONDENSATION CASE

This case elaborates the example illustrated at the beginning of this chapter (pp. 109–110). (For a description of the unit, see Kenyon, Schwarz, and Hug 2008). The fifth-grade class was studying what happens to the liquid in a solar still. The teachers and students were addressing 5-PS1-1, "Develop a model to describe that matter is made of particles too small to be seen."

Throughout a six- to eight-week time frame, the unit followed a curricular sequence that asked students to engage in cycles of constructing and revising their models over time to better answer the question about what happens to the liquid and why. This sequence is described in Baek et al. (2011) in greater depth. The curriculum followed a sequence that supported this cycle of revision in the following ways:

1. Teachers pose a central question about the phenomenon of water seeming to disappear and appear in different places throughout the solar still apparatus.

2. Teachers ask the students to develop the initial diagrammatic model of evaporation (or condensation) based on what they know so far to explain how and why the water disappears and appears in the phenomenon.

3. Teachers support students at conducting empirical investigations about the phenomenon, and students can use this information in later model revision.

4. Teachers and students interact with computer simulations and theoretical ideas with model revision and evaluation.

5. Student groups and teachers work together to develop a consensus model for why and how the phenomenon occurs.

6. Students apply their models to other related phenomena.

7. The sequence is repeated with condensation.

Let's unpack this sequence to see what this looked like in this case: Teachers and students started the unit with a question about some phenomena. In this case, the anchoring phenomenon was water movement in the solar still and the central question was "Would you drink the liquid in the bottle cap from a solar still?" (See Figure 6.4.)

Figure 6.4
Diagram of the solar still apparatus

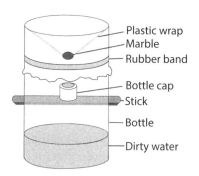

Figure 6.5
A student drawing of what happens when a puddle dries up

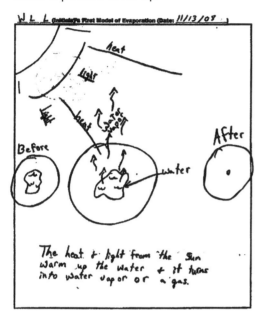

Because students cannot drink the liquid to test it, ideas needed to be developed about the invisible processes involved. The teacher asked the students to develop an initial model of what might be happening to the dirty water at the bottom next to the air in the container (evaporation). One way to start modeling is to simplify this situation and ask students what happens in any phenomenon in which water seems to appear and disappear—such as puddles on the playground. Students wrote and drew their initial ideas about the answer to that question, such as the one illustrated in Figure 6.5, in which a student shows what happens when a puddle dries up. This is a fine answer for most classrooms, except that it doesn't explain in much detail exactly how or why this happens or address the performance expectation for the grade at this point.

How might a classroom move from here? How might learners figure out if this is accurate or how it happens? Since there are likely to be alternative views of how evaporation happens under what conditions, it is useful to test some of the most common ideas using investigations. Measuring water vapor is very difficult under many circumstances, but there are some ways to do it with some help from old and new technology. One way is to mark a water level line in an open cup and closed cup to see how the water levels change over time. This helps test whether the water actually leaves the container when it looks like it disappears. Another is to measure the weight of the water as it evaporates. With a very sensitive scale, one can actually "see" the weight getting lighter. In addition, cobalt chloride strips, which change color when they detect water vapor in the air, can be used to test for evaporation. Students can investigate this next to a humidifier. Finally, digital probes with humidity detectors are extremely useful for collecting real-time water vapor data. They can measure the amount of water vapor in the air under various conditions (e.g., hot water, cold water, larger surface area, and smaller surface area). Figure 6.6 shows the use of probes.

Figure 6.6
Probes measuring water vapor

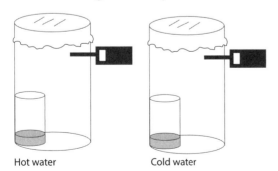

Hot water   Cold water

In this scenario, students and the teachers used stations where they collected the information and looked at the patterns they saw to inform their models. They observed that the cold water still evaporated even though there was not a direct heat source. It just happened slower. They also found that the water didn't disappear; it just changed location from the container with liquid to the air.

Figure 6.7
Student working on model revision

At this point, students went back and revised their models to consider what they had just found. The evidence pointed to some clues as to how water movement occurred, but they still did not have an answer for exactly why it was happening. Figure 6.7 shows an example of a student's revised model.

To help students find out more about how and why the water was moving, the teacher introduced some scientific information. Some of this information involved a theory that the teacher explained to the students: "Water is made of tinier parts of water (water droplets), and the tinier parts are again made of even tinier parts. (We can call them 'bits of water.') Those tiny bits are too small to see with our eyes. When the tiny, tiny bits are next to the air, they spread out into the air. They are so small that you can't see them, and so small that they float. When water does this, it has turned into a gas called water vapor. This process is called evaporation." In addition to this explanation, the teacher and students used a computer simulation software called Molecular Workbench, from the Concord Consortium, and asked students to interact with it (as shown in Figure 6.8). In this simulation, students can begin to visualize what these tiny bits of water might be doing as they move between the liquid and gas phases in the test tube. (See *www. concord.org/molecularworkbench*.)

Figure 6.8
Screenshot of the Concord Consortium's Molecular Workbench

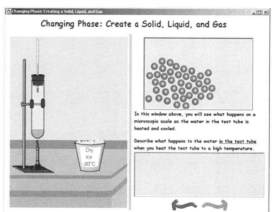

Figure 6.9
Initial and revised models after working with the Molecular Workbench simulation

(a)

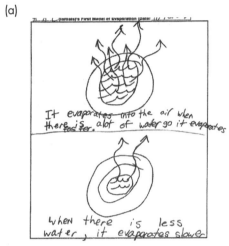

(b)

Once the students visualized those bits of water moving in the simulation, students revised their models again and addressed the phenomenon using ideas about the particle nature of matter. Figure 6.9 shows a student's initial model and the model right after the introduction to idea of water bits in the unit.

PEER COMPARISON AND EVALUATION TO CONSTRUCT A CONSENSUS MODEL

Finally, the classroom worked together to create a consensus model of evaporation and, later, another for condensation. While some teachers ask their students to create consensus models in small groups, others do so as an entire class. The process of negotiating ideas in consensus models is sometimes challenging, though critical for helping students understand that the model needs to be consistent with the evidence they collected and needs to predict and explain the phenomenon. Here is how one small group in class negotiated its evaporation consensus model—within a classroom where the teacher emphasized the importance of showing how and why the phenomenon happens in the model and that it can be used for reasoning about other phenomena in the world:

Ben: "Should we label right here and write "no direct heat source?"

Teacher: "Sure, Ben. Your air molecules are too close together. Remember in the simulation how they spread out?"

Ben: "Yeah, but we don't have that much room. ..."

Teacher: "Okay, we can make a note there that they eventually spread out."

Jack: "Why don't we just put an explanation on it?"

Ben: "Well, this is all the explanation."

Jack: "All right. You need to explain that a little bit more."

Teacher: "We have to explain it didn't seep through the cup, if someone asked that. Our model cannot explain that."

Jack: "Well, does this explain how paint dries?"

Teacher: "Yes, the water molecules are leaving. This explains how nail polish dries. It also explains how you can smell stuff, because molecules go away carrying scent."

After the final consensus model in the unit, the students then applied this to the solar still to determine where the water came and went. In that sense, they used their models to create an explanation of the solar still.

HIGH SCHOOL EVOLUTION CASE

A group of 36 ninth- and tenth-grade students entered the room. It was the third week of school, and the teacher had worked with the students to build a classroom community in which the students expected that they would be asked to wonder about some phenomenon in the natural world and seek to figure out how it works. This day was no different. Ms. C began by asking the students to recall the "big, huge driving question" about biology that they had developed and posted on the wall based on previous lessons. Amber raised her hand and said, "Well, I think what we decided yesterday is that we are trying to figure out how all living things can be so crazy different from each other and at the same time they have a lot in common, too!" Other students nodded their heads, and Ms. C pointed out the piece of poster board she had tacked up toward the back of the room with their "big, huge driving question" written on it.

Ms. C began the main lesson by saying, "So, today we are going to get started on figuring some of this out by looking at some organisms and what happened to them over time." She then shared three stories about change over time: She showed pictures and briefly told the story of peppered moth distribution in England in the 1800s; she told a story about antibiotic resistance; and she showed images and presented information about a population of some finches on the Galapagos Islands that had a measurable change in average bill depth across the population over a three-year period. At the end of her presentations, she asked the students to wonder about these three stories, consider the big driving question they had discussed before, and brainstorm some questions about the commonalities in the scenarios they just discussed. After about 10 minutes of pair discussions and whole-class conversation, they arrived at a consensus question: "How do populations change in their characteristics over time?" At this point, Ms. C told the students that to begin to explore this question, they would need look at data from one of these populations in depth, the Galapagos finches. She divided the students into groups of nine.

"I'm going to pass out a data set to each group. Look at the screen—I've got a little bit of introductory information for you before we get started." From here, she showed a few slides that illustrated where the Galapagos Islands are located, and she told them that the data they would be receiving were gathered by a couple of scientists named the Grants over several years of careful observation of some birds, the medium ground finch, that live on the island of Daphne Major.

Ms. C continued: "Your task is to look over the data and first get a sense of what happened to this population of finches over time on the island. What was the specific change in the population? Once you are clear about that, look over the other data about feeding behavior, rainfall, and survivorship and see what you can piece together about what may have caused the change. Use your whiteboards and the timeline I've provided to collect your initial ideas."

The students got to work and spent the remainder of the class period examining the data and discussing what happened to the finches and why. The following day, the students entered the room ready to continue working with the finch data. They pulled out their smartphones to look at the images they had snapped the day before of their whiteboards, and they took out their paper timelines. Ms. C told them that their task in the next 20 minutes was to take their ideas from yesterday and weave them into a "how and why" story about the change in the average finch beak size from 1976 to 1978. They wrote their first drafts on their whiteboards, and then, once they were satisfied with the stories, they transferred them onto butcher paper. Once all nine groups had their stories put together, they posted them around the room.

Ms. C said, "Okay, now we need to take a look. We are going to do a gallery walk and examine one another's work. We are looking for both commonalities and differences. Ultimately, our task is going to be to figure out some of the things that might be applicable beyond just the finches. What might be some rules that govern a change in the distribution of a trait over time? First, let's take a look at commonalities and differences. Take your assignment sheet and look at four posters besides your own, and write down the things you see across them that seem to be common and things that are unique to one or two."

The students stood up and examined other posters. The room was mostly quiet as students looked over the different posters around the room and wrote down their ideas. This took the rest of the period, and just before the bell rang, Ms. C. asked the students to come in the following day with a first draft of some of the general characteristics they saw in the posters.

The following day, after some introductory comments, Ms. C had the students return to their groups with their homework ideas and work together to come up with a list of the main ideas around how and why the finches changed over time. They shared their ideas and refined them, using the whiteboards at each table. Ms. C then called the group together to gather their ideas. She wrote notes on the board as the groups gave her one or more of the statements they had developed. After about 10 minutes, she had a list, as shown in Figure 6.10.

"So, as I look at this list, I see some things that are specific to the finches and some things that we might think of as more general. Can we make the whole list into a general one that we might be able to use to explain any population change over time? Take a moment and write some ideas in your notebook about how to make some of these ideas that are specific to the finches into more general statements about the conditions that would lead to change over time for some other population."

Figure 6.10

Notes written on the board after group discussion

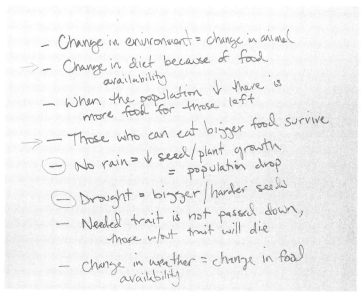

She continued, "Let me give you an example. Here it says there was a drought on the islands. What might be a more general way to say that? Remember the story about the peppered moths? What happened there?"

Gina said, "There was a lot of pollution?"

Ms. C replied, "Yes, pollution, lack of rainfall—how might we say something about that more generally?"

Alex said, "Well, they both have to do with the environment, is that what you mean?"

"That's it, what happened to the environment—it was pollution-free and there was a certain amount of rainfall that was normal, so what would we say happened to the environment in each of these cases?"

Min said, "It changed?"

Ms. C replied, "What do you all think, does that capture it? Could we say something about a change in the environment instead of just saying change in rainfall?" Several students nodded their heads and muttered agreement. "Okay, so see what you can do with the rest of this list to make it more general like that."

The students worked with their partners for about five minutes, and after that, Ms. C ended the class period by getting their revised statements up in a column next to the original list.

The following day, the students came in and began a more in-depth exploration of each of the ideas they had put forward as part of the model. Ms. C had them go through a series of activities that allowed them to investigate the importance of variation, competition for resources, and heritability. They then decided on a final form of the idea for their developing model of natural selection (see Passmore et al. 2013).

After several days, they had one final opportunity to refine and apply their complete model to another phenomenon. This scenario is based on actual classroom events and addresses the *NGSS* performance expectations HS-LS4-2 and HS-LS4-4.

TAKEAWAY POINTS ABOUT THE CASES

Each case illustrates a general instructional sequence that helps support sense-making about phenomena through modeling. There are several important aspects in the cases examined in this chapter:

- Engaging in modeling is a multiday endeavor. It takes time to ask students to represent and revise their ideas. But, it's worth it! Students learn and make sense of phenomena in much more powerful ways that may stay with them longer. They also gain a richer and more personal connection with science.

- It is important that the modeling work in the classroom is always connected to a phenomenon and clear questions about it, so that students can track their progress on understanding how and why the phenomenon behaves the way it does.

- Modeling is contextualized and interacts with all the other practices for the goal of making sense of phenomena. You cannot separate the practices from one another in any meaningful way.

- Modeling is a social practice. At its best, it involves exchanging ideas, opinions, theories, and critiques with others—especially peers with the goal of advancing those ideas. This is not always easy, but it's worth teaching and attending to in the classroom. There are several aspects of the practice of scientific modeling that are critical social processes, important for advancing students' sense-making. Those include evaluating and revising models—and developing and using consensus models with a class. Each of these modeling practices requires that learners engage in argumentation about such things as the features of models and the application of models while engaged in doing things like comparing and contrasting models. (See Cheng and Brown 2015 for modeling criteria; another example is in Forbes et al. 2015.)

How Can We Work Toward Equity With Regard to Modeling?

We think that centering classrooms on participating in scientific and engineering practices in general, and modeling in particular, can create more equitable spaces for students. Engaging in the modeling practice is to engage in a very personal, though socially negotiated, process. No longer is the authority for ideas vested solely in the teacher. Instead, the classroom is centered on the collective endeavor of making sense of the world, our world, the one we experience every day. We must remember that all students have relevant life experiences to bring to this work. It is then our job to create space for those experiences to be seen as productive resources from which to build. Engaging students as the generators and evaluators of knowledge can be a very important way to help them see themselves as agents of their own learning. Education is not something that should be done to kids. We must work to find ways to bring them into the process, and engaging them in modeling is one powerful way to do so.

At the same time, it is important to note that modeling might take different forms for different cultures and students. For example, it is important to help students relate abstracted representations (particularly classic scientific models) with story-telling narratives and other ways of figuring out how and why the world works the way it does. It is important to leverage students' resources in the models and build on the ones that help students' sense-making—rather than shutting down this sense-making process. This can be tricky, particularly when engaged in wanting to converge toward particular ideas in science such as in a consensus model. It is important at that time to really decide what ideas and reasoning are critical for students to be able to leverage later, and which ones are likely to resolve on their own—or to be unimportant to subsequent learning. Please refer to Chapter 3 (p. 33) for more ideas about these kinds of connections.

How Can I Support and Assess Developing and Using Models in My Classroom?

To focus and clarify exactly what you will be doing with students in a modeling unit, you need to consider the phenomenon you will be centering your instruction around and the specific question(s) about that phenomenon that will focus the modeling. As the teacher, you have to be clear about the model you are aiming toward; the ways that the model can be represented; and how you will guide students in developing, testing, revising, and extending these ideas. This may seem daunting at first, but once you do it a few times, it can become more straightforward.

One important aspect of supporting learners in the modeling practice is to make sure that the developing ideas are written down and accessible as you move with your students through the unit. Information and ideas should be recorded by individual students in their notebooks, and we have found that displaying key ideas on a wall in the classroom keeps everyone grounded and makes the models accessible and useful. The teachers with whom we work often use summary tables like the one described in "The Modeling Toolkit" (Windschitl and Thompson 2013).

Assessment in the modeling classroom can be a challenge at first, but we've found that when students are truly engaged in this practice, there are many opportunities to see their thinking. These opportunities can lead to both formative and summative assessment opportunities. Consider the drawings and demonstrations that students create as part of their modeling endeavors as artifacts that can be used for assessment purposes.

Perhaps you are concerned about the fact that many of these artifacts may have been created by a group, making evaluations of individuals difficult to make. We've seen teachers employ some very creative ways to address this. Some teachers require an individual written product in addition to the group product, perhaps a quick write-up at the beginning of class or a short homework assignment. Another strategy is to provide mini-challenges for model use sprinkled throughout the unit that function like quizzes. For example, in the Earth–Moon–Sun astronomy unit, each time the students agreed on an addition to their model, the teacher would present them with a few thought scenarios to write about. In these scenarios, they were typically asked to think through an alternative to the model idea they had just come up with. So, if they had just figured out as a class that the Moon orbited the Earth once every 28 days or so, then the teacher might ask them to individually write about what we would see from the Earth if the Moon orbited twice as fast. Or, in the case of the solar still investigation, the teacher could ask the students to think through what would happen if the apparatus were put in a giant see-though freezer outside on a sunny day. These kinds of opportunities are important for students to solidify their own understanding and make it clear to the teacher whether the students are really tracking the ideas or merely parroting them.

How Do I Get Started With Modeling?

To get started with the practice of Developing and Using Models, we encourage you to make sure that you are viewing learners as developers and evaluators of knowledge, not just consumers. All disciplines in science have at their core a central activity of *making sense* of our world and why things work the way they do. School should *engage* students in doing this sense-making, not just hearing about how others have done it. We suggest a few strategies to consider as you begin to align your instruction with the vision for science education described in the *Framework* and the *NGSS*.

As you plan your modeling instruction, be sure to do the following:

- Focus on phenomena and data from those phenomena.

- Include the opportunity to develop a driving question based on the phenomenon that addresses a big and important idea and provides coherence in the unit.

- Engage students in repeated cycles of model evaluation and revision, and emphasize that models are based on empirical data and evidence.

- Ask students to use models to explain specific phenomena in the world around them.

- Engage students in the social nature of modeling—argumentation is involved in evaluation and consensus in building and applying models.

The modeling practice is powerful for students and teachers (Passmore, Stewart, and Cartier 2009; Schwarz et al. 2009). It is aligned with authentic scientific reasoning in many important ways, as we have described throughout this chapter. Look at what one teacher wrote as a testimonial to her use of modeling in the classroom:

> *Oftentimes, students only experience learning science as memorization of facts. It's quite frustrating as a teacher when we bring up a concept and immediately a student will say, "Oh, I already know that, or I already learned that." Upon further questioning they undoubtedly respond ... "it's just too hard to explain."*
>
> *Yes, because they don't really understand the things they've memorized.*
>
> *This is where models play a critical role in helping uncover what the kids "think they know" and how the revisions help them develop a conceptual understanding of the topic in which to apply to teaching (us) about the phenomena in general. I've seen this play out in my own classroom using models and although the process takes time, the students develop a strong sense of seeing themselves as scientists and understanding the world around them. The benefits to developing a consensus model encourages much more than just a scientific understanding. Students learn how to give and receive feedback, how to create and develop a "tool" to explain their understanding, and most importantly, students learned that they were scientists!*

As this teacher points out, engaging in the modeling practice allows students to be the sense-making agents in the classroom and creates a context for developing scientific understanding of the phenomena in the world. For teachers, models can provide windows into students' thinking, and models can also serve to make ideas and contributions from students in the class public—and potentially accessible as a tool for everyone in the classroom. The practice of Developing and Using Models can provide an anchor for engaging in the full range of science and engineering practices in the classroom and fulfilling the vision of a new kind of science education set forth in the *Framework* and the *NGSS*.

Acknowledgments

We wish to acknowledge the contributions of many teachers, students, and colleagues with whom we collaborated and thank them for opening their classrooms to us. This material is based, in part, on work supported by the National Science Foundation under Grant No. DRL-0554652 and Grant No. DRL-13489900 to the University of California at Davis, Grant No. DRL-1020316 to the Scientific Practices Project at Northwestern University, and Grant No. ESI-0628199 to the MoDeLS Project at Northwestern University. The opinions expressed herein are those of the authors and not necessarily those of the National Science Foundation.

References

Baek, H., C. Schwarz, J. Chen, H. Hokayem, and L. Zhan. 2011. Engaging elementary students in scientific modeling: The MoDeLS fifth-grade approach and findings. In *Models and modeling: Cognitive tools for scientific enquiry*, ed. M. S. Khine and I. M. Saleh, 195–218. New York: Springer-Verlag.

Cheng, M. F., and D. E. Brown. 2015. The role of scientific modeling criteria in advancing students' explanatory ideas of magnetism. *Journal of Research in Science Teaching* 52 (8): 1053–1081.

Forbes, C., L. Zangori, T. Vo, and C. Schwarz. 2015. Supporting students' scientific modeling when learning about the water cycle. *Science and Children* 53 (2): 42–49.

Gopnik, A., A. N. Meltzoff, and P. K. Kuhl. 1999. *The scientist in the crib: Minds, brains, and how children learn*. New York: William Morrow & Co.

Kenyon, L., C. Schwarz, and B. Hug. 2008. The benefits of scientific modeling. *Science and Children* 46 (2): 40–44.

National Research Council (NRC). 2012. *A framework for K–12 science education: Practices, crosscutting concepts, and core ideas*. Washington, DC: National Academies Press.

NGSS Lead States. 2013. *Next Generation Science Standards: For states, by states*. Washington, DC: National Academies Press. *www.nextgenscience.org/next-generation-science-standards*.

Passmore, C., E. Coleman, J. Horton, and H. Parker. 2013. Developing and using the natural selection model as an anchor for practice and content. *The Science Teacher* 80 (6): 43–49.

Passmore, C., J. S. Gouvea, and R. Giere. 2014. Models in science and in learning science: Focusing scientific practice on sense-making. In *International handbook of research in history, philosophy and science teaching*, ed. M. R. Matthews, 1171–1202. Dordrecht: Springer Netherlands.

Passmore, C., J. Stewart, and J. Cartier. 2009. Model-based inquiry and school science: Creating connections. *School Science and Mathematics* 109 (7): 394–402.

Schwarz, C., B. Reiser, B. Davis, L. Kenyon, A. Acher, D. Fortus, Y. Shwartz, B. Hug, and J. Krajcik. 2009. Designing a learning progression for scientific modeling: Making scientific modeling accessible and meaningful for learners. *Journal of Research in Science Teaching* 46 (6): 632–654.

Windschitl, M., and J. J. Thompson. 2013. The modeling toolkit. *The Science Teacher* 80 (6): 63–69.

7

PLANNING AND CARRYING OUT INVESTIGATIONS

MARK WINDSCHITL[1]

Ms. Smith's third-grade students had been reading the children's book *Varun's Quest: Into a Bee Tree and Other Adventures* by Timothy Goldsmith (2013). The book begins with Varun's grandfather spinning a story that sends the young boy into a dream world where he becomes just a few inches tall. In the dream world, Varun meets an elf named Aubrey, and together they begin an adventure of making sense of the living world. Aubrey is very good at asking Varun questions, ones that engage his thinking about nature. With the elf's guidance, Varun discovers how bats find their way around at night and how crickets can escape the clutches of a praying mantis.

In the book, the elf gives Varun some advice to help him understand nature—"Now, here is rule number one: You can learn a lot just by looking. This is the starting place for trying to figure out how the world works." Inspired by this idea, Varun walks into a nearby garden and begins observing flowers and insects. In time, Varun meets a bee and comes to understand more about this creature, just by observing. He learns about the bee's legs, antennae, and eyes, and where the bee lives. As the story continues, Varun learns about flowers and the different behaviors of bees. Aubrey then introduces Varun to other ideas such as the bees' role in pollinating plants.

After learning the first rule—that you can learn a lot by just looking—Varun learns a second rule—ask questions. At this point in the story, Ms. Smith stopped to introduce some ideas to her class. She used this moment to share some scientific ideas about how animals and plants depend upon one another, and that science is a way of explaining many things about the world around us. Ms. Smith told her class that the next adventure in the book would show an example. In the next adventure, Aubrey planned and carried out an investigation using colored paper cut in the shape of a flower and a small container of sugar water at its center to see if bees in the neighborhood could find this artificial flower and return to the hive. But Varun was puzzled. How would we know it was the sugar water that attracted the bees to our flower? Could it be the color of the petals? The shape? Aubrey replied, "That's what an experiment is. It's a way of asking a question of nature and getting new kinds of information that help us explain things." Using this episode in the book, Ms. Smith then introduced her students to the idea of planning and carrying out scientific investigations. She used the context of the flower

---

1. The author thanks Richard Duschl and Rodger Bybee for their important contributions to this chapter.

experiment to explain that a major practice of science is planning and conducting systematic investigations.

In this chapter on the practice of Planning and Carrying Out Investigations, we share how different parts of investigations can be designed so that they work together and help students answer questions. In particular, we describe several ways to design effective investigations using examples from elementary classrooms through high school.

The Start to Planning and Carrying Out Investigations

Planning and carrying out investigations requires us to figure out what kind of information and observations we need to address our questions about a phenomenon and to decide how to systematically collect and record it.

From the systematic observations used in ancient times for charting the movements of planets, stars, the Moon and Sun, to the current use of computers and other advanced technologies to map the human genome, our quest for understanding nature and for solving problems has been based on Planning and Carrying Out Investigations. Investigations are at the core of the scientific enterprise because all forms of knowledge in the discipline (e.g., explanations, theories, models) are judged in part by how consistent they are with *observations* about the real world. These forms of knowledge often include claims about events and processes that are *not directly observable* because they are inaccessible (e.g., the layers of the Earth or hormonal reactions in the body), they are too small (e.g., atomic structures or chemical reactions), they happen on a vast scale (e.g., the blocking of the Sun's light during an eclipse) or over long periods of time (e.g., stellar life cycles, evolution, or continental drift), or they are conceptual (e.g., selective pressure in ecosystems, sound waves, or unbalanced forces). Scientists, however, make claims with some degree of confidence because patterns and trends that we can detect in the natural world give us clues as to what is happening at levels beyond what our senses and our instruments can detect. In this way, science is the coordination of the observable and the unobservable. Without data, science could not evolve.

Planning and Carrying Out Investigations is a practice that is integrated with other sense-making activities to help us explain the natural world. For example, to conduct investigations, decisions have to be made about the guiding question; about using scientific models to help frame those questions; and about interpreting data from the investigation, using these data to form or revise an explanation, and communicating these ideas to others. Through measurements and observations derived from investigations, we test and make sense of questions, models, and hypotheses about nature.

To anchor our descriptions about the design of investigations, we'll refer to some common scenarios that are part of science learning. We've chosen situations in which students start to plan for different types of investigations and, as a result, use different types of data and information as evidence. As you read the following vignettes, consider the kinds of conversations you would want to have with these students—conversations that help them link their questions with what they already know and with what is possible to learn from the collection of data.

Sound Energy Example

This is a case from a fourth-grade unit on the physics of sound. In this scenario, young learners were trying to figure out how a singer can break a glass with just the sound energy from his or her voice. They had watched a video of this event and discussed how sound travels in waves. After this initial lesson, students became aware of sound in their everyday world. One day soon after the unit began, several of them came in from recess to share with the teacher that they could hear a soccer ball being bounced on the pavement, no matter where they were standing. One student suggested that sound travels like waves on the surface of a lake, out from the source in all directions. Another student added that she thought the waves travel equally quickly in all directions. These hypotheses became the basis for several experiments by the students on the playground.

Cellular Respiration Example

During a seventh-grade unit on cellular respiration, a teacher had her students mix dried yeast and sugar in a flask of warm water. They then attached a balloon to the top of the flask. As students watched the balloon inflate, they hypothesized about what they were seeing. One group of students, knowing that warm air tends to rise, believed that this was causing the inflation. Another group of students thought that somehow the yeast was giving off a type of gas. The teacher highlighted these two reasonable hypotheses and started a conversation about how each could be tested.

Gravity Example

In a ninth-grade unit from an Earth and space science class, students had been exploring the way gravity shapes events and processes in our solar system. They had just learned about Newton's laws of gravitation but were confused about whether small bodies of mass in our solar system could exert gravity on larger bodies of mass. They wondered, for example, whether the Moon exerts a pull on the Earth. This became the basis for a series of thought experiments and web searches for "models" of phenomena like this elsewhere in the universe. The teacher then introduced a computer application that could simulate how gravity affects different bodies in a solar system. Before using the simulation, the students had a conversation about how to be systematic in collecting data, even if they weren't using a typical experimental design.

Ocean Example

This vignette is from an 11th- and 12th-grade Advanced Placement (AP) class on humans and the environment. This curriculum was project based, and a major portion of the year was devoted to the health and ecologies of our oceans. During this project, students learned that oceans are becoming more acidic over time and less habitable by hundreds of species of organisms. The focus of their explanations was determining why this is happening. Several students were trying to make the case that human-induced changes in the atmosphere have increased ocean acidification. The teacher asked students what type of evidence would convince them that this hypothesis is true or what evidence might convince them that some other mechanisms are affecting our oceans.

What Is the Planning and Carrying Out Investigations Practice All About?

Before we talk further about our scenarios, we revisit a question that has been posed several times in this book: How is the *Next Generation Science Standards* (*NGSS*) vision for these practices different from what might currently be going on in our classrooms?

As teachers, we have all gotten our students excited about hands-on work in one way or another. The *NGSS* vision is, in part, to ensure that our students are also engaged in specific types of intellectual work and talk. Much of the new vision is not about the collecting of data per se, but about what leads up to this activity and how hands-on work is linked with the development of "big" science ideas.

The new vision for investigative practice can be summarized in just a few principles. First, let's look at the broader picture—the development of big ideas in science usually requires multiple investigations, and those investigations need to be coordinated with one another to build ideas over time. During a unit of instruction, students should be focused on developing well-integrated explanations for a complex and contextualized event or process that is anchoring their collective work (such as in the elementary classroom where students were explaining how a singer could break a glass with his or her voice). Developing such in-depth explanations and models requires that evidence is generated by *multiple* investigations and that *several* new ideas are developed through cycles of developing hypotheses, designing studies, collecting new data, and representing and communicating findings. While it is possible to create a "small" explanation for a single investigation's outcome or to create a model of what just happened in a single lab experience, the *NGSS* presses students to create *more comprehensive explanations and models,* constructed over several days or weeks, that tell us why a complex phenomenon unfolds the way it does.

Second, decisions about what to investigate and how to investigate should be *motivated by questions arising from students' current explanations of phenomena and shaped in part by new science ideas* that have been introduced. Another way of saying this is that investigations should not simply be scheduled in because "it's Tuesday" or they come next in the curriculum. When investigations can be developed or at least be modified from existing materials based on students' questions and interests, they are no longer classroom events that are separated from conceptual understanding. Rather, students can learn to identify where their current understanding has holes and use this knowledge together with new conceptual ideas to talk with one another about the kinds of questions that are now possible to explore and how they might collect data given the available resources. In the scenarios described previously, students in these classrooms used science ideas that were introduced by the teacher to design meaningful investigations to further their knowledge. The elementary students who were investigating sound used the teacher-introduced idea of *sound as waves* to set up their playground study. The students hypothesizing about yeast later set up an experiment based on knowledge about the *chemical basis of respiration.* Students examining gravity in solar systems used *Newton's law of gravitation* to make sense of the design and outcomes of their computer simulation investigations. And students in the AP chemistry class used the idea of the *solubility of gases* to create controlled experiments about how carbon dioxide is absorbed into water. All of these classes used science ideas in their investigations, but none of their outcomes, as you will read about soon, were simply confirmatory. The science ideas were levers for reasoning about the design of the investigations and their outcomes.

Third, apprenticing young learners into this scientific practice requires *explicit conversations about why and how investigations are carried out.* It's not just about following procedures or using process skills such as formulating hypotheses, deciding how to measure variables, controlling variables, or measuring accurately. Yes, these skills are important, but too often they take precedence over the kinds of conversations that help student understand *why they would do a particular study in a particular way at a particular time in the inquiry process.* These are questions such as "What kind of investigation would help us fill a gap in our current understanding?" "In what ways should we make observations so that we can have credible data to explore later? How?" "Can we design circumstances to collect data that are similar to authentic circumstances in the real world?"

And finally, a word about curricula that tend to oversimplify the practice of scientific investigation. The intent of the *NGSS* and *Framework* is to avoid doing investigations that present science knowledge and inquiry as a straightforward path to truth and to unambiguous explanations. Students who routinely follow a set of procedures outlined by someone else get the impression that science investigations typically "work" and the anticipated outcomes are usually achieved. We caution, then, against the use of "cookbook" exercises. Such activities strip out the sense-making complexities of doing science and leave students with fewer skills or methods to figure out how to make sense of complexities in the world—and a false impression of the nature of scientific practices.

We should note, however, that "lab activities" are different from the scientific practice of Planning and Carrying Out Investigations. The meaning of "lab activity" differs across schools, regions, and grade levels. But for the sake of clarity, in this chapter we use the phrase "lab activity" to mean having students work with materials to demonstrate or develop a known idea or to build a skill. Lab activities typically ask students to use materials to conduct observations in a particular way, with limited possible opportunities for student exploration beyond what is prescribed. There is nothing wrong with lab activities; if thoughtfully designed, they can be appropriate for demonstrating or deepening understanding of specific concepts like conservation of mass, air pressure, pH, carrying capacity in ecosystems, and unbalanced forces. These activities, however, should not substitute for engaging students in authentic forms of investigation in which they are working together to figure out what they need more information about, planning a way to get that information, and carrying out the plan. Concepts developed through lab activities should be *used* in Planning and Carrying Out Investigations to reason about why phenomena happen the way they do and how investigations might be planned.

We also recommend avoiding investigating arbitrary questions. The investigations that scientists perform are part of a bigger picture than just the singular investigation. Science does not involve questions such as "Will my bean plants grow faster listening to rock and roll music or classical music?" A question like this, although testable, has little to do with the development of any coherent understanding of underlying causes. If students had some scientifically valid reason for believing that music affects plants, it could change the question from arbitrary to purposeful. In other words, if the investigation is connected to ongoing work on model development and an explanation for how or why something occurs, then it is part of a sense-making system. If it is a stand-alone lab on a single question (often with only correlational data available), then it is usually not part of a broader enterprise of figuring out how some aspect of the world works. Similarly, investigations outside the bounds of the natural world are not helpful for advancing understanding of natural science. The natural sciences do not investigate questions such as "How many students prefer pizza versus tacos for lunch?" or "Does extrasensory perception really exist?" because these questions relate to social science behaviors and to untestable metaphysical questions. Although these questions can be motivational hooks for students, they are essentially inquiries without links to important disciplinary scientific content.

What Is *Not* Included in the Practice of Planning and Carrying Out an Investigation

- Cookbook labs in which students follow directions without considering how the investigation helps them figure something out about the system under study.

- Labs that are primarily aimed at teaching students procedural skills like how to use a graduated cylinder, how to measure, how to use a balance or microscope, or how to graph.

- Labs that ask students to draw or write descriptions of items provided to them in the absence of some clear purpose for those descriptions.

- Activities that are not clearly linked to knowledge building about science ideas in the classroom. In other words, "cool" activities that have no clear purpose are not part of the investigating practice.

How Can I Support the Practice of Planning and Carrying Out Investigations in My Classroom?

The practice of Planning and Carrying Out Investigations begins with asking testable questions that can inform some part of a model or explanatory story. Because Asking Questions is itself a science practice and was discussed in Chapter 5 (p. 87), we start our discussion of the investigating practice after questioning but suggest that you also consult that chapter for ideas about how these two practices are connected. We can engage students in a variety of different planning and data collection conversations. You'll want to gradually give your students more responsibility to take charge of these conversations and to make decisions about the conduct of the investigation. We name and describe three of these possible conversations below. You don't need to navigate your way through all of these for every investigation, but perhaps you can feature one or two conversations for each round of inquiry.

WHAT KINDS OF DATA OR OBSERVATIONS WOULD HELP US ANSWER OUR QUESTION?

Some data collecting is designed to help us see how a measurable part of an event or thing changes over time ("How does the Moon change its appearance over the course of a month?"); some data collecting is designed to help us see how things are distributed over geographic space ("Where in our neighborhood has the Himalayan blackberry taken over and why?"); some data collecting is meant to help us see if two variables are correlated ("Is the decrease of the volume of a container related to the changing air pressure inside?"); and some data collecting is meant to help us test a causal question ("Do pill bugs hide because they prefer dark places?").

Not all investigations are controlled experiments. Many scientists, particularly those who do field work, do not actively manipulate variables and maintain "control" and "experimental" groups. Scientists in astronomy, genetics, field biology, oceanography, geology, and meteorology routinely create models of phenomena not by controlling conditions, but rather by selecting naturally occurring observations and looking for descriptive, correlational, or causal trends in those observations. As an example, a researcher may be interested in the relationship between air quality and the growth of lichens on trees. In her study, she would not be able to manipulate air quality around entire groves of trees. Rather, this researcher would identify areas of high air pollution (perhaps near a freeway or an industrial area) and areas of low air pollution. Then she would consider how to take into account potentially confounding variables such as species of trees, rainfall in the area, or amount of sunlight. She would then select similar trees for study that were living in comparable conditions, except of course for their location in an area of high or low air pollution, and compare the amount of lichen growth, thus choosing one focus variable to be measured in each of the "two groups" of trees. Other scientists also conduct investigations in which they try to create purely descriptive models of some natural phenomena. A classroom example of a descriptive study is creating a profile of the presence of macro-invertebrates along the length of a river. These types of studies result in averages, medians, ranges, and maps that tell a "what is happening story" and often generate enough data to help pose meaningful correlation or comparative questions as follow-ups. Many scientists are now doing investigations in which data are generated by elaborate computer models. These are simulations, generated from computational parameters based on previously collected data about phenomena like ocean currents, population dynamics in ecosystems, and planetary motion. Questions can be asked and tested within these simulations as they might be in the real world. So, while controlled experiments are an important type of investigation for students to understand and use in science, it should become clear throughout their schooling that other types of investigations are valuable as well.

Regardless of the type of investigation you plan, part of an initial conversation with students is to determine what the goals are for your data collection. Once this is determined, you can follow up with questions such as "Should we create a special situation that gives us an opportunity to collect data, or should we observe some naturally occurring event without manipulating it?" "If we do the former (perhaps a controlled experiment), then how could we create a situation that allows us to measure what we think is important?" "Which variables will be treated as the outcomes of the investigation?" "Which conditions would we vary to see if they have any effect on the outcome variable?" "What are all the other variables or conditions that should be held constant during the investigation?"

You'll want to make sure your students know that data are observations that are systematically collected *for a purpose*. Observations can be taken by using one of your senses directly (sight, sound, touch, smell, taste) or by using an instrument that extends your senses (a microscope, pH paper to test whether something is acidic or basic, a thermometer, an electronic probe, a digital sensor like the camera on a phone, satellite imagery). Wrestling with these questions, then, leads to a second kind of conversation.

SELECTING PROCEDURES AND TOOLS TO MEASURE AND COLLECT DATA

"What kinds of measurements should we take?" "What instruments or tools should be used to make such measurements?" "How can we all measure the same way, using the same procedure?" Here, precision is important, as the goal is to measure and record as accurately as possible and eliminate as many sources of error as possible. Inventiveness may be needed as you consider how to collect data. Often, scientists and teachers have to engineer the circumstances in which to collect data and design specialized ways and tools to collect the data. You'll see examples of students doing this in the examples below.

SYSTEMATICALLY IMPLEMENTING THE INVESTIGATION (RECORDING RESULTS AND OBSERVATIONS)

"How can we create a plan for taking data in an organized way and record the data so we can make sense of it later?" When we have worked with students on the collection of data, a good exercise is having them create a data table. The table has to be labeled with the event or thing being measured (e.g., speed, temperature, distance, or "yes/no" that something happened). It should include the frequency with which the readings are taken. The table also should have separate places for data if you are comparing different conditions. Creating this table should be first modeled by the teacher, and then the responsibility for its construction can be gradually turned over to students as they learn more (this kind of turning over responsibility to students can apply to any aspect of designing and carrying out investigations). The creation of a data table is *not just a procedure* with formatting rules—it requires students to think about being systematic in the collection of data and about what the actual design of data collection should or could be.

As you consider which of these conversations to have with students and what aspects of investigations to highlight, keep the long view in mind. Early in the year, for example, choose a couple of the ideas in these conversations to focus on and see how students respond. Mix in other aspects of the conversations when you feel that you want to deepen their experience or to give your students more autonomy in some aspect of designing and carrying out investigations.

What Does the Practice of Planning and Carrying Out Investigations Look Like When It Happens in Classrooms?

In this section, we share some authentic examples of how investigations were designed in a number of different classrooms, and then we refer to the conversations described above to make sense of the scenario. We'll start with the fourth-grade classroom in which students have questions about how a bouncing soccer ball creates sound. This is an example of firsthand data collection from a single event (not a traditional experiment with a control group and a comparison group).

Sound as Waves

The teacher discussed the idea of a fair test with students: "If some of us think sound waves go out in all directions with equal speed, how could we test that with the soccer ball on the playground?" Some students suggested that one of them stand in the middle of the playground with the soccer ball and bounce it once. The rest of the students would stand in different places and shout when they heard the bounce. The teacher knew the limitations of this but allowed the students to try it out.

The teacher in this unit used two related performance expectations in the *NGSS:*

1. 4-PS3-2. Make observations to provide evidence that energy can be transferred from place to place by sound, light, heat, and electric currents.

2. 4-PS4-1. Develop a model of waves to describe patterns in terms of amplitude and wavelength and that waves can cause objects to move.

On the playground, the students realized that it was not "fair" because some students were close to the ball and others were farther away. They wanted to test if sound traveled in all directions with equal speed, but if some students were closer than others to the ball, it would affect who heard the bounce first. After several discussions and trials, they formed a large circle about 50 yards in diameter with the student bouncing the soccer ball at the center. With their eyes closed, they quickly raised their hands when they each heard the bounce. Three students were observing when their peers raised their hands. They recorded whether all students raised their hands, and if students in any part of the circle raised their hands later than the others. They repeated this data collection over 10 trials. When the students went back into the classroom, they decided to represent the data as a drawing that showed who raised their hands earlier than others and who raised them later, to see if there were any real differences in the direction or speed of sound (Figure 7.1). They also had a conversation about other factors that may have affected the data, such as the attention kids were paying or their reaction time.

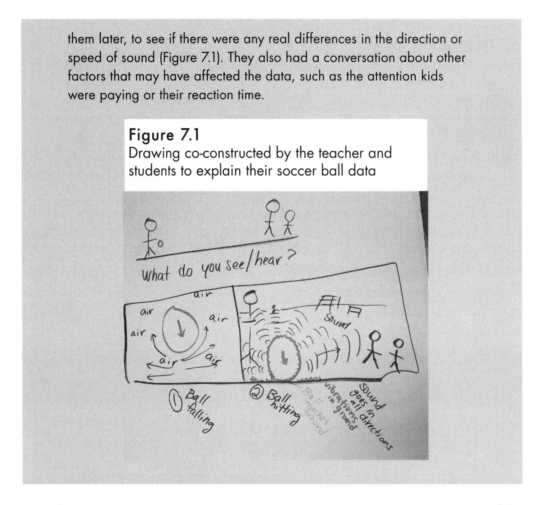

Figure 7.1
Drawing co-constructed by the teacher and students to explain their soccer ball data

In this scenario, we can see opportunities to engage students in several aspects of the conversations we outlined in the previous section. They discussed how to measure sound traveling and what to measure, and they developed their own procedure for measuring those things. Following this experience, the students decided the data were credible and then used what they had found to construct an explanation with their teacher's help.

Cellular Respiration

In the seventh-grade life science classroom, students collected firsthand data from a set of "proof-of-concept" experiments. One group of students believed that the balloon on the top of the flask was inflating due to warm air rising. Another group believed it was due to the yeast giving off some kind of gas. The teacher decided to arrange students in groups of four, two of whom believed the "warm air" hypothesis and two who favored the "yeast-gas" hypothesis (a good move by the teacher to bring advocates of each hypothesis together to design investigations). The teacher asked them to consider the question "How do you know it is the warm air causing the balloon to inflate and not some gas being given off by the yeast?" Over the next couple of days, the class read more about cellular respiration by fungi. The students who favored the yeast-gas hypothesis began to reason that the gas might be carbon dioxide.

The teacher in this unit used three related performance expectations in the *NGSS:*

1. MS-LS1-2. Develop and use a model to describe the function of a cell as a whole and ways parts of cells contribute to the function.

2. MS-LS1-3. Use argument supported by evidence for how the body is a system of interacting subsystems composed of groups of cells.

3. MS-LS1-7. Develop a model to describe how food is rearranged through chemical reactions forming new molecules that support growth and/or release energy as this matter moves through an organism.

When the groups of four got together again, they came up with two experiments. The first was to test the warm air hypothesis. They placed a two-holed rubber stopper on top of a flask with a small thermometer in one of the openings, suspended above the mixture of yeast, sugar, and warm water. They placed the balloon over the whole apparatus and recorded the air temperature as the balloon inflated. They continued with the readings to see if the balloon would remain inflated even after the air temperature had dropped back to normal levels. The students conducting this warm air experiment found that the balloon remained inflated long after the air in the flask had dropped

Figure 7.2

Increase in balloon circumference versus the internal air temperature of the flask to test hypothesis about warm air rising and filling balloon

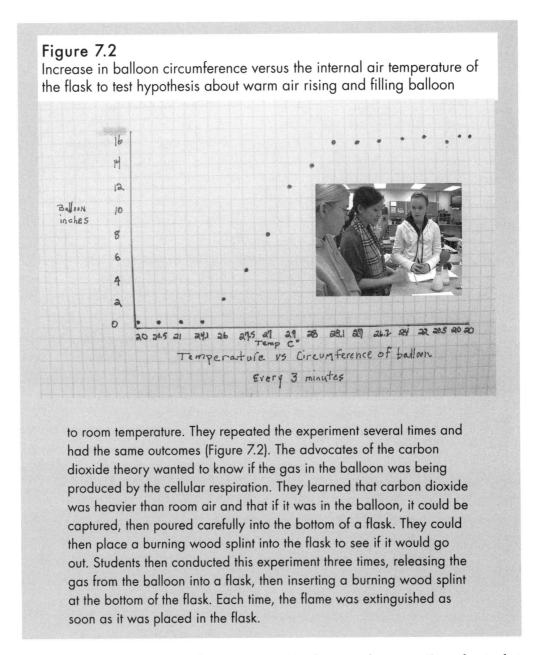

Temperature vs Circumference of balloon

Every 3 minutes

to room temperature. They repeated the experiment several times and had the same outcomes (Figure 7.2). The advocates of the carbon dioxide theory wanted to know if the gas in the balloon was being produced by the cellular respiration. They learned that carbon dioxide was heavier than room air and that if it was in the balloon, it could be captured, then poured carefully into the bottom of a flask. They could then place a burning wood splint into the flask to see if it would go out. Students then conducted this experiment three times, releasing the gas from the balloon into a flask, then inserting a burning wood splint at the bottom of the flask. Each time, the flame was extinguished as soon as it was placed in the flask.

In this example, we can clearly see opportunities for several conversations about what and how to measure and what specific observations are important. The students also attended to selecting procedures and tools to measure and collect data, and they figured out how to systematically record results and observations.

The Role of Gravity in Our Universe

In the ninth-grade Earth and space science classroom, students knew that they could not do any kind of hands-on experiment with planets and stars. But they could collect data in a systematic way with a computer model. They found a simulation developed by a well-regarded university astrophysics department that would allow them to create their own solar system (Figure 7.3). They could designate how much mass each body had, how far planets would be from the host star, and the speed of the planets' orbits. They then collected data on the movement of the star as planets of various sizes orbited. They found that under certain conditions, the star appeared to be pulled in a small elliptical orbit. This seemed to be most noticeable when there was a planet of large mass that passed close to the star.

Figure 7.3
Two of the computer simulation screens used to test hypotheses about small bodies in space exerting gravitational pull on larger bodies

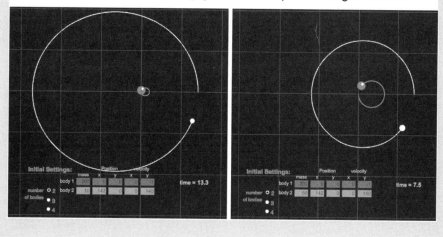

The teacher in this unit used two related performance expectations in the *NGSS*:

1. HS-PS2-4. Use mathematical representations of Newton's laws of gravitation to describe and predict the gravitational forces between objects.

2. HS-PS2-1. Analyze data to support the claim that Newton's second law of motion describes the mathematical relationship among the net force on a macroscopic object, its mass, and acceleration.

The students decided to run a kind of controlled experiment with the simulation. They set up conditions in which a planet of small mass orbited the star; they then took data on any perceivable elliptical motion of the star. If there was movement, the direction was noted at several points in time, and this was mapped against where the planet happened to be in its orbit. They repeated this scenario on several computers. They then collected data in the form of (1) the planet's mass, (2) the star's mass, (3) the distance between the planet and star, (4) the size of the "wobble" in the star's movement, and (5) the direction of the star's movement at three different points in the planet's orbit. This was repeated for three planets of differing masses. They used the diagrams of each system to make sense of what was happening and used ideas from Newton's law of gravitation to argue that, yes, small bodies in space exert a gravitational pull on larger bodies.

We note here that computer simulations produce very "clean" data that are controlled by the underlying algorithms of the program. This certainly masks the complexity of the real world and requires us to trust that the simulation outcomes would occur in authentic circumstances. In this scenario, we see students attending to all of the conversations relevant to investigations. Specifically, they discussed what and how to measure, they decided to employ a simulation in their investigation, and they figured out what to record from the simulation.

Ocean Acidification

In the AP humans and the environment class, students decided to collect data in two different ways to test the claim that ocean acidification was linked to human activity. One group of students looked up historical data on how the oceans have become increasingly acidic and compared that against other tables and graphs of data showing the total amount of greenhouse gases in the atmosphere over the past 100 years. Another group of students decided to create a small-scale replica of the ocean by using an aquarium. They filled it with water and recorded its pH. They then placed a lid on the tank and pumped small amounts of carbon dioxide into the space above the water. They recorded the pH of the water twice a day for about a week and found that the water did become more acidic over time. They were not sure, however, if this was due to something other than the carbon dioxide. They then conducted parallel trials with the same

The teacher in this unit used two related performance expectations in the *NGSS*:

1. HS-LS2-7. Design, evaluate, and refine a solution for reducing the impacts of human activities on the environment and biodiversity.

2. HS-ESS3-5. Analyze geoscience data and the results from global climate models to make an evidence-based forecast of the current rate of global or regional climate change and associated future impacts to Earth systems.

equipment but without the carbon dioxide. They found no increase in the acidity of the aquarium water.

The teacher asked them if they were creating conditions for data collection that were analogous to what happens in the real world: "Is there a 'lid' on our ocean?" "Doesn't wave action increase the dissolving of gases into the ocean?" Students themselves noted that additional trials may be needed. The teacher had earlier asked the students to look at a poster she created to help them collect data that could be useful in a scientific argument (Figure 7.4). The students were later able to use this scaffold to talk about how multiple forms of evidence supported their hypotheses.

When we look at all four classrooms, we see a wide variety of legitimate strategies for collecting data (Table 7.1). In nearly every case, the teacher and students had to decide how to create the conditions for data to be generated in the first place. There were opportunities for students to talk about accurate and reliable data, but to also look forward to defending their claims with these data—what would count as credible evidence and why? And across all these examples, there would be chances for students to reflect back on the design of the investigation as well as look forward to what they still needed to know to build the disciplinary core ideas.

Table 7.1
Strategies for generating data to be used as evidence

Scenario	Key concepts used to design and make sense of investigation	How data were generated or used
Sound energy unit	Sound as waves of energy	Firsthand data collected, each student's response to sound treated as a data point
Cellular respiration unit	The chemical basis of respiration	Firsthand data collected from "proof-of-concept" investigations
Solar system gravity unit	Newton's law of gravitation	Experimental data generated by a computer model of a real system
Ocean acidification unit	The solubility of gases	Secondhand historical data gathered. Firsthand data gathered by using a physical model in a controlled experiment

Figure 7.4
Teacher's scaffolding poster

Here is my claim [... we believe that X is caused by ... *or* we believe that Y has a role in how Z happens ...].

If this claim or explanation is true, then when I look at this data, I would expect to see [this particular result or this outcome].

The reason I'd expect to see this is because I collected data from a situation that is really close to the real thing we are studying, and if we had these outcomes, it would mean that [state a brief causal chain of events—this chain has to be consistent with known science ideas/facts].

We did see the data pattern we expected. We believe this supports our claim.

If our claim was not true, then I'd expect to see [a different set of patterns in the data or a particular outcome]. But we didn't see that outcome, so this reasoning also supports our claim.

There may be other explanations for the data, such as _____ or _____, but this does not seem likely because _____.

Note that the last type of data collection with the aquarium was the only one of our examples that could be considered a traditional controlled experiment. None of the investigations were "cookbook," and none were simply "confirmatory" of someone else's ideas. In the table, you can see the range of different ways that students can collect data. Table 7.1 also shows a summary of how science concepts were introduced so that students could use these to reason about the design of their investigations and develop explanations for the phenomena they were studying.

Equity in Designing Investigations

Excitement around investigations can sometimes lead some students to dominate the action. It is helpful to provide structured opportunities for all students to participate. For example, earlier in this chapter we showed three different types of preparatory conversations for students (under the headings "What Kinds of Data or Observations Would Help Us Answer Our Question?" "Selecting Procedures and Tools to Measure and Collect Data," and "Systematically Implementing the Investigation" [pp. 142–144]). Rather than throwing those topics out to the whole class, they could be posted at the front of the room. Students could have time to think about how they would contribute to the conversation. English language learners, socially marginalized students, girls, and students of color often feel reluctant to participate, but given private time to compose something to say, especially with a partner, they will be more likely to join the discussion. The talk environment also is made safer by maintaining norms for referring to one another's contributions. Teachers we know have had students create four kinds of posters with sentence stems on them. They are titled "How can we politely add to another person's ideas?" "How can I ask for clarification about an idea?" "How can I politely disagree?" and "How can I ask for evidence?" Under the evidence poster, for example, students have written stems like "I like what you are saying, but can you tell me what makes you think _____?"

Because so much happens in small groups during investigations, and this is a place where some students can push back from the table or be given menial tasks to do in the group, we have developed roles for students. These roles are not simply about managerial duties, such as the note taker, the supply getter, and the procedure reader. Rather, they are about students taking responsibility for different parts of the science talk that moves everyone's thinking forward. Here are some examples of roles for intellectual work:

- **Big ideas (BI) person**. This person pulls the group (occasionally) back to the scientific purpose of the activity. (Often a group will get too wrapped up in the rote execution of the directions.)

- **Clarifier.** This is a role of monitoring everyone's comprehension about one or two key science terms related to the investigation.

- **Questioner.** This person asks probing questions during the activity, listens for questions posed by other group members, and then revoices the questions to make sure that the whole group takes a moment to hear and entertain questions from everyone.

- **Skeptic.** This person tries to strengthen the group's work by probing for weaknesses in the developing investigation.

- **Progress monitor.** This person ask others to periodically take the measure of the group's progress.

These roles have helped many of our students participate, and some students actually take up these roles later in the school year without being asked.

How Do I Get Started With Students in Planning and Carrying Out Investigations?

Consider these goal statements for each grade band that appear in the *NGSS* for Planning and Carrying Out Investigations. Students should be involved in the following:

- Investigations based on fair tests to support explanations or design solutions (K–2),

- Investigations that control variables and provide evidence to support explanations or design solutions (3–5),

- Investigations that use multiple variables and provide evidence to support explanations or design solutions (6–8), and

- Investigations that build, test, and revise conceptual, mathematical, physical and empirical models (9–12).

By grade 12, students should be able to do the following:

- Formulate a question that can be investigated within the scope of the classroom, school laboratory, or field with available resources and, when appropriate, frame a hypothesis based on a model or theory.

- Decide what data are to be gathered, what tools are needed to do the gathering, and how measurements will be recorded.

- Decide what amount of data are needed to produce reliable measurements and consider any limitations on the precision of the data.

- Plan experimental or field-research procedures, identifying relevant independent and dependent variables and, when appropriate, the need for controls.

- Consider possible confounding variables or effects and ensure that the investigation's design has controlled for them.

We offer a note of clarification here. Every performance in the lists above is, in some age-appropriate way, within the grasp of students as young as third or fourth grade and certainly by upper elementary. Over the past 20 years, research programs and ambitious teachers have documented that young learners can construct and test models of natural phenomena, design controlled experiments, create novel and productive ways of representing data, and argue convincingly with evidence (see, e.g., Lehrer and Schauble 2005; Magnusson and Palincsar 2005; Metz 2004; Smith et al. 2000)—these capacities should be fostered long before middle and high school.

The *NGSS* set a high bar for students, but if we as teachers can coordinate, within our schools and districts, the instructional efforts at each of the grade levels, then the chances for students' cumulative success are magnified greatly. We can be intentional about addressing various dimensions of scientific practice across the K–12 spectrum, rather than leaving it up to chance that students have had particular experiences before they get to your classroom.

Very early in the K–12 trajectory—in elementary school—students should be given opportunities to decide what data are to be gathered, what variables should be controlled, and what tools or instruments are needed to gather and record data with precision. As students begin to develop and test hypotheses, they should be encouraged to explain their reasoning, to justify their choices, and to relate their thinking to a well-developed model or theory. At all levels, there needs to be a balance between the investigations structured by the teacher and those that emerge from students' own questions.

We have tried to make clear in this chapter that teachers are not just consumers of curriculum. They are decision makers who modify their materials, and they rearrange activities, readings, discussions, and other practices to help students build explanations and models in cumulative and coherent ways. Groups of teachers planning together should agree to discard activities that do not clearly advance students' thinking about a set of big ideas that anchor the unit. One of the primary messages threaded throughout the *Framework* and the *NGSS* is that *less is more*. Our message is that teachers have the specialized knowledge to make choices about their students' instructional experiences.

This chapter started with the story of a young boy who began investigating the world in his own backyard. The simple questions he posed about the flower and the bee represent a starting place for us, as teachers, to ask, "How can we systematically support the ability of students to test their ideas about things that matter to them?" and, just as important, "How can we keep curiosity alive for learners of all ages?" Engaging students in the practice of Planning and Carrying Out Investigations is key to fostering these scientific dispositions.

References

Goldmith, T. 2013. *Varun's quest: Into a bee tree and other adventures.* Branford, CT: Blue Ring.

Lehrer, R., and L. Schauble. 2005. Developing modeling and argument in elementary grades. In *Understanding mathematics and science matters,* ed. T. A. Romberg, T. P. Carpenter, and F. Dremock, 29–53. Mahwah, NJ: Lawrence Erlbaum.

Magnusson, S., and A. Palincsar. 2005. Teaching to promote the development of scientific knowledge and reasoning about light at the elementary school level. In *How students learn science in the classroom,* ed. M.S. Donovan and J. Bransford, 421–474. Washington, DC: National Academies Press.

Metz, K. 2004. Children's understanding of scientific inquiry: Their conceptualizations of uncertainty in investigations of their own design. *Cognition and Instruction* 22 (2): 219–290.

Smith, C., D. Maclin, C. Houghton, and M. G. Hennessey. 2000. Sixth-grade students' epistemologies of science: The impact of school science experience on epistemological development. *Cognition and Instruction* 18 (3): 285–316.

8

ANALYZING AND INTERPRETING DATA

ANN E. RIVET AND JENNY INGBER

Nia and Jessica took the geographic information system (GIS) plots of temperature and precipitation data for their region and placed them next to each other on their desks. "What is our question again?" asked Nia.

"We are asking if it is going to rain tomorrow," responded Jessica. The two girls were silent for a minute.

"Well," said Nia, "we know that warm, moist air rises, and then cools, and then forms clouds and rain, right? This maps shows that it's warm over here and cooler over here." She pointed to locations on the temperature map. "And that's where the rain is," she continued.

"Wait," interrupted Jessica, "so does that mean that that is where a cold front is?" The two girls pondered the information in front of them.

"I think so," said Nia.

"Which would mean it will likely rain tomorrow, because cold fronts move west to east, and we are located here, east of the rain," Jessica stated as she pointed to the temperature map. "So as the cool air runs into the warm air over us, it will make it rain like it's doing over there," pointing to the precipitation map.

"Yeah, I see it too," said Nia. "Let's write that down."

Data are everywhere all around us, all day, every day. Data are also very common in science classrooms. Students observe things, measure things, and calculate things all the time. Scientists, engineers, and students use data in an array of different forms to identify and document phenomena and to explain why and how it occurs. These data are facts, statistics, observations, or items of information that come from both the natural and built environment. But how do scientists, engineers, and students make sense of all this information? How can we use it to better explain and deepen our understanding of our world? The key processes that link this information to questions, models, explanations, and understanding encompass the practice of Analyzing and Interpreting Data.

What Is the Practice of Analyzing and Interpreting Data?

Problem-Solving Approaches

Scientists do very particular things with data in order to extract meaning and develop evidence related to a question or problem, including the following:

- Looking for patterns in the data

- Identifying significant features

- Describing relationships

- Highlighting trends

- Identifying anomalies

Each of these ways that scientists and engineers examine data reveals different things about the nature of or relationships among elements of the data and what the data mean in terms of the specific research question being investigated. A single data set can result in multiple different kinds of evidence, depending on how the scientist, engineer, or student looks at it.

Data come in a variety of forms such as, but not limited to, pictures, measurements, behaviors, maps, and calculations. "Analyzing" data involves studying or determining the nature of the relationship between objects, aspects, or parts (such as parts of a system). "Interpreting" data refers to how we explain the meaning of these relationships. Thus, data analysis and interpretation describe the process we use when we assign meaning to collected information and determine the significance and implications of the findings in the context of a question or problem. Data analysis and interpretation are key scientific practices and contribute to our ways of thinking about, and working with, science concepts to understand and explain how our world works.

Importantly, a key goal of science is to connect information (in the form of data) to a claim, explanation, or model that addresses a question or problem of interest and informs new kinds of questions. However, to do this, the relevant information needs to be identified and put in a form so that its meaning can be recognized and described. This process is the practice of Analyzing and Interpreting Data. Similarly, engineers strive to develop the best model to solve a problem; data analysis and interpretation are used to inform and revise multiple versions of their designed solutions. This is accomplished through repeated cycles of design, data collection and analysis, and redesigns; as such, the analysis and interpretation of the data are also central to the processes of developing and improving model solutions. The practice of Analyzing and Interpreting Data in both science and engineering is guided by questions such as "What do the data we collect mean?" "How do these data help me answer my question?" "What new questions come out of the data?"

This practice is central to the activities of scientists and engineers and should hold a prominent place in science education. Through the practice of Analyzing and Interpreting Data, we make connections between abstract, theoretical ideas and concrete, real-world phenomena with the aim of answering questions or solving problems. This interplay with the abstract and the concrete helps us develop and refine our understanding of how the world works, or determine *how* a design solution functions in a particular way as well as explain *why*.

There is no single "right way" to engage in Analyzing and Interpreting Data. Rather, scientists and engineers select from a wide array of approaches, tools, algorithms, processes, and reasoning strategies available to best connect the question or problem at hand with the data available.

When considering the practice of Analyzing and Interpreting Data, it is important to stress the distinctions among the data gathered through investigations, tools used for the analysis of data, and the analysis and interpretation itself. **The Analyzing and Interpreting Data practice highlights the act of ascribing meaning to relationships in data, supported by a wide range of tools and processes, including statistics, graphs, visual displays, and other mathematical tools.** It is closely related to the practices of Planning and Carrying Out Investigations and Using Mathematics and Computational Thinking, but it is distinct in its role for understanding how the world works.

> ## Tools
>
> There is also a wide array of tools that can be used in the practice of Analyzing and Interpreting Data. Such tools include the following:
>
> - Tables
>
> - Graphs
>
> - Mathematics
>
> - Computer-based "visualization tools"
>
> - Statistical analysis tools and techniques
>
> Each of these tools provides scientists and engineers with different perspectives on the relationships among and between the data, which may be more or less effective for addressing a particular investigation or design question at hand.

For instance, the act of identifying and gathering data that align with a question is not the same thing as analyzing and interpreting the data in relationship to that question. The former identifies the information needed, while this practice translates that information into evidence that can be used to support explanations and arguments. Specifically, in the introductory vignette (p. 159), the question guiding the students' investigation required spatial GIS data, but just having those data in hand was not analysis and interpretation.

Likewise, the tools employed in the process of Analyzing and Interpreting Data, and the mathematical and computational reasoning needed to effectively use those tools, are different from the process of ascribing meaning to the data. While mathematics and computational reasoning allow the relationships in the data to come to light, the products of those tools and processes are not in and of themselves conceptually related to the question being investigated. Rather, it is the analysis and interpretation that link those identified relationships with conceptual ideas and give meaning to those relationships. Again, in the introductory vignette (p. 159), the students employed computational reasoning to identify a relationship between the temperature and precipitation data. However, it was the examination of that identified relationship with respect to their understanding of the water cycle and weather fronts that allowed the students to analyze and interpret the relationship in a way that allowed them to address their question.

Thus, scientists and engineers need other practices to effectively engage in the practice of Analyzing and Interpreting Data. Those who are fluent with this practice draw from an array of knowledge about problem-solving approaches and tools that interrelate the data with the initial question and goals to gain new insights. We strive to develop this expertise in our students across their K–12 science learning experiences.

Key Features of Analyzing and Interpreting Data

As scientists or engineers engage with the practice of Analyzing and Interpreting Data, their activities have the following characteristics:

1. **Scientists and engineers work with data toward a goal.** A primary feature of the practice is that scientists and engineers themselves actively engage in working with data for the purpose of answering a question or solving a problem. They are not given data and shown the meaning of the data. Rather, they figure out relationships in the data in the service of making sense of how some aspect of the world works. The important feature of the practice is the thinking and reasoning around the data toward a goal that the scientist or engineer has, not just the presence of data in the investigation. For example, scientists and engineers engage differently with data if the aim is to uncover a previously unknown relationship in the data versus to demonstrate a relationship that has already been established by others.

2. **Scientists and engineers use a range of tools for analysis and interpretation.** Scientific tools are not limited to only data collection instruments. Critical to the practice are tools that assist with Analyzing and Interpreting Data. Scientists and engineers use many different visualization tools to represent relationships in data, including Venn diagrams, bar and line graphs, and GIS images. Mathematics is also a key tool, including averages, correlational statistics, function fits, and the like. These tools enable different kinds of reasoning about the data, and they allow evidence identified from the data to be linked to an increasingly wider array of questions.

3. **Scientists and engineers are engaged with multiple practices when they analyze and interpret data.** The practice of Analyzing and Interpreting Data is related and connected to all other scientific practices. Scientists and engineers analyze data as they attempt to answer a question or solve a problem. In turn, the analysis and interpretation may lead to new questions. Beyond just equations, mathematical thinking is a key tool used to analyze and interpret data. Emerging from the analysis is evidence that is then employed in explanations and arguments. It is virtually impossible to isolate this practice from the others; to do so would render it meaningless from a science perspective.

4. **The practice of analysis and interpretation is not a solo act.** Scientists are social beings; communicating, collaborating, and sharing are part and parcel of how they do their work. Engaging in this practice together in small teams and as part of the larger professional community can take many forms. Scientists and engineers often work together to contribute their individual data to a larger data set, which adds the ownership and identity of each individual to the resulting findings through the analysis process. The acts of comparing analyses and debating various interpretations engage their reasoning and discourse skills, along with developing more robust understandings of the concepts. In a collaborative and supportive environment, scientists and engineers bring different perspectives to bear on making meaning of the data, which is at the crux of new science discovery.

What Does the Practice of Analyzing and Interpreting Data Look Like in Classrooms?

To highlight the development of this practice across K–12, we present a series of classroom examples of Analyzing and Interpreting Data. Each example is followed by a commentary that highlights the salient features of the example as related to the key aspects of the practice. Later, we look across the examples to discuss particular challenges around supporting students' learning and development of the practice, interactions with disciplinary concepts, and assessment.

Example 1: Ms. Stevens's Second-Grade Science Class

Ms. Stevens's second-grade class engaged in a life science unit on interdependent relationships in ecosystems. Specifically, the unit targeted the development of students' understanding of *NGSS* standard 2-LS4-1, "Make observations of plants and animals to compare the diversity of life in different habitats." Water was used as a key connecting theme across many aspects of the second-grade curriculum, so for this unit, students started with the following guiding questions: Where is water found in both natural and urban environments? What kinds of living things live in and around the water? Part of this learning experience included students gathering data from two places, a local urban garden and a forest outside the city. The students used the observations they made in these two different places to compare the diversity of life in different habitats and analyze how this related to the water present in those places.

Trip 1: Urban Community Garden or "City" Garden. While visiting a local urban community garden, the students drew illustrations to record their observations, guided by the following questions: Where is standing water? Where is water being collected by people? What types of plants and animals do you observe living where you see water in the city? The students drew pictures of human-made objects that held water such as buckets, fire hydrants, hoses, and faucets. They also drew images of places where water could be "standing," such as in street puddles and in puddles in potted soil. Illustrations of the animals and plants they saw in the garden included worms, birds, vines, flowers, ants, butterflies, and bees.

Trip 2: Forest Outside the City. On a trip to a river in the forest, the class was asked to observe, illustrate, and record what they saw and answer the following questions: Where is the water? What lives on, in, or near the water? What is in the water (rocks, leaves, insects, fish)? The students drew pictures of the river and some of the animals and objects they saw in and around the river. They drew frogs, acorns, spiders, rocks, and bugs on their observation sheets. They also documented their observations by writing down other things they saw or heard. Some said they heard birds, saw logs, saw a lot of leaves, and saw a butterfly.

Analyzing Their Observations. After visiting the garden and the forest, Ms. Stevens collected and reviewed the pictures her students had drawn. She printed out her own digital photos, which she had taken during the two trips, that matched her students' observations. The pictures included trees, salamanders, frogs, spiders, birds, fish, pond algae, and butterflies from the forest trip, and spiders, butterflies, ants, flowers, and worms from the garden trip. When the students came back to class, she put a large Venn diagram up on the board and distributed the pictures to her students. She labeled one circle of the diagram "Forest" and the other "City Garden." She labeled the middle "Both Forest and City Garden." She asked the children to select pictures of two things they saw in each place and stick them on the board in the place they belonged.

After the students put their pictures up, Ms. Stevens asked them why they thought they saw some animals in the forest and not in the garden, with the aim for students to use their observations to compare the diversity of life in different habitats. She began asking about the fish, which were found in the forest but not in the garden. Students pointed out features of the habitats that could explain the presence or absence of fish. One student said that the fish could not swim to the garden because all of the water was brought there by people or came through hoses, but there could be fish in the garden if people brought them there. Another student said that the food that the fish eat is in the river or the pond and that there was no food for the fish in the garden. Ms. Stevens then asked why the vegetables were seen in the garden and not in the forest. A student said that the vegetables were brought there by people and that there could be vegetables in the forest if people brought them there. Another student responded, saying that the vegetables might not live in the forest even if people brought them because they need sunlight, and the trees make it too shady for some vegetables. Finally, Ms. Stevens asked why they thought that butterflies lived in both the garden and the forest. A student said that butterflies could fly from the city to the woods, and they looked for plants. Through this conversation, Ms. Stevens began to help her students understand that there was greater diversity in the forest than in the garden because the kinds of organisms in the garden were, generally, limited to what people brought there. They continued this work in future lessons, comparing the diversity of life in additional habitats and considering different factors, such as water, that affected this diversity.

ELEMENTARY SCHOOL: COMMENTARY ON MS. STEVENS'S SECOND-GRADE EXAMPLE

Kindergarteners come into school having made observations of the world around them but may not have systematically collected, recorded, or shared these observations with other people. In the early years of elementary school, children should learn about different kinds of data that can be collected using their senses. For example, we may ask children to observe the weather for one month each season. They may observe it with their eyes and document these observations by drawing, painting, or taking camera pictures of the sky. They may write a sentence or some simple words describing the way it smells or the sounds they hear such as raindrops falling. They can compare these data by looking at how their pictures, descriptions, or charts changed from one season to the next. In this example, students used their observations to describe patterns in the natural world to answer the scientific question "How does weather change from season to season?" While much of the data that younger students use are qualitative, the students can also begin to start working with simple measurements, such as measuring the heights of plants as they grow and using the data to explain that as the plant gets older, it also, typically, gets taller.

In the example presented above, the students in Ms. Stevens's class were able to generate evidence and compare the diversity of organisms in different habitats (in this case, human-made and natural habitats) through the process of analyzing and interpreting their observational data. While the teacher selected the Venn diagram as the analysis tool, the students were the ones who actively made decisions about where in the Venn the images belonged. They were able to look at the Venn diagram and recognize that there were similarities and differences between the two environments they had visited and were able to use the data they had gathered to show their understanding. Using the Venn diagram as a visual to compare the two sites, the students then made conjectures about why they saw some organisms in the garden and others in the forest.

These activities built the foundation for helping students generate evidence-supported explanations about the diversity of organisms in different habitats further in the lesson sequence.

A key aspect of this investigation was the *comparison* of two sites. The process of students' Analyzing and Interpreting Data using a Venn diagram was a necessary extension of the data collection, as it helped students demonstrate that they could differentiate between the different sites and the animals that lived there. If the students had simply looked at their own observations—rather than the observations of the entire class—and not used an analysis tool such as the Venn diagram, they may have missed the opportunity to see the numerous examples of similarities and differences between the sites. The statements they could make about the locations would have been limited to students saying simply what they saw in each place, rather than more generally how the two places compared or differed. Ms. Stevens's selection of the Venn diagram was important also because it emphasized comparing and contrasting as the goal of this lesson, and not, for instance, categorizing the kinds of animals in each place. Also note that Ms. Stevens reviewed her students' observations before providing them with images that were similar to what they saw. At this juncture, her students were still grappling with what qualifies as an observation. Many students this age still have active imaginations and will include, in their drawings, things they like to draw and things they wish they had seen (e.g., we commonly see the Sun shining in a child's picture, even if the day had been really cloudy).

Example 2: Mr. Kay's Sixth-Grade Science Class

Mr. Kay used project-based science approaches to many of his science units. In addressing the *NGSS* standard MS-PS3-1, "Construct and interpret displays of data to describe the relationships of kinetic energy to the mass of an object and to the speed of an object," his sixth graders focused on the science of bike riding. The class worked with ramps and carts as simulations of riding bikes on hills, to describe the speed of moving objects and differences in speed between riding down a gentle ramp/hill and a steep ramp/hill. The class went on to discuss energy as what can cause things to happen or change. Chris shared that he broke his arm when he fell off his bike and asked if energy caused this. To explore this idea, Mr. Kay gave the class dried spaghetti, and they found that it was easier (used less energy) to break a single strand of spaghetti as compared to being much harder (used more energy) to break several strands of spaghetti together. This led the class to ask the question "Do moving things (like bikes) have energy? If so, how could they measure it?" They came up with an investigation using the ramps and carts and dried spaghetti as a way to quantify the amount of energy the cart had at the bottom of the ramp. Mr. Kay first demonstrated the process of using clamps to set the strands of spaghetti across the bottom of the ramp (Figure 8.1). With the ramp set at 15 cm high, the class rolled the cart down the ramp first with one strand of spaghetti at the end. The strand broke easily, indicating that the moving cart had more energy than was needed to break one piece. They repeated the experiment with two, three, four, five, and six strands of spaghetti. The cart had enough energy to break three pieces but not four pieces. The class hypothesized that faster carts (higher ramps) would break more spaghetti, and slower carts would break less. To test this hypothesis, Mr. Kay directed the class to expand the experiment. Each group was given a different height of the ramp (different cart speed) to explore, ranging from 5 cm to 30 cm. At least two groups explored the same ramp height. For each height, the groups needed to determine how much energy (in units of broken spaghetti pieces) the cart had at the bottom of the ramp. They conducted multiple trials and recorded their data in a group data table. The data were then collected across groups on the whiteboard for discussion and analysis.

Mr. Kay first had the class stop and look carefully at the data they collected. She asked the following questions: Were the measurements in each of the columns similar? What was the range (the difference between the largest and smallest values)? Were there any data points that were noticeably different from each other? Why weren't the measurements between groups with the same height ramp exactly the same? The class noticed that Trevor's group's measurements were much smaller than the others. Mr. Kay called this data point an "outlier," which is one that doesn't fit with the general pattern of the rest of the data. Trevor pointed out that he thought the clamps weren't

Figure 8.1
Clamps are used to set the spaghetti at the bottom of the ramp

holding the spaghetti strands right. Mr. Kay acknowledged that this could have been the case, as one cause of outliers in data is that equipment or measuring tools are not working properly. The class brainstormed other possible causes of outliers in the data, including writing down the wrong measurements or having something else affect the experiment (like someone pouring oil on the ramp as a joke). Mr. Kay explained to the class that this data point could be removed because it was so different, but they needed to write in their report why they did not include this measurement.

Reminding the class that scientists have tools to help them look at data to see what it means, Mr. Kay then asked the class for ideas for how they could better see if there were any patterns from the numbers in a table. The class decided to graph the data. Volunteers averaged the data for each ramp height, then each group created a bar graph to display the relationship between height of the ramp and number of spaghetti pieces broken. Mr. Kay asked Anny's group to share its graph (Figure 8.2). After confirming that this plot was similar to those of the other groups, Mr. Kay asked Anny to describe the trend in the data. "It goes up," Anny stated. "What goes up?" Mr. Kay asked. Anny hesitated. Mr. Kay directed the groups to work together to use the graphs to state a relationship between ramp height and spaghetti pieces broken. Through discussion, the class came up with this claim: As ramp height increases, the amount of spaghetti broken increases. "And what does the ramp height mean for motion?" asked Mr. Kay. The class responded, "Speed of the cart!" "And what does the broken spaghetti represent?" "Energy!" shouted the class enthusiastically. So Mr. Kay asked the class to interpret the relationship between speed and energy based on their data. Jordan stated, "The faster the cart, the more energy it has, because the graph goes up." Mr. Kay agreed and posed the big question: "So what does this mean for riding your bike down a hill?" Anny then piped up, "So when you go down a steep hill, you have more energy!" Mr. Kay smiled and gave her a big high-five.

Figure 8.2
Anny's group's graph

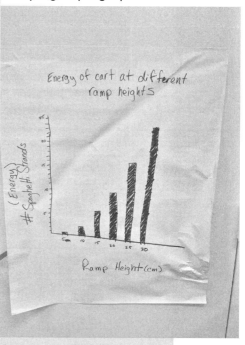

MIDDLE SCHOOL: COMMENTARY ON MR. KAY'S SIXTH-GRADE EXAMPLE

In the example presented above of Mr. Kay's sixth-grade science lesson on energy and motion, the students were actively engaged with multiple aspects of the practice of Analyzing and Interpreting Data. They looked at consistency and outliers in a data set, used mathematical tools to average data points, and created bar graphs to see the relationship between the data they collected during the investigation. There were several goals for engaging students with this opportunity for data analysis and interpretation. Through gathering, analyzing, and interpreting their own data, they were able to develop both a deeper sense for what motion and energy are and a sense that real relationships can be identified and explored through data. In this particular case, one experiment at a single ramp height would not have been sufficient for students to grasp the power of comparing data and generalizing across specific instances.

Overall in the middle grades, students use what they learned in the lower grades about using their senses and making qualitative observations to compare and contrast multiple trials or multiple organisms, objects, or phenomena. For example, students may observe images of four different fossils and then be asked to compare and contrast these fossils to each other and with similar organisms that live today and determine the nature of the environment in which they lived. These older students may look at more than just the qualitative physical features but also use measurements to notice that the fossilized organism was significantly larger or smaller than similar organisms found today. In the middle grades, students also begin to explore more extensive data sets and use the data to evaluate claims or refine design solutions. Students at this age can collect data in small groups and then compare the data by discussing the similarities and differences in their findings. The data that students gather can be organized into tables and graphs to help them identify patterns and relationships. Whereas younger students look at more at qualitative features of the weather by stating whether is it cloudy, rainy, sunny, and so forth, older students look at numerical data sets, such as temperature, precipitation, and wind direction, to describe the weather. For example, monitoring and graphing temperature from the beginning of the school day to the end of the school day over the course of a week would likely help students notice that it is, typically, cooler in the morning at the start of the school day than it is around lunchtime. With these data they could evaluate the claim that as the sun gets higher in the sky, the temperature increases.

As they advance in middle school, students also begin to use more sophisticated and precise tools for data analysis. They increase engagement with quantitative investigations as they begin to recognize the power in describing relationships through mathematical means. They may make use of basic statistical techniques (i.e., mean, median, mode, and variability) to describe a data set and how it relates to observable traits of the phenomena under study. Students can use such tools to distinguish between linear and nonlinear relationships, and they can begin to recognize differences between simple correlation and cause and effect. The nature of the research questions posed also expands, engaging students in explorations around patterns and variations in data across space and over time, and they can begin to use graphical displays as analysis tools, including line graphs and maps, for such purposes. Middle school students also now approach the analysis and interpretation of data with different goals in mind, as they respond to the increased range in research questions posed. They may attend to similarities or differences in their data, or they may analyze data to define the ideal range for a proposed tool, object, system, or process that meets criteria for success. At this stage students also should become more critical of their data analysis, understand data limitations, and work to improve precision and accuracy.

Example 3: Ms. Green's Ninth-Grade Life Science Class

Ms. Green has been teaching at the same suburban high school for seven years. Each year, Ms. Green's students conduct an investigation into the quality of the water in the small creek that runs behind the school. Teams of four are each assigned a different segment of the creek to investigate. Students collect data from the creek three times a year—fall, winter, and spring—using a variety of digital and analog tools to gather measurements of temperature, salinity, dissolved oxygen, turbidity, nitrates, phosphates, and pH. They also conduct biodiversity counts of macroorganisms in the creek and along its banks. The goal of this extended task is to analyze and interpret the data to generate evidence that shows how available resources, such as dissolved oxygen, nitrates, and phosphates, affect the populations of plants and macroorganisms present in the creek. Student groups complete interim analysis reports after each creek visit, and they produce a final report that synthesizes the findings across the visits in the spring. Ms. Green saves the data each year so they are available to subsequent classes and can be included as part of their analysis. This investigation addresses aspects of multiple life science learning performances in the *NGSS*, including HS-LS2-6, "Evaluate the claims, evidence, and reasoning that the complex interactions in ecosystems maintain relatively consistent numbers and types of organisms in stable conditions, but changing conditions may result in a new ecosystem."

This spring, Ms. Green got the idea for students to add the use of digital cameras to document observations of the creek and the organisms within it. The pictures could serve as a source of additional evidence for their claims about the relationship between the resources and the populations living in the creek. To begin integrating the digital photos into the study, Ms. Green asked the class to brainstorm the kinds of data they might be able to capture with images. Students talked about the numbers of different plants or animals, how muddy the water was, and any signs of trash that could lead to pollution. Ms. Green asked them to think more about the measurements they were already collecting. How could the images that they collect support the measurements of temperature, salinity, dissolved oxygen, turbidity, nitrates, phosphates, and pH? She asked the students to work in their teams to develop two questions about the creek's water quality and the populations of organisms living in the creek that could be explored by combining both the quantitative measurements and digital images. After talking in groups for several minutes, teams posted their questions on the board: "Are there more plants or macroorganisms present when the dissolved oxygen levels are high?" "How does a change in the amount of nitrate in the creek affect the number of plants in the creek?" "Does murkier water hide more macroorganisms from predators?"

The next day, the teams went out to gather their data. In addition to recording the measurements for their section of the creek, the students took several pictures. Not all pictures were directly related to the students' research questions, but the pictures showed the range of abiotic and biotic factors of interest to the students once they were in the field. Some focused on the big picture: the shape of the creek, the contour of the land around the creek, and the houses and buildings that were nearby. Other students focused on the close-up, taking pictures of individual plants, macroorganisms, and rocks. Some focused on trash and bottles that were found in the water in one part of the creek. One student took a picture of a frog in the weeds and excitedly showed it to several of his classmates.

Back in the classroom, students began to work on the analysis of both the quantitative measurements and the images, in preparation for their final spring report. While they were primarily analyzing the relationship between resources and populations of organisms, students examined all of the data they collected and considered how the data could impact what was living in the creek. Students compared temperature measurements from different points in the creek and graphed their dissolved oxygen levels in comparison with measurements from the fall and winter. They spent significant time poring over the digital images and figuring out how to understand this new data source. They commented that they liked the ability to take their time looking at the photographs, and it allowed them to observe different things than they had noticed out in the field. A group of girls wrote in their report, "The picture of the side of the stream caving in helped us to rate turbidity." Several students talked about how the images helped them develop a big-picture view of the creek and "notice that the water quality of the creek was a mix of things as a whole, not just data points." The images also helped connect pieces of evidence into claims. Two groups were debating the cause of increased nitrate measurements and increased appearance of algae in the spring as compared to the fall and winter. One boy was arguing that it came from pollution from lawn fertilizers in nearby yards. Pointing to a photograph of the condominiums next to the stream, he stated, "This photo shows that it definitely slopes down from the condos, we have talked about that a long time. This picture proves it."

Students also became aware of the limits of the observational data. As they did not have images to compare with fall and winter, the pictures did not help as much with the overall yearlong analysis of resources and populations. Instead, the students went back to previous years to look at data from earlier projects. They found that the patterns of temperature, dissolved oxygen, and other factors across seasons were similar to those in past years, but not exactly the same. For example, three years ago the creek was much colder in the winter than it was this year. Ms. Green recalled how three years ago there had been a big storm and a deep freeze right before the class went out for data collection, and most of the creek was frozen over at that time, while this winter had been relatively mild. The students wondered how changes in temperature may have affected the populations of organisms and plant and algae growth.

Considering the conversation about weather and the levels of nitrates in the creek, a student hypothesized that maybe this year the homeowners had used lawn fertilizers earlier than in previous years because it had been so warm. He pointed out that more fertilizer could explain why they saw more plants and algae in the creek this year. Ms. Green noted that this could be a good hypothesis and asked what information would be needed to confirm it. The class suggested weather data for each year and digital pictures so they could better compare the conditions for each year's data collection. Ms. Green agreed and stated that she would try to incorporate digital pictures into each year's creek project from now on.

HIGH SCHOOL: COMMENTARY ON MS. GREEN'S NINTH-GRADE EXAMPLE

Ms. Green's yearlong creek study exemplifies several ways in which students engaged with the practice of Analyzing and Interpreting Data in developmentally appropriate ways. The key questions driving this investigation reflected the need for a deep understanding of how the interactions of multiple elements of the complex ecosystem could be evidenced through relationships of measurements of environmental factors. Thus, students were engaged with both temporal (over time) and spatial (across distance) analyses of the creek. Ms. Green supported temporal analyses with both the connections across the three data collection periods and the comparisons to the archival data. The spatial analysis, in particular, she facilitated with the use of digital images as data, as students were able to use the images to gain a big-picture perspective on the creek's resources. It is important to note that the images themselves were not separated from the more quantitative data. Rather, Ms. Green set the expectation at the beginning of the lesson that the observations and measurements should be working in tandem to help students understand the overall phenomena more completely and together provide ways of understanding the nature of the data that would not be possible by keeping the data types separate. Additionally, with the teacher's encouragement, the class was able to recognize how the images supported some kinds of claims but did not help with other questions they were pursuing in this extended investigation.

As students pursue science classes in high school, students' engagement with the practice of Analyzing and Interpreting Data becomes not only more sophisticated but also more integrated with the disciplinary understandings and the other science practices. Students at this stage rely more frequently on statistical analyses and computational models to assist with revealing the relationships, connections, and meanings in complex data sets. Mathematics becomes a key analysis tool, with function fits to data (i.e., slope, intercept, and correlation coefficients) used to identify and describe relationships. Similarly, students engage the power of mathematics to identify and describe the limits of data to address particular questions, such as the impact of small sample size or measurement error on the strength of a relationship or confidence in interpretations. Comparing across different data sources is emphasized throughout high school, as students recognize how scientists substantiate claims with multiple sources of evidence. However, it is not just the sheer volume of evidence that matters; it is the nature of the relationships between sources of evidence and the insights that emerge through bringing them together that leads to new understandings.

Common Challenges in Analyzing and Interpreting Data

Although the practice of Analyzing and Interpreting Data is a central scientific practice and should be deeply engaged by students across all of K–12 science education, that does not mean that it is easy or straightforward to implement. There is an array of known challenges that both students and we, as teachers, face when planning for and engaging in this practice across classroom settings. The good news is that with a little awareness and some planning, many of these challenges can be anticipated and effectively addressed to create quality learning opportunities for all students.

CHALLENGE: HOW DO WE HELP OUR STUDENTS REALLY OBSERVE IN A WAY THAT RESULTS IN RICH SUBSTANTIVE DATA, SO THEY CAN DO THINGS SUCH AS IDENTIFY PATTERNS OR CAUSE-AND-EFFECT RELATIONSHIPS?

Observing is something that we think we do every day. However, many of our students approach the act of making and recording observations in a very superficial manner. Observing is a learned skill that needs to be developed over time with ongoing support. Observations are also not typically conducted in an open-ended manner; rather, one observes a specimen or phenomenon *for a purpose*. In that way, observations are guided by questions and are connected to a theory or model that students are trying to understand. Thus, it is important for us to support students by asking them to articulate ahead of time *what* they are looking for and *why*. Once they have gathered their observations, ask them to share their data with the class or in small groups, paying attention to what others observed and why they observed what they did. Students might need multiple experiences observing the same thing to find a pattern or recognize a relationship between the data and the theory or model under investigation. Additionally, students might need practice in differentiating between observations (what we see, smell, hear, feel, and taste) and inferences, or what we think based on those observations. For example, when we walk outside and see that the ground is wet, we have made an observation, whereas when we suggest either that the sprinkler system was on or that it was raining, we have made an inference. Practice in clarifying this difference reminds students to focus on what they observe and not jump straight into making inferences.

CHALLENGE: WHAT DO WE DO WITH STUDENTS WHO UNDERANALYZE OR OVERANALYZE DATA?

We've worked with students who try to use a single data point to substantiate a claim. We have also had students who want to include all of the available information in their analysis, regardless of whether it is relevant to the investigation. Additionally, we know students who simply bypass the interpretation stage altogether and connect claims to questions irrespective of the data at hand. Each of these scenarios is common and appropriate in the early stages as students learn the difficult task of supporting claims with evidence. In most of these cases, the students were missing an understanding of the nature of data as a collection of information gathered for a purpose. Demonstrating how to engage in the practice multiple times, explicitly articulating the connections between the data and the analysis, and giving meaning to those relationships is one way we have addressed this common set of challenges.

CHALLENGE: HOW DO WE HELP STUDENTS UNDERSTAND THE VARIETY OF ANALYSIS TOOLS AND PROCEDURES AND WHAT TOOL TO USE WHEN?

As described earlier, there is a wide array of tools and procedures that are available to both scientists and students to assist with data analysis. We noticed that our students have a tendency to pick the first tool they think of and use that, rather than considering which approach would be the most appropriate for their question. Usually more than one analysis is needed to address most questions, so part of our challenge is to help students recognize the need for multiple tools and how they can work together to address specific questions. Students may also lack mathematical skills, which limits their ability to understand and engage with some important analysis tools. Any time students begin to use a new analysis tool or approach, they will need support through demonstration and example. However, as students gain more opportunities to use the same tools and approaches across a school year, their work with such tools should become more independent and self-guided. One strategy we used is to consistently ask students to justify their selection of tools and procedures. Why are you using a line graph for this data? Why are you adding up the total amount rather than comparing the means? What will using a map of the data tell you that a table might not? By asking students to be reflective of their choices, they may become more aware of the benefits and limitations of individual tools and discriminate in their future selection.

CHALLENGE: HOW DO WE HELP STUDENTS RECOGNIZE AND ACCOUNT FOR POTENTIAL ERRORS AND LIMITS IN THE DATA?

Recognizing and accounting for errors and limits in the data is a real challenge for students at all stages. In early grades, students tend to have difficulty understanding variability and how it relates to the precision of measurements. With older students, even when they can state possible sources of error, students often do not know how to take those into account as limiting the extent of the claims that can be made with the data. There are also times when the data that students are working with, either collected by themselves or gathered from other sources, simply do not demonstrate the disciplinary concept or relationship under study. Each of these challenges can thwart a teacher's best attempts to engage students with the practice. One approach we use is to relate concepts of error and limitations to experiences that students may have in everyday life, outside of science class. When dealing with outliers, as illustrated in the fourth-grade example, decisions to keep or toss the anomalous data points are discussed explicitly with the class and are based on information about how the data were collected and what could have influenced those results. These concepts are developed over time and across multiple learning opportunities, as we encourage students to continuously reflect on the nature of the data, the assumptions therein, and the goals for examining it.

ASSESSING STUDENTS' ANALYSIS AND INTERPRETATION OF DATA

Assessment of this practice is focused on students' awareness of the relationship among questions, data, analysis tools, and resulting interpretations within the context of examining and testing science concepts, theories, and models. Below, we describe some approaches that we use to assess this practice.

- Ask students to explain, in detail, the steps in their analysis process. "How did you get to that interpretation?"

- Ask students to provide a rationale for the analysis tools and approach they used. "Why did you choose that kind of graph?" "Why did you average?" "Why did you select the way you did?" "How do these tools and procedures relate to the goals of your analysis?"

- Ask students about other considerations during their analysis. "What could be sources of error in your investigation?" "How confident are you in these findings?" "What things make you unsure?" "What are the limitations on the claims from this analysis?" "What further information do you need to address the question?" For younger students, the language of these questions could be adapted to be less judgmental of their effort (e.g., "What could be done to make your data better?"). However, this language is appropriate for older students working with statistics and other kinds of analysis, where error and limitations can (and should) be described in mathematical terms.

How Can We Work Toward Equity With Regard to Analyzing and Interpreting Data?

The process of Analyzing and Interpreting Data lends itself to providing inclusive and equitable opportunities for learning science. We strive for equity by providing learning opportunities that are likely to align with the needs of all students, including English language learners, learners with special needs, ethnically diverse populations of learners, and talented and gifted learners. Specific strategies lend themselves well to supporting student learning. Below, we highlight two examples as they relate to the cases in this chapter.

SITUATING THE LEARNING IN A LOCAL CONTEXT

In all of the examples provided in this chapter, students were considering the data they collected in relation to their local environment or in relation to problems they perceived as meaningful. Ms. Stevens's focus on a local garden and a forest were situated in venues that were somewhat familiar and meaningful to the students in her class. The opportunity for integrating students' personal experience with such locations allows students to see science as something that is tangible and taking place around them, and that they are making sense of something that they have seen outside of school. This relevance triggers personal connections and helps students activate their prior knowledge. It makes the content and the practices more accessible to students who might otherwise view science as something outside of their reach or interest.

STRATEGIES FOR LITERACY SUPPORT AND DISCOURSE

Talking through data and using a variety of representations of the data lends itself to both challenges and opportunities for language development. In Mr. Kay's sixth-grade class, for example, there was a rich dialogue around the results of the experiment that were depicted on the bar graph. The fact that Trevor, in this case, had a data point that was clearly different from that of his classmates opened the door for Mr. Kay to introduce the term "outlier" to his class. He had a specific example of an outlier and several examples of nonoutliers. This was a memorable moment for his students. Both learning the new word and seeing the examples allowed students to see and talk about potential outliers in their own data in the experiments that followed. Mr. Kay also had his students practice describing what was happening with their data by having them write sentences. Finally, Mr. Kay used the materials in the laboratory setup to help his students connect what they observed to what their data meant. This is especially helpful to those students who need to connect the words they are using to something they can see. By providing such supports, Mr. Kay made the content and ideas learned through the data analysis processes more accessible to his students. Knowing his students and their language needs, Mr. Kay made several decisions that supported his students' language development, such as introducing new terms when they were relevant to the experience and taking advantage of the visual setup of laboratory materials for helping his students describe their findings. Depending on the robustness of students' language, additional scaffolding may also have aided their participation in the discussion. Use of "sentence starters" or common ways to start sentences, such as "I think _____ because _____" or "If _____ then _____," can provide additional frameworks for supporting ideas with evidence or demonstrating causal relationships.

Conclusions

The practice of Analyzing and Interpreting Data is central to both science and science learning. The most important point regarding this practice is that in science class, students *must* work with data in significant and meaningful ways. It is not sufficient for students to see data being displayed or to simply conduct rote calculations with data presented to them. The focus for students' activity must be on identifying and explaining the connections between the question or problem, the data itself, and the claim or solution that arises from the data. This is must be an active, concerted effort on the part of the students. It cannot be accomplished by passively observing others engaged with the analysis or only being demonstrated by the teacher.

A second key point is that there is a distinction between the tools for analysis and the analysis itself. Statistics, graphs, visual displays, and other mathematics are tools that allow for and facilitate meaning-making around the data. These tools are not the goal of the practice. Thus, the increasing sophistication and robustness of reasoning around data should be the primary focus of curriculum and assessment related to this practice, supported by learning about an increasing array and complexity of tools and procedures. The tools should not become the driving force in either curriculum or assessment.

The practice of Analyzing and Interpreting Data is complex and must build over multiple supported experiences across years of schooling. However, as exemplified by the individual cases presented in this chapter, there are lots of potential applications of this practice across the curriculum. By incorporating this practice throughout a teacher's science instruction, students will gain not only expertise at working with data but also a deeper understanding and appreciation for the interconnections between science concepts and the real world.

Acknowledgment

We would like to thank Jeff Wuebber, Earth science teacher at New Rochelle High School in New Rochelle, New York, for his valuable comments and suggestions on drafts of this chapter.

Suggested Further Reading

Bybee, R. W. 2011. Scientific and engineering practices in K–12 classrooms. *Science Teacher* 78: 34–40.

Krajcik, J., S. Codere, C. Dahsah, R. Bayer, and K. Mun. 2014. Planning instruction to meet the intent of the Next Generation Science Standards. *Journal of Science Teacher Education* 25 (2): 157–175.

Osborne, J. 2014. Teaching scientific practices: Meeting the challenge of change. *Journal of Science Teacher Education* 25 (2): 177–196.

9

USING MATHEMATICS AND COMPUTATIONAL THINKING

MICHELLE HODA WILKERSON AND MICHELLE FENWICK

A group of high school students is conducting a study of air quality in their city. They are interested in mapping where air quality is better and worse, finding out how it is changing over time, and identifying potential causes for poor air quality.

Before they start collecting data, the students work with their instructor and science experts to decide what information they need to answer their questions. They choose to focus on areas around the public transit system, and they carry GPS units and particulate matter sensors in their backpacks as they travel to key locations. During their visits, they take observational field notes and photographs. As they begin to notice patterns and factors that might influence air quality, the students record features of each location: whether it is indoor or outdoor, coastal or inland, suburban or urban. They begin to more systematically take air-quality measurements, ensuring that sensors are positioned both inside train cars and on train platforms for predefined periods of time. They develop systems to keep track of observations they make in the field, such as how crowded subway trains were, or how intense train cars and stations smelled, at different points during the day (Figure 9.1, p. 182).

During these investigations, the students use a mobile mapping technology called Local Ground to organize their measurements, notes, and observations. The tool allows users to make sketches and notes on paper maps, scan, and compile them to create a collection of annotations on a virtual, shared map (Figure 9.2, p. 182). Students also take photos and make audio recordings using their own mobile devices, which they can then link to the air-quality measurements they have collected with the sensors in their backpacks. They look for patterns in data collected for different parts of the city and times of day and develop codes for qualitative observations about train car

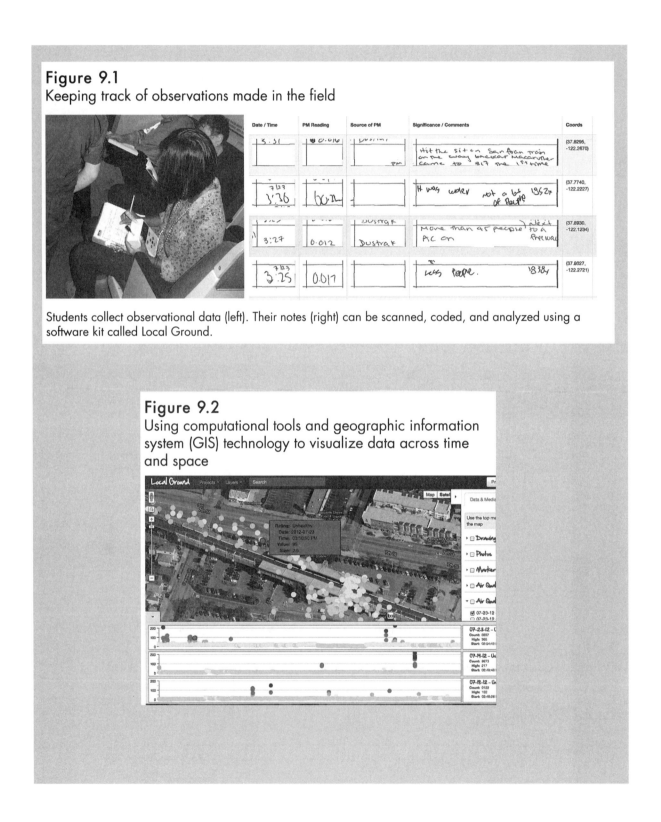

Figure 9.1
Keeping track of observations made in the field

Students collect observational data (left). Their notes (right) can be scanned, coded, and analyzed using a software kit called Local Ground.

Figure 9.2
Using computational tools and geographic information system (GIS) technology to visualize data across time and space

smell and crowdedness so that those observations become comparable and replicable. The students also begin to hypothesize about causal relationships—for example, whether air quality near a power plant is worse than in other areas.

By finding ways to organize their data and turn observations into measurable quantities, the students can then conduct a more systematic inquiry. They compare air-quality measurements; the features of the trains, platforms, and traffic patterns at stations they explored; and their observations in the field. Across these data, the students notice a dramatic difference in air quality between underground and above-ground stations (Figure 9.3). Even when taking other factors into account, such as time of day, number of cars on the trains, and other sources of pollution such as freeways and power plants, underground stations consistently produced more hazardous levels of air quality than their outdoor counterparts.

Students decided to conduct more focused investigations to learn about the source of air particulates in train cars and stations. One thing they found was that air particulate levels fluctuated dramatically *inside* trains each time they stopped. In a follow-up investigation, students hold sensors near seats that they hit deliberately. They used this evidence to argue that air-quality fluctuations inside trains were in part caused by particulates trapped in padded cloth seats, released by passengers as they sat and got up. The students present their findings to the local port authority and transit authority, as well as at a national research conference. They make recommendations for addressing the problems they found, including providing better ventilation for underground stations and cleaning or changing the seating materials inside of subway cars.

Figure 9.3
Using data plots across study sites to support a scientific argument

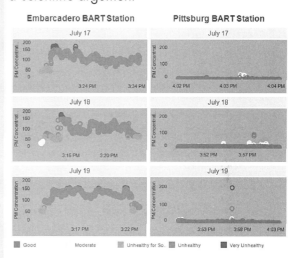

This vignette is based on an actual investigation done by high school students (Cheon et al. 2013). It is connected to performance expectations where students use mathematics and computational tools to explore the influence of human activity on Earth systems (HS-ESS3-6) and to propose and test solutions to complex problems that involve many factors (HS-ETS1-4). It would be hard to imagine how these students would have been able to do such an investigation *without* Using Mathematics and Computational Thinking. Mobile technology helped them collect qualitative and quantitative data that were distributed across space, time, and multiple investigators. It helped them consolidate and visualize dramatically different types of information (transit, air quality, cleanliness, behavior on train cars). Mathematical tools and representations allowed the students to systematize and quantify their observations, and then to find and compare the patterns they noticed.

These kinds of investigations are not limited to just older students. More recently, a fourth-grade class has been using Local Ground to organize its investigation of soil-based ecosystems by developing measures and mapping relationships between biotic (insects, plants, worms) and abiotic (moisture, compactness) indicators around their school (Lanouette, VanWart, and Parikh 2016).

Why Is the Practice of Using Mathematics and Computational Thinking Important?

Often, when we begin to explore a natural event or think about solutions to a problem, we are not just interested in describing *what* is happening. We are also interested in *how much, how fast, or how frequently* something has happened, and how it may happen in the future or in a different circumstance. Mathematics and computational thinking offer ways to do this by allowing scientists and engineers to build precise, predictive models; conduct investigations; and analyze data in new ways.

The Using Mathematics and Computational Thinking practice is all about finding precise ways to describe the patterns and processes that make up scientific and engineered systems. Calculus was originally developed to study and better understand the motion of planets. Biologists have been able to explore new population models because advances in statistics and computation allow them to work with larger and more complex types of data. In the environmental sciences, researchers use geographic information systems (GIS) and sophisticated sensors to model global climate trends and ecosystem dynamics.

In the same way that becoming proficient in a language involves learning how to both *read* and *write*, the practice of Using Mathematics and Computational Thinking is about learning how to both *apply* formulas and tools that already exist and *create* new ones. In this chapter, we focus on creation. Mathematics and computation offer special ways to propose and investigate scientific relationships and to make predictions. By exploring how mathematics and computation represent scientific ideas and help them become more precise, students can begin to understand how even the most complex mathematical formulas or computer simulations are fundamentally connected to observations, experiences, and ideas about the world around us and help us explain the natural and designed world.

BUILDING TESTABLE, PREDICTIVE REPRESENTATIONS OF MODELS

Both mathematics and computational thinking are ways to represent models we have about how the world works using precise, shared languages that can be interpreted without having the original creator around. Mathematics is sometimes described as a "universal language" that focuses on quantities and relationships. Similarly, computational thinking is about decomposing and describing processes using specific rules, to use programming or "teach" the model to a computer so that we can explore what happens over time or in new conditions.

Mathematical Modeling

Consider how with just a few mathematical symbols, the equation $p = mv$ (momentum = mass × velocity) can say a lot about how physical objects behave. It describes something even young children intuitively know: It is much harder to stop a heavy object from moving than a light one. This is represented by the direct relationship between p and m; if one side of the equation increases, so does the other. It also represents a model that can explain surprising or unexpected outcomes. If a heavy ball is rolling very slowly toward an object and a light ball is rolling very quickly, the light ball may still create more of an effect on the object than the heavier ball. This is because if velocity, v, decreases as mass, m, stays the same, momentum p decreases. If velocity increases as mass gets smaller, the total momentum may increase, remain the same, or even get smaller depending on *how much* each of these parts of the system changes relative to the others.

Using mathematics to describe relationships precisely is useful both for understanding scientific systems and for making engineering decisions. If we want to design a machine that can pitch balls of *different* mass so that they have the same momentum, we can find out exactly how much to change the pitch velocity to balance the change

Figure 9.4
Computational models of predator–prey dynamics

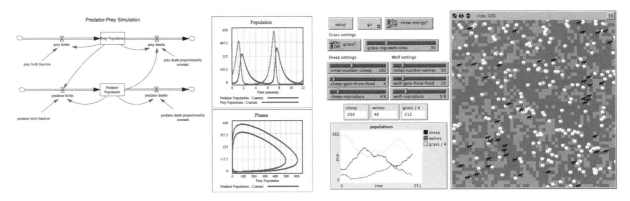

A systems dynamics model in Vensim (left) and an agent-based model of predator–prey dynamics in NetLogo (right) are shown.

in mass. Depending on the mathematical tools students have at their disposal, students can express the very same mathematical relationships in different ways. Elementary students who have not yet been formally taught algebra can create data tables or plot the outcomes of experiments using marbles of different mass to explore mathematical relationships. High school students able to work with vectors can use the same equation $p = mv$ to explore the motion and interaction of objects in 2-D and 3-D space.

Even with all of this power, mathematical models like $p = mv$ tell only part of the story. In a given situation, friction, air resistance, or the elasticity of materials might affect how a system or machine works. In this way, every mathematical model—like a scientific model in general—is incomplete. Depending on the questions someone has about a system. They might also offer powerful ways to calculate, visualize, or organize data.

Computer Modeling

Computational representations like simulations or data visualizations also allow scientists and engineers to express and test models in powerful and precise ways. These descriptions might include rules for actions such as movement or cause-and-effect relationships between parts of a system. They might also offer powerful ways to calculate, visualize, and organize data.

Figure 9.4 shows two simulations of a simple predator–prey system. Both can be used to explore ecosystem dynamics, but each emphasizes different aspects of the system. The simulation on the left focuses on relationships between various rates and quantities in the system. Using that simulation, someone can quickly explore how combinations of different birth, death, and predation rates affect overall population patterns. The simulation on the right focuses on how individual predators and prey interact over time: When a predator comes into contact with prey, the prey is eaten, and the predator gains energy and reproduces. This emphasizes the interactions (predation, energy transfer, density) that create a scientific pattern. It also reflects how stable or unstable a system might be, and it illustrates how small changes to behavior (such as whether and how a predator might chase prey) can change what happens to the system as a whole.

Although computational models can exist in many different forms, one thing they have in common is that they can free people from repetitive, computationally intensive parts of scientific and engineering tasks. For example, representing some models of systems requires people to do many difficult calculations or to imagine every possible interaction between many objects such as molecules or cells. Computational models do this *for* us, so that we can spend more time making sense of the results of these relationships and interactions. In fact, scientists' understandings of large systems such as insect colonies or engineers' understandings of the stability and failure of power grids would be almost impossible without computational models.

CONDUCTING INVESTIGATIONS

Mathematics and computational thinking, and the models that can be constructed with these tools, also provide new ways to collect and analyze data. They allow people to explore and test otherwise unobservable aspects of scientific systems. For example, epidemiologists have found ways to predict the spread of diseases such as the common cold by measuring and analyzing how frequently people use certain words in their social media and investigating how those words spread through a network. Computer simulations allow scientists and engineers to explore "what if" scenarios and conduct virtual experiments that may be impossible in real life and compare solutions to large-scale and even global problems.

Similarly, mathematics and computational thinking can help students collect, organize, and make sense of data. Simple tools like spreadsheets allow students to organize and visualize data easily, and publicly available data are increasingly accessible on the internet and through educational software tools. Digital probes and sensors can be connected to computers so that students can easily collect detailed data, and GIS allows students to explore large-scale or global environmental patterns. More advanced data analysis and visualization tools allow people to uncover hidden and unexpected patterns and relationships deserving of further study, as the students did in the opening vignette (pp. 181–184).

What Is the Practice of Using Mathematics and Computational Thinking All About?

Many people remember using mathematics in science class by plugging numbers into an equation or using particular formulas to solve science-related word problems. Similarly, they might think about using computer simulations as a way to view and interact with scientific processes that are too small, complicated, fast or slow, or otherwise difficult to observe or interact with in real life. These applications are useful, but Using Mathematics and Computational Thinking is not just about getting answers or seeing what can't be seen. Instead, it is a collection of ways that learners can theorize, test, and refine their own scientific understandings about the patterns, relationships, and processes they notice in the world.

When we focus on mathematics and computational thinking as ways to describe, make comparisons between, and test predictions about systems in the world, then it is easy to see how students are naturally inclined to think mathematically and computationally. As soon as children say something like "the heavier car will hit the wall harder than the light car" or "the smaller ice cube will melt faster than the big one," then they are on their way to thinking mathematically—in terms of relationships—about how specific quantities (mass, volume, surface area, time) might be related. In fact, much of Piaget's work explored exactly this—how young children's intuitive senses of quantity developed into more robust mathematical understandings (Piaget 1970). Similarly, as soon as children begin to describe instructions like "every time a predator catches a prey, it gains energy to live for a few more months," play Simon says, or make plans like "my robot's motor should turn faster when there is more light," they are thinking computationally about rules and ways that components of a system interact with each other.

The practice of Using Mathematics and Computational Thinking provides tools and techniques to turn these early noticings into powerful ways of thinking about, representing, and testing scientific and engineered systems. Different branches of mathematics provide tools for thinking about different things, such as shape (geometry) or change (calculus). The same is true for computation—each programming language is "like a natural, human language in that it favors certain metaphors, images, and ways of thinking" (Papert 1980). Together, they offer a myriad of ways to organize students' thinking about the following:

- What are a system's **key components:** the matter, energy, organisms, materials, or other parts that together make up a system or design? Examples are atoms and molecules in chemical interactions; mass, force, and energy in a physical system; and predator and prey levels, birth rates, death rates, and predation rates in a population dynamic system.

- What are the important **features or properties** of those components that might influence how the system works? Examples are the structure or mass of atoms and molecules; density or elasticity in a physical system; or patterns of movement, predation, and the local environment in population systems.

- What are the **relationships** between different parts and properties of a system? Example questions might be Do changes in one component always cause changes in another? Do components change over time? What is the "shape" of change: linear, exponential, or *S*-shaped?

- How can properties and relationships be **mathematically or computationally described** in a way that allows for meaningful comparisons across situations or object types?

- How do components and relationships **interact and combine** to create patterns? Example questions might be What happens to components over time? Are there chains of cause and effect that might explain surprising or unexpected results?

There are some specific mathematical formulas and computer tools that are especially important in science and engineering—such as recognizing and applying Newton's second law (*force = mass × acceleration*) or using spreadsheets to organize and visualize data. However, the practice of Using Mathematics and Computational Thinking is about having access to a toolkit of resources that help students make sense of the data and make progress. Arithmetic, algebra, geometry, calculus, and statistics are all parts of this toolkit. So are simulations, data analysis tools, programming environments, spreadsheets, and probes and sensors. Later in this chapter, we review a few strategies and resources for building an accessible math and computing toolkit in your classroom.

Even though here we present mathematics and computational thinking separately, they are often interconnected. Computational tools can be used to collect, organize, visualize, and analyze data, and computational simulations often generate quantitative data and graphs as part of their output. Similarly, some computational simulations are programmed using mathematical expressions, and many mathematical analysis tools and statistical analysis apps include computer programming languages or features.

MATHEMATICS

Using mathematics is about describing a system quantitatively. This requires students to search for and take note of patterns and trends that might be important for better understanding or building a system. It also involves finding ways to measure those patterns and to express measurements as quantities in units that different people can use to compare their results with one another's consistently. Sometimes these measurements are straightforward, like measuring the height of plants using a ruler or using a scale to find mass. Other times they can be more complex, like calculating the density of a substance using measurements of mass and volume or developing a new measure that students decide is important, but may be difficult to measure (such as the "smelliness" of trains in the opening vignette [pp. 181–184]).

Once patterns and quantities are identified, students need to describe the relationships between them using the language and symbols of mathematics. Arithmetic, algebra, and geometry are all ways to describe and predict how quantities are connected through physical or causal relationships. Combining objects or substances of like units can be expressed using arithmetic addition. Algebra or graphs can be used to describe a proportional relationship in which an increase in one variable corresponds to an increase or decrease in another. As more data are collected, students can test or adjust the mathematical relationships they describe. For example, students may notice that a relationship they first believed was linear—such as the growth of a population—is actually speeding up and might be better described as exponential.

These aspects of using mathematics do not necessarily happen in order. Even in professional science, while there are many long-established ways of taking measurements, new measuring devices or techniques are being developed all the time even for well-known systems. Or a mathematical model might be developed based on theoretical conjectures about physical or causal relationships rather than measures from data, to be validated against empirical data later. Using mathematics is a process of working within and constantly building connections across these aspects, rather than completing each as a linear process.

COMPUTATIONAL THINKING

While mathematics focuses on quantities, computational thinking focuses on processes. Students engaged in the practice of computational thinking break a complex problem or process up into smaller steps to better understand, describe, or explain it. They think about how computer tools and algorithms—specific instructions for how something should be done—can be used to make jobs like data collection and analysis or theory testing easier, more manageable, or more powerful.

One way that students can engage in computational thinking is by using existing computer models and simulations to explore, test, and better understand scientific and engineered systems. There are many freely available simulations and computer tools that can help students conduct explorations and collect and analyze data (we list a few in the "How Do I Get Started?" section, p. 200). Some allow students to conduct virtual experiments, while others allow students to visualize specific parts of systems or models of scientific phenomena. Figure 9.5 shows three different types of computer simulations designed for classroom use.

Figure 9.5
Computational models of gases

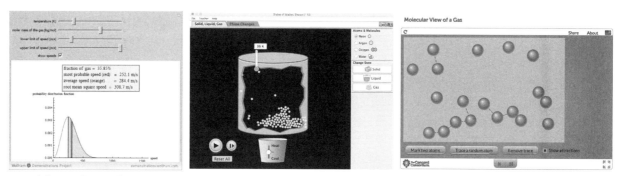

From left to right: Wolfram Demonstrations model of Maxwell-Boltzmann speed distribution, PhET Phase Change Simulator, and Molecular Workbench gas simulation

Figure 9.6
Simulations

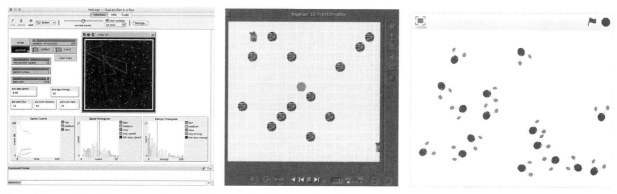

From left to right: NetLogo simulation of Maxwell-Boltzmann distribution modified by a high school student, Stagecast Creator simulation of diffusion created by a group of middle school students, and Scratch simulation of water created by a Scratch community member

Like mathematics, computational thinking is not just about using tools that already exist, but also about building your own. Many computer environments exist that allow students at even the elementary level to create their own models of scientific systems. Usually, students do this by thinking about what objects in their systems are important and defining how those objects should behave using text computer code or visual instructions. As they add more objects to their systems, they can think about the relationships and interactions between them, and they can run their models to see how each piece interacts and to test whether their models behave the way they expect. Figure 9.6 shows three different programs designed for students to use to create computational models, each with a student-produced or student-modified model of molecules acting together as a gas. NetLogo (left) allows students to write models with text code. Stagecast (center) allows students to physically "teach" objects how to move by dragging them on the screen (middle). Scratch (right) allows students to write programs by putting together puzzle blocks. NetLogo is often used at the middle and high school levels; Stagecast and Scratch were designed to be accessible to elementary students.

Although computational thinking, like mathematics, involves learning about and using formal symbolic languages, there are a few important differences. Computational models are often used to explore problems that are too complex to describe mathematically or systems that have random or probabilistic elements. For example, the predator-prey system described earlier might have very different outcomes depending on how predators and prey are distributed in space. Simulations allow this uncertainty to be represented and explored. This can help students understand the fragile and at times unpredictable nature of some complex systems.

How Does Using Mathematics and Computational Thinking Relate to the Other Practices?

Like all of the *NGSS* practices, Using Mathematics and Computational Thinking is likely to interconnect with other practices in many ways, depending on the topics students are exploring and the problems they are working to solve. The practice includes specialized ways to *develop and use models* that are powerful and predictive. Because of this, the practice shares many features with the modeling practice, and we refer readers to Chapter 6 (p. 109) for more information.

Using Mathematics and Computational Thinking also provides learners with a powerful way to *engage in argument with evidence*. Students can use mathematical representations or simulations to generate theoretical data that they can use to support their own scientific claims or challenge those of others. Computational models can generate theoretical data about systems that might be otherwise difficult to interact with, like geological or population dynamic systems. Mathematics and computation also offer new ways to connect real-world evidence to theoretical models: Some tools even allow learners to link computer models with experiments and measurements conducted in the real world, to test the validity of their models and compare how idealized models do and do not reflect what happens in the "messiness" of real life.

Relationship Between Mathematics and Computational Thinking and Modeling

There is a special connection between the Using Mathematics and Computational Thinking practice and the Developing and Using Models practice. As illustrated in this chapter and in Chapter 6 (p. 109), there can be a great deal of overlap in the intellectual work of students (and scientists!) when they engage in these two practices. The essence of the modeling practice is to develop and use specific ideas about theoretical and actual objects and the relationships between and among them to account for the behavior of systems in the natural and designed world. Very often, those relationships can be specified in mathematical or computational terms, so the two practices can become completely intertwined. Mathematical relationships and computational processes are often powerful ways to represent, share, and test our ideas about how and why a phenomenon happens. It is important to note, however, that not all models can be expressed mathematically or computationally, and not all mathematical expressions or simulations are necessarily models. To reiterate a point from Chapter 6, it depends very much on how the student *thinks about and uses* the mathematical or computational representations.

Finally, Using Mathematics and Computational Thinking is closely related to the practices of Analyzing and Interpreting Data and Communicating Information. Mathematical methods, data collection and analysis tools, and visualizations all provide ways that students can work with large quantities of data. And students can use mathematical representations, data displays, simulations, and graphical representations to communicate their findings in precise ways that might be difficult to do with text or spoken language alone.

```
┌─────────────────────────────────────────────────────────┐
│                                                           │
│           What Is Not Included in This Practice           │
│                                                           │
│   •  Using simulations or data visualizations to illustrate│
│      a target scientific phenomenon or pattern, without   │
│      allowing students to pursue their own questions or   │
│      theories or explore how the phenomenon works or      │
│      why the pattern holds                                │
│                                                           │
│   •  Using spreadsheets to input data and perform         │
│      calculations, without having students reason about   │
│      what those calculations mean scientifically          │
│                                                           │
│   •  Having students complete simple word problems or fill│
│      out predefined data tables to reinforce a given formula│
│                                                           │
│   •  Using computer-based flashcards, quizzes, wikis, or  │
│      videos to introduce science concepts                 │
│                                                           │
└─────────────────────────────────────────────────────────┘
```

What Does the Practice of Using Mathematics and Computational Thinking Look Like When It Happens in Classrooms?

Mathematics and computational thinking should be used in the science and engineering classroom when they can help students understand, describe, predict, and change the world around them. Here, we provide an example from a late elementary school classroom where students used computational thinking to make sense of a scientific system. At the end of this section, we talk more generally about what teachers can expect across K–12.

AN EXAMPLE FROM ELEMENTARY SCHOOL

A fifth-grade science class had been working in small groups to model evaporation and condensation using animation and computer simulation as representational tools. The students had already explored condensation by creating models of why they think droplets form on a cold bottle of soda when it is taken out of the fridge. During that part of the activity, they described how particles of water (what they called water vapor) are always in the air around us, and these particles stick to the surface of the bottle. Next, the students were asked to show their ideas about what happens to puddles of water outside during a sunny day. The students had used a modeling toolkit called SiMSAM (Simulation, Measurement, and Stop Action Moviemaking) and craft materials to create different stop-motion animations of their evaporation models.

After a gallery walk during which they were able to inspect their peers' work, the students had many questions and comments for one another. Some of these questions dealt with what exactly was happening in the animation: What were the cotton balls meant to represent? Why did things seem to move more slowly at some times and faster at others? Should only one water particle leave a puddle at a time? Many of these questions were posed because of the way students' models were represented: While animation is good at showing how things change over time, it is difficult to create animations that are consistent or that involve many moving pieces. These sorts of questions and needs motivate computer simulation, which allows students to write automatic rules for when and how interactions between objects take place.

Students selected and cropped objects from their animations that they thought were most important for modeling the evaporation process. They could then visually demonstrate how those objects should behave, by double-clicking and moving objects on the screen. Objects could change position, turn a certain amount or randomly, duplicate, change size, or create other objects. The students gave each object in their simulation a rule for how it should behave when it is alone and how it should behave when

Figure 9.7

An example of an animation (a) and simulation (b, c) constructed by one fifth-grade group

(a)

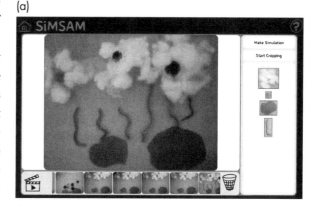

(b)

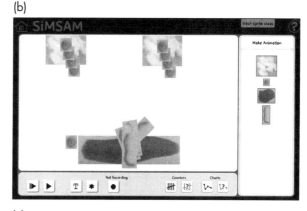

(c)

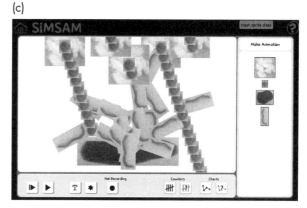

it bumps into other objects. For example, in the simulation shown in Figure 9.7, water vapor (represented by pipe cleaners) is emitted by the puddle, and water droplets are released by clouds. As water vapor objects come in contact with clouds, more clouds appear in the simulation.

After student groups each created their own simulations, one (Figure 9.7) was projected to the front of the room as a basis for further discussion. The students agreed with several of the features included in the simulation. They agreed that clouds should increase as water evaporates from the puddles, and that puddles should emit vapor. However, they were dissatisfied with how "clean" the process was: They felt that the vapor should "move everywhere" because there is always water in the air around us. Some commented that the simulation did not show enough of the *process* of evaporation; that is, when, why, or how vapor comes out of the puddle. Several wanted to introduce more precise quantitative descriptions to the simulation. For example, they argued that one "vapor" object should not be enough to create a new cloud, and some wanted more vapor objects to come from larger puddles than from smaller ones. Their conversation was much more focused on objects, interactions, and qualitative and quantitative differences than it was before.

Toward the end of the class discussion, one student, Emily, suggested that the puddles should be made up of many vapor objects placed tightly together. She wanted to show that the puddle itself was made up of many water vapor objects (molecules), and that evaporation was the result of these objects breaking off into the air. She further noted that this way, the puddle would not have to be given a separate instruction to get smaller—it would do so automatically as vapor pieces break off from the group. Emily's proposal synthesized many of the ideas the students were exploring: the connections between matter of different states, evaporation, and the water cycle. Her proposal also represented a shift in how she was thinking of scientific models—from simply showing a physical situation to proposing ways for explaining *how* the situation works.

On the last day of the activity, we asked the class to watch a time-lapse video of a new evaporation situation. The video showed two beakers full of water, one covered and one uncovered, heated over several days so that the water level of the uncovered beaker was reduced over time and the covered beaker appeared to "sweat" from the inside. This time, we asked students to create paper simulations to show what was happening using index cards instead of computers (Figure 9.8). Building on their experiences with

Figure 9.8
Paper simulation

Omar's group builds a paper simulation that combines its exploration of evaporation in beakers with condensation on cold drinks to show that the same idea explains both.

simulations on computers, many students created paper objects representing water molecules that would either leave or be trapped inside of the beaker.

One group completed its paper simulation quickly and was encouraged by the teacher to include a different object in its new "simulation": the soda bottle from the group's very first animation task. One student, Omar, quickly noted that water particles are everywhere in the air, and they all act the same way. So he decided to show that while water particles in the covered container are trapped, the water particles in the uncovered container "go up" and leave. However, he noted, they don't just go up, but *everywhere*, and may even stick to the soda bottle. Here, using computational thinking—specifically, thinking about how rules and interactions might work in new and different arrangements—led Omar to connect and generalize his model across different contexts.

This example is related to the performance expectation that students "develop a model to describe that matter is made of particles too small to be seen" (5-PS1). It illustrates how, by articulating the specific rules needed to build computer simulations, students started to think in detailed ways about how molecules behave during the process of evaporation and condensation, and about what matter is made of. Wilkerson-Jerde, Gravel, and Macrander (2015) explore in detail how these ideas develop as students model and remodel scientific systems using tools like animation and simulation.

THINKING ABOUT YOUR OWN CLASSROOM

Appendix F of the *NGSS* provides some insight into how the practice of Using Mathematics and Computational Thinking might unfold over students' K–12 experiences. In early elementary grades, students should be able to record information based on qualitative and quantitative amounts and use counting numbers to find patterns in scientific phenomena. By upper elementary, they should be able to determine if certain data are relevant to understanding a given system and should become comfortable organizing data graphically and describing measurements. At the middle level, students are expected to begin to use digital tools to collect data. They are also expected to use simple mathematical concepts such as ratios, percentages, averages, and basic operations to prepare scientific arguments and construct tests for engineering designs.

By the time students leave high school, they should be able to use mathematics and computational thinking to predict and describe the world around them. This includes creating and revising simulations to accurately reflect the scientific phenomenon; using algebra to solve and scientific and engineering problems; and applying ratios, percentages, and unit conversions to complicated mathematical scientific problems. However, given the wide applicability and flexibility of this practice and the collection of mathematical and computational tools available, we encourage you to think about ways you can use mathematics and computation to support and build on the sense-making you see in your own classroom.

How Can We Work Toward Equity in Using Mathematics and Computational Thinking?

There are a number of ways to make sure that Using Mathematics and Computational Thinking is done equitably and inclusively in the science classroom. Perhaps most important, this practice—like all of the practices—is about giving students *ownership* over science ideas and explorations. The practices are ways that students can make and evaluate their own claims and evidence and develop their own theories and solutions to problems, rather than always looking to their teacher or other authorities for all the answers.

Mathematics and computation are popularly known languages of science and offer students a visible and respected way to convince others of their findings. As students learn how to speak these languages, they can use them to explore and argue about issues they care about. In our introductory vignette (pp. 181–184), high school students used research software, computer sensing devices, and mathematical representations to explore air quality in their own community. They found ways to report their observations and evidence so that they are verifiable and replicable and so that anyone can use the same tools, measures, and methods to challenge or support their claims. They were also able to use these tools to make convincing recommendations about how those issues might be improved.

Mathematical and computational representations, simulations, data visualizations, and formulas all provide students with *more* ways to show and share their ideas. This can be especially important for engaging English language learners. Focus on students' arguments, gestures, questions, ideas, and claims rather than vocabulary. If ideas can be expressed more precisely, try revoicing ideas in a way that introduces mathematical language subtly. Rather than making sure students use technical terms or phrases, focus on having them explain what those terms mean in their own words.

Finally, understanding how mathematics and computational thinking are used in science and engineering can help students become critical consumers of popular science and media. More than ever, students are exposed to conflicting information about controversial topics—for example, climate change, vaccination, and nutrition—that can affect their future decision making. Being able to critically analyze statistics, recognize and explore mathematical trends, and recognize the benefits and limitations of computer tools and simulations can help students make informed decisions for themselves and their communities.

How Can I Support and Assess Using Mathematics and Computational Thinking in My Classroom?

Supporting your students in this practice is all about helping them structure their thinking, observations, and arguments in ways that can be described and tested using mathematical and computational tools. Be on the lookout for student observations, comparisons, and descriptions about qualitative patterns that lend themselves to quantitative specification. Think about how you can challenge or ask your students to elaborate their ideas about patterns. For example, if students note that something in an exploration you have conducted happens faster than something else, encourage them to think about measuring and quantifying that: "So you say it was faster; can we think about ways to find out how much?"

Once you have found these ways to connect to students' observations and questions, give them ways to organize and formalize their observations. If students are given a prefabricated chart that tells them what information they need to collect, they may take a "fill in the blank" approach instead of a mathematical thinking mode. Similarly, if they are simply given a formula, they may apply it without understanding what the results mean. Instead, have a conversation about what representations make sense for a given investigation or scientific question. If you are making a data table, what values should be recorded and how should they be measured? What do the variables in an equation represent, and what do results mean in terms of the physical, biological, chemical, or engineering system being studied? Have students interpret formulas and predictions based on qualitative trends: "So, if mass gets larger but velocity stays the same, this formula tells us that momentum should do what?"

When supporting mathematical thinking, there is a fine line between allowing flexibility and supporting students as they gain proficiency. Remember that sometimes a wrong turn can be a learning experience. If students collect measurements or include variables in a mathematical model that prove extraneous, this helps them hone their skills in deciding what to include and what not to in the future. Your main goal should be to make sure students are able to justify their answers and make connections to the science and engineering concepts.

Think of your one-on-one conversations with students and student groups, classroom discussions, and the written work students produce as opportunities for formative assessment. Some things you may want to check for include the following:

- Are students connecting what they are doing with mathematics and computation to the scientific ideas they are exploring?

- Can they identify appropriate mathematical tools and computational techniques to tackle a given problem?

- Are they checking their work using common sense and reason?

- Can they recognize and diagnose errors in others' mathematical solutions or reasoning?

- Are they using mathematics or computational information as evidence to support arguments during discussion?

- Are they considering how they might extend or apply mathematical and computational ideas in new situations to make predictions or comparisons?

These questions show that Using Mathematics and Computational Thinking is difficult to assess on its own, without thinking about the concepts and ideas it is linked to. Because of this, the performance expectations of the *NGSS* are nice examples of summative assessment. Each performance task is worded so that it includes a practice, disciplinary core idea, and crosscutting concept. There are many performance tasks that require explicit use of mathematics and computational thinking to conduct particular kinds of inquiries, provide evidence for arguments, develop solutions, or communicate results. Use these as an example, or template, for how you can build these types of performance expectations into your own curriculum.

How Do I Get Started?

Getting started Using Mathematics and Computational Thinking in your own classroom involves three interrelated issues: promoting student sense-making, fostering a classroom culture, and finding tools and resources that work for your classroom and curriculum.

EXAMPLE: USING "SCIENCE STORIES" TO MAKE MATHEMATICAL CONNECTIONS

A seventh-grade science class was about to start a unit on line graphs as a way to display and analyze quantitative data. Before the students started, they did a short activity called "Showing Science Stories," where they invent their own representations of scientific systems. They were given three stories involving scientific systems that exhibit patterns of change over time: one that involved the position and velocity of a traveling car, one about a population of animals responding to changes in birth and death rates, and a third about a collection of plants grown by children over the summer. (These stories were adapted from research studies in mathematics and science education.) Their task during the class period was to find a way to show the scientific system described, so that someone who did not know the story still could understand how the car's speed, total population of animals, and plants' heights changed over time.

Even though these students hadn't yet used graphs in their science class, they came up with a number of useful ways to represent quantities that changed over time. Some students were already familiar with graphs and quickly recognized how they could convert the patterns described in the stories to graphical form. Others developed innovative ways to show how different quantities in the story changed over time.

Many of the displays the students came up with were not conventional. Some might even at first glance seem outright wrong or confusing. However, if we look closely, they

Figure 9.9

Invented representations of qualitative and quantitative changes in different "science stories" created by seventh-grade students during an introduction to graphing activity

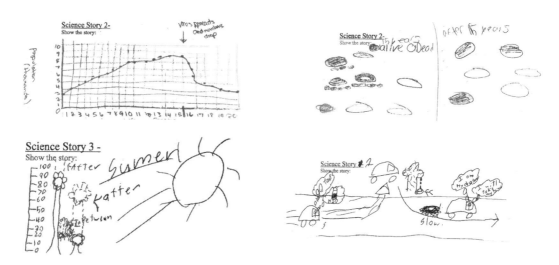

tell us a lot about how the students were thinking about the patterns and quantities in each system. Some students, such as the one who produced the conventional line graph of population growth in the upper left of Figure 9.9, already had a good understanding of how graphs could be used to show trends in very different systems. Others, like the student that produced the display in the lower left, made less scientifically conventional representations that nonetheless tell us a lot about what this student was thinking. In particular, this student's representation is already organizing the plants into a maximum, minimum, and some sort of measure of center (indicated by the small cluster of plants labeled "In Between")—ideas that connect naturally to statistics. The representation also contains information about what the student thinks might be *causing* patterns of change over time, sunlight.

Even representations that looked less like what we would expect to see in a science textbook still tell us a lot about what mathematical ideas students might be ready to explore and what qualitative and quantitative measures they believe are important to communicate. The student who created the display on the upper right used circles of different colors to represent the number of animals that lived versus died during different periods of the story (which connects well to ideas of ratio), as well as the number of offspring they expected from living animals (which connects to exponential models). The comic-like display in the lower right uses the thickness of the arrow in different parts of the image to represent differences in the car's speed and uses the convention of left to right to represent the passage of time. Even if students don't use the *right* visual features to show quantitative differences, there are ways to build on what they do know. Thinking of the height of a point as representing the same thing as the thickness of an arrow might give this student one way to start to make sense of line graphs to represent velocity.

Unlike the extended explorations we presented at the beginning of this chapter and in this section, this activity took only one day in a classroom. In that short time, the classroom teacher was able to learn a lot about what her students thought was happening mathematically in these systems: what qualitative and quantitative patterns to pay attention to, how those data can be represented visually, and even how they might want to organize and explore the data more systematically using statistical analysis. They did this even for systems that involved complex, interrelated patterns that all unfolded together over time. Research suggests that this classroom is not unique—other, more developed examples can be found in diSessa (2004) and in Lehrer and Schauble (2004).

Short activities like these can form the basis for more extended and rigorous discussions of how mathematics can be used in scientific exploration. Students can do a gallery walk to see and critique one another's displays or have a class discussion about which ones are clearest to understand. For example, while the image in the lower left of Figure 9.9 includes many interesting ideas, it also features an axis with numbers that are not connected to a particular unit of measurement. This omission can become the focus of a discussion about why units are important. Similarly, the two displays on the right side of Figure 9.9 only show snapshots of the system over time, rather than describing patterns of change. This sort of activity can also serve as a brainstorming session that helps a whole class think together about how the students might organize and display data during a more in-depth scientific investigation. Because these representations start with students' drawings, they are more likely to recognize and understand the links between the mathematical representation that is used and events in the scientific story.

This example shows how, in just one day, students were able to find ways to model the important quantities and relationships in a variety of situations studied in the science classroom. Because of the richness and familiarity of the situations used, students' models then revealed a number of connections that can be made not only to mathematics and computation (through the use of visualization or spreadsheet tools to conduct data analysis) but also to the relevant disciplinary core ideas the underlie each situation. For example, many of the students' representations of the plant and population situations revealed some foundational ideas that can lead to explorations and discussions about flow of energy and patterns of interactions in ecosystems (MS-LS2).

INTRODUCING THE PRACTICE INTO YOUR OWN CLASSROOM

More generally, we suggest a few principles to get started on introducing the Using Mathematics and Computational Thinking practice into your own classroom. First, it is important to motivate your students and recognize their interest in the patterns and trends that characterize scientific and engineered systems. Do they notice patterns or have questions that mathematics or computational tools can help answer? Can you present demos or ask questions in a way that moves beyond *what* happens to *how much* or *how intensely* it happens, which would, in turn, make qualitative and quantitative differences clear and open for debate and exploration?

Second, work to establish a classroom culture where students are expected to use mathematics and computation as ways to tell scientific stories, test ideas, and make predictions. Have students practice making and evaluating one another's qualitative and quantitative observations and mathematical claims. Do not focus just on data or the results of mathematical procedures but also on how data are obtained through measurement and how results can be interpreted in terms of scientific predictions. Offer students opportunities to use simulations or data visualizations as part of scientific discussion. Build a shared toolkit of mathematical and computational tools—software, sensors, measures, data displays, and techniques—that students have available to refer to during discussions and investigations.

Third, find out what resources work best for your classroom and curricular plans. There are many modeling tools, data analysis tools, and simulations that have been designed especially for K–12 students. Many of these tools also have dedicated educator communities that can help you get started. Below we list just a few tools that represent a wide range of subjects and student levels and are free for educational use. But as the example above shows, even paper and pencil can get you quite far—what is important is how well the tools allow students to share and refine their models and make connections to the disciplinary core ideas under study.

- **Concord Consortium Simulations** (*concord.org*): Online simulations and curriculum resources.

- **Google Spreadsheets** (*www.google.com/sheets.about*): Online spreadsheet tool to organize, analyze, and visualize data.

- **NetLogo** (*ccl.northwestern.edu/netlogo*): Programmable agent-based modeling environment. The download includes many prebuilt simulations that users can use or modify, and users can start fresh to build their own.

- **PhET Simulations** (*phet.colorado.edu*): Educational computer simulations in physics, biology, chemistry, and Earth science.

- **ScratchEd** (*scratched.gse.harvard.edu*): Curricular resources and how-to guides for the Scratch drag and drop programming environment.

- **Vensim** (*vensim.com/vensim-software*): A systems dynamics modeling environment.

In doing all this, you shouldn't feel like you are alone. More than for many of the other practices, teaching the practice of Using Mathematics and Computational Thinking is about working in partnership. Talk to your fellow mathematics and technology teachers, coaches, and specialists about what is reasonable to expect from your students at different grade levels. Consult the *Common Core State Standards for Mathematics* and specific state guidelines to get a sense of what your students might have already learned. Find out what technology experiences your students might already have, and think about how they can work in your own classrooms. Try developing a shared language across classes that helps students recognize connections.

Acknowledgments

Thanks to Julia Svoboda Gouvea, who provided feedback on drafts of this manuscript. We are grateful to Sarah Van Wart and Tapan Parikh for sharing their experiences with Local Ground and associated images to use as a basis for the opening vignette (pp. 181–184).

Funding for Wilkerson's research came from the National Science Foundation under Grant No. IIS-1217100 for the SiMSAM project. Funding for the vignette featured at the beginning of this chapter came from the National Science Foundation under the Grant No. IIS-1319849 for the Local Ground project. The opinions expressed herein are those of the authors and not necessarily those of the National Science Foundation.

References

Cheon, U., N. Williams, M. Quintana, J. Thompson, R. Quartey, A. Gray, Q. Ma, C. Lin, D. Yee, and N. Biswas. 2013. Particulate matter 2.5 and black carbon concentrations in underground San Francisco Bay Area Rapid Transit stations. *http://static.lawrencehallofscience.org/ays/research/papers/2013_AGU_BART_Poster.pdf*.

diSessa, A. A. 2004. Metarepresentation: Native competence and targets for instruction. *Cognition and Instruction* 22 (3): 293–331.

Lanouette, K., S. VanWart, and T. Parikh. 2016. Supporting elementary students' science learning through data modeling and interactive mapping in local spaces. In *Transforming learning, empowering learners: The International Conference of the Learning Sciences (ICLS) 2016.* Vol. 1, ed. C. K. Looi, J. L. Polman, U. Cress, P. and Reimann, 570–577. Singapore: International Society of the Learning Sciences.

Lehrer, R., and L. Schauble. 2004. Modeling natural variation through distribution. *American Educational Research Journal* 41 (3): 635–679.

Papert, S. 1980. *Mindstorms: Children, computers, and powerful ideas.* New York: Basic Books.

Piaget, J. 1970. *The child's conception of movement and speed.* New York: Basic Books. First published 1946.

Wilkerson-Jerde, M. H., B. E. Gravel, and C. A. Macrander. 2015. Exploring shifts in middle school learners' modeling activity while generating drawings, animations, and computational simulations of molecular diffusion. *Journal of Science Education and Technology* 24 (2–3): 396–415.

10

CONSTRUCTING EXPLANATIONS

KATHERINE L. MCNEILL, LEEMA K. BERLAND, AND PAMELA PELLETIER

In this chapter, we examine student engagement in the science practice of Constructing Explanations. (The engineering practice of Designing Solutions is described in Chapter 13, p. 283.) We also try to tease apart Constructing Explanations from some of the related science and engineering practices like Engaging in Argument From Evidence and Developing and Using Models. What does it look like to work on constructing a scientific explanation? How can our classroom culture help support students in this process? What types of instructional strategies can we use to support students in Constructing Explanations? To begin, let's consider a vignette from Ms. Garcia's 11th-grade classroom.

Ms. Garcia's environmental science class is investigating this question: "Is the Earth's climate changing?" They have been examining the topic for one week. She began the unit by having the students share their initial ideas about whether or not they believed the climate was changing and why. The majority of students concluded that it was changing and provided a variety of explanations for what they thought might be causing the climate changes. Then she had the students research air and water temperature using data from the National Oceanic and Atmospheric Administration (NOAA) to develop patterns and initial models about the flow of energy into and out of Earth systems. She decided to return to their overarching question in a class discussion to explore potential alternative explanations for the factors that might be a cause of climate changes that they would continue to revisit throughout the unit.

Ms. Garcia said to the class: "Now that we have looked at some empirical data and learned more about energy in the Earth's systems, I would like us to revisit this question—"Is the Earth's climate changing?" So far, by examining the data, we have figured out that the climate does seem to be changing. So *our question now is why*. I want you to share and critique each other's explanations for what is causing the climate to change. Who would like to start us off by sharing a potential explanation?"

Nina responded: "I think the tilt of the Earth is causing the climate to change. In middle school, we learned that the tilt of the Earth causes the seasons. We saw in the NOAA data that the temperature is increasing, so I think that increase in temperature is because of the tilt of the Earth."

Brayden: "I think the amount of carbon dioxide in our atmosphere is the reason the climate is changing."

Ben: "I agree with Nina that the NOAA data shows the climate is changing, but I disagree with her explanation. Like Brayden brought up, I think the climate is changing because there is more carbon dioxide in the atmosphere, and carbon dioxide is a greenhouse gas."

Ms. Garcia: "Who can add to this thinking using the science ideas from our model of energy? Why would carbon dioxide make a difference?"

Sophia: "Our model shows that the carbon dioxide molecules in the air absorb the sun's energy and start vibrating. They move faster."

Olivia: "Yeah. And moving faster increases the heat energy, which makes the temperature go up. That is why the NOAA temperatures are going up. Our model helps us explain the data."

Nina: "I disagree that carbon dioxide explains why this is happening. There has always been carbon dioxide in the air. The amount is not changing that much."

Ms. Garcia: "What does everybody else think? Let's recap where we are and see what we agree with so far, and what questions we have."

At this point, the students decide they are all in agreement that the climate really is changing beyond the historical variation, but they are not agreed yet on why. Some students are convinced by the carbon dioxide explanation, and others are not. So they decide to explore more about the historical presence of carbon dioxide and the role of carbon dioxide in the atmosphere.

Ms. Garcia hoped that the discussion would help students consider several causal factors, which the students would continue to explore throughout the climate change unit as they worked toward developing a consensus explanation (e.g., tilt of the Earth versus amount of carbon dioxide). This class discussion illustrates how students can collaboratively make sense of phenomena in the world and work toward constructing an explanation for this phenomenon. This dialogue also shows students engaged in several different complementary scientific practices. So let's tease apart these practices.

Students are constructing an explanation in this example. There are two important parts of their work on an explanation. First, they are focusing on *a question about a specific phenomenon*: Why is the Earth's climate changing? Second, they are constructing a *how or why account* of that phenomenon. These accounts are based on understandings drawn from concepts such as the tilt of the Earth or the role of carbon dioxide in atmospheric temperature. For example, Sophia and Olivia discuss the science ideas related to why an increase in carbon dioxide would alter the climate. Nina also brings up the tilt of the Earth in relation to the seasons, although she does not describe these science ideas in depth. Explanations need to bring scientific ideas (sometimes from models) to make sense of a phenomenon. The core of explanation is showing how a scientific idea (such as "carbon dioxide traps heat") can lead to, or account for, what we see in the phenomenon (our data).

But now that we have multiple ideas on the floor, students need to use argumentation to compare their explanatory ideas. Thus, students engage in argumentation to attempt to question, support, and critique possible explanations. They did this by bringing in *evidence* that supported parts of their explanation and showing how that evidence connected to their claim. In this case, the students used evidence that the amount of carbon dioxide had risen. They tried to show that what we know about these two factors—carbon dioxide traps heat and therefore would be expected to cause temperature increases—matches the available data.

The example helps pull out the central aspect of explanation—developing an account of how or why some phenomenon occurred. Supporting and evaluating that account may also bring in argumentation. But as we shall see in Chapter 11 (p. 229), one can argue for many different things—an interpretation of data, a question that we should investigate, or an experimental design. To consider the argumentation to be part of explanation construction, it is essential that what is being asserted includes an account of how or why something (such as climate change) happens and not simply *that* it is happening. **Explanations focus on a specific question about a phenomenon and construct a how or why account for that phenomenon.**

We will revisit and discuss characteristics of an explanation in more detail throughout the chapter. We will also further explore how the classroom culture, particularly the "talk moves" used by the teacher (see Chapter 14, p. 311), can help encourage students as they collaboratively develop and refine scientific explanations.

Why Is Constructing Explanations Important?

Constructing Explanations is a key practice of science and lies at the core of what the discipline is about. Scientists try to build knowledge that can answer questions about how or why phenomena occur in the world around us. For example, currently scientists are trying to understand questions such as "How and why do patients develop heart disease?" or "Why do some patients with heart disease live longer than others?" This might lead to helping address a design challenge: "How can we help prevent heart disease?" Other questions that scientists might ask are "Why are tsunamis that hit certain coasts, such as those of Japan, stronger than others?" and "Could this help us predict where other powerful tsunamis might occur?" Engineers often need to understand the workings of phenomena to help design solutions to problems. For example, developing theories of electromagnetic radiation has helped design important devices in the world around us, such as microwave ovens, cell phones, and RFID (radio frequency identification) devices that can track where we left our keys or help make our credit cards more secure.

Often, when we find explanations at work, we will also see argumentation as a key part of developing explanations. Our reasoning and evidence do not lead us through a single path directly to the best explanation, so scientists frequently engage in argumentation to compare multiple, competing explanations. When engaged in this argumentation, they use evidence and theories to negotiate or advance ideas for the best explanation. Answering questions like these enables scientists to better understand and make sense of the world, which ultimately can also have important implications for society.

Engaging in explanation construction can have multiple benefits for students, such as developing a stronger understanding of the natural world as well as helping them understand how knowledge is produced in science (McNeill and Krajcik 2012). Students can see science as a static set of facts that need to be memorized or a list of terms to define. The chapters throughout this book portray the vision of science in the *NGSS* as a practice of sense-making—understanding the world around us. Developing explanations is a key way to capture what sense we have made. It is difficult for most students to memorize explanations as simple products without working through the logic of these ideas. Studies of learning across the last several decades have shown than students understand more deeply and remember longer when they actively construct explanations about the world around them.

Furthermore, engaging in explanation construction helps students see how scientific knowledge is constructed. Scientific understandings continually change and are refined as scientists collect new evidence and refine their theories. If students better understand the practice of Constructing Explanations and have frequent opportunities to engage in building and then revising these explanations (as with building and revising models, described in Chapter 6, p. 109), we can help students develop a richer understanding of the dynamic nature of science and become more critical consumers of scientific media. Developing expertise in this practice supports greater science literacy as well as 21st-century skills that are essential for students both inside and outside of the science classroom.

What Is a Scientific Explanation?

Although the term *explanation* has multiple meanings in everyday life, *A Framework for K–12 Science Education* (National Research Council [NRC] 2012) states, "Scientific explanations are *accounts that link scientific theory with specific observations or phenomena—for example, they explain observed relationships between variables and describe the mechanisms that support cause and effect inferences about them*" (p. 67; italics added). This definition differs from the everyday use of explanation, which can often just refer to a description. For example, at a new school, one might ask a colleague, "Can you explain the procedure we need to use to sign up for professional development days?" This is a request for the procedure or rules to be followed, rather than a request for a causal account for why the system is set up the way it is. Even in classrooms, explanation is often used to simply mean asking students to give reasons for an answer; for example, "Is the disease a dominant or recessive condition? Explain your answer." The key difference in the use of "explanation" as a science practice is that students need to include not only their ideas about what something is or does but also the *how* or *why* that caused a particular example or phenomenon. In the dominant and recessive disease example, an explanation has to go beyond simply answering "How do you know?"—such as saying, "Oh, because neither parent had the disease, so it must be recessive"—and get to how and why the disease happened, tied to ideas about how traits are determined from alleles. We want students to go beyond just naming the factor ("if parents can pass on the disease without having it, the disease must be recessive"), which could be a memorized or

Table 10.1
Key elements of Constructing Explanations

Question about phenomenon	Explanations address a question about a specific phenomenon. They are not abstract descriptions or definitions of a science concept. Rather, they are explicitly linked to a context or real world example. • For example, an explanation might address the question "Why does a metal nail left outside start to turn orange?" • In contrast, "What is oxidation?" is not a question that leads to explanation building.
How or why account	Explanations include a *how* or *why* account of the phenomenon that draws on a scientific model or generalized principles that use disciplinary core ideas. • For example, "I think what happened when the nail turned orange is that when the nail sat in the moist air, the material in the nail (the iron) interacted with the water and oxygen in the air. Some of the matter that makes up the nail and the air (the iron, the water, and the oxygen) chemically reacted (the matter mixed and rearranged its structure) to form a new substance—iron oxide or rust, which is the orange stuff on the nail." • Notice that this example requires scientific ideas related to oxidation and chemical reactions, but it does not stop at just stating these ideas. Instead, they are used to construct a causal account.
Based on evidence	Explanations are based on evidence. This connection to evidence can occur in different ways such as the following: 1. Evidence to be explained: Evidence may be part of the starting question we need to address, communicating specifics about the phenomenon that need to be explained. The explanation we construct has to fit the data we have about the phenomenon. • For example, the prompt for the explanation refers to one piece of evidence—that *the nail turned orange*. The explanation needs to fit this observation. 2. Evidence to provide support: When explanation is combined with an argument that supports it, evidence may be included to provide support for steps in the explanation. • For example, the student may support the identification of iron, water, and oxygen as the components of the chemical reaction with evidence: "We conducted an investigation to determine the reaction needs both oxygen and water, because when an iron nail was exposed to only air or only water, no iron oxide formed. When the nail was exposed to both air and water, a new orange substance—iron oxide—appeared on the nail."

poorly understood rule, and actually have students walk through the process of how the phenomenon occurs.

There are several characteristics of explanations to consider when asking students to construct and revise explanations, summarized in Table 10.1.

We will discuss each of these characteristics in more detail, and illustrate them with examples.

EXPLANATIONS ANSWER A QUESTION ABOUT A PHENOMENON.

Explanations have to be *about* something. Explanations involve bringing scientific ideas to bear to explain things that can be observed in the natural world—phenomena. Scientific explanations address questions about a particular phenomenon or class of phenomena. For example, consider the performance expectation (PE) 3-LS3-2, "Use evidence to support the explanation that traits can be influenced by the environment." The phenomena referred to in the disciplinary core idea (DCI; LS3.A, LS3.B) are cases where a characteristic that can be inherited is also influenced by the environment. Notice that because the PEs are general descriptions of what students should be able to do, rather than specific curriculum goals, there are many different examples that could be used to teach and assess this idea (such as different kinds of organisms, different traits, and different mechanisms by which the environment could affect those traits). A third-grade explanation should be able to start with the idea that some traits are inherited, such as the size of an animal; for example, dogs are larger than insects but smaller than elephants. The explanation also needs to bring in a causal factor (in this case, the environment) and say how that factor would result in the target phenomenon (e.g., variation in dog sizes). A student might explain that what happens in a particular dog's environment, such as the amount of food available and the amount of exercise, could influence whether the dog is lean or overweight.

Here is another example at the middle school level. The PE MS-ESS2-2 asks that students "construct an explanation based on evidence for how geoscience processes have changed Earth's surface at varying time and spatial scales." The phenomena to be explained are various kinds of changes in the Earth's surface (e.g., changing coastlines, growth of a mountain range). What needs to be explained about each phenomenon is how and why this phenomenon occurred. For example, students might investigate the question of what geological processes led to the formation of the Grand Canyon.

It is important to stress that not *all* questions about phenomena lead to explanations. For example, think about science questions such as "Is making lemonade by squeezing lemons into water a physical or a chemical change?" or "What forces are acting on a rolling ball?" These questions are about scientific phenomena. They may be fine questions to include in a lesson, but they do not engage students in the science practice of

What Does *Not* Count as Explanation in the *NGSS*

The term *explanation* has a variety of meanings in everyday life and in classroom contexts. However, in terms of a scientific practice, we are trying to convey a specific meaning to help students become more competent at this key element of science. An explanation is always about a specific phenomenon or an example. An explanation articulates how or why something occurs. There are many things that an explanation is *not*.

Facts or definitions: Answers that stop at labeling a phenomenon are not reflecting the explanation practice. For example, if one asks, "How does a plant get the energy it needs?" simply answering that "plants get energy through photosynthesis" does not reflect the full explanation practice. All the students have done is label the mechanism, but they have not provided the cause-and-effect account that addresses how plants get energy. In addition, if a student simply defined photosynthesis as "the process that plants use to create food from sunlight, carbon dioxide, and water," that is also not an explanation. Simply stating facts or definitions does not reflect the practice, because students are not providing a causal or mechanistic account that explains why the phenomenon occurs.

Evidence for a claim *without* a how or why account: Simply providing evidence for a claim, without providing the how or why account, does not reflect the full practice either. In recent years, the claim, evidence, and reasoning (CER) framework has helped many teachers bring argumentation and explanation into their classrooms. However, using CER does not always align with the science practice of Constructing Explanations. For example, suppose students conduct an experiment to compare different thermal insulators (e.g., exploring PE MS-PS3-3) and find that a wool covering keeps warm liquid warmer over time than cotton does. Students then summarize their results using CER: "My claim is that wool is a better insulator. When we wrapped the beaker in wool, the temperature dropped only 4 degrees in 5 minutes, compared to 8 degrees in 5 minutes when we wrapped the beaker in cotton. Since the wool led to less change in temperature, it is the better insulator." This CER is a scientific argument—it uses evidence to support the claim that wool is a better insulator. However, the students' work does not contain an account for how or why the temperature changed over time, or why one material differed from another in affecting that change. It does not say what is going on behind the scenes that led to this result. In short, this CER labels the phenomenon as insulation but does not explain why the phenomenon occurred (i.e., how insulation works). It reflects only the Engaging in Argument From Evidence practice and not the Constructing Explanations practice.

> Descriptions of processes or data: Students will often just describe how they did an experiment, which also does not count as an explanation. Instead, students need to make sense of the phenomenon they explored to provide an explanatory account. For example, after investigating how the size of a force affects how far a car travels, elementary students described the procedure for the car setup such as how many trials they completed and how they applied different forces to the car. To be a scientific explanation, the students would need to explain how the larger force causes the car to travel farther.

Constructing Explanations, because these questions do not focus on *how* or *why* the phenomenon occurs (the second key element of explanations).

EXPLANATIONS INCLUDE A HOW OR WHY ACCOUNT OF THE PHENOMENON THAT MAY DRAW ON A SCIENTIFIC MODEL OR GENERALIZED PRINCIPLES.

A second critical characteristic—perhaps the most important aspect—of scientific explanations is that they include an explanatory account that articulates how or why a natural phenomenon occurs. As the definition from the *Framework* cited earlier states, an explanation needs to link scientific ideas "with specific observations or phenomena." These ideas should "explain observed relationships between variables and describe the mechanisms that support cause and effect inferences about them" (NRC 2012, p. 67). Thus, the goal of an explanation is to include some level of mechanism or a chain of cause and effect that leads to what we observed about the phenomenon. This goes beyond just *naming* what happened with the science word. For example, suppose we ask, "Why does a metal nail left outside start to turn orange?" Answering by simply labeling the process "because it underwent a chemical reaction" is not much better than saying "because it rusts." So far, all the student has done is to label an everyday phenomenon with a scientific term. Perhaps he or she knows much more, but simply labeling it with the chemical process doesn't articulate how that process leads to the phenomenon. It leaves out the *how* and *why* story, the mechanism. Let's say the next step the person takes is to define that scientific concepts: "A chemical reaction is a process when two or more substances interact to form a new substance." This is a step forward but has not applied this scientific idea to the phenomenon. How do substances interacting lead to what we saw—the nail turning orange?

Instead, constructing an explanation entails articulating a chain of events behind the cause of a natural phenomenon. For example, students could construct an explanation to address this question of why an iron nail turns orange in some environments. To be a strong scientific explanation, the students' explanation would need to include a cause for the change in color that goes beyond naming the process to the *how* and *why*. For example, a student might say the following:

> The iron nail turns orange because a chemical reaction occurred and formed a new substance. The iron reacted with both oxygen and water to form a new orange substance called iron oxide or rust. When a chemical reaction occurs, the atoms that make up the molecules in the old substances combine in new ways to form the molecules of the new substance, which results in the new substance having properties, such as color, that differ from the original substances.

This example specifically ties the science back to the phenomenon to say *why* a change in color occurs.

In providing this explanatory account, the explanation often draws on scientific models contained in the DCIs. For instance, in the example above, the student includes the cause of change in properties: "When a chemical reaction occurs, the atoms that make up the molecules in the old substances combine in new ways to form the molecules of the new substance, which results in the new substance having properties ... that differ from the original substances." (See the diagram in Figure 6.3 in Chapter 6, p. 120, related to creating explanations by using models to explain patterns in observations or phenomena.) The use of the DCIs as part of the scientific practice of Constructing Explanations is essential: Students' explanations need to be consistent with and apply the scientific models or principles that they are learning. Consequently, the how and why parts of scientific explanations in the *NGSS* draw on and use scientific ideas.

EXPLANATIONS ARE BASED ON EVIDENCE TO BE EXPLAINED OR USED AS SUPPORT.

In addition to a focus on the how or why account and use of DCIs, the *Framework* emphasizes that explanations should connect to evidence. For example, the *Framework* states that students should be able to "construct their own explanations of phenomena using their knowledge of accepted scientific theory and linking it to models and evidence" (NRC 2012, p. 69). The *NGSS* state that students at the K–2 level, "use information from observations (firsthand and from media) to construct an evidence-based account for natural phenomena" and that students at the 9–12 level "construct a scientific explanation based on valid and reliable evidence" (NGSS Lead States 2013, Appendix F, p. 27).

Why do the *Framework* and the *NGSS* connect the idea of evidence to explanation? Constructing Explanations requires a shift away from seeing science as set of facts or even explanations that need to be memorized to students actively using disciplinary knowledge to build, test, and revise explanations of phenomena. A scientific explanation is not a definition, but rather an explanatory account of a real phenomenon. Building that explanation requires reasoning about scientific ideas to see how they can apply to the phenomenon, rather than staying at the general level of defining science ideas.

Making sense of the phenomenon needs to be constrained by evidence and needs to fit aspects of the phenomenon that are what we are trying to explain.

In the example about the nail (Table 10.1), the prompt for the explanation already includes evidence about the phenomenon that the explanation needs to fit—we need to account for why the orange substance appeared. Besides fitting these constraints, we also bring in evidence to support the particular chain of ideas in the explanation we are constructing. In building science knowledge, we need to defend our reasoning with a logical and empirical argument. The move from learning explanations to constructing them means that we also want students to *defend* how they know what they know (i.e., present an argument for their explanation). We want students to go beyond memorizing facts that state that changes like rust are chemical reactions; students need to be able to articulate how one can provide support for that idea and say how that idea fits the particular case we are trying to explain. Evidence provides a lever to connect the explanations to the natural world and to support students in moving away from seeing explanations as disconnected facts from a textbook or other authoritative source that need to be memorized.

Consequently, a more complete scientific explanation for why an iron nail turns orange in some environments could include the use of evidence to support the explanation. For example, the following explanation includes additional evidence to provide support for several steps of the explanation:

> The iron nail turns orange because a chemical reaction occurred and formed a new substance. The iron reacted with both oxygen and water to form a new orange substance called iron oxide or rust. When a chemical reaction occurs, the atoms that make up the molecules in the old substances combine in new ways to form the molecules of the new substance, which results in the new substance having properties, such as color, that differ from the original substances. <u>We know that oxygen and water are needed for the chemical reaction, because we conducted an investigation where we tested whether iron oxide would form in different conditions. When the iron nail was exposed to only air or only water, no iron oxide formed. When the nail was exposed to both air and water, a new orange substance—iron oxide—appeared on the nail, suggesting that the chemical reaction needs both oxygen and water to combine with the iron to form the iron oxide.</u>

In this example, the student adds evidence to the explanation to provide support for the details of the causal mechanism that was responsible for the color change. In this way, the student provided an argument, from evidence, for the step in the explanation citing iron, oxygen, and water as the components of the chemical reaction. Often we want students to do more than generate a plausible explanation—we ask them to make sure the explanation is consistent with the evidence we have and to use evidence to help flesh out the explanation. So, for rich questions like this, we are often asking students to develop an explanation (the Constructing Explanations practice) and to support it with evidence (the Engaging in Argument From Evidence practice).

Explanations, such as this one about the iron nail, are developed and refined over time in classroom contexts such as the vignette (pp. 205–206) from Ms. Garcia's classroom. The process of Constructing Explanations engages students in sharing and debating different explanations using evidence and scientific ideas to defend, question, critique, and then revise their explanations. Students consider questions such as "Does the explanatory account explain all of the data?" "Does the explanatory account consider all of the scientific ideas?" "Are there alternative explanations that better align with the available evidence and scientific ideas?" This process of co-constructing, critiquing, and revising explanations supports students in developing a stronger understanding of the DCIs as they engage in sense-making about the world around them.

How Does Constructing Explanations Relate to the Other Practices?

The eight scientific practices do not work in isolation or as discrete steps in a scientific method; rather, as Bell et al. (2012, p. 18) argued, the interrelatedness of the practices includes "an unfolding and often overlapping sequence, or a cascade." Engaging in explanation in the science classroom typically relies on the use of other scientific practices. For example, we began the chapter by introducing a vignette from Ms. Garcia's 11th-grade science classroom in which the students constructed preliminary explanations about what might be causing the climate to change. We will use this example to illustrate the relationship between explanation and the other seven scientific practices. In Ms. Garcia's classroom, the unit focused on the practice of Asking Questions and Defining Problems around the overarching question "Is the Earth's climate changing?" Finding that yes, the Earth's climate is changing, led to asking why it is happening. The students refined and evaluated this *why* question throughout the climate change unit as they developed their explanations. Furthermore, the students used the practice of Developing and Using Models to generate models about the flow of energy into and out of Earth systems, which informed their explanations about what causes climate change. They used the models to develop mechanistic accounts of what was causing the change. In terms of the practice of Planning and Carrying Out Investigations, later in the unit (after the discussion in the vignette), Ms. Garcia had the students design and conduct investigations using plastic 2-liter bottles as representations of the Earth's systems to explore how different variables affect temperature change. Students then used the practice of Analyzing and Interpreting Data from their investigations as well as secondhand data from other sources (like the NOAA website) to inform their climate change explanations. This analysis required the students to engage in Using Mathematics and Computational Thinking as they revised their explanations based on the patterns and trends that emerged. Throughout the unit, the students were Engaging in Argument From Evidence as they constructed and revised their explanations. For example, the initial vignette illustrates the students engaging in argumentation about two explanations—the tilt of the Earth and the amount of carbon dioxide—offered by the students as the cause of the climate change. Finally, the students employed the practice of Obtaining, Evaluating, and Communicating Information throughout the process of constructing their explanations as they read and made sense of texts, evaluated information from multiple sources, and communicated their explanations to their peers. Consequently, the students utilized many if not all of the scientific practices as they engaged in sense-making to construct their explanations of what is causing the climate to change.

Although all of the practices are related, the practices that involved explanation, modeling, and argumentation are closely linked and can happen simultaneously in a science classroom.

How is a scientific explanation different from a scientific model? As Chapter 6 (p. 109) discusses, a scientific model is a type of representation that focuses on critical features or interactions of a system and is used to predict and explain systems. A model is essentially a piece of a scientific theory. In contrast, an explanation draws ideas from a model to create an account for a particular phenomenon. In other words, **the explanation is the "playing out" of the model to answer a particular problem or question. The explanation is the instantiation of the model for a context or example.** In reality, scientists often work on both models and explanations at the same time—creating and revising model-based explanations or explanatory models. Students in our classrooms do the same. If students are working on developing or refining a general idea, then typically they are developing and revising models. If students are answering a specific question, they are ideally applying the model to create and revise an explanation. Sometimes this model is implicit in the work of the explanation.

How is a scientific explanation different from argumentation? Argumentation involves persuading and justifying ideas. Explanation and argumentation depend on each other, because the development of an explanation includes the comparison and critique of multiple explanations through the practice of argumentation (Reiser, Berland, and Kenyon 2012). As we saw, Ms. Garcia's students argued about two alternative explanations—the tilt of the Earth and the amount of carbon dioxide. When scientists develop an explanation for how or why a phenomenon occurs, they engage in the same process as they consider and debate multiple alternative explanatory accounts. The explanatory account (or claim) scientists put forth is critiqued and evaluated in light of all available evidence and theory. As the *Framework* states, "Deciding on the best explanation is a matter of argument that is resolved by how well any given explanation fits with all available data, how much it simplifies what would seem to be complex, and whether it produces a sense of understanding" (NRC 2012, p. 68). Scientists come to accept a particular explanatory account of a phenomenon through the process of argumentation. Furthermore, they realize that any explanation can change over time as new evidence becomes available or new scientific ideas arise that question the current explanation and provide support for an alternative explanatory account of the phenomenon. This is similar to the process that occurred in Ms. Garcia's classroom throughout the climate change unit as students gathered new evidence and refined the models that they used to revise their scientific explanations.

What Does Constructing Explanations Look Like When It Happens in the Classroom?

In this section, we use examples of student work from elementary, middle, and high school to illustrate what Constructing Explanations can look like in the classroom as well as how they can increase in complexity across the grades. One of the authors of this chapter, Pamela Pelletier, is the director for science and technology/engineering in the Boston Public Schools (BPS). These examples come from BPS teachers who have been working hard to integrate Constructing Explanations into their classroom instruction. Recent initiatives in BPS have included a focus on scientific practices as well as creating greater alignment across science and literacy (McNeill, Katsh-Singer, and Pelletier 2015). We focus here on students' written products to more easily illustrate the three characteristics of explanations. However, in all three cases, students developed and refined their explanations in a similar process to that illustrated in Ms. Garcia's classrooms in which the students collaboratively discussed and revised their explanations.

SECOND-GRADE EXPLANATION ABOUT SEEDS

The first example aligns with the second-grade *NGSS* PE 2-LS2-1, "Plan and conduct an investigation to determine if plants need sunlight and water to grow." The second-grade classroom was investigating what happens to seeds in the presence of water. The teacher, Mr. Williams, gave each group of students a different type of seed (e.g., lima bean, popcorn). The students planned and conducted investigations in which they watered and observed the seeds for a week. After completing their observations, Mr. Williams asked the students to construct scientific explanations using their observations from their investigation to explain how seeds are affected by water. This illustrates the strong relationship between explanations and the other practices, such as planning and conducting investigations. Figure 10.1 includes an example from one student, Lin.

Figure 10.1
Second-grade explanation about seeds

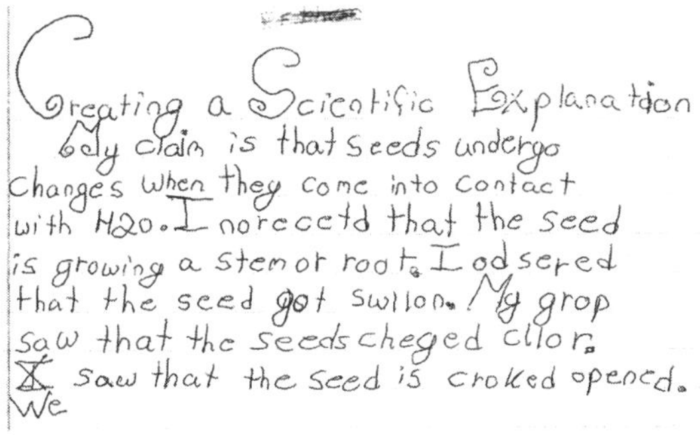
Creating a Scicntific Explanation
My claim is that seeds undergo
changes when they come into contact
with H2O. I norecctd that the seed
is growing a stem or root. I odsered
that the seed got swllon. My grop
saw that the seeds cheged cllor.
I saw that the seed is croked opened.
We

Lin starts her explanation by providing an explanatory account that "seeds undergo changes when they come into contact with H_2O." In early elementary school, students' explanations should provide an account of how or why a phenomenon occurs, though they will typically not include a complex causal mechanism behind that account. Consequently, Lin's explanation is appropriate for her grade level, by linking the changes in the seed to the cause of "when they come into contact with H_2O." (This could have been a more explicit causal account if she had phrased her first sentence as "Seeds undergo changes *because* they come into contact with H_2O.") She incorporates appropriate science ideas in relation to the question about the specific phenomenon including the external parts of plants, such as a stem and root, in describing her observations of the phenomenon. Furthermore, she uses her direct observations as evidence to elaborate the story about how the seed changed—growing a stem or root, becoming swollen, changing color, and cracking open. Although this example is not complex, it clearly illustrates an early elementary student successfully using her observations to explain how a phenomenon (plant growing from a seed) occurs.

SEVENTH-GRADE EXPLANATION ABOUT SEEDS

The second example builds toward the middle school PE MS-LS1-5, "Construct a scientific explanation based on evidence for how environmental and genetic factors influence the growth of organisms." We selected the second example because it also focuses on students' explanations about how seeds are affected by water; however, this example is from a seventh-grade classroom and is thus more complex. It is a nice comparison with the second-grade example, illustrating the increasing sophistication of Constructing Explanations across the grade levels. In this lesson, Ms. Davis had her students conduct an investigation similar to what the second graders did, in that they observed over time what happened to seeds when they were exposed to water. Although the investigation was similar, the questions being asked and the students' explanations were more complex, particularly in terms of the explanatory account that incorporated scientific ideas. Kris wrote the following for his explanation:

> For seeds to germinate, they need water. The Rye grass seed was put in the minisprout with a paper towel and water it. Then we put it inside the chamber for dark and on October 21 to 26 the root grew fast but the shoot were growing slow so we put the minisprout upside down in the chamber and now the root is growing up and the shoot is growing down. Germination is the start of growth and development of a seed. So in order for a seed to grow and develop it needs water first and the water softens the coat seed. The cotyledons then contains food to nourish the embryo during the germination it soaks up water, swell, split the seed coat and the seed start to grow.[1]

In writing his response, Kris provides an explanatory account of what happened to the rye seed. He writes, "So in order for a seed to grow and develop it needs water first and the water softens the coat seed. The cotyledons then contains food to nourish the embryo during the germination it soaks up water, swell, split the seed coat and the seed start to grow." In this section of his explanation, Kris discusses why the water causes the seed to grow. Unlike the second-grade example, he provides a mechanism that articulates how the water affects both the seed coat and cotyledon, which then enables the seed to grow. His response also demonstrates a more complex understanding of the scientific principles or models in his first statement explaining what germination is and also threaded throughout his explanatory account in which he illustrates his understanding of the structure and function of the components of a seed, such as the seed coat and cotyledons. Furthermore, Kris provides evidence for his explanation from the observations he collected during his rye seed investigation. Notice that the explanation does a good job unpacking how structures of the plant's seed (containing food, seed coat) enables it to perform the functions needed and identifies how the environmental factors (water) play a role in that process. The explanation does not make explicit the role of genetic factors in this process. While the student work is a clear explanation for the lesson, building toward the PE, other investigations would need to bring in the genetic factors to fully meet the PE.

NINTH-GRADE EXPLANATION ABOUT FORCE AND MOTION

The last example is from Mr. Randall's high school class and continues to illustrate increasing sophistication. The example also illustrates what the practice looked like in a different science content area, physics. In this example, students conducted investigations examining what happened to their "passenger" in a toy car when they used

---

1. The spelling, grammar, and punctuation are from the student's original writing.

different materials for the seatbelt during a collision. This lesson builds toward the high school PE HS-PS2-3, "Apply scientific and engineering ideas to design, evaluate, and refine a device that minimizes the force on a macroscopic object during a collision." After completing the investigation in which the students examined the effectiveness of the different seatbelts, Mr. Randall asked the students to construct explanations about how seatbelts impact injuries during collisions. Leon wrote the following evidence-based explanation:

> Seat belts are used in cars to lessen the impact of an injury received from a collision. The outcome of a crash depends on the type of seatbelt being used by the passenger. My experiment proved that a wire, twine, and paper seatbelt have very different outcomes. A wire seatbelt has less area and applies more pressure. Twine seatbelt does not hold the passenger firmly. Paper seatbelt works the best but it is soft and may rip. When the play-doh passenger's cart crashed the passenger continued to move forward because of Inertia and Newton's 1st law. The more area a seatbelt has the less pressure is applied to the passenger. Even if there is less area there is the same force but the pressure is not spread and there can be more damage during the collision.[2]

Similarly to the last example, Leon includes an explanatory account near the end of his explanation when he writes, "The more area a seatbelt has the less pressure is applied to the passenger. Even if there is less area there is the same force but the pressure is not spread and there can be more damage during the collision." In this section, he explains why a seatbelt with more area will cause less damage because the pressure is spread over the passenger. He offers a mechanism for why the paper seatbelt, which had the largest area, provided the least injury to his Play-Doh passenger. He also applies important science ideas where he mentioned inertia and Newton's first law as well as in his discussion of force, pressure, and area. The explanation would be even stronger if he more clearly articulated why inertia and Newton's first law were important for his explanation. Leon also includes evidence to argue for his explanation in his discussion of the results from his experiments using wire, twine, and paper seatbelts in the collision. The evidence provided could also be richer if he included more data, such as quantitative measurements of the thickness of the seatbelts and qualitative observations of the impact of the collision on the Play-Doh passengers for the three conditions. Although his explanation could be

---

2. The spelling, grammar, and punctuation are from the student's original writing.

more sophisticated, it illustrates how the characteristics of an explanation can become more complex in high school.

In all three of these examples of students' written explanations, we see students answering a question about a phenomenon, including a how or why account, and connecting to evidence that guided and supports their explanation (Table 10.1, p. 210). It is important to note that in order for students to complete these writing tasks, they were engaged in the process of developing their explanations—talking and listening, investigating and observing, comparing, arguing, and revising their ideas. This process is essential and requires considerable teacher planning and support.

How Can We Work Toward Equity With Regard to Constructing Explanations?

Constructing Explanations is an accessible practice for all learners, including students with culturally and linguistically diverse backgrounds as well as students with special needs. Similarly to the other scientific practices, engaging in scientific explanations includes particular norms that may be similar to or different from the discourse in students' everyday lives. Two instructional strategies that can benefit all students, but particularly those with culturally and linguistically diverse backgrounds, include (1) connecting students' everyday practices with scientific practices and (2) making the implicit rules or characteristics of the practices explicit (Michaels, Shouse, and Schweingruber 2008). In terms of connecting to students' everyday practices, we have already discussed how the word *explanation* can have a very different meaning for students in their everyday lives than in science or in a science classroom (McNeill 2011). Consequently, in teaching about Constructing Explanations, it can be important to understand students' prior ideas and discuss with them how those everyday connotations are similar to and different from scientific ones. This strategy connects to the second strategy, which is to make the implicit rules or characteristics of explanations explicit to students. Making your expectations explicit for students about the structure of an explanation as well as the classroom norms for constructing them can better enable all students to successfully engage in the practice.

In addition, students with learning disabilities can have a variety of challenges such as difficulty organizing concepts, making connections, and expressing ideas (Steele 2005). The strategies we discuss in the next section, particularly around scaffolding, can help decrease the complexity as well as offer different representations that are accessible to diverse learners. Providing a variety of techniques and strategies will support all students in successfully engaging in Constructing Explanations.

How Can I Support and Assess This Practice in My Classroom?

There are many strategies you can incorporate into your classroom instruction to support students in Constructing Explanations in science (e.g., McNeill and Krajcik 2012; Zembal-Saul, McNeill, and Hershberger 2013). We summarize three different types of strategies that we have found to be particularly important for students successfully engaging in Constructing Explanations: (1) developing "good" questions, (2) developing talk moves and classroom culture, and (3) scaffolding student writing. In addition, we discuss ways to assess students' explanations to assist you in modifying your instruction to better meet your students' needs and challenge them moving forward.

DEVELOPING "GOOD" QUESTIONS

Designing appropriate questions is essential for providing students with opportunities to construct explanations. Considering the three characteristics of explanations in the *NGSS* can be helpful in the design. Identify opportunities in the science curriculum that allow students to (1) answer a question about a phenomenon, (2) develop a how or why account, and (3) provide scientific data about a phenomenon that the explanatory account must fit. In addition, it is important to consider the clarity of the question. If the wording of the question is too vague or general, students may be unsure of what they are being asked to do. Table 10.2 includes some examples of weak questions as well as potential revised questions that address the identified issue.

Table 10.2
Ineffective questions for Constructing Explanations

Issue	Weak explanation question	Revised explanation question
Lacked question about phenomenon	Does a DNA molecule resemble a spiral staircase? Why or why not?	Why does Susan have a hitchhiker's thumb when neither of her parents have this trait?
Lacked evidence	Why is a volcano different from a mountain?	What caused volcanoes to form in the Azores?
Lacked how or why account	What will happen when you roll a ball on different surfaces?	Why does a ball roll faster on some surfaces and slower on other surfaces?

In some cases, these examples could be productive questions, but they are not specifically helpful for supporting the practice of Constructing Explanations. For instance, the first question asked whether a DNA molecule resembled a spiral staircase, which is an interesting analogy but does not specifically target how or why something occurs in the world around us. To construct an explanation, the question needs to focus on a specific genetic phenomenon. The revised question focuses on having students analyze heredity data from a family in which a daughter, Susan, has the recessive trait of a hitchhiker's thumb when neither of her parents have the trait. This revision does shift the DCI away from just knowing the DNA model and toward using that model to explain. Another way to alter that question, while still focusing on the DNA model, would be to ask, "How does the structure of a DNA molecule help explain the behavior of this molecule?" Consider opportunities in the science curriculum that provide opportunities for all three characteristics of explanations.

The second question focuses on describing why a volcano is different from a mountain, but unfortunately, it basically results in students defining the two terms. This is interesting because it does use the word "why," but it does not result in a causal account, due to the lack of a connection to a phenomenon and lack of evidence. For instance, in the revised Azores question, students can analyze secondhand data such as evaluating maps that show the distance of the islands from plate boundaries, the location of the plates over time, and the activity of the volcanoes over time.

Finally, both versions of the last question attempt to get students to consider the difference between mixtures and chemical reactions. However, the first version of the question is less demanding, in that it essentially asks just for "the right answer" without asking for an explanation of how the particles and salt are interacting and how that connects to the ideas of mixtures and chemical reactions. The revised version of the question is more explicit, going beyond just using definitions and instead asking students to develop a causal account.

DEVELOPING TALK MOVES AND CLASSROOM CULTURE

Developing a classroom culture that includes a focus on Constructing Explanations can help students develop an understanding of the characteristics of explanations and incorporate these ideas into their talking and writing. Engaging in this practice should not just happen at one discrete moment but should be threaded throughout instruction whenever students are making sense of phenomena and using evidence to support those explanations. One way to help students with this is by including specific talk moves or questions into your classroom discussions to model these characteristics and encourage students to consider them as well. Table 10.3 includes some sample questions that you can use to guide whole-class or small-group discussions. A strategy we have used is to create posters for the classroom with these questions or with sentence starters to help guide students as they work.

Table 10.3
Talk moves and sample questions

Focus	Sample questions
Refocus on guiding question	• How does this help us answer our overarching question: _____?
Consider alternatives	• Are there other potential explanations for this event (or for these data)? • What is an alternative reason for why or how _____ occurs?
Include evidence	• How does our data either support or refute this explanation? • What other evidence should we consider as we construct our explanation?
Use scientific ideas	• How does this connect to the big ideas we have been learning about in science? • How can we use our science knowledge to help explain _____? • How can we use our model to support or refute these explanations?

Source: Adapted from Zembal-Saul, McNeill, and Hershberger 2013.

The questions in Table 10.3 encourage students to consider multiple explanations as well as how to support those different explanations using evidence and scientific ideas. Incorporating questions like these can help students understand science as a practice that is constantly developing and refining explanations. This can help students see that science is not the memorization of discrete facts but rather a way to understand the world around us.

SCAFFOLDING STUDENT WRITING

Specifically, in terms of supporting students' written explanations, using scaffolds can help students understand the characteristics of an explanation as well as what those characteristics look like in different content areas and in different contexts (McNeill and Krajcik 2012). Written scaffolds can be sentence starters, questions, other prompts, or visual representations that provide students with hints about what to include in their scientific explanations. When designing scaffolds for students, we consider multiple characteristics. Specifically, we consider (1) general and content support, (2) detail and length, and (3) fading. In terms of general and content support, we often include language in the scaffolds that provides both a general description of the characteristics of explanation (e.g., "Remember to include how or why the event occurred") and specific language for that particular content or lesson (e.g., "You should explain why the nail turned orange"). Using both aspects helps students develop a general understanding of an explanation as well as what specifically counts as an explanation for that particular lesson. In terms of detail and length, it is important to consider the age and abilities of students when designing the scaffolds. Sometimes we are tempted to include too much support in the scaffolds, which results in lengthy prompts or questions that the students do not read. Consequently, there is a tension in providing enough support that is helpful, but not so much detail that the students just skip over the scaffolds. Finally, *fading* means that we use the scaffolds as temporary supports that we reduce over time. The ultimate goal is for students to be able to construct explanations independently without any additional support. We often start the school year by providing more detail and support in the scaffolds, then decrease the amount as the students become more comfortable and proficient with the practice.

ASSESSING STUDENTS' EXPLANATIONS

An essential part of providing appropriate support for students is being able to assess the strengths and weaknesses of their explanations and design instruction to address those needs. Focusing on the three elements in Table 10.1 (question about phenomenon, how or why account, and based on evidence) in assessing students' explanations can enable you to determine whether students have more difficulty with one of the characteristics as well as the quality of each characteristic in their explanation construction. This information can then be used to inform your own instruction.

In addition, the three characteristics can also be used as a checklist for assessing the process of Constructing Explanations during whole-class or small-group discussions. We began the chapter with a vignette (pp. 205–206) from Ms. Garcia's classroom, in which the students discussed potential explanations for what causes climate change. All three characteristics are prevalent in that student discussion. In addition, the development of the students' explanations includes the comparison and critique of multiple explanations through the process of argumentation. This process of engaging in argumentation is an essential practice to help students (and scientists) develop and revise their explanations for natural phenomena. Consequently, the development of explanations should also include the evaluation and critique of multiple explanatory accounts as students revise their explanations over time in light of new evidence and scientific ideas.

The practice of Constructing Explanations in science can be challenging for students. Initially, you may find that you and your students will struggle with many aspects of it. With practice, you will create better questions and supports, and your students will learn to develop explanatory accounts efficiently and effectively. As you incorporate different strategies into your instruction and your students gain more experience with this scientific practice, all students will become more successful at developing and revising their scientific explanations.

Acknowledgments

This material is based, in part, on work supported by the National Science Foundation under Grant No. DRL-0836099 and Grant No. DRL-1020316. The opinions expressed herein are those of the authors and not necessarily those of the National Science Foundation.

References

Bell, P., L. Bricker, C. Tzou, T. Lee, and H. Van Horne. 2012. Exploring the science framework: Engaging learners in scientific practices related to obtaining, evaluating and communicating information. *Science Scope* 36 (3): 17–22.

McNeill, K. L. 2011. Elementary students' views of explanation, argumentation and evidence and abilities to construct arguments over the school year. *Journal of Research in Science Teaching* 48 (7): 793–823.

McNeill, K. L., R. Katsh-Singer, and P. Pelletier. 2015. Assessing science practices: Moving your class along a continuum. *Science Scope* 39 (4): 21–28.

McNeill, K. L., and J. Krajcik. 2012. *Supporting grade 5–8 students in constructing explanations in science: The claim, evidence and reasoning framework for talk and writing.* New York: Pearson Allyn & Bacon.

Michaels, S. A. W. Shouse, and H. A. Schweingruber. 2008. *Ready, set, science! Putting research to work in K–8 science classrooms.* Washington, DC: National Academies Press.

National Research Council (NRC). 2012. *A framework for K–12 science education: Practices, crosscutting concepts, and core ideas.* Washington, DC: National Academies Press.

NGSS Lead States. 2013. *Next generation science standards: For states, by states.* Washington, DC: National Academies Press. *www.nextgenscience.org/next-generation-science-standards.*

Reiser, B. J., L. K. Berland, and L. Kenyon. 2012. Engaging students in the scientific practices of explanation and argumentation: Understanding *A Framework for K–12 Science Education. Science Scope* 35 (8): 6–11.

Steele, M. 2005. Science sampler: Teaching science to middle school students with learning problems. *Science Scope* 29 (2): 50–51.

Zembal-Saul, C., K. L. McNeill, and K. Hershberger. 2013. *What's your evidence? Engaging K–5 students in constructing explanations in science.* New York: Pearson Allyn & Bacon.

11

ENGAGING IN ARGUMENT FROM EVIDENCE

LEEMA K. BERLAND, KATHERINE L. MCNEILL, PAMELA PELLETIER, AND JOSEPH KRAJCIK

Engaging in Argument From Evidence in the Classroom

What is the practice of Engaging in Argument From Evidence? What does it look like in a class discussion or in students' writing? How does Engaging in Argument From Evidence differ from other class discussions? What strategies can you use to successfully engage all of your students in this scientific practice? Let's consider a vignette from Ms. Smith's second/third-grade class.

> This mixed-grade class of English language learners illustrates the ways in which Engaging in Argument From Evidence can help younger students use their observations of the world to engage in argumentation. In this particular case, the students have been studying the caterpillars in the back of their room. They noticed that the milkweed plant in the caterpillars' cage was disappearing. The transcript picks up as the students begin discussing their explanations for why the milkweed was disappearing.
>
> Jay: "The milkweed disappears into the caterpillars' tummies. They eat like us! It goes into their bodies."
>
> Calvin: "Right! It all disappeared. Because when the larva eats it, it's gone."
>
> Jay: "Not gone, Calvin. It's there in the tummy."
>
> Suki: "The milkweed makes them fatter because the caterpillars ate the leaves. The caterpillars are going to be fat and big."
>
> Ms. Smith: "What can you add? What do you think happens to the milkweed? Amari?"
>
> Amari: "It will be gone. It will get rotten and crunchy. We might throw it away."

Benita: "But, I saw the milkweed, it had little holes. And ... the caterpillars are bigger."

Ms. Smith: "You have some good evidence, Benita. Adam?"

Adam: "It goes inside to their stomachs and some comes out as poop just like human beings."

Ms. Smith: "Did you see poop?"

Suki: "Yes. They have a lot of poop. Some of the milkweed is probably poop."

Amari: "Oh, I saw the poop, too. It is the brown bits on the leaves."

In this short excerpt, the students are engaged in an age-appropriate scientific argument in which they are co-constructing an explanation about why the milkweed is disappearing. In this exchange, we see two possible explanations emerging:

Claim #1: Most of the students are claiming that the caterpillars ate the milkweed.

Claim #2: Amari claims that the milkweed rotted and was thrown away.

In response to Amari's alternative claim that the milkweed was removed from the cage, Benita, Adam, and Suki support their claim that the caterpillar ate the milkweed using evidence and disciplinary core ideas (DCIs). In terms of evidence, Benita discusses her observations of the holes in the milkweed and the size of the caterpillars, and Suki states that she observed the poop accumulating in the cage. In addition, Adam supports this claim by connecting to DCI LS1.A regarding the structures organisms have (in this case the caterpillars' stomachs) and how that helps them survive (in this case, the work of digestion). Thus, through this short exchange, we see the students supporting their claims with evidence and DCIs.

In addition, we see two instances in this brief exchange in which the students critique one another's ideas. In particular, when Calvin states that the milkweed is "gone," Jay disagrees, saying, "Not gone, Calvin. It's there in the tummy." In addition, Amari offers a counterargument when he introduces the alternative claim: Maybe the caterpillars are not eating the milkweed but humans are removing it instead. These critiques suggest that the classroom has a culture in which students are listening to and evaluating whether they agree with one another's ideas.

Finally, this episode also shows the students working toward the reconciliation of their differing ideas. In particular, in the last line of the transcript, Amari agrees with the evidence that the caterpillars are creating a lot of waste and states that he has seen this. In doing this, we see Amari taking a first step toward reconciling his understandings with those of his classmates: Maybe the caterpillars are eating the milkweed.

We selected this vignette to illustrate the process of Engaging in Argument From Evidence, in which students work together to make sense of the world around them and to illustrate specific strategies teachers can use to support this practice. In this particular case, the students argued about their explanations about why the milkweed plant is disappearing. As we will discuss below, this practice entails making and supporting claims, evaluating one another's ideas, and working toward reconciling their differences. In addition, this vignette demonstrates how the teacher can work to establish a classroom culture that supports argumentation. For example, in this brief exchange, we see the teacher prompting students to contribute to the discussion and, in particular, selecting Amari to speak. This selection is purposeful, as the majority of students agreed with one another, and the teacher's invitation to Amari provided the opportunity for the students to discuss an alternative explanation. The teacher's two other contributions focused on the students' evidence: The teacher requested evidence and positively evaluated the evidence provided. In focusing on the evidence rather than the explanations about why the milkweed was disappearing, the teacher helped create an expectation that students will support their ideas with evidence and conveyed that she values evidence-based supports over simply knowing a right answer.

Why Is the Practice of Engaging in Argument From Evidence Important?

Scientific sense-making happens in communities. Through this process, questions and disagreements arise. As seen in the vignette, the practice of Engaging in Argument From Evidence is how members of the scientific community—from scientists to students— reconcile their disagreements to reach the strongest answers to those questions. In other words, scientific argumentation is how scientists and students collaboratively build scientific knowledge—it is how we learn together.

We know that scientific knowledge is not a static or final form body of facts; rather, scientists revise old ideas and develop new understandings over time. But we have also all seen classrooms depicting science as a set of facts that others figured out a long time ago. In these classrooms, the science is presented as content for students to memorize rather than ideas that they can co-construct and use to explain new phenomena, learn new ideas, and solve problems. On the other hand, when students participate in scientific argumentation, they are part of the process of developing new ideas by revising old ones. When students argue, they are *producing and critiquing knowledge* rather than *receiving final form ideas* that others have constructed. This shift toward knowledge producer and critic helps students engage with the DCIs deeply—applying the DCIs to support and question their explanations about why a specific phenomenon occurred, the validity of a research method, or the veracity of their models. This shift also enables students to experience scientific knowledge as tentative and revisable—a key understanding about the scientific endeavor.

In *A Framework for K–12 Science Education (Framework)*, guiding the development of the *Next Generation Science Standards (NGSS)*, the National Research Council (NRC) explains the ways that the practice of Engaging in Argument From Evidence supports student knowledge construction:

> *As all ideas in science are evaluated against alternative explanations and compared with evidence, acceptance of an explanation is ultimately an assessment of what data are reliable and relevant and a decision about which explanation is the most satisfactory. Thus knowing why the wrong answer is wrong can help secure a deeper and stronger understanding of why the right answer is right. Engaging in argumentation from evidence about an explanation supports students' understanding of the reasons and empirical evidence for that explanation, demonstrating that science is a body of knowledge rooted in evidence. (NRC 2012, p. 44)*

As such, scientific argumentation creates opportunities for students to construct and apply DCIs—it is a rich opportunity for students to learn.

In addition, the role of critiquing the ideas being discussed enables the student to become a "critical consumer of science" by critiquing and evaluating "the merits of any scientifically based argument" (NRC 2012, p. 71). By engaging in critique and considering the evidence for different scientific ideas, students become scientifically literate (American Association for the Advancement of Science 1990).

What Is the Practice of Engaging in Argument From Evidence All About?

Scientific argumentation occurs when students are unsure about the idea they are constructing (because there exist multiple possible answers or because they simply haven't convinced themselves yet). In argumentative interactions, students develop more confidence in the ideas they are constructing through defending, evaluating, critiquing, and revising those ideas. A written argument is the culmination of these components—it reflects the student's idea as well as the possible defenses of it and critiques of alternatives.

While many examples of argumentation focus on instances in which the idea about which students are arguing are explanations, scientists engage in argumentation around all of the practices: They might argue about which interpretation of the data is most consistent with shared scientific understandings, which investigation will result in the most useful data, which model best represents the phenomena being studied, or why a question is important to investigate. For example, students in the introductory vignette (pp. 229–231) argued about why the milkweed was disappearing. We could easily imagine them arguing about how to best investigate that topic—one student might want to explore whether the caterpillars were growing, while another could be interested in how humans interact with the cage (e.g., do they clean it frequently?). In addition, after concluding their investigations into this specific phenomenon, they might argue about how to best model it. Thus, argumentation can occur around any and all of the other seven scientific practices discussed in the *Framework* and the *NGSS*.

Engaging in a scientific argument requires first that ideas—or claims about investigation designs, interpretations of data, explanations, design solutions, questions, or models—be treated as tentative and subject to revision. We call the idea (i.e., the proposed investigation plan, research question, explanation, model, or design solution) being questioned and revised the *claim* of the argument. The expectation that ideas are worth questioning and revising leads to the components of argumentative interactions:

1. Claims must be *supported* to communicate why they should be accepted.

2. Claims and their supports are *evaluated and critiqued* to identify strengths and weaknesses of each claim.

3. Differing claims are *reconciled* such that the community will make progress on the problem at hand and determine its next steps.

As we will demonstrate below, each of these components can be fulfilled in a variety of ways. In the following sections, we briefly describe this variation and what these key components—supporting, critiquing, and reconciling—entail when Engaging in Argument From Evidence.

Three Components of Scientific Argumentation

1. **Supported claims:** Students describe why the claim should be believed. Claims can be about any of the other seven scientific practices identified in the *NGSS*. Depending on the available information and the focus of the claim, the defense entails some combination of available evidence, DCIs, and logical accounts.

2. **Evaluation and critique:** Students indentify strengths and weaknesses of the supported claims.

3. **Reconciliation:** When multiple possible claims are discussed, students will eventually reconcile these claims in order to make progress on the problems about which they are arguing.

SUPPORTED CLAIMS

A claim is any idea that students are supporting. In the vignette (pp. 229–231) at the beginning of this chapter, the students are supporting their claim for why the milkweed was disappearing, and we see two different claims being discussed. The first claim is that the caterpillars are eating the milkweed, and the second suggests that humans are removing the rotten milkweed. Students can also make claims about possible research questions to explore, investigation designs, interpretations of data, models, and design solutions.

When Engaging in Argument From Evidence, one must do more than offer claims, because when a student offers a claim with no support, there is little opportunity for ideas to be questioned and revised (Berland and McNeill 2010). That is, there is little opportunity for students to work collaboratively to improve on one another's ideas—to learn—when claims are not supported. In fact, the *Framework* makes the case that students should

> go beyond simply making claims—that is, to include reasons **or** references
> to evidence and to begin to distinguish evidence from opinion. As they grow
> in their ability to construct scientific arguments, students can draw on a

wider range of reasons or evidence, so that their arguments become more sophisticated. (NRC 2012, p. 73; emphasis added)

We see in this quote that claims are supported with a combination of "reasons" and "references to evidence." Thus, the first component of Engaging in Argument From Evidence is to both offer a claim and support that claim with evidence or reasons or both.

As seen in the above quote, the claims are supported with two types of information: the reasons and evidence. Supports based on reasons involve student use (implicitly or explicitly) of DCIs to logically support the claim. For example, in the introductory vignette, Adam supported his claim that the caterpillars were eating the milkweed by connecting to DCI LS1.A. regarding the structures organisms have to perform the functions necessary for survival. In this case, Adam described what happened to the milkweed after the caterpillars ate it: "It goes inside to its stomach and some comes out as poop just like human beings." This is not something Adam observed but is instead a logical construction of what might have happened to the milkweed based on Adam's knowledge of the digestive system. Evidence-based supports, on the other hand, are grounded in actual data or observations students have made. We also see Suki using evidence to support Adam's claim when she states that she saw "a lot of poop [in the caterpillars' cage]." We typically see the definition of evidence shifting across the grades: In the younger grades, experiences would count as evidence, whereas students in the upper-grade bands would be expected to provide increasingly reliable and rigorous empirical data.

While Engaging in Argument From Evidence and the performance expectations associated with it often emphasize evidence-based supports, it is not always necessary for an argument to include both DCIs and data-based evidence. The importance of these types of information depends on the claim being discussed. For example, we find that it is often not possible to support a claim about the research question or investigation design the class should pursue with evidence—it is likely that students do not have any evidence available to support such claims. Instead, they will rely on their shared understandings of the DCIs, or reasoning, to support their claims about what to pursue next and how to do so. On the other hand, when arguing about a scientific explanation of a phenomenon they all observed, students will have much more evidence upon which they can draw—they will have their observations of the phenomenon. For example, in the introductory vignette, Benita used evidence—her observations of the milkweed—to support her claim when she reminded her classmates that the milkweed leaves have holes in them. We imagine that if they were arguing about what research question to investigate, they wouldn't have gathered this evidence yet and instead would support their claims using DCIs about what animals need to survive (i.e., connecting to the idea that animals must eat to survive—LS1.A—would support a claim that they should investigate whether caterpillars eat milkweed). In this way, we do not expect all scientific arguments to use the same types of information to support all claims, but one can expect that all scientific arguments will include a claim that is supported. Table 11.1 illustrates this idea by identifying possible claims and supports for various performance expectations found in the *NGSS*. Note that we use performance expectations that highlight a range of the scientific practices—not just argumentation—to illustrate the ways in which argumentation can be seen across the practices.

EVALUATION AND CRITIQUE

After a claim has been articulated and supported, students should evaluate and critique the claim and support for that claim. When engaged in an argumentative interaction, this would entail evaluating and critiquing one another's arguments. For example, the *Framework* states, students "should learn how to evaluate critically the scientific arguments of others and present counterarguments" (NRC 2012, p. 73). However, it is important to recognize that this evaluation and critique can be a part of written arguments as well—critiquing alternative ideas will strengthen one's argument in any form.

We've seen these critiques taking many forms: evaluative statements, questions, counterarguments, and refutations of other possible claims. In addition, in early grades, the evaluation and critique might look more like a comparison of possible claims than a critique of them. In all of these moves, students are stating whether they agree with the claim being offered and why or why not. In addition, counterarguments offer an alternative claim to be supported and discussed.

We see an evaluation in the introductory vignette, in which Jay disagrees with Calvin by saying that the milkweed is "not gone." In addition, Amari offers a counterargument when he introduces an alternative claim: Maybe the caterpillars are not eating the milkweed but humans are removing it instead. We illustrate additional possible ways to communicate evaluative or critical responses to an argument in Table 11.2 (p. 238). In this table, we focus on the fictional argument illustrated in Table 11.1 in which a student might argue, "We should use more sandbags to keep the Mississippi River from flooding the fields because we observed that sand can absorb and block water. So, I believe that the sandbags will soak up all the extra water and keep it from going into the farmers' fields."

Table 11.1
Possible claims and supports to fulfill sample performance expectations

Number	Performance expectation	Possible claim	Possible supports for that claim
K-ESS2-2	Construct an argument supported by evidence for how plants and animals (including humans) can change the environment to meet their needs.	Student claim: "Squirrels don't need our help surviving in the winter. They can make their own warm homes."	• Evidence from their observations of squirrels dens • Might refer to DCI that animals have to fulfill certain needs to survive (LS1.A), and for squirrels, staying warm is one of those needs
2-LS2-1	Plan and conduct an investigation to determine if plants need sunlight and water to grow.	Student claim: "I think we should place some plants in a dark closet and others under our classroom lights. Compare the plants to determine which ones are healthier."	• No student evidence for these claims • Could support their claims using reasoning about what counts as "light" (PS3.A) (i.e., are classroom lights equivalent to sunlight?)
3-ESS3-1	Make a claim about the merit of a design solution that reduces the impacts of a weather-related hazard.	Student claim: "We should build walls to keep the Mississippi River from flooding the fields."	• Evidence from experiments showing that sand is more absorbent than the soil naturally found on the banks of the Mississippi
MS-ESS1-1	Develop and use a model of the Earth–Sun–Moon system to describe the cyclic patterns of lunar phases, eclipses of the Sun and Moon, and seasons.	Student uses Styrofoam balls to represent the Earth and Moon and a light bulb to represent the Sun in order to illustrate underlying ideas about the interactions between these bodies. Student uses model to propose an explanation for the phases of the Moon by exploring how the Moon is illuminated by the Sun.	• Evidence from student observations of the Moon over the past month to demonstrate that his or her representation is consistent with what happens in nature
HS-LS4-2	Construct an explanation based on evidence that the process of evolution primarily results from four factors: (1) the potential for a species to increase in number, (2) the heritable genetic variation of individuals in a species due to mutation and sexual reproduction, (3) competition for limited resources, and (4) the proliferation of those organisms that are better able to survive and reproduce in the environment.	Student constructs an explanatory account of a particular instance of evolution. For example, after exploring evidence from Galapagos finches, a student might claim, "The average length of a Galapagos finch beak increased after the drought in 1976 because the birds with longer beaks were able to eat the seeds that survived the drought. So, the birds with longer beaks also survived the drought, while birds with shorter beaks did not. This means that birds with longer beaks passed this trait on to the offspring, increasing the average beak length of the Galapagos finches in the next generation."	• Evidence regarding the drought and the seeds that survived the drought • Evidence showing that birds with longer beaks were able to eat surviving seeds • Reference to DCI LS4.B, which discusses the link between survival and passing on of genetic traits

Table 11.2
Possible ways to evaluate and critique arguments

Evaluative or critical response	Example
Comparison	"You think the sandbags can soak up all the water, and I think that the sandbags do not soak up enough water." (This comparison focuses on identifying the student's key disagreement and might help move them forward to discussing why they have these different claims.)
Evaluative statement	"I disagree with you because I don't think sandbags absorb or block enough water."
Question	"What happens when the sandbags fill up and there is still more water coming?"
Counterargument	"I was thinking we should build a wall because we saw videos of farmers using sandbags to protect their fields and still getting flooded."
Refutation	A student might refute the above counterargument by stating: "But, we did research showing that walls are too expensive for the farmers and they break. Sandbags might not work all the time, but they work most of the time and are affordable."

In these hypothetical examples, the students are all worried about whether the sandbags can hold back all of the floodwater, but they are communicating their concerns with different levels of complexity and detail. In each of these, the students are engaging in the evaluation or critique of an argument.

RECONCILIATION

As discussed, the goal of Engaging in Argument From Evidence is to construct a claim that aligns with the data or DCIs that students are constructing and collecting—these claims can be a research question, investigation design, data interpretation, explanation, design solution, or model. If there are multiple possible claims being discussed, this process entails reconciling the different claims that emerge. When students are working to convince themselves of one possible claim, this reconciliation means that they are resolving their doubts. In both cases, students are revising the claim, and supports for that claim, in ways that are consistent with the available evidence and DCIs.

The term *reconciliation* suggests that all of the students will eventually be convinced of a single claim. We all know that this ideal will occur only infrequently. Moreover, it is not always ideal. In many instances, the goal is for students to explore the realm of possibilities because there is not *one* right answer (e.g., imagine arguments about engineering design solutions or research designs) or because the argument and gathering of supports enables students to explore content before they are ready to understand all the complexities associated with agreeing upon one answer. Thus, we use the term to suggest movement toward reconciliation rather than complete reconciliation in all arguments—this movement suggests that students are making progress on a problem. For example, the students in the vignette (pp. 229–231) have begun reconciling their opposing claims when Amari states that he has observed the poop—a by-product of eating—and thereby indicates that he might see the strength of his classmates' claim that the caterpillars eat the milkweed. In this case, Amari has not revised his original claim—he does not agree with his classmates' claim—but he is showing movement: He is listening to his classmates' claims and supports. This openness to alternative arguments can be difficult for students to maintain and is the first step toward reconciliation.

In addition, this sort of movement is how students construct knowledge. Imagine a different sort of conversation in which the teacher is pushing Amari to accept that the caterpillar ate the milkweed. In this case, Amari might repeat the teacher's claim, but he probably won't understand why it is true, how his observations of the caterpillars support the claim, or how the claim relates to the structure of the caterpillars (DCI LS1.A). Thus, we use the term *reconciliation* to indicate that students are engaging with the various claims being discussed and demonstrating small movements in their own arguments as they gradually shift their understandings toward those that align with their current understandings of the DCIs and evidence. It is this gradual process that indicates that students are developing and applying deep understandings of the science.

Of course, reconciliation doesn't stand alone. The three components of Engaging in Argument From Evidence (supporting claims, evaluating and critiquing, and reconciling) together create opportunities for students to treat science knowledge as something they are able to construct and question. In addition, engaging in each of these aspects of argumentation requires that students synthesize all of the available information and make sense of what they've been experiencing. In other words, it is through these components of argumentation that students construct knowledge.

Some Points of Clarification

- **Arguments are not the process through which explanations (or other knowledge products) are made.** Argumentation is a process—it is the process by which individuals discuss their tentative ideas and the supports for them. However, arguments can easily be—and often are—recorded in a final written form. In short, arguments are both a process and a product. This is similar to constructing a model (process) and the model (product).

- **Arguments do not require disagreement.** While arguments do not make sense if there is only one right answer with which everyone already agrees, it does not require that the students be debating multiple possible claims. Instead, argumentation requires that the students be unsure of their claim, and that they work to gain confidence in that claim by either reconciling it with alternatives or bolstering the supports for it.

- **You can (and should) engage in scientific argumentation around issues that have a right answer.** Although it is easy to imagine facilitating argumentation around those issues that have no right answer, argumentation is a key practice for constructing understandings of all sorts. It is how we figure out an answer, and it should be used as such. In fact, it can help students develop a richer understanding of the answer, because of their consideration of alternative claims.

- **Argumentation does not require that students construct an explanation.** While explanation and argumentation are often seen together (for reasons discussed below), they are two distinct practices. Argumentation must occur in conjunction with one of the scientific practices (there must be something around which the students are arguing), but it can occur around any of the other seven scientific practices, not just explanation.

How Does the Practice of Engaging in Argument From Evidence Relate to the Other Practices?

Individuals never engage in scientific argument from evidence as a stand-alone practice. Instead, they are argue with and around their work in the other practices:

> Arguments can be … about the best possible explanation. Argumentation is also needed to resolve questions involving, for example, the best experimental design, the most appropriate techniques of data analysis, or the best interpretation of a given data set. (NRC 2012, p. 71)

In other words, we engage in scientific argumentation to make sense of the question and to produce the best research questions, investigation designs, data interpretations, explanations, models, and design solutions. Thus, as described above, the claim is a product of the accompanying practices, while the supporting, evaluating, critiquing, and reconciling of the claim are the argumentation. This argumentative work can be represented in writing (to form an argument) or through classroom discussions (as argumentation). The examples in the following sections illustrate how argumentation might look around a range of practices and across writing and verbal interactions.

A Note About the Form of the Argument

Much of the *NGSS* and this chapter focus on argumentation as a verbal exchange. This argumentation, or arguing, is the process through which students, working as a scientific community, construct the best claim—the best research question, design solution, explanation, or model. This arguing occurs in small- or large-group discussions (the vignette at the beginning of this chapter [pp. 229–231] illustrates argumentation in the context of a whole class discussion). During these discussions, students collaboratively engage in the three components of arguing (supporting claims, evaluating and critiquing, and reconciling).

Students may not need to produce a formal written argument when engaging in argumentation. In fact, depending on our goals as teachers, we might want students to focus on recording their notes and thoughts before engaging in an argument and then verbally reconciling their differences and collaboratively constructing the best claim. In these instances, students might formally record only their final claim, or their final research question, design solution, explanation, or model.

However, this does not mean that the practice of scientific argumentation refers only to the discourse. Arguments can be, and often are, *written*. Written arguments include the students' claim and supports for that claim. This document could also include the other components of scientific argumentation by describing possible counterarguments and identifying rebuttals that explain why their claim is better than alternatives. (Vignette 3 [pp. 248–249] illustrates this written argument product.)

As discussed in Chapter 12 (p. 259), the practices of explaining and arguing are often linked in curricular materials and in research. This occurs because both explanations and arguments entail DCIs and evidence. However, the evidence and DCIs play different roles in the two practices: When constructing an explanation, evidence might be the phenomenon being explained, and it might be used, in conjunction with DCIs, to figure out the how or why account of the phenomenon; when constructing an argument, on the other hand, evidence and DCIs are used to defend the claim. In this way, while there is a large overlap between the two practices, there are important distinctions. Constructing an explanation requires that students construct a how or why account about a phenomenon. Arguments have no such requirement. Instead, arguments require that students support their claims with evidence and scientific ideas, and that they include the components of critique and evaluation and of reconciliation.

What Does the Practice of Engaging in Argument From Evidence Look Like When It Happens in the Classroom?

In this section, we offer three vignettes of the practice of Engaging in Argument From Evidence that we have observed through our research in classrooms. These vignettes show what argumentation can look like in different settings. We picked these examples to highlight the ways in which the components of Engaging in Argument From Evidence (i.e., supported claims, evaluation and critique, and reconciliation) might change throughout students' schooling as well as the ways in which argumentation can vary when done around different practices.

VIGNETTE 1: UPPER-ELEMENTARY STUDENTS ARGUING ABOUT THEIR MODELS

We describe students arguing about the models they are constructing in the context of a mixed-grade classroom of fifth and sixth graders enacting the *Investigating and Questioning Our World Through Science and Technology* curriculum (Krajcik and Reiser 2004). In this case, the students are exploring the particle nature of matter (DCI PS1) by constructing a model of how odor moves across a room. The students come to the activity depicted below after some in-class activities exploring how odor travels and after constructing models of the odor traveling individually. They are now sitting in groups of four, comparing their models so that they can converge on a single model of odor moving throughout a room.

While in their group, working to construct a single model, Linda and Mikey argue about whether the "nothingness" between the air molecules needs to be represented. This argument begins after Mikey describes his model of odor traveling through the air by pointing at different aspects of his drawn model and saying, "This is the nose, this is the ... odor. Those little dot things are nothingness. This is air ..."

At this point, Linda interrupts Mikey, questioning the idea that the "dot things are nothingness." She says, "Nothingness couldn't be able to be seen. You can't see nothingness. Are you kidding me?"

Thus, we see these two students arguing about how to represent odor in a room: Mikey believes that you should depict the nothingness between the air and odor molecules, while Linda argues that nothingness cannot be seen, implying that it should not be represented in their model.

Mikey challenges Linda by pointing to his model, saying, "Yes you can [see the nothingness]. Those are little dots of nothingness." Stephanie (another group member) then clarifies that Mikey's model "is a figure for the nothingness. It is not saying that this [the dots] is what nothingness looks like."

In saying this, Stephanie makes clear that Linda and Mikey may not disagree about how odor travels. Instead, they disagree about how to model this phenomenon: Linda is saying that you cannot see "nothingness" in the real world, while Mikey is arguing that you can see it in the model.

Linda responds to this clarification by shifting to focus on the representation and saying that "there can't be dots of nothingness." And Mikey disagrees, stating simply, "Yes there can."

At this point in the conversation, there is a brief teacher interruption. This seems to give the students some space to consider their positions. When they return to the conversation, Mikey concludes the argument by joking, "You can see nothingness. There's one. There's one. There's one." He points at the air around him and laughs.

In this, Mikey is not yet resolving the question of whether the nothingness should be represented in their model. Instead, he focuses on their general agreement that there is nothing between the particles and that this cannot be seen in the natural world.

Shortly after Mikey makes this joke, Linda notices the similarities across the four students' individual models and says, "They're all very similar. I like everybody's. ... They're all very similar, we even use dots and stars [to represent different types of molecules]."

Upon realizing that they have a common base of elements, the group quickly shifts gears to construct its final consensus model. In this process, Mikey demonstrates that he has come around to Linda's idea that the "nothingness" did not need to be represented in their group's model, stating, "Can I do the Xs and Os [the symbols representing the air and odor molecules]? No little nothingness," he says, laughing.

While Mikey does not explain *why* he shifted to accept Linda's claim that the nothingness should not be represented in their model, his joke earlier in the exchange suggests that he agrees that the nothingness is not a *thing* in the real world and that it therefore need not be represented in the model.

As seen in this exchange, the main area of disagreement surrounds the question of whether and how to represent the "nothingness" between the air molecules. Mikey's claim is that the nothingness should be represented, while Linda's claim is that it cannot be represented. Linda begins by *critiquing* Mikey's idea that nothingness should be represented. She *supports* her claim that the "nothingness" doesn't need to be represented in the model by asserting that "you can't see nothingness." Stephanie and Mikey *support* Mikey's claim that the nothingness can be represented with little dots by asserting that the dots are a "figure for the nothingness."

Given the question at hand, these supports do not draw on evidence or DCIs. That is, the disagreement is about *how* to represent the thing in the world, not *what* that thing is or how it works. Thus, the students support their claims by appealing to their intuitive rules for representations (i.e., whether nothingness can be depicted). Even so, the students are focused on a DCI that is challenging for students: The question of how to represent the space between the particles creates opportunities for students to think about what is between the particles and how that relates to particle motion (PS1).

In addition, throughout this vignette, the students are critiquing and evaluating one another's claims. Moreover, it concludes with Mikey reconciling his thinking with that of his classmates—picking between the alternatives, selecting the strongest case. Thus, we see all three components of scientific argumentation, and it is a strong example of scientific argumentation around models.

VIGNETTE 2: MIDDLE SCHOOL STUDENTS ARGUING ABOUT THEIR EXPLANATIONS

This vignette is similar to the vignette at the beginning of the chapter, in that the students in this vignette are engaged in a whole-class argumentative discussion to co-construct an explanation. This example comes from a sixth-grade classroom in the Boston Public Schools in which the teacher was piloting a middle school science curriculum, developed through a collaboration between the Learning Design Group at the Lawrence Hall of Science and Amplify Learning (Regents of the University of California 2012). Throughout the argument, we see students making connections to DCIs regarding the role of water in the Earth's surface processes (ESS2.C) and weather and climate (ESS2.D).

This group of students is working to explain what makes the Atacama Desert so dry. Early in the conversation, Jose states that "one of the reasons the Atacama Desert is the driest place on Earth is because of the mountains surrounding it. So even if there is some precipitation, the water will go on the mountain, because it is like the rain shadow effect."

As seen here, Jose believes that there are factors in the desert that can produce rain, but that in the Atacama Desert, the surrounding mountains cause the rain to fall before the rain can get to the desert (i.e., the rain shadow effect).

Danny and Sheila disagree with Jose. Danny and Sheila critique Jose's idea by constructing a counterargument:

Danny: "I agree and disagree. I disagree because when I was looking at the map I saw by the Atacama Desert the ocean currents were cold so that means, umm, the cold water and cold water doesn't evaporate and it is dense. And it was warm air. It has to be warm water to evaporate."

Sheila: "I agree with Danny because if you can't have evaporation … if the water goes up and you have no evaporation, you can't—you don't have no water to support the clouds to make rain. So if the water, the cold water can't evaporate, you can't have rain. Because evaporation has to happen."

Danny: "I agree. I agree, because like you can't have rain. It's not rain before. Rain happens by evaporation."

In this exchange, we see that Danny and Sheila disagree with Jose's explanation for why the Atacama Desert is so dry. Instead, Danny and Sheila argue that there is no evaporation around the Atacama Desert because the ocean currents are too cold for the water to evaporate. Since, as they argue, evaporation is a necessary precondition for rain, there is not enough water in the atmosphere around the Atacama Desert to produce rain.

After some additional discussion, Jose responds to Danny and Sheila's fundamental assertion that there is little evaporation around the Atacama Desert, stating, "I think that I disagree because you say there is no precipitation. But there [pointing at the map of the ocean currents around South America] if you see there are warm currents on the top of South America and there are lots of prevailing winds. So there are warm currents and evaporation happens. And then the cold gathers and the wind takes it across the Andes Mountains."

Here, we see Jose arguing that evaporation could occur in the warm currents north of the Atacama Desert ("on the top of South America") and that the "prevailing winds" would blow the evaporated water vapor toward the Atacama Desert. In saying this, Jose is further supporting his claim that the factors necessary to produce rain exist in the Atacama Desert and the intense dryness is produced by the rain shadow effect.

Throughout this exchange, we see all three students stating claims and supporting those claims with evidence and DCIs. For example, Jose begins by supporting his claim with a reference to the mountains surrounding the Atacama Desert—evidence the students gathered through their observations of a map of the region. Danny similarly connects to evidence gathered from maps. In his case, he is focused on the surrounding ocean currents. In addition, Danny discusses the conditions needed for evaporation, and Sheila focuses on the conditions needed for rain to occur (DCIs ESS2.C and D).

Furthermore, these students are *critiquing* one another's ideas in sophisticated ways. For example, Danny musters evidence and DCIs to directly challenge Jose's claim when he discusses the maps of ocean currents and what is necessary for evaporation to occur. And, Jose responds directly to their counterargument, explaining that there are other warm currents, but there is still no rain. Consequently, Jose believes that cold currents alone are not a sufficient explanation for why there is no rain in the Atacama Desert.

Given the presence of the components of scientific argumentation, this exchange is a strong example of students engaging in scientific argumentation. Moreover, the claims about which the students are arguing (i.e., Jose's claim that there are factors in the desert to produce rain but that the rain falls on the surrounding mountains rather than in the desert) are accounts of how a phenomenon occurs. Thus, these students are constructing both arguments and explanations: They are engaging in an argument to reach consensus on which explanation best uses the known DCIs and available evidence.

VIGNETTE 3: HIGH SCHOOL STUDENTS ARGUING FOR AN ENGINEERING DESIGN DECISION

Our final vignette comes from a 10th-grade chemistry classroom from the Boston Public Schools. In this example the students are working to construct an engineering design solution. In particular, they are designing a more efficient biodiesel fuel. Figure 11.1 presents one group's argument for its biodiesel recipe—the group's solution.

In this written argument, we see the students *supporting* their claim that their recipe is the best with specific evidence from their various tests (i.e., measurements of heat of combustion). They further *support* their claim with reasons about why their evidence is related to their claim (connecting to DCI PS1.B). Through this, the students have supported their claim about the effectiveness of a design solution. In addition, this group has presented rebuttals to counterarguments that emerged through class discussions, thereby *evaluating* their ideas. In particular, this group states that "even though the yield is the lowest amount using the 10 ml methanol, it has the most energy and that's mostly what matters." In this, the students have identified what others might find to be a weakness in their work and explained why it is actually a strength; this is a first step toward *reconciliation* of differing ideas, as it begins to depict perceived weaknesses in the alternative claims.

Figure 11.1
Written argument for an engineering design

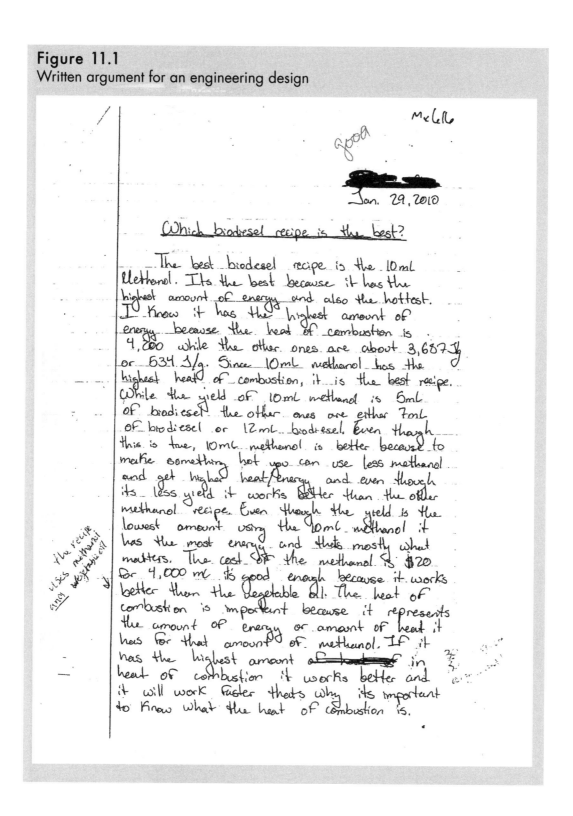

What Does *Not* Count as Scientific Argumentation

When students argue, they are supporting their claims, evaluating and critiquing possible alternatives, and reconciling disagreements. However, as seen throughout the examples, the kind of information found in the claims, and the ways that students support their claims, can vary depending on what information is available. In addition, the evaluation of alternatives can take the form of building on or directly disagreeing with one another's ideas, and reconciliation may or may not be necessary—depending on the degree of disagreement.

Given all this room for variation, what doesn't count?

Our experience suggests that at least three common variations of this practice do not align with the *NGSS* vision of this practice. Each of these variations is problematic because it fundamentally does not provide students opportunities to engage in sensemaking around the scientific ideas under study. Instead in these variations, students are arguing or constructing final form arguments, which are removed from those core scientific ideas.

1. **Constructing arguments that are unrelated to disciplinary core ideas.** For example, students might practice arguing about a "black box" problem or some socioscientific questions that motivate students to support their claims using information about social aspects of the situation rather than scientific observations and ideas. In these cases, students are learning some of the discourse moves associated with the practice of scientific argumentation, but they are not doing so to construct knowledge about scientific content or to make progress on a bigger question. As such, this falls short of the *NGSS* vision of scientific argumentation.

2. **Student groups presenting their final arguments with little discussion or feedback from their peers.** In these cases, students are focused on constructing arguments that demonstrate mastery over the content, not on evaluating, challenging or learning from one another's ideas. This is a common adaptation of the argumentative practice because the student presentation is a familiar classroom activity; however, it falls short of the *NGSS* vision of scientific argumentation because the presentation does not align with the argumentation learning goals and the practice of argumentation is treated as separate from the work of learning the DCIs.

3. **Arguing about claims about which students have few concerns.** Students are often asked to construct arguments for relatively simple problems for which there is one clear right answer and few questions. That is, students are asked to construct arguments about which the class is confident of the claim. Similarly to the previous point, this provides little need for students to attend to one another's ideas and makes the argumentation a skill to demonstrate rather than a practice that is purposeful.

How Can We Work Toward Equity With Regard to the Practice of Engaging in Argument From Evidence?

In some respects, Engaging in Argument From Evidence is a powerful practice with respect to promoting equity in the classroom. It promotes a classroom environment in which all ideas are useful because the best ideas emerge out of the comparison, evaluation, and revision of multiple ideas and evidence. As such, scientific argumentation can support participation by all students.

However, it is important to note that some students—particularly those that are often underrepresented in science—may think that openly disagreeing with others' ideas is disrespectful. In addition, some students may be uncomfortable evaluating ideas, and they may find offering their own ideas up for evaluation to be threatening. Research suggests two possible ways of addressing these particular difficulties: (1) Ensure that there are multiple ways and opportunities for students to engage in argumentation so that students that are uncomfortable in one situation (e.g., whole-class discussions) have other opportunities to participate and demonstrate their competence. (2) Explicitly, and repeatedly, discuss the norms and expectations of scientific argumentation. Making the expectations explicit enables students to name the disconnects between their expectations and those of the teacher, rather than experiencing them tacitly. This can enable students to begin to take on the new norms and expectations. The next section, "How Can I Support and Assess This Practice in My Classroom?" offers additional teaching strategies for supporting students in overcoming these particular challenges and gradually developing a classroom environment that empowers all students to construct understandings of the DCIs through argumentation.

Practicing argumentation in classrooms with large numbers of English language learners or individualized learning plans poses additional challenges. In particular, we have found that argumentative discussions are language intensive and can be quite meandering—students may respond to one another's claims, but they may also respond to someone's evidence (i.e., question whether the evidence supports the claim or is correct). In addition, they might respond to the immediately preceding comment or an idea that was expressed two minutes ago. As such, students might need extra support in argumentation (González-Howard, McNeill, and Ruttan 2015). Thus, when supporting argumentative interactions, we suggest that teachers make the focal question clear—write it on the board, give students sentence stems that emphasize the question, have them record it, and so forth. In addition, useful strategies for supporting all of your students in participating in argumentative discussions include recording key areas of agreement and disagreement, so that students can help track the ideas that have been discussed, and revoicing students' ideas in a way that emphasizes the main claims and questions. These strategies are also consistent with the *Universal Design for Learning* framework (Rose and Meyer 2002), which suggests that representing ideas in multiple ways can support students that have different needs.

In addition to providing students with multiple instructional supports, we suggest that teachers provide multiple ways for students to engage in the argument—from independent construction of initial ideas to small groups in which those ideas can be discussed and debated to whole-class discussions that drive consensus. Not all students will excel in all formats, but creating multiple opportunities for students to engage in the argumentation will mean that all students will find a mode in which they are comfortable.

How Can I Support and Assess This Practice in My Classroom?

Engaging in Argument From Evidence, as envisioned by the *NGSS*, requires a transformation in how students interact with their teacher, each other, and the science content. In particular, this practice requires that students and teachers perceive and treat the scientific knowledge as something that they can use to explain and investigate natural phenomena, something that will improve through collaboration, something that is worth questioning and revising, and something that they construct. However, this approach to scientific knowledge and learning can be unfamiliar to and uncomfortable for all of us. For example, students might not want to publicly admit when their ideas are changing because they are used to demonstrating that they understand rather than that they are working to make sense of something. In other words, when students are accustomed to classroom discussions that reward them for knowing the right answer, it can be threatening to offer an idea with the expectation that peers will evaluate and revise it. Similarly, students might not be used to being the audience members for one another's work—it is much more common for teachers to take the role of evaluating and validating student contributions. As such, they might not be comfortable stepping into these new, expanded roles.

Summarizing Perceptions About Knowledge in Scientific Argumentation

Scientific argumentation requires that students and teachers perceive and treat the scientific knowledge as something that

- can be used to explain and investigate natural phenomenon,

- is worth questioning,

- can and should be improved as new information (e.g., evidence) is collected, and

- can be constructed.

There are a number of strategies teachers can use to overcome these challenges and foster a classroom environment in which students are empowered to argue with one another's ideas:

- When discussing the claims, evaluation should not focus on canonical accuracy. Instead, evaluation and critique should examine whether student ideas are sensible and consistent with the available evidence, and DCIs. The opening vignette (pp. 229–231) has a nice example of this when the teacher says to one of the students, "You have some good evidence."

- Engage students in multiple activities around these rich phenomena with varied group sizes. This will give students a chance to construct their initial ideas, share and evaluate alternative ideas, and work toward reconciliation. This is seen across the examples in which we see small-group and whole-class argumentation as well as an argument product that was produced by an individual student.

- When in small groups, students often share their ideas and offer cursory feedback without truly comparing or evaluating one another's ideas. In these situations, it might be helpful to ask the students to reach consensus by constructing a shared product—a research question, investigation design, explanation, model, or design solution—with which the entire group agrees. Vignette 1 (pp. 243–244) illustrates this sort of consensus-building task.

- Students should be working with tentative claims (research questions, investigation designs, explanations, models) such that they will have questions and concerns to work through by arguing from evidence.

- When engaging with the student ideas, emphasize "why" questions that create an expectation that students will support their claims. As you do this, increasingly expect students to use evidence when supporting their ideas. This can be done through questions such as the following:
  - What evidence do you have?
  - Why do you agree or disagree? What are your reasons? What is your evidence?
  - What could be some other possible claims? Do you have evidence?
  - Do you agree with the points being made? Why?
  - Who has a different opinion? What is it? How is it different?
  - Why are you using that as evidence and not the other data? How would your claim change if you used all the data?

- How is that idea related to what was previous discussed? What reasons do you have for saying that?

• Encourage students to question your ideas and continually demonstrate what it looks like to support the ideas with evidence. This lets students see that ideas are evaluated on whether they can be supported with evidence and scientific concepts rather than their alignment with a textbook or outside authority.

Summary of Strategies for Supporting Scientific Argumentation

• Promote argumentation in multiple activity types (i.e., individual, small group, and whole class).

• Evaluate student ideas on whether they align with available evidence and shared disciplinary core ideas.

• Ask student groups to construct a single product about which they all agree.

• Encourage students to question your ideas and demonstrate how to support those ideas with evidence and reasoning.

• Explore phenomena that are complex enough to create tentative claims that students can question and resolve.

• Frequently ask students to support their ideas with evidence and disciplinary core ideas.

When assessing the way students engage in argument from evidence, we can evaluate the students' participation in argumentative conversations or their written arguments. Regardless of the format, assessment should focus on the coherency of students' arguments rather than final accuracy—we have seen this shift in emphasis for students to engage in argument from evidence as an opportunity to construct knowledge rather than as an opportunity to demonstrate final form knowledge. The assessment could examine the three components of an argument from evidence—depending on the context of the argument:

- Assessing the supported claims could be broken into two components:
  - ○ Claim: The idea being supported. This could be an explanation, a model, a question to investigate, a proposed investigation plan, or an engineering design solution.
  - ○ Support: Statements used to convince someone of the strength of a claim. Depending on the claim and the information available, supports will include evidence or disciplinary idea(s) or both.

- The assessment of the evaluation and critique could similarly involve two components:
  - ○ Critique: Identification and critique of alternative ideas. Students should evaluate and ask questions of each other's claims as well as provide potential counterarguments for those claims.
  - ○ Response: A response to the critique. Where critiques to a student's own claim have been identified, the student might respond to these challenges, explaining why the idea remains sound.

- Reconciliation: When possible, the teacher might reward students for publicly revising their claims to account for weaknesses identified through the argumentative process.

Summary

As we discussed throughout this chapter, the practice Engaging in Argument From Evidence is a key opportunity for students to engage in sense-making. In other words, it is through the active work in supporting their claims, evaluating and critiquing the claims and supports of others, and reconciling their ideas that we have seen students construct rich understandings of the science content. Moreover, we see argumentation as a flexible practice—students can argue about their investigation plans, models, data interpretations, explanations, or design solutions. This flexibility enables us to incorporate this practice throughout the curriculum, helping shift the entire classroom culture to one in which the students are active participants as the authors of science knowledge.

Acknowledgments

This material is based, in part, on work supported by the National Science Foundation under Grant No. DRL-1119584 and Grant No. DRL-1020316. The opinions expressed herein are those of the authors and not necessarily those of the National Science Foundation.

References

American Association for the Advancement of Science. 1990. *Science for all Americans: Project 2061.* New York: Oxford University Press.

Berland, L. K., and K. L. McNeill. 2010. A learning progression for scientific argumentation: Understanding student work and designing supportive instructional contexts. *Science Education* 94: 765–793.

González-Howard, M., K. L. McNeill, and N. Ruttan. 2015. What's our three-word claim? Supporting English language learning students' engagement in scientific argumentation. *Science Scope* 38 (9): 10–16.

Krajcik, J., and B. J. Reiser, eds. 2004. *IQWST: Investigating and questioning our world through science and technology.* Ann Arbor: University of Michigan.

National Research Council (NRC). 2012. *A framework for K–12 science education: Practices, crosscutting concepts, and core ideas.* Washington, DC: National Academies Press.

Regents of the University of California. 2012. *Plate tectonics.* Filed trial version of middle school science unit developed by the Learning Design Group. Berkeley, CA: Lawrence Hall of Science.

Rose, D. H., and A. Meyer. 2002. *Teaching every student in the digital age: Universal design for learning.* Alexandria, VA: ASCD.

12

OBTAINING, EVALUATING, AND COMMUNICATING INFORMATION

LEAH A. BRICKER, PHILIP BELL, KATIE VAN HORNE, AND TIFFANY L. CLARK

Consider the following classroom scenario. A group of four high school students decided to learn more about herd immunity for a project in their biology class as part of an infectious disease unit focused in part on ideas listed in two disciplinary core ideas (DCIs): LS2.C and ETS1.B (NGSS Lead States 2013). Their teacher encouraged them to play the game POX (*www.tiltfactor.org/game/pox*), which simulates the relationship between herd immunity and vaccinations within a community, and through their game play, the students learned more about what herd immunity is and how it functions. The students also watched a TED Talk by Nicholas Christakis (*www.ted.com/talks/ nicholas_christakis_how_social_networks_predict_epidemics*) and learned that events like the spread of infectious disease take place within social networks. The students and their teacher, after consultation with a local scientist who uses social network analysis in her work, decided that the students could map the social network of the freshman class (i.e., who interacts with whom most frequently). Students then used this network model to help them think about herd immunity, vaccination, and infectious disease transmission in their school.

To continue to learn about herd immunity, epidemics, vaccinations, and social network analysis, students had to do the following:

- **Obtain information** from a variety of sources (e.g., websites, online talks, magazine articles, textbook chapters, interviews with scientists and public health officials).

- **Evaluate that information** so they could decide not only what information was scientifically credible but also what information was relevant to their specific project and thus useful to their goals.

- **Communicate information** throughout their project. In this classroom example, students had to communicate what their project was about to the scientists they interviewed and to their classmates who agreed to participate in the social network survey. Students had to communicate updates to their teacher as the project developed. They shared a draft of their research findings with the local scientist they talked with initially, and she provided feedback on their ideas and writing. Students then used that feedback to finalize a scientific abstract about their project for publication in the school's newsletter, as well as for the creation of a public service announcement for their local community.

During these various activities, students engaged in a range of the disciplinary practices—but the practice of Obtaining, Evaluating, and Communicating Information played a central role. This practice factored into how students learned about relevant science-related information, how they made sense of that information in relation to their investigations, and how they shared the products of their investigations with others.

What Is the Practice of Obtaining, Evaluating, and Communicating Information All About?

Building on the National Research Council's *A Framework for K–12 Science Education* (*Framework*; NRC 2012), the *Next Generation Science Standards* (*NGSS*) (NGSS Lead States 2013) incorporates the practice of Obtaining, Evaluating, and Communicating Information throughout the K–12 spectrum and among a wide variety of performance expectations situated in different scientific and engineering disciplines. The following performance expectations illustrate how the practice of Obtaining, Evaluating, and Communicating Information appears in the *NGSS*:

- Communicate solutions that will reduce the impact of humans on the land, water, air, and/or other living things in the local environment (K-ESS3-3, Kindergarten; Earth and Human Activity).

- Gather and synthesize information that sensory receptors respond to stimuli by sending messages to the brain for immediate behavior or storage as memories (MS-LS1-8, Middle School; From Molecules to Organisms: Structures and Processes).

- Evaluate the validity and reliability of claims in published materials of the effects that different frequencies of electromagnetic radiation have when absorbed by matter (HS-PS4-4, High School; Waves and Their Applications in Technologies for Information Transfer).

As readers will notice, students across the grade levels and irrespective of DCIs are expected to obtain (from a variety of sources), evaluate (for credibility and for fit with the task at hand), and communicate (in a variety of ways, to a plethora of different audiences, and for myriad purposes) information as it relates to the science and engineering ideas they are learning and the phenomena they are explaining. **The practice of Obtaining, Evaluating, and Communicating Information involves students in gathering, critically examining, and using resources to further their collective investigations and sense-making about the natural and designed world.**[1] In this chapter, we describe this practice to give science educators a better sense of what is meant by performance expectations like the examples just listed. In other words, what does it look and sound like for students to engage in this practice in the multitude of ways that are intended, as well as for student sense-making and communicative purposes? What might not be intended by this practice as it is specified in the *Framework* and the *NGSS*? What are some challenges associated with this practice? In what follows, we explain more about this practice and how scientists and engineers participate in it. We also provide examples from different grade levels of how educators have helped students as they obtained, evaluated, and communicated science-related information. Last, we provide additional resources that educators can use to help students engage productively with this practice.

Why Is the Practice of Obtaining, Evaluating, and Communicating Information Important?

Like the other practices outlined in the *Framework* and the *NGSS*, the practice of Obtaining, Evaluating, and Communicating Information represents work that scientists and engineers routinely undertake to conduct their research; design and test their solutions, tools, and the like; and communicate information throughout the course of their work to each other, to others they work with, and to the general public (e.g., Bazerman 1988; Olson 2009; Sismondo 2010). By some accounts, over half of scientists' and engineers' time is associated with Obtaining, Evaluating, and Communicating Information (NRC 2012; Tenopir and King 2004). This practice involves important learning processes related to interpreting information, synthesizing personal understanding, and learning to make one's own thinking visible to others. Thus, the practice of Obtaining, Evaluating, and Communicating Information is useful to individual scientists and engineers as they make sense of the world. This practice is also essential to the ongoing work of the scientific and engineering communities as they collectively develop ideas and engage in design-related work. As one of the key practices of science and engineering highlighted in the *Framework* and the *NGSS*, this practice should be a prominent part of the sense-making students do during their K–12 science education.

As for what type of information students should have experience obtaining, evaluating, and communicating, we know that science- and engineering-related information is not composed of words alone; it also includes diagrams, graphs, charts, equations, interactive models, and the like. K–12 students learning and participating in science and

---

1. Readers might choose to explore various resources that outline possible progressions specific to this practice, such as the following: *http://ngss.nsta.org/Practices.aspx?id=8* and Appendix F of the *NGSS*.

engineering have to know how to find the information they need, how to interpret and evaluate it, and how to effectively communicate it using a variety of media, such as written text (words, symbols, diagrams, graphs), oral presentations, and multimedia productions. These disciplinary literacy-related skill sets (see Moje 2008) are valuable not only to those wanting to pursue careers in the sciences and engineering but also to *all* people, as everyone should know how to critically obtain and consume scientific and engineering-related information and products as a function of actively participating in local and global conversations, and as a function of personal and societal decision making.

Students should learn to obtain, evaluate, and communicate scientific and engineering-related information throughout their preK–12 educational careers. To fully engage in this practice, students need many and varied opportunities to learn how to effectively utilize the different skill sets encompassed by the practice. Students also need opportunities to understand that different disciplines in the sciences and engineering make use of different symbols, for example, and therefore, students need to know which symbols are appropriate for which disciplinary landscape, so that they can effectively obtain, evaluate, and communicate science- and engineering-related information. For example, chemistry is heavily focused on the coordinated use of multiple representations for atoms, molecules, and reactions. In another example, communicating solutions to engineering problems requires visual displays of diagrams further described by text and numerical values.

Working with text is another key competency related to Obtaining, Evaluating, and Communicating Information. Throughout their science education careers, students must read, interpret, and produce scientific texts, and they need support to become skilled in these areas. The term *text* in the *Framework* and the *NGSS* encompasses a large set of products (e.g., textbooks, trade books, films, blogs, public service announcements). Students need to work with texts in ways that make sense given the specific goals of their grade level or class. As science educators, we should not assume that helping students participate in Obtaining, Evaluating, and Communicating Information, as they engage in extended reading and writing tasks, is solely the responsibility of the English language arts teachers.

With that said, there is significant overlap between the practice of Obtaining, Evaluating, and Communicating Information, as discussed in the *Framework* and the *NGSS*, and the standards outlined in the *Common Core State Standards, English Language Arts* (*CCSS ELA*; NGAC and CCSSO 2010). As readers may be aware, the *CCSS ELA* contains a special section called Science and Technical Subjects, which was written exclusively for grades 6–12. This section contains standards relevant to reading, writing, speaking, and listening in science and engineering. *Literacy for Science: Exploring the Intersection of the Next Generation Science Standards and Common Core for ELA Standards* (NRC 2014) contains a table that shows the relationship between the various science and engineering practices in the *Framework* and the *NGSS* and the standard(s) in the *CCSS ELA* (NGAC and CCSSO 2010). With respect to Obtaining, Evaluating, and Communicating Information, the applicable *CCSS ELA* standards are (a) gathering relevant evidence and (b) translating information from one form to another.

People who actively engage in scientific communication themselves or who have helped support students learn the skill sets related to this practice can attest that learning how to read, interpret, and produce scientific and engineering-related text is challenging. This is because the language used in those texts (words, as well as other types of symbols) and the way that language is structured (e.g., passive voice, lengthy sentences, verbs used as nouns, arguments threaded throughout) can be intimidating, confusing, and strange (see Gee 2008). If students are not given ongoing opportunities to practice the various skills embedded in Obtaining, Evaluating, and Communicating Information, at increasing levels of complexity throughout the preK–12 spectrum, scientific and engineering-related communication will remain difficult.

How Can I Support and Assess the Practice of Obtaining, Evaluating, and Communicating Information in My Classroom?

What is involved in Obtaining, Evaluating, and Communicating Information? We provide various examples and resources later in the chapter, but we would first like to outline some details about how capacities related to the practice build over the preK–12 grade span. Even preK students, who may not yet be fluent in reading and writing, have developing literacy skills that enable them to understand and communicate information through visual representations (e.g., photographs, illustrations, graphs), discussions, and short text. Thus, students in the early grades (preK through third grade) are more than capable of participating in this practice and should be given ample opportunities to do so. For example, students can obtain books (including picture books) and other resources, such as science-related drawings, videos, and product information (e.g., labels on various food products). As the *Framework* notes, "Students [in the early grades] should be asked to engage in the communication of science, especially regarding the investigations they are conducting and the observations they are making" (NRC 2012, p. 76). Students should learn how to carefully detail their observations (in words or in other ways) and learn how to express their ideas about those observations (e.g., begin to formulate explanations). Students should be given opportunities to "both refine [their ideas] in response to questions and to ask questions of others to achieve clarification" (NRC 2012, p. 76).

In upper elementary and middle school—or before, depending on whether students and teachers feel that students are ready to developmentally engage—students should begin to learn how to interpret scientific and engineering-related texts. This should include explicit teaching related to how to read these types of texts, knowing that students have to learn how to not only read the words but also interpret the graphs, figures, diagrams, and other representations. Students need to learn how to decode the meanings of technical terms, as well as the meanings of more general academic terms (e.g., annotate, attribute, critique, generalize, qualify). However, decoding is only the first step. Students also need to learn how various conceptual ideas, represented by technical terms and representations, relate to each other and how we can use various elements of scientific language to convey these relationships (see Lemke 1990).

Scientific and engineering-related information needs to be critically interpreted, and thus students in these grade levels need to begin to learn how to evaluate scientific and engineering-related information. For example, how does one know whether information he or she located on the internet is scientifically accurate? What types of sources are scientifically reliable and suitable for any given task? In addition, students need explicit instruction about how to effectively search for and select sources—from using different search engines to locating people who might be helpful to scanning the tables of contents and indexes of books.

At the high school level, students should continue to develop and practice these skill sets. Students should locate

> more complex texts and a wider range of text materials, such as technical
> reports [and] scientific literature on the Internet. Moreover, students need
> opportunities to read and discuss general media reports with a critical eye
> and to read appropriate samples of adapted primary literature (Yarden 2009)
> to begin [to see] how science is communicated by science practitioners [i.e.,
> scientists and engineers]. (NRC 2012, p. 77)

In addition to obtaining, interpreting, and evaluating various types of information, students at all grade levels should also produce information in various forms and then communicate it to different audiences for a range of purposes. This may include sharing their initial ideas about a phenomenon with a peer or teacher or making a detailed presentation to an audience of community members. Students' production should further help them learn to "read" various types of scientific and engineering-related information (e.g., recognize structural elements, understand technical terms, and learn how to thread an argument throughout text and how to adequately support that argument with applicable evidence). Scientists and engineers communicate differently to different audiences. They communicate their knowledge to the broader public through events like science cafes. They share their research findings and conclusions with other scientists in their peer-reviewed journal articles. Therefore, students should also practice producing communications for different audiences and purposes.

In Tables 12.1–12.3 (pp. 266–268), we talk more about how and why scientists and engineers obtain, evaluate, and communicate information. Based on that, we note what students could do in science classrooms to participate in this practice. We also note some challenges students typically face during their participation.

There are various science-specific resources available to help students learn how to obtain, evaluate, and communicate information. For example, *Front-Page Science: Engaging Teens in Science Literacy* (Saul et al. 2012), a science writing and journalism resource, helps teachers and students think about the nuances associated with Obtaining, Evaluating, and Communicating Information and learn how to do that in the context of science writing for a public audience. In addition, there are a myriad of resources available that help students use science notebooks to communicate information (e.g., for materials applicable to grades K–5, see Fulwiler 2011; for materials applicable to middle school grades, see Marcarelli 2010).

Besides various science-specific resources, there are resources available that are associated with the fields of information processing and library sciences.[2] Granted, science teachers will need to modify and customize resources and tools found on these types of websites because, as noted, they are not always science specific, but we think learning more about information literacy in general is hugely helpful with respect to better understanding how to obtain, evaluate, and communicate science- and engineering-related information. For example, the Big Six (*http://big6.com*) is a website created by two educators, Mike Eisenberg and Bob Berkowitz. The website details various literacy goals for students (including information-seeking strategies, using information, and evaluating information). The site also provides lessons for teachers, resources that many might find useful (free handouts, presentations, videos), and information about literacy in general.

The Association of College and Research Libraries devotes a section of its website to information literacy resources (*www.ala.org/acrl/issues/infolit*). On this website, teachers can learn more about information literacy, access resources, and review standards for information literacy. This group has also developed "Information Literacy Standards for Science and Engineering/Technology" (*www.ala.org/acrl/standards/infolitscitech*).

---

2. We wish to thank our colleague, Sarah Evans, for providing the resources discussed in this section.

Table 12.1
Obtain scientific and engineering-related information

Use in science and engineering	Scientists and engineers are constantly obtaining information to inform and situate their work. For example, scientists might read research to better understand how their research question relates to other questions that have previously been investigated. Engineers might talk with those who will ultimately use their designs (i.e., clients or users) to better understand their needs. The process of obtaining information happens throughout the inquiry and designing process (not simply at the beginning).
Science classroom examples	• Young science learners can begin to consult resources (books—including picture books—and the internet) that teachers, librarians, parents, and others help identify, to purposefully gather information. • As students get older, they should obtain information from a variety of sources (magazines, texts, newspapers, the internet), and learn how to conduct fruitful searches using various databases and search engines. • In addition to text-based sources, students should also have practice conducting interviews with appropriate people—given the question(s) students are researching. Also, students should have opportunities to mine other types of sources (e.g., video, audio, photographs, graphical representations) for useful information.
Possible learner challenges	Teachers should consider not always giving students all of the information they will need to participate in any given activity. Students need to learn how to obtain information for various purposes. However, there are some known challenges when students look for information: • Some students are not aware of the variety of resources available to them or resist asking for expert help (e.g., librarians) when obtaining information. Students need to learn the range of advice and help available to them and where to look for support (in addition to their teachers). • Many students have difficulty knowing exactly how to search for needed information online (e.g., what key words to use, which search engines will be most helpful given the task, how to interpret and filter search results). • Students may not always know how to identify the most helpful types of sources to use for any given investigation or exploration.

Table 12.2

Evaluate scientific and engineering-related information

Use in science and engineering	Once scientists and engineers locate information to use as part of their investigative and design work, they need to evaluate that information to be certain that it is maximally helpful with respect to their work. Two issues can arise: (1) Information might not be credible, or (2) the information may be credible but not a good fit for the task at hand.
Science classroom examples	• Students can be asked to compare and contrast examples of scientifically credible and noncredible sources, and discuss the features of each. Teachers can model for students their own materials and thought processes as they decide whether a source is credible. That way, students will have access to their teachers' practices and thinking related to judging whether a source is credible. • Students should have ample opportunities to evaluate the credibility of any given source relative to the investigative task at hand. Again, teachers can model how to do this as part of instruction.
Possible learner challenges	• Students do not always know how to judge whether information they have obtained is credible. • Students may have trouble evaluating what information (within any given credible source) is actually valuable to the task at hand.

Table 12.3
Communicate scientific and engineering-related information

Use in science and engineering	Scientists and engineers are constantly communicating information. They do this in a variety of forms (e.g., via e-mail, phone calls, videoconferencing sessions, conference presentations; during research group meetings; on research posters; in papers; and on blueprints and other types of design specification documents). They communicate to a myriad of audiences (e.g., other scientists and engineers, members of the general public) and for a variety of purposes depending on their audiences. Scientists and engineers communicate at all stages of their investigative and design work. Good communication is essential, as it can serve to teach others about what one is investigating or designing, help ensure that everyone involved is making sense of the task, and highlight differences in interpretation, as well as help ensure that the work runs smoothly.
Science classroom examples	• Students need ample grade-level appropriate practice communicating the same information to different audiences and at different times throughout their investigative work (i.e., not only at the end of that work). They can then reflect on how their communication might change depending on audience and purpose. • Students need practice constructing different kinds of communication (e.g., oral presentations, written documents, drawings of figures) and reflecting on why a certain form of communication might be ideal given audience and purpose. • Students need practice with all technical aspects of communicating (e.g., learning how to properly cite sources, e-mail etiquette, and how to properly format a research paper and a science notebook entry).
Possible learner challenges	• Students do not always know how to correctly attribute information (e.g., proper format for citations) when they communicate their investigative work. • Students sometimes struggle with communicating the same information but for different purposes to different audiences (e.g., communicating to an audience of scientists versus an audience of younger students). • Students need practice with different communication types (e.g., oral presentations, written research papers, science notebook entries, proposals for funding, and drawings of models).

Potential Misinterpretations of the Practice of Obtaining, Evaluating, and Communicating Information

We have spent time describing the practice of Obtaining, Evaluating, and Communicating Information so that readers can better understand what it involves. We think it is equally important to spend time discussing what we believe the practice does not intend. First, this practice is part and parcel of students' investigations and design work in the sciences and engineering and should not be treated as an addition that could potentially be cut from students' experiences if students and teachers are short on time. When many of us were in school, it was common to select or be assigned a topic in science class that we would research using a resource like the *World Book Encyclopedia*, and then write a paper detailing what we learned. Although obtaining, evaluating, and learning from resources is certainly an aspect of scientific and engineering work (e.g., conducting a literature review as part of a research study, learning more about something observed during an observation, practicing techniques used in science journalism or other types of science writing), we do not believe that this practice is code for the more traditional idea of "report writing." The skills involved in the practice of Obtaining, Evaluating, and Communicating Information are critical to actively constructing knowledge, and then authentically communicating ideas and understandings to others. Thus, the practice involves students gaining experience using a variety of scientific and engineering texts (and not simply a single textbook) as part of their sense-making relative to DCIs and crosscutting concepts.

Additionally, we have already discussed the importance of technical vocabulary in the sciences and in engineering. One certainly has to know the languages of the sciences and engineering to interpret texts, effectively produce them, and communicate one's ideas. However, the practice of Obtaining, Evaluating, and Communicating Information is not simply about "memorizing vocabulary words." If students are only memorizing terms, the meanings of those terms (e.g., in relation to important DCIs, in relation to their investigative work) are lost, and the exercise becomes a memory task instead of a task situated in larger investigative and communicative practices. Scientific language takes on conceptual meaning only through repeated attempts at using language in the context of real science activity—for example, expressing one's ideas to others, documenting an investigation and explaining natural phenomena, and communicating the details of scientific investigations and engineering designs.

What Is *Not* Intended by the Obtaining, Evaluating, and Communicating Information Practice

- Interaction with scientific information as an add-on or in ways that are not integrated with ongoing sense-making in the classroom

- Stand-alone reports of science facts from online or print resources

- A focus on decontextualized vocabulary work

How Can We Work Toward Equity With Regard to Obtaining, Evaluating, and Communicating Information?

Information and our ways of communicating it are cultural artifacts (see Medin and Bang 2014). The science and engineering practices generally hold the promise of supporting important cognitive, social, and cultural learning processes. With respect to the cultural dimensions of these practices, scientists and science learners alike bring their worldviews, interests, language repertoires, and developing expertise to their participation in scientific practices. There is often an artificial distinction between what counts as science and what is not considered science (Calabrese Barton 1998; Rosebery et al. 2010; Warren et al. 2001). This can especially be true of the Obtaining, Evaluating, and Communicating Information practice with its specific use of technical terms, unfamiliar sentence structures, and specific genres. It is important to realize that learners bring significant knowledge and reasoning strategies that can be leveraged as they obtain, evaluate, and communicate information. The *Framework* states, "Recognizing that language and discourse patterns vary across culturally diverse groups, researchers point to the importance of accepting, even encouraging, students' classroom use of informal or native language and familiar modes of interaction" (NRC 2012, p. 285). Classroom instruction should leverage how youth have learned to talk about nature and to communicate with others.

It is also important to realize that scientists often engage in creative ways of communicating their ideas related to natural phenomena. There can be a tendency to focus too much attention on the "final form" written products of science and engineering as we engage students in this practice, and not enough on the everyday talk and gestures that scientists and engineers use to grapple with their ideas. Students can feel alienated from learning science by the cultural mismatch between their orientation to interpreting and communicating about the natural world and approaches to Obtaining, Evaluating, and Communicating Information that are thought to be "culturally neutral."

Last, and as we have previously discussed, it is important for students to communicate about their work with a wide variety of audiences and for different purposes. If students throughout their preK–12 career are only obtaining, evaluating, interpreting, and communicating scientific and engineering-related information to and for their teachers and so that they can receive a grade, much of the authenticity of this practice will be lost. When possible, students should be practicing the various skill sets associated with this practice by repeatedly communicating with each other, parents, community members, scientists and engineers, other teachers, and so forth—in addition to their own teacher.

What Does It Look Like When Students Participate in the Practice of Obtaining, Evaluating, and Communicating Information?

In this section of the chapter, we use illustrative examples of students participating in activities where they are obtaining, evaluating, and communicating science-related information. We have created these examples based on some of the classroom work we have codesigned with teachers and have implemented with them and their students. In each case, we describe an aspect of the classroom work and its connection to this practice.

OBTAINING, EVALUATING, AND COMMUNICATING INFORMATION AS PART OF A PRE-K RESEARCH ACTIVITY

Young children are curious about the world around them and participate in many activities that can be related to science and engineering in a variety of ways (e.g., with respect to ideas and concepts, but also with respect to science and engineering practices). The *Framework* and the *NGSS* call for a significant focus on providing science learning opportunities in preschool and early elementary school, so it is important to consider how our youngest students, who are still learning to read and write, can engage in the practices of science. In this example, teachers from two preK classrooms, collaborating with university researchers, developed an approach to science instruction that aligns with the vision in the *Framework* by incorporating students' science-related interests and experiences while engaging them in practices and helping them develop an understanding of core ideas and make connections to crosscutting concepts.

In the spring of their preK year, the students were engaged in a unit on garden ecosystems. This unit aligned with the kindergarten performance expectation K-LS1-1, which asks students to "use observations to describe patterns of what plants and animals (including humans) need to survive." Following a field trip to a nearby garden, students had the opportunity to discuss their observations from that day and began to raise many questions about insects and other living creatures found in a garden (e.g., aphids, bees, worms, spiders). Given the unit's focus on identifying what plants and animals need to survive, the students were very interested in what particular animals in the garden might eat. To allow students to investigate their own questions, the teachers offered what they called a Research Day.

Earlier in the year, they had primed their students for this work by leading a whole-class discussion about the differences between fiction and nonfiction books as a way to help learners begin to understand different sources of information. They used books about animals as examples and asked the students to think about features that would help them distinguish the difference between fictional storybooks and nonfiction, informational

Figure 12.1

Eleanor dictating her research findings about ladybugs to a teacher

books. Following that discussion and after hearing the kinds of questions students had previously asked, the teachers and the school librarian preselected relevant nonfiction books for students to use as resources on this Research Day to investigate their individual questions. Students then drew, dictated, and shared their research findings with their peers.

To learn more about the organisms they were seeing in the garden, the teachers and librarian preselected relevant books after hearing the kinds of questions students had asked to use as resources on this Research Day. One student, Eleanor (all names are pseudonyms unless otherwise noted), was immediately attracted to a book with colorful illustrations of ladybugs in a garden—an insect she had wondered about previously. A teacher came over to read the text to her, and Eleanor, satisfied with the information, drew a detailed picture of a ladybug surrounded by aphids on her research paper. She then dictated information she had just learned about ladybugs to be written down on her paper by a teacher (see Figure 12.1): "Sometimes ladybugs' food runs out and there are not enough aphids to go around. The ladybugs gather in a swarm and fly off somewhere near to survive."

Here, the teacher's support of the students' individual interests allowed Eleanor to find information that provided further evidence related to DCI LS2 (Ecosystems: Interactions, Energy, and Dynamics) in their garden ecosystems unit: Animals depend on their surroundings for survival.

With Research Day, all students were given opportunities to obtain information from their school library resources related to the phenomena in the world that they were investigating. Though they only used one type of resource (nonfiction books), the teachers and students also discussed other sources where they might find information (by speaking with other people, searching the internet, or making their own observations). The preK students were not yet able to fully evaluate the credibility of their sources or critically interpret the information gathered; however, they did begin thinking about the differences between fictional and nonfiction books—a starting place for thinking about the credibility of a resource. In addition, they were evaluating the content in front of them in terms of determining whether the resource provided information that would answer their individual questions (e.g., because Eleanor was interested in ladybugs, she bypassed the books on other kinds of insects). The students also had multiple opportunities to communicate the information they gathered. During the activity, the students dictated information to a teacher and used drawings to illustrate the information. At the conclusion of each Research Day, the students were asked to stand in front of the class and share their research papers with their peers, describing their drawings and explaining what they learned that day. Later, the teachers compiled the research papers into a book that was displayed in the classroom. Each Research Day resulted in a collection of student research that was displayed in the classroom and revisited by the students and their parents. Students were supported in an initial form of the Obtaining, Evaluating, and Communicating Information practice, using books purposefully to learn about topics of their own interest and collectively sharing their knowledge with teachers, peers, and families through their writing, drawing, and speaking.

OBTAINING, EVALUATING, AND COMMUNICATING INFORMATION AS PART OF A FIFTH-GRADE PERSONAL HEALTH EXPLORATION

The aim of this fifth-grade unit about various topics and concepts of microbiology (e.g., the distinction between animal and plant cells and between disease-causing pathogens and beneficial microorganisms) is to engage students in personally consequential science, while providing opportunities for them to practice different techniques (e.g., using a microscope, culturing microorganisms, obtaining applicable information on the internet). Ultimately, the unit is meant to help them learn disciplinary knowledge and conduct research. This unit was collaboratively designed by teachers and researchers and has been used in various classrooms since 2007. This unit targets several DCIs, such as LS1.A (Structure and Function). Students participated in a variety of activities to learn about personally consequential microbiology, from culturing microorganisms found in their schools to conducting investigations with yeast to conducting hand-washing investigations. As shown in Figure 12.2 (p. 274), the students' culminating project was a public service announcement (PSA) about a microbiology-related topic of choice (e.g., food poisoning). Students ultimately took the message noted on their PSAs out into their communities and engaged various audiences with microbiology concepts and practices (often related to human health).[3]

During the course of the unit, students engaged in aspects of the Obtaining, Evaluating, and Communicating Information practice to make sense of relevant information sources, to develop and articulate their scientific ideas, and to communicate their understanding to others in multiple forms. They participated in this practice in the usual ways we might anticipate given standard practices in K–12 science classrooms. For example, they read various materials to learn information, and they documented the results of their investigations and their related scientific explanations in science notebooks. However,

---

3. See Bell et al. 2012 for more information about this unit and its connection to the practice of Obtaining, Evaluating, and Communicating Information.

Figure 12.2

Public service announcement created by students about a health topic of personal interest

they also made personal and community-related connections to the unit by taking photographs of objects, practices, products, and the like that represented student, family, and community thinking about what it takes to stay healthy or get better when sick. As a way to make sense of these photographs and evaluate them with respect to their connections to unit themes, students collectively analyzed their class sets of photographs—in small groups and then as whole classes—to look for distinct categories and emergent patterns. Students communicated the range of family and community health practices through their photographs and the descriptions of their photographs. These picture-taking activities took place toward the beginning of the unit so that students' photographs and students' analyses of these photographs could be used throughout the unit as sense-making objects and as examples of how microorganisms both positively and negatively affect students' lives. Students also used their photographs to generate ideas for microbiology-related research projects that they conducted and that served as the bases for their PSAs. Recall that the Obtaining, Evaluating, and Communicating Information practice is not solely associated with culminating course projects, artifacts, or activities. Students can and should be engaging in this practice throughout the instructional sequences associated with their learning experiences, especially as a strategy for documenting and communicating their developing scientific understanding.

OBTAINING, EVALUATING, AND COMMUNICATING INFORMATION AS PART OF AN EIGHTH-GRADE CLASSROOM DEBATE

This example highlights how three scientific practices—Obtaining, Evaluating, and Communicating Information; Constructing Explanations and Designing Solutions; and Engaging in Argument From Evidence—can be productively sequenced to support students' conceptual learning. Scientists often communicate and discuss evidence-based arguments that support or critique one or more explanations for the causes of prior events or natural phenomena when they give talks, present posters, publish papers, or have research meetings. We want students to engage in the science and engineering practices in similar, coordinated ways.

For three decades, Doug Kirkpatrick (his actual name; he's known as "Mr. K") taught middle school physical science. For more than two decades, he collaborated with a research team from a nearby university to develop curricula that extensively used computer-learning environments to support students' science investigations (Linn and Hsi 2000). Each semester, Mr. K spent considerable effort turning each of his six periods of eighth-grade students studying physical science into "scientific communities writ small." He wanted students to produce, share, debate, and refine their ideas about the natural world in ways similar to how practicing scientists do it—by working with their peers to develop shared causal explanations for scientific phenomena.

Mr. K taught a light curriculum unit where students conducted four weeks of hands-on experiments related to the properties of light, embedded in DCIs PS4.B and PS4.C (e.g., light intensity over distance, how light travels through space from distant stars, reflection, absorption, and energy conversion). Students ended the unit by engaging in an eight-day debate project as a way to integrate their understanding of how light works. The debate was pedagogically framed around the scientific model of light (i.e., that light travels forever until absorbed) versus a counter position that mapped onto many students' intuitive ideas about light (i.e., that light "dies out" as it travels away from a light source). Students evaluated disparate sources of information—from their classroom experiments, numerous web sources and advertisements, and their own life experiences—according to scientific criteria. In addition, they evaluated a shared corpus of science-related information, data, and evidence. They then constructed, tested, and refined explanations for science phenomena and, finally, engaged in two days of whole-class debate about how light works (for more information about this example, see Bell 2004).

Figure 12.3
Written explanation produced by student pair as they analyze a piece of evidence from a shared corpus

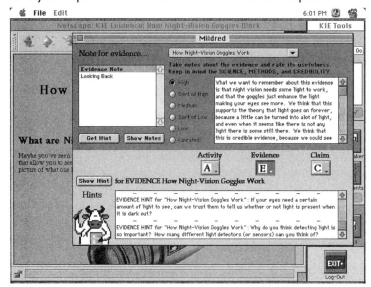

Figure 12.3 shows the written argument created by one student pair (out of 15–16 groups in a class). For each piece of evidence in the set, students were given the sentence-starter, "We think this supports the theory ____ because … " In addition to this "causal explanation prompt," students also reflected on, and learned to apply, multiple relevant criteria—related to how well the evidence fit with scientific knowledge, whether appropriate methods were used, the trustworthiness of the source, and the usefulness of the information for the debate topic.

Each student pair created an argument map using a software tool called SenseMaker where they related pieces of evidence (shown as dots) to conceptual claims (shown as boxes) by writing a causal explanation (see Figure 12.4). These argument maps allowed for an easy comparison of students' ideas during the classroom debate by making student thinking visible.

In a moment of classroom debate, Eli (a student) argued that a piece of evidence was irrelevant to his position after he had evaluated the information it contained. That piece of evidence showed that it is much more difficult to see an individual far away on a field using a smaller light than a larger light. He said this evidence did not help distinguish between the two theories (light goes on forever until absorbed or it dies out). Another student, Kathryn, provided a different perspective, saying that the light intensity drops off over distance until you can no longer see it although it is still there, which led Eli to reconsider the evidence. This approach to drawing the relationships between conceptual ideas and evidence allowed for more focused questions to be posed to peers (e.g., sharing different explanatory perspectives or criteria for interpreting evidence), and the detailed written arguments allowed students to share and refine their conceptual ideas at a deeper level. In this kind of discussion, the desire is to have students be *hard* on the ideas—yet pushing for a shared consensus of understanding—but *easy* on the people. By Obtaining, Evaluating, and Communicating Information, students synthesized what they knew and developed an integrated conceptual understanding of how light works. Students were also able to develop knowledge about the enterprise of science—that it is a social enterprise that progresses through the evaluation of evidence, systematic argumentation from evidence, and the collaborative debate of ideas (Bell and Linn 2002).

How Can I Get Started on Engaging Students in the Practice of Obtaining, Evaluating, and Communicating Information in the Classroom?

The obtain, evaluate, and communicate tables in this chapter (see Tables 12.1–12.3, pp. 266–268) showcase some common challenges that students tend to face

Figure 12.4

SenseMaker argument jointly constructed by a student pair for use in a classroom debate about the properties of light

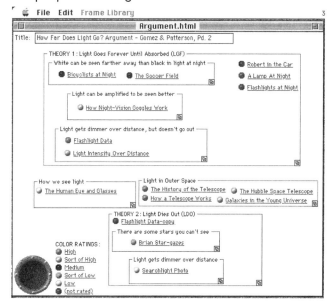

when learning the nuances of this practice. In this section, we want to address two others: (1) reading, comprehending, and interpreting expository, multimodal texts, and (2) enacting this practice when students' first language is not English. Those familiar with these challenges know that there are whole fields devoted to researching elements of them, as well as designing and developing tools, strategies, and other materials to help support students and teachers with respect to these challenges. Although it is beyond the scope of this chapter to adequately describe the plethora of research and development efforts related to these two challenges, we do want to share some general strategies that teachers and students might find helpful. Readers might also wish to consult *Literacy for Science* (NRC 2014).

READING, COMPREHENDING, AND INTERPRETING EXPOSITORY TEXT

It is well known that many students struggle to read, comprehend, and interpret expository text, and this seems especially true of students in middle and high school. We have collected example strategies that teachers might use to help students, including citation information so that teachers and students can learn more about them:

- Prediction guides, anticipation guides, and question guides as tied to any particular text (see Martin 2002)

- Learning logs to help students select particular aspects of different texts that seem particularly helpful to their sense-making of DCIs as related to their investigative or design work (see Vacca and Vacca 1999)

- Graphic organizers (e.g., concept maps, flowcharts, tables, matrixes; see Coburn 2003)

- Text annotation and text summaries (see Gomez et al. 2010)

As mentioned previously, science and engineering texts are not only expository in nature but also multimodal, meaning that they are composed of words in addition to graphs, tables, charts, diagrams, and the like. Interpreting multimodal texts is not trivial because students have to interpret the words and the visuals, and then make sense of how the words and visuals work together to convey meaning, support an argument, and so forth (see Lemke 2002). Students at all grade levels need substantial and repeated practice reading and interpreting these types of texts. Of course, reading and interpreting scientific and engineering-related texts is an important skill to learn that will help students make sense out of these texts and help them better understand their investigative or design work. However, learning to master the art of reading and interpreting expository, multimodal text is also essential to learning how to produce these types of texts. As part of their investigative and design work, students should produce a variety of textual products (e.g., research design plans, science notebook entries, scientific abstracts, proposals for funding, scientific posters, research papers, videos, public service announcements, and newspaper articles for lay audiences). Learning what these various scientific genres of writing look like structurally (e.g., what structural elements are present in each type of scientific or engineering text, where these structural elements are located in the text, what their functions are within the text) is critical to being scientifically literate.

SUPPORTING STUDENTS WHO ARE LEARNING ENGLISH AS THEY LEARN SCIENCE

It is important to realize that learning science by engaging in the disciplinary practices is highly language intensive in general. Given the rapidly increasing level of linguistic diversity in the United States, it is increasingly crucial for teachers to be able to support students in science who are also English language learners (ELLs). As Lee, Quinn, and Valdés (2013) note, the act of helping science learners who are ELLs needs to be reframed from "the traditional emphasis on language structure (phonology, morphology, vocabulary, and syntax) to an emphasis on language use for communication and learning" (p. 223). These scholars urge teachers and others supporting students who are

ELLs to help students understand what one *does* with language in the science classroom. In other words, obtaining, evaluating, and communicating information are active and social processes that are given meaning through activity, such as science investigations. Students who are ELLs can be supported in learning both science and English through their participation in scientific practices.

Many students will struggle to express in English what they understand or are interested in. It is important to not presume a lack of science interest or ability in science because a learner lacks fluency in English—and may not be able to produce canonical oral or written language responses. Students who are still learning English can reason deeply about science, and language development supports should be provided to help them express their understanding.

Concluding Remarks

In this chapter, we have outlined the details of the practice of Obtaining, Evaluating, and Communicating Information and provided examples and resources related to implementing the practice. We hope that the information here will help teachers and others learn more about this practice and learn ways to support students as they participate in this practice as part of their investigative work in K–12 science classrooms. As is the case with all of practices outlined in the *Framework* and the *NGSS*, students will need support and a myriad of opportunities to engage in the practice when learning how to effectively obtain, evaluate, and communicate scientific and engineering-related information. Yet, it is worth the effort on the part of both students and teachers because the skills and competencies associated with this practice are useful not only to students in their K–12 science education but also to a variety of other ventures, both in and out of school, in which students will participate both now and in the future.

Acknowledgments

We extend deep gratitude to the children, youth, families, and teachers who participated in our research. We also gratefully acknowledge the intellectual influence of our colleagues. Funding for research reported in this chapter came from the National Science Foundation as part of the KIE and WISE projects at the University of California, Berkeley, under Grant No. RED-9453861 and Grant No. MDR-8850552; as part of the Learning in Informal and Formal Environments Science of Learning Center under Grant No. SBE-0354453 and Grant No. SMA-0835854; and from the Bill and Melinda Gates Foundation as part of the Educurious project. The opinions expressed herein are those of the authors and not necessarily those of the foundations and other agencies that helped fund this work.

References

Bazerman, C. 1988. *Shaping written knowledge: The genre and activity of the experimental article in science.* Madison, WI: University of Wisconsin Press.

Bell, P. 2004. Promoting students' argument construction and collaborative debate in the science classroom. In *Internet environments for science education*, ed. M. C. Linn, E. A. Davis, and P. Bell, 115–143. Mahwah, NJ: Lawrence Erlbaum.

Bell, P., L. A. Bricker, C. Tzou, T. Lee, and K. Van Horne. 2012. Engaging learners in scientific practices related to obtaining, evaluating, and communicating information. *Science Scope* 36 (3): 17–22.

Bell, P., and M. C. Linn. 2002. Beliefs about science: How does science instruction contribute? In *Personal epistemology: The psychology of beliefs about knowledge and knowing*, ed. B. K. Hofer and P. R. Pintrich, 321–346. Mahwah, NJ: Lawrence Erlbaum.

Calabrese Barton, A. 1998. Reframing "science for all" through the politics of poverty. *Educational Policy* 12 (5): 525–541.

Coburn, D. G. 2003. Using graphic organizers. *Science Scope* 27 (1): 46–48.

Fulwiler, B. R. 2011. *Writing in science in action.* Portsmouth, NH: Heinemann.

Gee, J. P. 2008. What is academic language? In *Teaching science to English language learners: Building on students' strengths*, ed. A. S. Rosebery and B. Warren, 57–70. Arlington, VA: NSTA Press.

Gomez, K., J. Sherer, P. Herman, L. Gomez, J. W. Zywica, and A. Williams. 2010. Supporting meaningful science learning: Reading and writing science. In *Science education as a pathway to teaching language literacy*, ed. A. J. Rodriguez, 93–112. Rotterdam, The Netherlands: Sense.

Lee, O., H. Quinn, and G. Valdés. 2013. Science and language for English language learners in relation to the *Next Generation Science Standards* and with implications for *Common Core State Standards for English Language Arts and Mathematics. Educational Researcher* 42 (4): 223–233.

Lemke, J. L. 1990. *Talking science: Language, learning, and values.* Westport, CT: Ablex.

Lemke, J. L. 2002. Travels in hypermodality. *Visual Communication* 1 (3): 299–325.

Linn, M. C., and S. Hsi. 2000. *Computers, teachers, peers: Science learning partners.* Mahwah, NJ: Lawrence Erlbaum.

Marcarelli, K. 2010. *Teaching science with interactive notebooks.* Thousand Oaks, CA: Corwin.

Martin, G. 2002. Reading, writing, and comprehending: Encouraging active reading in the science classroom. *The Science Teacher* 69 (7): 56–59.

Medin, D. L, and M. Bang. 2014. The cultural side of science communication. *Proceedings of the National Academy of Sciences* 111 (Suppl. 4): 13583–13584. *www.pnas.org/cgi/doi/10.1073/pnas.1317510111.*

Moje, E. B. 2008. Foregrounding the disciplines in secondary literacy teaching and learning: A call for change. *Journal of Adolescent and Adult Literacy* 52 (2): 96–107.

National Governors Association Center for Best Practices and Council of Chief State School Officers (NGAC and CCSSO). 2010. *Common Core State Standards*. Washington, DC: NGAC and CCSSO.

National Research Council (NRC). 2012. *A framework for K–12 science education: Practices, crosscutting concepts, and core ideas*. Washington, DC: National Academies Press.

National Research Council (NRC). 2014. *Literacy for science: Exploring the intersection of the Next Generation Science Standards and Common Core for ELA Standards*. Washington, DC: National Academies Press.

NGSS Lead States. 2013. *Next Generation Science Standards: For states, by states*. Washington, DC: National Academies Press. *www.nextgenscience.org/next-generation-science-standards*.

Olson, R. 2009. *Don't be such a scientist: Talking substance in an age of style*. Washington, DC: Island Press.

Rosebery, A. S., M. Ogonowski, M. DiSchino, and B. Warren. 2010. "The coat traps all your body heat": Heterogeneity as fundamental to learning. *Journal of the Learning Sciences* 19 (3): 322–357.

Saul, W., A. Kohnen, A. Newman, and L. Pearce. 2012. *Front-page science: Engaging teens in science literacy*. Arlington, VA: NSTA Press.

Sismondo, S. 2010. *An introduction to science and technology studies*. 2nd ed. Malden, MA: Wiley-Blackwell.

Tenopir, C., and D. W. King. 2004. *Communication patterns of engineers*. Hoboken, NJ: Wiley.

Vacca, R. T., and J. L. Vacca. 1999. *Content area reading: Literacy and learning across the curriculum*. 6th ed. New York: Longman.

Warren, B., C. Ballenger, M. Ogonowski, A. Rosebery, and J. Hudicourt-Barnes. 2001. Rethinking diversity in learning science: The logic of everyday sensemaking. *Journal of Research in Science Teaching* 38 (5): 529–552.

Yarden, A. 2009. Reading scientific texts: Adapting primary literature for promoting scientific literacy. *Research in Science Education* 39 (3): 307–311.

13

ENGINEERING PRACTICES

CHRISTINE M. CUNNINGHAM

One novel aspect of *A Framework for K–12 Science Education* (*Framework*; NRC 2012) and the new *Next Generation Science Standards* (*NGSS*; NGSS Lead States 2013) is that engineering holds a more prominent position than in past science education standards. Students are now asked to learn not only about the natural world in which they live through practices of science but also about the human-made, or engineered, world that surrounds them by solving problems through the practices of engineering design (NGSS Lead States 2013). The *Framework* is also concerned with helping build students' awareness of the type of work engineers do, stating that "engaging in the practices of engineering … helps students to understand the work of engineers" (NRC 2012, pp. 42–43).

For many educators, introducing engineering and engineering practices into the classroom may be new. In this chapter, I explain some defining features of engineering practice and provide illustrative examples of how teachers can frame activities to engage children in engineering practices and sense-making. The chapter concludes with a look at how an engineering context can invite children to learn and apply science ideas as they engage in science and engineering practices.

First, it is important to understand that engineering and science are distinct but related fields (Cunningham and Carlsen 2014). In particular, science and engineering have different goals: Scientists aim to describe, explain, and predict the natural world; engineers aim to solve problems. As a result of these goals, the outcome of scientists' and engineers' work is also different. Scientists work toward producing new knowledge; engineers work toward producing new technologies (objects, systems, or processes). However, in the real world, scientists and engineers may move back and forth between both types of pursuits as they undertake their work. For example, scientists often use instruments to measure or study physical phenomena. They may need to design and construct new instruments tailored to their research—so they engineer the cutting-edge tools they then use to collect data. In response, the new information gathered from this new technology advances their data collection, the quality of the data and patterns from those data, and the related scientific theories.

Similarly, developing effective solutions often requires engineers to use scientific information. For example, biomedical engineers developing a new type of bandage to aid wound recovery in burn victims need to draw on their scientific knowledge of biology and chemistry as they design their product to better determine the most effective ways that the bandages can function. As they conduct investigations, engineers develop more advanced solutions for the problems. At the same time, they may also develop new understandings of the natural systems they are working with, thus contributing to the description of the natural world in the process of engineering.

Although the purposes and outcomes of their work may differ, scientists and engineers use many similar practices, and they engage in multiple practices as they work (Kelly 2011; Kelly and Chen 1999). Students in elementary, middle, and high school should begin gaining capacity in these practices as they participate in science and engineering design activities. To encourage educators to develop students' science and engineering skills and processes to make sense of the world and develop solutions, the *Framework* and the *NGSS* highlight eight practices that are common to both fields. However, while many of the practices that children use to make sense of their natural and physical world are similar, the *NGSS* also explicitly recognizes that the goals and outcomes of science and engineering can be different by stating that "engineering design is not just applied science … the practices of engineering have much in common with the practices of science, although engineering design has a different purpose and product than scientific inquiry" (NGSS Lead States 2013, p. 103).

These differences in goal and outcomes manifest directly in two of the eight *NGSS* practices, Asking Questions and Defining Problems (practice 1) and Constructing Explanations and Designing Solutions (practice 6). Each of the titles of these practices contains two clauses; the latter is included to foreground practices prevalent in engineering. Engineers not only ask questions throughout their work but also need to define the problem to be solved. Engineers may construct explanations about how a system or technology works, but they do this as they strive to create solutions to the problem at hand. While engineers engage in their design process, they also use the other six practices highlighted in the *Framework* and the *NGSS*. However, they do so in the service of designing technologies.

In the first part of the chapter, I explain the importance of the two practices that include elements designed to address the different goals and outcomes of engineering. What might these practices look like in classrooms? How can they contribute to students' sense-making of the world in which they live? Later in the chapter, I share a classroom case that illustrates the entire design cycle process and call out instances where each of the eight *NGSS* practices is occurring.

Asking Questions and Defining Problems

Ms. Martinez's second graders are embarking on a unit that explores the basic life cycles of plants and pollinators. She frames the unit with a problem that she needs her children's help to solve: She has a plant that is not producing berries. She asks the children to help figure out why this is happening and to help her solve this problem.

After Ms. Martinez lays out the general challenge, she asks, "What questions do you have that might help you solve this problem?" To scaffold her young children's responses, she explains that they will address this question in two parts. First, they will focus on understanding why this phenomenon is happening. Ms. Martinez asks her students what they'd like to know about the plant. As children call out questions, she writes them on the board:

- How does the plant usually make berries?

- How does the plant grow?

- When does it make berries?

- Why does it make berries?

- What does it need to make berries?

- Does the plant have everything it needs? If not, what is missing?

These questions begin a series of science investigations about the life cycle of plants. Once Ms. Martinez is confident that her students have built an understanding of the life cycle of a plant and particularly of the roles of flowers, pollen, and seeds in reproduction, she returns to the original challenge and asks students what they think the problem with her plant might be. Again, the students offer a wide variety of responses, some directly stemming from their science work and, of course, some from their own ideas and experiences. Class discussion helps all children understand that the plant lacks a pollinator— something it needs to make berries.

Ms. Martinez then focuses the class on the second part of the challenge. She explains to her children that now that they have identified the problem, they can help solve it by designing a hand pollinator that can move pollen from one plant to another. Again, she invites the children to brainstorm questions they'd like to know the answers to so they can complete this task. The children's responses include the following:

- What materials can we use?

- How many materials can we use? Are there limits?

- How much time do we have?

- How can we test our designs?

- Do we have to be able to use our pollinator more than once?

- Has anyone else ever solved a similar problem? What did she or he do?

After the class has created a list, Ms. Martinez reads each question and provides an answer. She makes clear the criteria for a successful pollinator. And through dialogue with her students, she identifies the constraints that will limit and shape children's designs. When the children have a clear understanding of the problem and task, they begin to work in small groups to generate ideas for how they might design a technology to solve the problem.

This scenario illustrates how a class of young learners works together to understand and define the problem they are going to tackle. Similarly to the students and classes described in Chapter 5 (p. 87), Ms. Martinez's pupils do this by asking questions. The role that questioning plays in unpacking an engineering problem is articulated by the *Framework*: "For engineering, [children] should ask questions to define the problem to be solved and to elicit ideas that lead to the constraints and specification for its solution" (NRC 2012, p. 56).

In this unit, Ms. Martinez is focusing on *NGSS* performance expectation 2-LS2-2: "Develop a simple model that mimics the function of an animal in dispersing seeds or pollinating plants" (NGSS Lead States 2013, p. 18). She has chosen to frame the unit with an engineering design challenge, which she sets in a real-world context—that of her berryless plant—to help engage her students. She knows this task will require the children to construct and use knowledge about the life cycle and basic needs of plants. As her students make sense of this task, they will need to draw on science ideas and engage in a range of science and engineering practices.

Because the children in her class are seven and eight years old, Ms. Martinez carefully scaffolds their questions, work, and investigations. Thus, after introducing the general question, she breaks it into smaller pieces. There are two kinds of problems that her children need to define. First, they need to identify what the problem is that is causing the plant not to produce berries. To do this, they need to understand the life cycle of a normal plant. So Ms. Martinez first prompts her students to ask questions about what they need to know to diagnose the problem. In this part of the unit, her students are engaging in Asking Questions and Defining Problems at the grade K–2 level, as specified by the *NGSS*. They "ask questions … to find more information about the natural and/or designed world(s)" and "ask and/or identify questions that can be answered by an investigation" (NGSS Lead States 2013, p. 51).

Determining the nature of the problem that needs to be solved is a critical aspect of the Defining Problems engineering practice. For example, some questions a teacher might pose include "What is not working or could be improved?" "What is our goal, or what does our new solution need to do?" "What do we already know that we can draw on to help us solve the problem?" These are all questions the students address as they struggle to begin their unit.

After the class has come to a consensus about what is "broken" in her plant's system, Ms. Martinez supports them as they grapple with their second problem, defining the parameters of a successful technology (a hand pollinator). This ensures that the students clearly understand the task at hand. This also reflects an *NGSS* recommendation for grades K–2 for this practice, which is to "define a simple problem that can be solved through the development of a new or improved object or tool" (NGSS Lead States 2013, p. 51). Because her children are young, Ms. Martinez has thought carefully about how to provide freedom for children's original explorations while also considering how to structure the class so students can learn from each other and eventually design a successful pollinator. Thus, as with many engineering tasks in the real world, after the children generate a list of questions about the challenge, the teacher provides specifications for some criteria and articulates the constraints that will underlie this challenge. One important part of orienting children to engineering challenges is helping them understand the parameters of the problem. A discussion of what their solution needs to do (criteria) and how they will be assessed helps focus children on the important features of a problem. Demonstrating the rubrics or tests that their solutions will be measured against should be part of the exploration of the problem. Similarly, reminding children of the limitations under which they are working (constraints), such as time, materials, or cost considerations, is important. Throughout the cycle of planning, designing, creating, and assessing the engineered device, Ms. Martinez will continue to encourage students' questions and draw out and explore the most salient concepts and processes involved in the design.

The types of questions and the role that students can play in defining a problem increases in complexity as they get older. By the time students are in high school, they themselves should be developing facility in "formulating, refining, and evaluating empirically testable questions and design problems using models and simulations" (NGSS Lead States 2013, p. 51). The questions high school students generate should "arise from careful observation … [and] from examining models or theory, to clarify and/or seek additional information and relationships" (NGSS Lead States 2013, p. 51). Teens should be able to evaluate a question to determine if it is testable and relevant and to ask questions that they can investigate with resources available at the school. Not surprisingly, the problems that high school students address are also more complex, involving processes and systems "with interacting components and criteria and constraints that may include social, technical, and/or environmental considerations" (NGSS Lead States 2013, p. 51).

As students and teachers define these problems, they can go back and forth between asking questions and designing solutions. This design process often involves many of the other practices, including collecting and analyzing data; constructing explanations; and communicating ideas, results, and recommendations.

Constructing Explanations and Designing Solutions

While specifying the design problem is critical to launching the engineering practices, the core focus of engineering is designing solutions. The following case illustrates the Constructing Explanations and Designing Solutions practice in the *NGSS*, how it intersects with other practices, and what it might look like at the secondary level.

> As the culminating experience for their energy, electricity, and magnetism unit, Mr. Washington challenges the students in his physics class to engineer an efficient and low-cost wind turbine. The students work in groups of three. Mr. Washington provides them with a range of materials they can use to design and construct the wind turbine's blades, gears, drivetrain, and tower. He also provides many possible materials from which the students can design and build an electric generator. Each of the materials has a financial cost associated with it. In this way, Mr. Washington has provided his students with a design problem and constraints.
>
> Mr. Washington explains that the written engineering journal that each student will keep needs to document the work, decisions, and thoughts that he or she and his or her team engaged in throughout the engineering process. The journal needs to explain how the energy from the wind is converted into electrical energy through the components of the group's turbine.

To assess the efficiency and cost of their solutions, students are expected to measure the wind speed and the power their solution generates. They must also calculate the economic and mechanical efficiency. They need to keep careful records of their plans, the decisions they make and why they make them, and the tests they conduct.

This engineering design task takes several weeks as students construct and test their wind turbines. Each group engages in redesign at least twice as it attempts to make its turbine more efficient and cost-effective. In their journals, students document how their next design choice was informed by physics knowledge or the tests and calculations they performed. They also offer explanations for why one design operates more efficiently than another.

As they engage in this complex challenge, Mr. Washington's students have the opportunity to demonstrate their proficiency in *NGSS* performance expectation HS-PS3-3: "Design, build, and refine a device that works within given constraints to convert one form of energy into another form of energy" (NGSS Lead States 2013, p. 97). The students in the class move back and forth through scientific and engineering ideas and practices as they engineer a model wind turbine. Their work is consonant with the vision articulated by the *Framework* that the goal of engaging in engineering practices is to design solutions:

> *In engineering, the goal is a design rather than an explanation. The process of developing a design is iterative and systematic. … Engineers' activities, however, have elements that are distinct from those of scientists. These elements include specifying constraints and criteria for desired qualities of the solution, developing a design plan, producing and testing models or prototypes, selecting among alternative design features to optimize the achievement of design criteria, and refining design ideas based on the performance of a prototype or simulation. (NRC 2012, pp. 68–69)*

Students can also demonstrate many of the components of the Constructing Explanations and Designing Solutions practice as outlined by the *NGSS* for the high school level during this challenge. As they conduct investigations of how to best design their blades or how the design of their generator affects the power output of their turbine, students will make a "quantitative and/or qualitative claim regarding the relationship between … variables" (NGSS Lead States 2013, p. 61). Students will need to "apply scientific ideas, principles, and/or evidence to provide an explanation of phenomena and solve design problems, taking into account possible unanticipated effects" (NGSS Lead States 2013, p. 61) as they explain the transfer and transformation of energy in their turbine. They will concurrently need to generate the type of explanations detailed in Chapter 10 (p. 205) of this book. Some of these explanations will focus on the scientific ideas underlying their designs. Others, however, may focus on the engineering components—for example, which materials were used or how the structural design or interaction of the components affected the performance of their turbine.

Throughout this engineering design challenge, the groups will "design, evaluate, and/or refine a solution to a complex real-world problem, based on scientific knowledge, student-generated sources of evidence, prioritized criteria, and tradeoff considerations" (NGSS Lead States 2013, p. 61). The physical artifacts resulting from this experience are both an engineering journal and a technology. At the project's conclusion, students will have designed a scale model of a wind turbine whose performance they can demonstrate (and explain) to their classmates. As students wrestle with capturing and converting the wind's energy, they will gain a new appreciation for the complexities of energy production in the real world. At the same time, they will come to better understand scientific ideas and principles related to air flow, energy, and electricity as they use them in their design solutions.

Engineering Design and Equity

As is the case with the two challenges described above, engineering design activities should be focused on real-world problems situated in local, regional, or global contexts. Children, particularly those from groups that are underserved or underrepresented in engineering or science, are often attracted and motivated by engineering challenges because they are situated in the real world (Cunningham and Lachapelle 2014). Grounding students' activities in a setting can help them make sense of what they are doing and why (Lachapelle and Cunningham 2014). Framing tasks as an engineering challenge also has the potential to increase student agency and responsibility for learning (Silk et al. 2009) and can help build children's understandings about relevant science ideas (Levy 2013).

Recognizing the power of engineering as a sense-making tool that can engage a diverse range of students, the *NGSS* state the following:

> The NGSS inclusion of engineering with science has major implications
> for nondominant student groups. From a pedagogical perspective, the focus
> on engineering is inclusive of students who may have traditionally been
> marginalized in the science classroom or experienced science as not being
> relevant to their lives or future. By asking questions and solving meaningful

problems through engineering in local contexts (e.g., watershed planning, medical equipment, instruments for communication for the deaf), diverse students deepen their science knowledge, come to view science as relevant to their lives and future, and engage in science in socially relevant and transformative ways. (NGSS Lead States 2013, p. 104)

The second part of this chapter steps back from a focus on individual *NGSS* practices to consider how engineering practices might be experienced by students as they make sense of the natural and designed world. In the classroom, students will likely move back and forth between practices as they work to engage in a task. The next sections explore what science and engineering practices look like as they are enacted in classrooms engaged in engineering design.

Engineering Design Fosters Engineering Practices
ELEMENTARY CHILDREN DESIGN A PARACHUTE

Elementary school children in grades 3–5 often study science ideas related to astronomy, structures of matter, and forces and motion. In this section, I describe an instructional unit from the Engineering is Elementary curriculum to illustrate how the use of engineering design can foster student learning of disciplinary ideas and engineering practices. The unit, *A Long Way Down: Designing Parachutes* (EiE 2011), was designed to enhance children's understanding of science ideas as they engage in engineering design. Table 13.1 (p. 292) summarizes the *NGSS* disciplinary core ideas addressed by the unit. As these ideas appear in the following description, the disciplinary core idea is referenced in parenthesis (e.g., ETS1.A).

Additionally, the unit invites students to use science and engineering practices as they develop solutions for their challenge. When the practices or key words related to them are mentioned in the following lesson descriptions, they appear in italics.

Here, we focus on a fourth-grade class that has been studying ideas related to astronomy in its science lessons. (To view video of this engineering activity in an actual fourth-grade classroom, please visit *www.eie.org/eie-curriculum/curriculum-units/long-way-down-designing-parachutes*.) In their classes, students have been exploring space and the solar systems; have discussed Earth, stars, and the planets; and have identified some of the similarities and differences between other planets and Earth. Through readings, videos, and discussions, the students have learned that the planets have very different atmospheres from each other. One attribute that varies is the density of each atmosphere: Some atmospheres are more dense or "thicker" than Earth's, and others are less dense or "thinner." The class has also discussed gravity and gravitational forces. It has been exposed to the idea that gravitational forces are different on different planets and that this force and the density of

Table 13.1
NGSS disciplinary core ideas consistent with *A Long Way Down*

Number	Disciplinary core idea	Sub-idea
ETS1.A	Defining and delimiting an engineering problem	Solutions are limited by available materials and resources (constraints). A successful solution is determined by considering desired features (criteria).
ETS1.B	Developing possible solutions	People brainstorm, test, and refine possible solutions. There are many types of models that can be used to investigate how a design might work, to communicate design ideas, or to compare designs.
ETS1.C	Optimizing the design solution	Different solutions need to be tested to determine which best solves the problem given the criteria and constraints.
PS2.A	Forces and motion	Forces act on objects. Forces can cause changes in an object's speed or direction of motion. The patterns of an object's motion in various situations can be observed and measure of future motion predicted.
PS2.B	Types of interactions	Objects exert forces on each other such as gravity and friction. The gravitational force of Earth pulls the object toward its center.
ESS1.B	Earth and the solar system	The solar system consists of the Sun and a collection of objects, including planets.

the atmosphere mean that objects can fall more quickly or more slowly than on Earth. All of these ideas lead children to wonder about visiting the planets and getting more information about these planets. They might wonder how a spaceship or rocket ship might get into the atmosphere of these planets and allow further exploration of the surfaces.

We join the class as the teacher begins the aerospace engineering unit "A Long Way Down," which is connected to the idea of atmospheres and how those atmospheres might affect parachutes and other objects traveling through them. The engineering challenge in this unit prompts students to think more about the forces acting on a parachute as it falls on Earth and other planets as the students design and test small parachutes. The children will need to draw on the science ideas they just learned about atmospheres and gravitational forces as they design solutions for the challenge.

As the unit continues, the teacher introduces a context within which students can learn about the design of a parachute and the processes involved. To help children understand the relevance of their activity as well as to set the context for their design challenge in an engaging way (Cunningham and Lachapelle 2014), the children's engineering unit begins with a reading a storybook, *Paulo's Parachute Mission*. The story introduces the engineering challenge the children will face in a general way (*defining a problem*; ETS1.A), and it also helps students see how the scientific ideas they have been studying, such as drag, gravity, and atmosphere, can be applied to solve a problem.

Figure 13.1
EiE's engineering design process

Figure 13.1
EiE's engineering design process

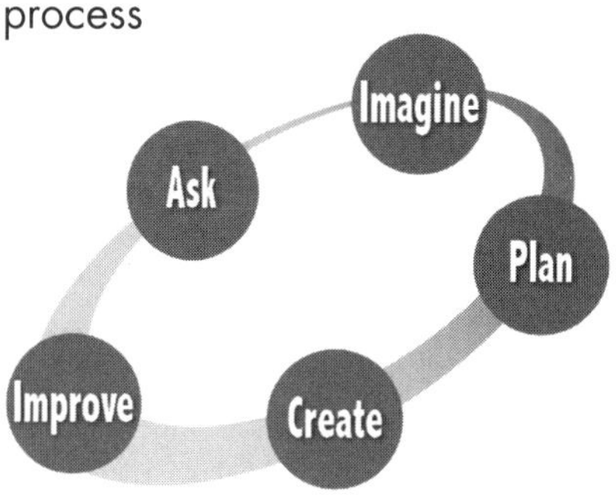

Because the curriculum is designed for elementary school children, the students use a five-phase process called the EiE engineering design process (Figure 13.1). It is similar to the science and engineering processes but modified in language to help students understand and monitor their way through engineering design. The steps are Ask, Imagine, Plan, Create, and Improve. Ask is similar to the *Asking Questions* science practice. Imagine includes some aspects of the *Designing Solutions* engineering practice and the *Developing Models* practice. Planning is similar to the *Planning and Carrying Out Investigations* practice. Create is a critical part of the *Designing Solutions* practice. Finally, Improve has similarities to the act of revising solutions.

In the first lesson, the engineers in the story evoke the engineering design process as a tool engineers use. The classroom children will themselves use this tool in a later lesson. After the teacher reads the story to the class—stopping frequently to ask questions—students work in pairs to reflect on what they have learned from the book. In particular, they consider the engineering design process and describe what the main character, Paulo, does in each of the five phases of the process. Worksheets and class discussions prompt the students to think more about aerospace engineering and the vocabulary, geography, and science topics featured in the story.

In the second lesson, students think more about the work of aerospace engineers. Before they turn their attention to engineering one particular type of technology—a parachute—that works in one type of environment, students are given the opportunity to think more generally about the kinds of work aerospace engineers do. The students learn that aerospace engineers often design technologies for varied atmospheres and extreme environments in our solar system. As the students act as aerospace engineers, they experience the way engineers think about things as they work to make sure their spacecraft designs are suited to the crafts' destinations.

The students recall what they have learned from their science study about the solar system (ESS1.B) and then brainstorm some features of planets. The teacher asks students to predict how these features might influence the design of a spacecraft traveling to that planet or celestial body. These are all important aspects of the engineering practice of *Defining Problems.* The following shows a possible questioning sequence:

- What do you think the word *spacecraft* means?

- As aerospace engineers, what do you think we need to know in order to design a spacecraft to explore part of our solar system?

- What do you think we need to know about our destination?

- How do you think the features of our destination might impact our designs? (questions adapted from EiE 2011, pp. 63–64)

With the class, the teacher creates a list of features of several celestial bodies (size, location, surface, atmosphere, and temperature) and then has the students think about how each design of a spacecraft might change depending on the feature. The students are divided into small groups, and each group is then assigned a celestial body as a destination for its spacecraft. With a sheet providing basic information about their celestial body (e.g., distance from Earth, temperature, atmosphere, characteristics of the surface), students *ask questions* about how these features will affect the design of their spacecraft (see Figure 13.2). They work as aerospace engineering design teams to *imagine* a spacecraft that will explore their destination. In addition to the features of their destination, they also consider the purpose of their mission (e.g., taking pictures, gathering samples) in their designs (see Figure 13.3). Students draw ideas for possible spacecraft designs— sometimes quite fantastical (*Designing Solutions*; ETS1.A, ETS1.B).

Figure 13.2
Fact sheet about Neptune

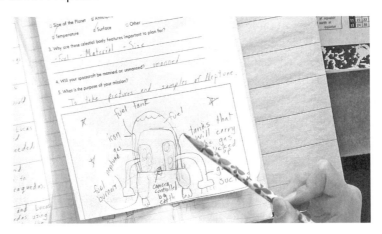

The entire class then comes together to reflect on the designs and the real-world criteria and constraints they would need to think about to make their spacecraft mission ready. The class discusses why brainstorming sometimes out-there ideas is important (ETS1.A, ETS1.B).

Now that the children have developed a larger understanding of the work of aerospace engineers, in the next lesson they home in on a more limited problem: space. The teacher *defines the general problem*: They will design a parachute for a mission to a planet with an atmosphere that is thinner than Earth's. To design an effective parachute, students will call on scientific knowledge, so this lesson focuses on helping children develop or refine their understandings of some of the scientific principles they will use.

The teacher starts by asking the class what they need to know to make the most effective parachute. As part of the Ask step, children iteratively *ask questions* that help them further *define the problem*, such as "How big can the parachute be?" "Where will it be dropped?" "What materials can we use?" Most of the ideas that the children generate focus on the atmosphere where the parachute will be dropped and the design of the parachute. Thus, the teacher articulates that the class will be exploring the question "How do the thickness of an atmosphere and the design of a parachute affect the speed of a falling parachute?"

Figure 13.3
Spacecraft designed for Neptune

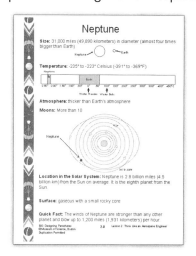

Source: EiE 2011.

To help answer these questions, children engage in science experiments. The first set of these focuses on the properties of atmospheres. The class will *investigate* how the thickness of an atmosphere affects the speed at which objects fall. The teacher initially asks students to recall what they have learned from their previous lessons, including how the storybook characters described the atmosphere (lesson 1) and whether the atmospheres on other planets were similar to or different from Earth's (lesson 2). Then the teacher draws students' attention to information in the storybook about aerospace engineering and the exploration of atmospheres (lesson 3). In the book, Paulo's mother, Mãe, an aerospace engineer, explains that it is easy to study our atmosphere, but exploring other planets' atmospheres can be difficult because they are so far away. Students are asked to recall how Mãe tested the technologies designed for use on other celestial bodies. This opens a conversation about physical *models* that mimic parts of the world that are difficult to observe or test. The children generate ideas about what they think a model is and why models are important to use in science and engineering. They then discuss why models might be useful for aerospace engineers.

The teacher then explains she is going to illustrate that objects, such as parachutes, fall more quickly in thinner atmospheres than thicker ones. She shows the children two clear plastic jars—one filled with water and one with air—that show physical models of a thinner and thicker atmosphere and asks the students how they can figure out which jar models which atmosphere. The students suggest they can drop something in each jar and see how it falls. The teacher produces two golf balls to drop and *questions* the students, asking them to predict what will happen when a ball is dropped in each jar. After the students observe the golf balls being dropped from the same height simultaneously a few times, the teacher leads a conversation, *asking* the children the following questions:

- What did you observe?

- Which jar do you think models a thicker atmosphere?

- Why does an object fall more slowly in a thicker atmosphere?

- Which celestial bodies could this model of a thicker atmosphere illustrate?

- Which jar models a thinner atmosphere?

- Why does an object fall more quickly in a thinner atmosphere?

- Which celestial bodies would this model of a thinner atmosphere illustrate? (questions adapted from EiE 2011, pp. 81–82)

During this conversation, the students discuss why they observed what they did: In the thicker, denser medium—water—there "was more to bump into," which slowed the ball down. The thicker liquid created more drag. Teachers and students can engage in rich conversation here, with students reflecting on structures of matter and how more particles create frictional forces (PS1.A, PS2.A). There are many forces acting on the ball as it falls, such as gravity and friction, which affect the speed with which it falls (PS2.A, PS2.B).

To help the children better visualize what is happening when the golf ball is dropped in the water, the teacher uses food coloring. She places a few drops at the top of the water in the cylinder and then has the students observe how the water behaves when the golf ball is dropped through it. They notice that only the water near the golf ball moves and that the water just under the ball is pushed out of the way (PS2.A). The teacher asks the students to make connections to the thinner atmosphere by asking them what they might see if we could color the air. The atmosphere investigation concludes with the students summarizing what they have learned about how the thickness of an atmosphere affects the speed of an object (such as a parachute) in a chart (see Table 13.2, p. 298).

The second *investigation* invites students to consider how the design of a parachute affects its speed. Again, the teacher anchors the students' activities in their larger task by asking them the goal of their parachute's mission. (It will be dropped on a planet with an atmosphere thinner than Earth's.) The students also review the questions they *asked* about parachutes. The teacher explains that they are now going to explore how the design of the parachute parts influences its speed. After reviewing the main parts of a parachute (which were introduced in the storybook—canopy, suspension lines, and load), the teacher asks the class to make predictions about how the design of each will affect how the parachute falls and why. For example, "Do you predict that the parachute will fall faster or slower as we increase the size of the canopy? Why?" The studentss engage in similar predictions for the canopy materials—they will test paper (coffee filters), plastic (garbage bags), and sheer fabric (sheer curtain)—as well as suspension line length.

The *why* questions prompt conversations that require students to call on the science knowledge they have learned. They discuss drag, surface area, and the idea that air has particles that can't be seen that are "trapped" by the canopy and push against it. The children talk about forces and the fact that gravity is pulling the parachute toward the Earth, but the air (and particles) caught in the canopy create friction that slows the parachute down. The children posit that the bigger the canopy, the more air gets trapped and so the greater the force pushing up against gravity that slows the falling object (the parachute and its load; PS1.A, PS2.A, PS2.B). Such conversations allow children to apply the science they have learned or to understand science ideas in new or deeper ways. This is also a place where a teacher could engage the class in additional science investigations to deepen understanding of science principles.

The teacher explains that each group will examine the effect of one variable on parachute drop speed. Each group will create and test three parachutes and record which one landed first, second, and third. Then the teacher asks the children to think about the design or *planning of investigations*: Are there variables that they should keep constant for all the groups? This leads into a conversation about controlling variables during experimentation and the importance of changing only one variable at a time. The children decide that the load, the drop height, the canopy shape, and the overall design of how the parachute is constructed (the construction technique) should remain constant. The children are assigned to groups in which they construct three parachutes that vary in one respect (e.g., small, medium, and large canopy). After teams test the materials by dropping each parachute three times and recording the fall times, they review what they have learned. The teacher adds to the results chart to summarize their findings.

The children compare how their predictions align with their observations. Then, the teacher reminds them of the role that the atmosphere plays in what they observed by asking them how the parachutes would behave if they had been dropped in a thicker or thinner atmosphere. Finally, the teacher asks, "If you were working as an aerospace engineer, why wouldn't you always just design a huge parachute with long suspension lines and materials without holes?" (EiE 2011, p. 97). This prompts the students to begin considering additional variables that aerospace engineers must grapple with—costs and space constraints—and segues into the final lesson.

Table 13.2

Results chart summarizing children's knowledge about parachute descent

How do the thickness of an atmosphere and the design of a parachute affect the speed of a falling parachute?	
Parachutes fall more **slowly**	Parachutes fall more **quickly**
• In thicker atmospheres • With larger canopies • With canopy materials without holes • With longer suspension lines	• In thinner atmospheres • With smaller canopies • With canopy materials with holes in them • With shorter suspension lines

Source: Adapted from EiE 2011, p. 96.

Now that they have used physical models, observation, and investigation to cultivate some science and engineering understanding, the children are ready to apply this knowledge to generate solutions to an open-ended engineering challenge.

The teacher begins lesson 4 by reviewing the engineering design process. Students think about each of the phases and why they are important.

Ask (Asking Questions):

- What's the problem?
- What have others done?
- What are the constraints?

Imagine (Generating Multiple Possible Solutions):

- What could be some solutions?
- Brainstorm ideas.
- Choose the best one.

Plan (Planning Investigations):

- Draw a diagram.
- Make a list of materials you'll need.

Create (Designing Solutions):

- Follow your plan and create it.
- Test it out!

Improve (Revising Solutions):

- Make your design even better.
- Test it out!

Source: Adapted from EiE 2011.

Students are challenged to use the engineering design process to solve a very specific problem. The teacher posts a guiding question for the activity that reads, "How can we use our knowledge of parachutes, atmospheres, and the Engineering Design Process to design a parachute that meets specific criteria for drop speed and parachute size?" (EiE 2011, p. 103).

As the teacher sets forth the problem or goal for her students, she asks students to remember what they learned about atmospheres and parachutes earlier in the unit when they were *asking questions*. Through the subsequent discussion, the teacher tackles another component of this practice—*defining the problem*—by determining the criteria for a successful solution and identifying constraints (ETS1.A). The lesson sets specific criteria that the designs should meet: Parachutes need to have a drop speed of five feet per second or slower and must be below a certain size. The teacher leads a discussion in which she explicitly defines criteria and constraints and introduces her students to the concept of trade-offs, in which engineers must compromise one aspect of a design to bolster another.

The teacher helps her students understand that they must consider two things, drop speed and parachute size. Bigger parachutes fall more slowly. However, any spacecraft has limited space. So, the children's designs must balance these variables. The teacher shares with the class the metrics it will apply to determine whether its solutions have been successful (ETS1.A). The students discuss how they will determine the drop speed or the rate at which the parachute is falling by measuring how much time it takes the parachutes to fall a certain distance and dividing distance by the time it takes (*using mathematics*). The teacher again reminds the students that they are creating a *model* parachute designed for another atmosphere and asks them to consider how fast the parachute might fall in a thinner atmosphere.

Students continue to engineer, moving on to brainstorm or *imagine* solutions (ETS1.B). Working independently, each student is asked to imagine two different solutions to the problem (Figure 13.4, p. 300). On the basis of the criteria that have been laid out, students think up ideas for viable solutions and sketch out their ideas (*planning investigations*).

During engineering design, students make diagrams and list materials needed for each solution they propose. Representing their ideas in detailed sketches or diagrams is one way that these students are *Developing and Using Models* that help them articulate and evaluate solutions. The students and teachers discuss why they, and engineers, use smaller-scale models as part of engineering.

Figure 13.4
Designs for parachutes imagined by students

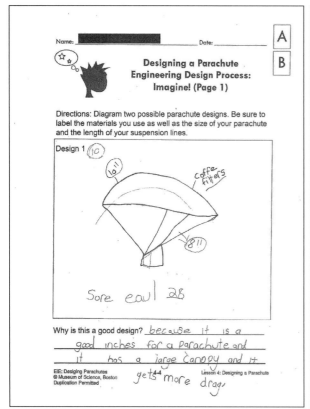
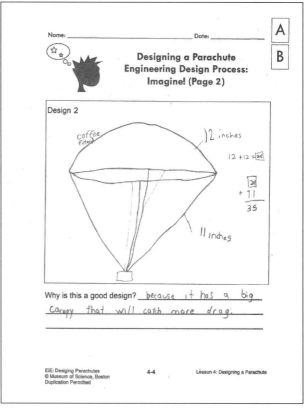

After each student has imagined solutions independently, the ideas are shared in groups. As a team, the students engage in *planning* by choosing an idea to further develop and test first (ETS1.B). Oftentimes, children have different ideas about how to proceed, frequently connected to different scientific understandings or different conceptions of how those ideas apply in a given situation. Thus, as individual students present their designs, ideas, and reasoning and try to convince others of their merit, they are *Engaging in Argument From Evidence*. During their discussions, children reference the tests they conducted in the previous lesson about designing parts of a parachute.

As part of their team deliberations, students practice *Using Mathematics and Computational Thinking*. Because engineering design emphasizes brainstorming and planning designs before building, students are forced to make very direct decisions about the speed and size of the parachute early in the process. One way engineers use numerical data is to help objectively assess which designs they should pursue further. Students engaged in this challenge are also asked to compare possible solutions on the basis of how well they meet space constraints (ETS1.B).

Each team must draw up a plan for its parachute and then assess whether it is mission ready—a determination that is made quantitatively—before the students are allowed to build and test it (see Figure 13.5).

Once the students on a team decide on their first design (*planning the investigation*) that is mission ready, they *create* it and test it (*carrying out the investigation*). The children construct their parachutes using the mission-ready diagram they agreed on. The parachutes the children build are themselves a type of physical model because they are not full size

Figure 13.5
Worksheets to calculate parachute-packing score and determine if the design is mission ready

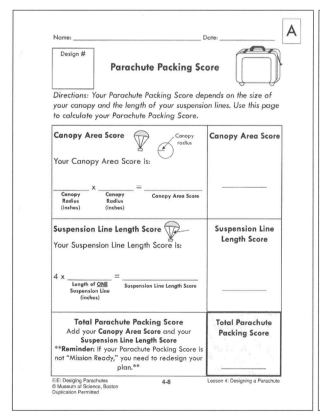

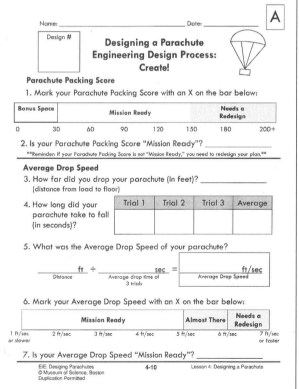

or to scale (*Developing and Using Models*). Physical models or prototypes are often used in engineering for analysis and evaluation of designs.

Finally, it's time to test the group's parachute design and gather data (ETS1.C). Convening as a class, the students and the teacher deliberate about what a fair test is and discuss

Figure 13.6
Students test their parachutes

why this is important for discovering weaknesses in a design, comparing competing designs, or evaluating whether changes produce improvements. The whole class discusses which parts of the parachutes need to align at a common starting point (the load). They determine how students will know when to stop timing (when the load hits the ground), and they agree that they need to be careful to just open their fingers to drop the parachute instead of pushing or throwing it, which will introduce additional forces. Then they try it out (*carrying out an investigation*; Figure 13.6)! They time the parachutes' descents as they float from the second floor to the ground in an open atrium (ETS1.C).

Test results reveal that some of the designs work better than others. With the results of all their drop tests in hand, the class turns to *Analyzing and Interpreting Data* (ETS1.C). To figure out how well their solutions met the criteria, individual teams share their data with the class. The teacher guides the discussion so that observations and conversations about trends across groups occur.

By pooling data and looking at each other's work, students are able to make some observations about trends in their data (Figure 13.7). The teacher asks the students to look carefully at the data. She asks, "Which parachutes had the slowest drop speeds? Is there anything that these slowest-moving parachutes have in common?" Students make some hypotheses about the relative sizes of the canopy and suspension lines, which reopens a conversation about drag and helps children notice that canopies that can open fully "catch a lot of air" and thus fall more slowly. They start to link the speed at which a parachute drops with the amount of drag operating on the parachute. They talk about the forces that are pushing "up" on the canopy of the parachute and how these can work against the gravitational forces that are pulling down on the parachute. The students discuss the effects of forces on the motion of a parachute (PS2.B).

Obtaining, Evaluating, and Communicating Information as a class is important because it allows students to use all of the groups' findings to help them improve their own technologies. The iterative nature of the engineering design process means students keep evaluating their designs to determine how they might improve and redesign their solutions. Thus, students learn from the designs built in their small group, the designs of the other groups, and the conversations about how the constraints were addressed across the different designs.

As the students review data and look at trends, they again need to practice *Engaging in Argument From Evidence* as they begin *Constructing Explanations and Designing Solutions*, which draws in science content. The students have a vested interest in figuring out how they might *improve* their designs, since they all want their parachutes to better meet the criteria. By carefully structuring her classroom and the discussion, the teacher encourages students to think about what they've learned and apply their knowledge to make informed decisions about their second, improved parachute designs, instead of just making random changes (ETS1.C).

After students build their improved design, it's time to test and reevaluate, which, of course, requires another round of asking children to engage in science and engineering practices. The iterative nature of engineering means that children should have multiple opportunities to engage in the practices, thereby refining their ideas and strengthening their skills.

As this activity walk-through suggests, engineering challenges can provide a rich opportunity for children to develop or use engineering and science disciplinary core ideas as they explore and make sense of their world. In this case, as students engaged with core engineering ideas, they also called on disciplinary ideas related to astronomy and space and forces and motion to make sense of their designs. Additionally, as students engineer their parachutes using an engineering design process, they move freely among the eight scientific and engineering practices.

Figure 13.7
Data table from parachute testing

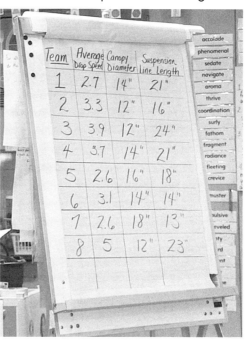

HIGH SCHOOL STUDENTS DESIGN A PARACHUTE

The *NGSS* describe one set of eight practices that elementary, middle, or high school students should be using throughout their educational career. Engineering problems can easily be reworked to be relevant and challenging for more advanced students. For example, high school students could also engineer a parachute to learn more about core ideas of science and engineering. In fact, one *NGSS* performance expectation for high school physical science suggests parachutes as a possible solution:

HS-PS2-3: Apply science and engineering ideas to design, evaluate, and refine a device that minimizes the force on a macroscopic object during a collision. [Clarification Statement: Examples of evaluation and refinement could include determining the success of a device at protecting the object from damage and modifying the design to improve it. Examples of a device could include a football helmet or a parachute.] (NGSS Lead States 2013, p. 94)

Clearly, the scientific and engineering principles and practices that high school students use will be more complex than those at the elementary level. For example, more advanced students could use Newton's second law and Newton's law of universal gravitation to develop mathematical models that describe or predict the motion of their parachute. They could design experiments to determine an algebraic formula for the drag force. Furthermore, the students might balance more constraints as they design their projects, develop models not only of the parachutes' physical structure but also their descent, conduct science experiments that gather information about how objects fall and how drag and friction affect drop speed, engage in mathematical models and explanation to predict and analyze their parachutes, and create more detailed analytical reports that compare the results of their tests. While the high school students consider more variables and conduct more complicated testing and analysis, the core practices that they engage in remain the same as those used by elementary students.

Conclusion

The new standards documents open the possibilities for the next generation of students to develop more robust understandings of engineering, the practices of science and engineering, and the interdependencies between these fields. The *NGSS* documents suggest that students across all grade levels should experience engineering and in so doing develop their comfort, familiarity, and fluency with engineering practices. Teachers can draw on the structures provided by the *NGSS*—its core ideas and eight practices—to foster science and engineering sense-making and practices in their students.

What an Engineering Activity Should Include

In thinking about how to integrate engineering into classrooms, it's important to consider elements that should be present. These help differentiate between "tinkering" and hands-on construction—which are not part of the *NGSS* expectations—and engineering. The three attributes below also support the development of engineering practices by students.

Engineering activities should rest on an *engineering design process*. This is one of the defining features of engineering. Engineers aim to develop solutions to problems that are bounded by criteria and constraints. The *NGSS* engineering disciplinary core ideas—define and delimit, develop, and optimize—articulate a process that students should experience. Providing scaffolding and structure throughout the process helps students build their familiarity and fluency.

Engineering activities should include a way to *assess the merits of a design solution*. As in the real world, the criteria and constraints of the problem need to be defined. Students should understand how they will be evaluating their solutions and what standards they are aiming to meet. They should be asked to use rubrics or metrics to assess and compare their designs.

Engineering activities should *connect with science or mathematics*. Engineers draw heavily on their knowledge of science and mathematics to design stable, strong, and efficient (among other things) solutions. Children need to see the connection between engineering activities and how science or mathematics knowledge can inform or improve them. In the real world, before a solution is selected (e.g., bridge, skyscraper, airplane), the science and mathematical underpinnings often need to be calculated.

It's Not Just Bridge Building and Egg Dropping! What Engineering Practices Are *Not*

While bridge building and egg drops can be fun and engaging activities, they don't always foster students' engineering practices. As the box "What an Engineering Activity Should Include" (p. 305) says, classroom activities need to go beyond tinkering and hands-on construction to include the design process, assessing the design solutions, and connecting with science or mathematics. It is also important to avoid doing activities for the sake of rehearsing individual practices (such as practicing defining problems or creating models) instead of engaging in engineering that asks students to draw on their science or math knowledge as they design and evaluate a solution to a problem. Just as experiencing the scientific method as separate, content-free steps does not build deep facility or knowledge, doing isolated parts of the engineering design process and the associated practices without the goals and purposes of the design makes the engineering practices much less effective and meaningful.

Students can and should engage in engineering throughout their K–12 careers. Engaging in engineering and design practices can prompt learners to more deeply understand scientific ideas. One way to incorporate engineering practices in science classes is to use design projects to frame science units: Set forth a challenge. Help children recognize that understanding the natural world will help them solve the challenge by strengthening their ideas and their solutions. Have them apply their science ideas to designing or improving the technology. Such engineering projects can increase students' motivation and engagement as they see the relevance and utility of the ideas they are studying. Finally, by expanding our instruction to foster in our next generation of learners understandings not only about the natural world (science) but also about the human-made (engineered) world in which they live, we equip them with tools, ideas, and practices that they can use to create the world of the future.

Acknowledgments

I would like to thank Ms. Jean Facchiano and her students for inviting us into their classroom.

References

Cunningham, C. M., and W. S. Carlsen. 2014. Precollege engineering education. In *Handbook of research on science education*, ed. N. Lederman, 747–758. Mahwah, NJ: Lawrence Erlbaum Associates.

Cunningham, C. M., and C. P. Lachapelle. 2014. Designing engineering experiences to engage all students. In *Engineering in pre-college settings: Synthesizing research, policy, and practices*, ed. S. Purzer, J. Strobel, and M. Cardella, 117–142. Lafayette, IN: Purdue University Press.

Engineering is Elementary (EiE). 2011. *A long way down: Designing parachutes*. Boston, MA: Museum of Science.

Kelly, G. J. 2011. Scientific literacy, discourse, and epistemic practices. In *Exploring the landscape of scientific literacy*, ed. C. Linder, L. Östman, D. A. Roberts, P. Wickman, G. Erikson, and A. McKinnon, 61–73. New York: Routledge.

Kelly, G. J., and C. Chen. 1999. The sound of music: Constructing science as sociocultural practices through oral and written discourse. *Journal of Research in Science Teaching* 36 (8): 883–915.

Lachapelle, C. P., and C. M. Cunningham. 2014. Engineering in elementary schools. In *Engineering in pre-college settings: Synthesizing research, policy, and practices*, ed. S. Purzer, J. Strobel, and M. Cardella, 61–88. Lafayette, IN: Purdue University Press.

Levy, S. T. 2013. Young children's learning of water physics by constructing working systems. *International Journal of Technology and Design Education* 23 (3): 537–566.

National Research Council (NRC). 2012. *A framework for K–12 science education: Practices, crosscutting concepts, and core ideas*. Washington, DC: National Academies Press.

NGSS Lead States. 2013. *Next Generation Science Standards: For states, by states*. Washington, DC: National Academies Press. *www.nextgenscience.org/next-generation-science-standards*.

Silk, E. M., C. D. Schunn, and M. S. Cary. 2009. The impact of an engineering design curriculum on science reasoning in an urban setting. *Journal of Science Education and Technology* 18 (3): 209–223.

SECTION 3

HOW CAN WE TEACH USING THE PRACTICES?

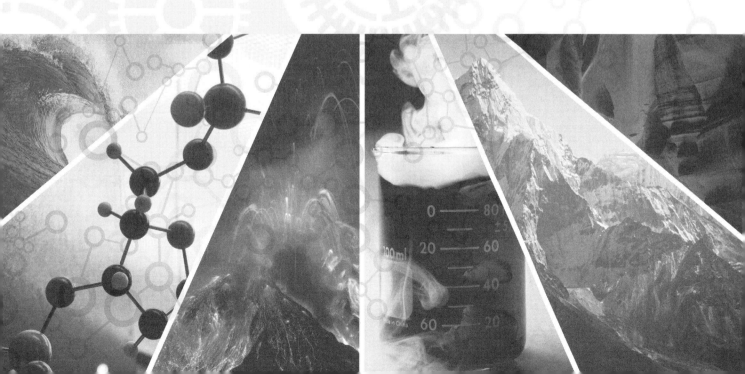

14

FROM RECITATION TO REASONING

Supporting Scientific and Engineering Practices Through Talk

SARAH MICHAELS AND CATHERINE O'CONNOR

This chapter is about fostering what we call *academically productive talk* in science classrooms to support students' engagement with the eight science and engineering practices. How do we establish a classroom culture in which all students feel engaged and able to think with others? What are the specific "high-leverage" talk tools that help teachers bring all students to a deep level of engagement with the *Next Generation Science Standards* (*NGSS*) science and engineering practices?

Why a Chapter on Classroom Talk?

Reasonable readers might ask, "Why devote a whole chapter to student and teacher talk? Isn't this a volume about the science and engineering practices? I can see the relationship between classroom discussion and practice 7 (Engaging in Argument From Evidence), but what about the others? What does classroom talk have to do with Developing and Using Models, Asking Questions and Defining Problems, or Using Mathematics and Computational Thinking?"

When most people first encounter the science and engineering practices, they may envision them as professional practices engaged in by actual adult scientists and engineers, with all their knowledge and expertise. Scientists and engineers don't have to talk or discuss to engage in these core practices; they can individually develop and use models, analyze and interpret data, and so on.

Our perspective on the practices is a bit different. We envision them as they *begin to be acquired*—in a classroom with a teacher and other students. Each of the eight practices, as it is introduced and elaborated and experienced in the classroom, requires that students *externalize their reasoning*. It requires that they *work with the reasoning of other students*. So in our view, teacher and student talk is the *vehicle* by which every student can make his or her way into a deep and productive relationship with the science and engineering practices. Becoming a full participant in the practices goes beyond the learning of new science content. It involves new ways of thinking, of relating with and interpreting others' thinking, and of communicating and acting.

It's true that practices such as Engaging in Argument From Evidence obviously require attention to group discourse, but there is a critical role for talk even beyond practice 7. Let's examine the practices that *don't* explicitly mention discourse, argument, reasoning, or talk in the *NGSS*, such as practice 2 (Developing and Using Models) and practice 3 (Planning and Carrying Out Investigations). To learn *how* to *model, analyze data,* or *use appropriate tools,* students have to *participate* in these practices—with others. And that participation happens primarily through talk, joint attention, and shared activity.

So talk and discursive practices (oral or written) are actually fundamental to all of the science practices. If teachers are going to induct students into these practices and support them in participating actively, there will have to be opportunities for *all* students to make their thinking visible and available to one another. Teachers will face the challenge of building a classroom culture of public reasoning, and that will require new forms of well-guided talk and writing, with a central emphasis on conversation and discussion of several kinds.

Note that this is not entirely different from what happens when the practices are used by mature professionals. Experienced scientists and engineers often work in groups, on teams, and in larger networks or communities, in which communication of their ideas, findings, and data is essential in advancing knowledge in the field. They communicate their thinking informally and formally, in face-to-face meetings, in e-mail communications, in formal conference presentations, in peer-reviewed journals, on the internet, and in books and other media. For evidence to have weight in these professional communities, it has to be explicated, argued for, and made public so that others can evaluate it and think about it. This requires dedicated and disciplined approaches to the explication and sharing of evidence and agreed upon ways of challenging or critiquing evidence in the effort to advance knowledge and understanding. Through well-structured talk, students are guided—or apprenticed—into the fundamental practices of these disciplines or fields.

There are measurable benefits as well. Researchers in a variety of fields relating to education have begun to converge on the finding that when teachers "open up the conversation" and get students to participate actively in reasoning with evidence and building and critiquing academic arguments, students make dramatic learning gains. Taken together, this body of work illustrates the importance of discourse-intensive teaching approaches that combine rigorous tasks with carefully orchestrated, teacher-led discussion and student-to-student pair and group discussion. These discourse practices have been shown to result in robust gains in academic achievement for students from a range of socioeconomic and linguistic backgrounds in mathematics, science, history, English, and English language arts (Adey and Shayer 2001; Reznitskaya et al. 2001; O'Connor, Michaels, and Chapin 2015; Resnick, Asterhan, and Clarke 2015).

In this chapter, we first introduce a picture of the most common varieties of classroom talk—*recitation*, or the IRE, and *lecture*. We contrast those with the kind of classroom conversation that can actually support the science and engineering practices, and we describe an approach to productive talk that undergirds many of the activities you will put in place as you engage your students in the intellectual practices at the heart of the *NGSS*.

The Most Common Forms of Classroom Talk

While many teachers intuitively feel that they use discussion in their classroom, a number of studies have shown that, instead, these teachers are spending most of their class time in an activity that researchers have called group recitation. Extensive research shows that this is the most common and, in fact, is often the default pattern of talk in classrooms throughout the country.

It's a very familiar scene: The teacher asks a question (typically a question the teacher knows the answer to), a student replies (usually a short reply), and the teacher evaluates (saying, "Right," "Not quite," or "Well … who else has an idea?"). Some people have talked about this as a teacher lecture elicited out of the mouths of the students.

This is often called the IRE pattern: *I* for the teacher's initiating move, *R* for the student's response, and *E* for the teacher's evaluation—right or wrong.

Teacher (I): "Who remembers one of the kinds of eclipses we talked about?"

Student (R): "Annual?"

Teacher (E): "Well … anyone else?"

The teacher does not have to explicitly say "wrong" to the student; everyone knows that asking for another response in this way means the answer was somehow inadequate. This "talk format" is deeply internalized by most students and teachers throughout the United States and in many parts of the world.

This is not to say that the IRE is intrinsically a "bad" practice. Many have noted that recitation, or the IRE, can be very helpful for reviewing material or checking to see what the students recall, and it does give the teacher a great deal of control over the topic and who speaks. However, in spite of these benefits, the IRE pattern does not support complex reasoning or the building and weighing of arguments. It emphasizes correctness over reasoning, and once the correct answer is offered, the conversation is closed down rather than opened up. The teacher then moves on to a different question and a different student. The conversation proceeds with the teacher holding a series of exchanges with individual students—without crosstalk among the students in which they consider others' ideas, agree or disagree, and explain their own reasoning. Indeed, in recitation, there is rarely any overt link between the ideas and answers of different students. Moreover, within each IRE segment, the teacher is always positioned as the final authority, the one who has the answer. The student is positioned as the "getter" of the answer in the teacher's head. Students are either correct or incorrect and thus are publicly shown to be either right or wrong (which often is interpreted as either smart or not smart). Typically, only a few students (and usually the same few) volunteer to take a turn.

Because of the emphasis on correctness over reasoning, research on student motivation links the IRE pattern to "performance goals" (whereby students act in such a way as to look smart) rather than to "learning goals" (whereby students participate so as to really understand and learn). In short, the IRE format doesn't create a classroom culture that promotes risk taking or effort, where students work hard at explicating their ideas, requesting clarification from others, responding to or building on the ideas of others, or building and weighing complex arguments with evidence.

The IRE is often used in reviewing material (such as what was done the day before), checking to see what students recall about a topic, or reminding them what they have already learned. It can be useful in these settings. However, there are hidden drawbacks: Students who do not feel confident do not participate, so their understanding is not assessed. Students who give correct answers might have serious misconceptions that are never voiced because their responses are not probed more deeply. Students, especially secondary students, often withdraw from talk in which they feel they are being "used" to make a teacher's point, or when they fear they might appear as "model students" in the eyes of the rest of the class. Finally, IRE talk reveals answers but it does not reveal students' knowledge nearly as well as more open-ended talk in which students draw on their prior knowledge to offer predictions or conclusions about a new problem.

And, of course, in middle and secondary school science classrooms, another dominant form of talk is the *teacher lecture*. While a coherent delivery of complex content can be accomplished, and the lecturer has a great deal of control over the talk (and can "read" from notes or projected slides or recite from memory), much research on human learning suggests that simply "telling" students information is not as effective as it feels. When students listen to a lecture, they are passive, and, typically, they are not making sense of the information as it comes in even if they are taking notes. It is an ineffective talk format if the goal is for students to develop deep and robust understanding and the ability to reason about the material in new contexts.

What Does Academically Productive Classroom Talk Look Like?

In contrast to the teacher lecture and IRE recitation format, academically productive talk involves students working hard to explicate their thinking, with evidence, whether in whole-class or small-group settings. It involves students listening to and responding constructively to the ideas of others, in the service of making progress around an intellectually rich problem, text, or investigation.

Characteristics of productive talk include the following:

- Students listening closely to one another

- Students doing the heavy lifting of

    ◦ explicating their ideas

    ◦ reasoning with evidence and models

    ◦ building on the thinking of others (agreeing, disagreeing, and questioning)

    ◦ making thinking—questions, models, data, arguments, explanations—public and available

- Students and teacher working together to clarify, challenge, and improve the group's thinking

- Equitable participation

- Risk-taking and opportunities for students to revise their thinking

Productive talk can take many forms, because the talk is always improvisational. There is no way to script academically productive talk because it is always the students, on the spot, who are contributing to the analysis and applying their reasoning to the thinking of others. But the talk is always about important academic content, and it is always focused around a rich problem or task designed to support reasoning and conceptual understanding.

This does not mean that academically productive talk is only student-to-student. The teacher is centrally involved in a variety of ways and formats. In the selection of the problem, task, or framing question, the teacher has a good deal of control. And in following up on and processing students' contributions, there are a number of strategies or "moves" that reliably help keep the conversation proceeding at a rigorous and productive level. These improvisational but strategic follow-up moves on the part of the teacher help keep the students tuned in to the contributions of others and guide the conversation so that it promotes reasoning with evidence, building toward conceptual understanding of key constructs or big ideas.

KEY COMPONENTS OF ACADEMICALLY PRODUCTIVE TALK

A Belief in the Possibility and Efficacy of This Kind of Talk

This first component is not something that happens in the classroom. It is a belief or mindset on the part of the teacher! For teachers to successfully take on this practice, they must believe two things, even if this entails a bit of a leap of faith at the outset: (1) All my students can learn from participating in well-structured discussions, and (2) my students are smart enough and capable enough to do this. In addition, a teacher must feel committed to two major learning objectives: (1) deep understanding of concepts, as contrasted with mere familiarity and ability to recognize concepts, and (2) students' ability to learn with increasing independence. Teachers who are successful in orchestrating academically productive talk believe that even very young children can tackle challenging, rich, and ambiguous problems and reason about them with evidence. They believe that if their students work hard at explaining their own ideas and their thinking with respect to the ideas of their classmates, they will become even stronger reasoners and learners, able to think for themselves about complex texts, problems, or situations. They believe that their students—even struggling students, English learners, or students with individualized education programs (IEPs)—are fundamentally sense-makers and that, with guidance, they all can engage in intellectually challenging and productive activities.

Well-Established Norms or Ground Rules for Talk

Before you can use talk reliably to promote learning, you have to have laid the foundation for talk by establishing a set of clear norms or ground rules for class discussions. There are three different kinds of norms that we have learned about from teachers who are successful at this. One is a norm about the focus of talk: students need to understand that classroom talk will *focus on reasoning*. It is important to establish this norm explicitly because, without it, students may expect the more typical focus—correct answers to the teacher's questions—to be in play. If students do not understand that the focus is on reasoning—their reasoning—they can be quite surprised by questions such as "Why do you think that?" or "How did you figure that out?" Some may even infer that you are trying to tell them that they are wrong.

Next, it is important that norms for *respectful talk* are in place—that is, that students will listen to one another attentively and respond respectfully. Students have to feel a sense of trust that their ideas will be taken seriously and that disagreements will be handled respectfully, so that ideas, not individuals, are challenged. Students have to speak loudly enough that everyone can hear (which is not easy for many students to do at first), and all students have to be on notice that if they can't hear something or don't understand what someone has said, they must speak up and ask for clarification.

Finally, students must understand that talk will be *equitable*: Students need to know that this kind of talk is not just for some—that is, the good talkers or the academically gifted. They have to understand that this kind of talk is expected of everyone, and everyone will have a chance to participate and express their ideas, perhaps not in every discussion, but certainly over the course of several days.

Establishing ground rules is particularly important in the secondary classroom, where students come with a long history of expectations about how to participate in science classrooms and a long history of expecting lecture and IRE recitation as the dominant mode.

Essential Goals for Productive Discussion

To support the kinds of talk we have been describing, there are four conditions that need to be in place. These are simple to state as goals, but they are not always easy to accomplish.

- **Goal 1: Help individual students share, expand, and clarify their *own* thoughts.** If a student is going to participate in the discussion, he or she has to be able to share thoughts and responses out loud in a way that is at least partially understandable to others. If only one or two students can do this, you don't have a discussion—you have a monologue or, at best, a dialogue between the teacher and a student.

- **Goal 2: Help students orient to and listen carefully to one another.** If a student is just sitting waiting to speak and is not *listening* to others and *trying to understand them*, he or she will not be able to contribute to a real discussion. Your ultimate goal involves sharing of ideas and reasoning, *not* simply a series of students giving their own unconnected thoughts one by one.

- **Goal 3: Help individual students deepen their own reasoning.** Even if students express their thoughts and listen to others' ideas, the discussion can still remain superficial or boring; it may fail to include solid and sustained reasoning. Most students are not skilled at pushing to understand and to deepen their own reasoning. Therefore, a key role of the teacher is to continually and skillfully press the students for reasoning and evidence.

- **Goal 4: Help students engage with others' reasoning.** The final step involves students actually taking up the ideas and reasoning of other students and responding to them. This is when real discussion can take off, discussion that will support robust learning. And it's exhilarating for students and teachers alike.

As teachers who are skilled at discussion know well, these four goals are conditions for academically productive talk and discussion, but they are not onetime goals. A teacher must keep them all in mind every day. Over time, your class may become a place where goals 1 and 2 are fairly stable. But in our experience, goals 3 and 4 require attention all year long.

Do these four goals all apply to each of the *NGSS* practices? Yes! Any time you are engaged in orchestrating a meaning-making conversation, in any of the practices, it will be critical that students actually talk and go public with their thinking, listen carefully to their peers, dig deeply into their evidence and data and reasoning, and build on and critique the thinking of others.

So how do teachers accomplish these goals? We have found that teachers who are skilled at consistently putting these goals in place use a variety of tools to help them. Some of the tools are norm-setting routines. Some are practices like think-pair-share, stop and jot, or wait time. Other talk tools are those we have come to call teacher talk moves, or talk moves for short.

What do we mean by talk moves? These are ordinary utterances (simple questions and statements) that build on what has come before in the conversation and are designed to get students to respond in productive ways. A simple example is the talk move we might call Why Do You Think That? It serves the purpose of getting a student to externalize his or her reasoning for the group. This move can be uttered in many different ways: "What's your evidence?" "What makes you say that?" "Did you find something in the text that made you think that?" "Can you explain your reasoning for us?" or "Talk us through your reasoning."

The talk moves we focus on all respond to a preceding student utterance and are designed to open up a space for one or more students to elaborate further on their own thinking or to connect with the thinking of others. We are not the first to use the term "move" in describing classroom talk. Bellack et al. (1966), in their description of classroom discourse, used the term "move" to evoke the image of a game, such as chess, in which a player makes one move expecting that his or her partner will make a move in response. Sinclair and Coulthard (1975), in an early and very influential analysis of classroom discourse, took up the term to describe "initiating" moves, which were intended to evoke "response" moves. (They were among the first to identify the IRE as a common sequence in classroom discourse.)

In the next section, we describe a number of these talk moves, and talk about their functions.

TALK TOOLS

Research over the past several decades and documentation of teachers who are particularly successful at facilitating productive discussions have led to the identification of a small number of general, all-purpose talk moves that are remarkably helpful tools for making discussions and conversations work. These talk moves can be used in any subject domain and are especially well-designed tools for multiparty talk in noisy and heterogeneous classroom settings. Successful discussion leaders use talk moves strategically to set students up to think, reason, and collaborate in academically productive ways. We will describe them against the backdrop of whole-class, teacher-led discussion, but they can be used within small-group work as well.

We will introduce these tools by listing them under the goal that they serve most obviously, but many teachers have pointed out to us that each tool can serve more than one goal. You will find, as you pick up these talk tools and work with them, that they can accomplish a number of complex purposes when used together or alone.

1. Talk Moves and Other Tools That Help Individual Students Share, Expand, and Clarify Their Own Thoughts

This "family" of talk moves sends the message that the teacher wants to understand the student's thinking. It sends a signal that the teacher wants more than just the nominally correct answer. It also gives the student time to regroup and clarify his or her thinking to formulate complex ideas so that others can understand.

Partner Talk

Let's start with a situation that causes anxiety for many teachers: You ask a question and no one says anything. No hands are raised. If you are taking on the challenge of the *NGSS*, your question is likely not one for which students can give a simple short answer. So it may be that they don't understand your question. After you clarify and make sure everyone understands the question, they may still not volunteer—they may be uncomfortable sharing their thinking with the whole group, or they may simply not have formulated a response they feel comfortable saying out loud.

At this point, a useful tool to get everyone ready, willing, and able to share his or her thinking is *Partner Talk*, also known as *think-pair-share,* or *consider and commit.* Tell students to talk to the person next to them for a minute or so (sometimes 30 seconds is enough!) and share their thoughts. After that time, many students will be ready to share something.

Say More (Asking a Student to Expand on What He or She Said)

Students often assume that their perspective is shared by everyone, so a student's response to a question is often very condensed and doesn't fully spell out his or her thinking. Because the student doesn't say much, it's hard to understand. We guarantee that if you start asking challenging questions, this will happen multiple times in every lesson!

So when someone is taciturn, you can use the Say More move and ask that student to expand: "Can you say more about that?" "Tell us more about your thinking." "Can you expand on that?" or "Can you give us an example?"

This move is also helpful when a student makes a contribution that you can't understand. And as any experienced teacher knows, this happens often! We have all used the tack of saying, "Hmm! Interesting! Anyone else?" in response to an unintelligible student utterance, but the Say More move is much more likely to result in that student trying to explain. And again, just because the *NGSS* asks students to share their reasoning, we have no reason to expect that they will be able to do so clearly every time. Thus, we need a tool that will help them clarify so that their thinking can support the work of the group.

VERIFYING AND CLARIFYING BY REVOICING (ASKING A STUDENT TO VERIFY OR CORRECT YOUR INTERPRETATION AND CLARIFY HIS OR HER THOUGHT)

When students talk about complex phenomena in science, it's often difficult to understand what they say. And if the teacher has trouble understanding a student's reasoning, the student's classmates will likely not do any better. Therefore, teachers need talk moves that can help them deal with the inevitable lack of clarity of many student contributions. They need tools that will allow them to interact with the student (without putting the student on the spot) in a way that will encourage that student to clarify his or her own reasoning.

One such tool has been called Verifying and Clarifying by Revoicing. Revoicing is *not* just repeating. In a Revoicing move, the teacher essentially tries to repeat some or all of what the student has said, and then *asks the student to verify* whether the teacher's representation is correct. In doing this, the teacher leaves room for the student to *clarify* the original intention.

2. Talk Moves That Help Students Orient to and Listen Carefully to One Another

WHO CAN RESTATE THAT? (ASKING STUDENTS TO RESTATE, REPEAT, OR REPHRASE WHAT HAS BEEN SAID)

When a student says something potentially important, whether it is correct or not, the teacher may want to make sure that everyone can engage with that idea. But if other students did not hear it or were not paying attention, they will not be able to take the next step and think about it. There are many ways to do this, using what we call a Who Can Restate That? move: "Who thinks they understood what Jashida was saying and can put it into their own words?" "Who can just restate what Jashida said?" "What do you think Jashida was saying?" or "That was interesting and complex! Who can restate just one thing Jashida said?"

Even in cases where the student is not correct, all students can benefit from understanding the reasoning behind the thought, particularly when a common misconception is at stake. And to understand it, they have to hear it. Even if the speaker is correct and clear, that does not mean that everyone else will hear and understand. Many students will tune out as they hear a classmate produce a long and complex piece of reasoning, with pauses and hesitations. This is an ideal time to use the Who Can Restate That? move, and ask for volunteers to put the student's ideas into their own words.

Some might object because this move takes extra time. It does take a few extra minutes of class time, but in our experience, everyone benefits. The student being repeated is honored by being taken seriously, and the student repeating has a chance to practice explicating a complex idea. And everyone in the group gets a second chance to hear and consider the idea. (In fact, this move can make a critical difference in inclusion for students learning English or students who need more time to process.) The entire group moves forward together toward a more academically productive discussion. It's important to note that "Who can repeat or put this into their own words?" is *not* a management move. Some teachers use this move to "catch" students who are not listening, but we recommend against using this as a management tool. Students will be more enthusiastic if you use it in a positive way, asking for volunteers who think they *have* understood to repeat the idea or put it into their own words.[1]

It's also important that this Who Can Restate That? move be used when students are correct *and* incorrect. If alternative conceptions or misconceptions are not explained and explored, students never fully come to understand what's problematic about them. It is through using the Who Can Restate That? move that the teacher can "set the table" for digging deeper into the data and letting different views to come into play.

3. Talk Moves That Help Students Dig Deeper Into Their Own Reasoning

ASK FOR EVIDENCE OR REASONING (ASKING STUDENTS TO EXPLAIN THEIR REASONING)

Even if students speak so that everyone can hear, and even if students listen carefully to one another, it's possible that the discussion will remain at a shallow or superficial level. To deepen the focus on shared reasoning, all students must get used to explaining *why* they say what they say and what the evidence is behind their claims. There are many ways to press for reasoning. Here are some examples:

―――――

1. At the beginning of your efforts to use productive classroom talk moves, some students may resist repeating. It's important to get across that they are allowed to say, "I didn't hear" or "I didn't understand," but they must then ask the person to repeat, and then you must follow up by asking them to repeat or put it into their own words.

- Why do you think that?

- What convinced you?

- Why did you think that strategy would work?

- Where in the text is there support for that claim?

- What is your evidence?

- What makes you think that?

- How did you get that answer?

- Can you prove that to us?

Some students are not used to explaining their thinking in this way and may at first be puzzled.[2] "How did you know?" "I just ... I followed the directions" or "I can't explain. I just know." So, it is important to be persistent in asking for reasoning.

CHALLENGE OR COUNTEREXAMPLE (PRESENTING A COUNTEREXAMPLE OR OTHER CHALLENGE)

Sometimes you will want to press students to dig more deeply into their reasoning by presenting them with conflicting evidence: "So, your claim says *XYZ*, but what about Sonia's example?" "Does it *always* work that way?" or "What if we used the copper cube instead? What would happen?"

4. Talk Moves That Help Students Think With Others or Apply Their Reasoning to the Ideas of Others

After all your students hear and understand the claim and the reasoning behind it, they are ready to think with that idea, to apply their own reasoning to the thinking of someone else.

DO YOU AGREE OR DISAGREE AND WHY? (ASKING STUDENTS TO TAKE A POSITION)

This talk move helps you bring the students into direct contact with the reasoning of their peers. There are a number of variants of this Agree or Disagree and Why? move. Other versions of this question include, "Who has a similar idea or a different idea about how this works, and how is it similar or different?" "Does someone want to respond to that idea and tell us why you agree or disagree?" Some teachers say, "Thumbs up if you agree; thumbs down if you disagree."

Note, however, that it is crucial that you follow up with the question, "*Why* do you agree?" or "*Why* do you disagree?" Otherwise, there's a chance that students will just "phone it in" and assert that they agree, without much thought. Moreover, asking, "Does everyone agree?" or "So, do we all agree?" and getting a chorus of yeses is *not* the same move. It telegraphs to everyone that there is one right answer, and students will stop pursuing their own ideas if they are different.

---

2. The question "Why do you think that?" is an ambiguous one. Students might at first think you are asking them whether they guessed, took someone else's idea, or figured it out for themselves, rather than explaining in words the reasoning behind their answer.

WHO CAN ADD ON? (ASKING STUDENTS TO ADD THEIR OWN IDEAS OR TAKE A POSITION)

Sometimes a student may explain his or her own reasoning or make a claim in a way that is clear enough and significant enough for others to respond to. This is a time when you can really help students engage with their classmate's reasoning and work to sustain and amplify the depth of the discussion. Asking, "Who can add on?" or "Who wants to respond to that?" invites anyone to join in and respond. You can also personalize this move by calling on a particular student.

5. Talk Tools That Apply to All Four Goals

WAIT TIME (3–5 SECONDS OF SILENCE; "TAKE YOUR TIME. WE'LL WAIT.")

This is perhaps an odd "talk tool" because it's actually silence: a pause in the talking. But providing time (3–5 seconds or more) after asking a question, as well as after a student has spoken, has repeatedly been shown to help students, particularly English language learners, expand, explain, and clarify their ideas.

Wait Time is a talk move that actually supports all four goals and can be used productively throughout a discussion. Wait Time is the most researched of all the talk tools, and it's been shown to have remarkable effects on the quality of both students' and teachers' thinking. Wait Time, as described in the work of Rowe (1986), involves waiting *at least* 3–5 seconds after you ask a question and then waiting again for the same interval *after* the student responds to the question before you respond.

The research on Wait Time is extensive. The research literature talks about two different kinds of Wait Time, both important and both powerful. The first is after you've asked a question, whether to the whole class or to a particular student. The second kind is after a student speaks, before you respond in any way to what the student has said. And of course, sometimes in the middle of a turn, a student pauses, and this second kind of Wait Time is important as well—that is, waiting after a student has paused or stopped talking.

The research—at all grade levels, and across all subject domains—shows that if you increase your Wait Time dramatic changes take place. Students say more. The length of student responses increases between 300% and 700%. They expand and clarify and explain their thinking, with evidence. The number of questions asked by students increases dramatically. Student-to-student talk increases. Increasing Wait Time *after* a student has talked is particularly powerful in increasing the complexity of student explanations and the depth of reasoning and in increasing the amount of student-to-student talk, where students spontaneously address a peer or ask a question of someone in the group (Rowe 1986).

Although the research is clear on the value of Wait Time, anyone who's tried to do it knows that it's difficult to change one's ingrained conversational style with respect to pausing. We tend to feel uncomfortable with silence, as though we are putting a student "on the spot." Yet few students can put together an answer to a complicated question after only a second or two. And English language learners may need even more time to formulate their ideas. So, if we do not use Wait Time consistently and patiently, students may give up and opt out of the conversation, assuming that someone else will carry the ball. If students opt out because they think they are not quick enough at formulating their ideas, they often stop listening closely to their peers. When this happens, everyone suffers. The discussion will not be enriched by the thinking of everyone in the group, and the talk will not lead to deeper learning for the entire group.

Poker Face/Evaluation Avoidance

This is the avoidance of the positive, smiling face and expressions of approval when a student is producing a "good" answer ("Yes! Right! Great!") or the grimace, wrinkled brow, and expressions of negativity that emerge when a student response is wrong, hard to understand, or incoherent ("Okay ... well ... someone else?")

Again, this is perhaps an odd "talk tool" because it's really about what is not said (positive or negative evaluations) and what is not expressed facially (again, evaluation). Earlier, we talked about the fact that the most common pattern of classroom talk (throughout the country and at all grade levels) is recitation—the IRE sequence, in which the teacher asks a question, a student responds, and the teacher evaluates the student's contribution, saying, "Good" or "Not quite. Anyone else have an idea?" Because this pattern is so deeply ingrained in teachers' and students' experience, it is very, very hard to change. But to orchestrate an academically productive discussion in working through a problem for which students have the tools to figure things out for themselves, the evaluation move (the E of the IRE) has got to go! And this is perhaps the most challenging but also the most transformational change in one's teaching as you take on this new discussion practice. Why should this be the case?

Many students are unaccustomed to explaining their ideas in detail and in depth, with evidence. Many are not accustomed to listening carefully to their peers, with interest and respect. A surefire way to shut down discussion is to focus too early on correctness or to telegraph the correct answer. This toolkit of talk moves helps you defer your evaluation of the students and instead helps you support the students in clarifying and formulating their own ideas. This positions the students to do the heavy lifting, taking seriously and evaluating their own and others' competing ideas in their strongest forms.

As we will discuss in the next section, a good framing question for a meaning-making discussion is, by design, one that will support *divergence* in student thinking: multiple solution paths, more than one interpretation, different ways of representing data, multiple models or explanations for a particular phenomenon, or different positions on the significance of some finding. The goal is for multiple student positions to emerge and get explicated and interrogated by the students, with the result that some ideas will be found to be compelling and others incorrect or inadequate. Some are going to be better than others, some will be mistaken, some will be unexpected, and some will be full of depth and cogency. But in all of this, the teacher's job in facilitating the discussion is to help the students clarify their ideas and ensure that they take each other's ideas seriously and critically evaluate the ideas. In the context of a problem designed to support student reasoning, the standard "evaluation" move (telegraphing correctness) on the part of the teacher can actually be *detrimental* to the process.

This is a strong claim and likely to be highly counterintuitive. Why would an evaluation move—a move that lets students know that they are on the right track or that they are mistaken—be a problem? Aren't correctness and understanding, after all, the goal here? The answer is a simple one. Reasoning and building and weighing arguments with evidence is more important in the long run than getting the right answer in the short run. Reasoning and argument will lead, over time, to deep and canonical (or correct) understanding of important concepts and will help students become powerful, lifelong thinkers and learners.

Teachers who have become successful leaders of academically productive discussions universally say that learning how to provide nonevaluative responses to students' ideas, in the midst of a discussion, is the single hardest thing to get the hang of. It's so contrary to what they have been doing for much of their teaching—that is, helping, nudging, suggesting, telegraphing, assisting, rephrasing their questions, reminding students what they did the day before, and so on—guiding students to get the preferred answer, interpretation, or line of thinking. Teachers say that they really struggle at first to provide a nonjudgmental response to a student's idea, especially if the student's idea is a correct and cogent one! These teachers have told us all sorts of strategies to avoid an evaluation or judgment. Instead of saying, "Great!" "Right," or "I like that idea," they say, "Hmm … interesting …" (in a thoughtful but neutral tone) and look down at their hands or off into the distance for a moment. Expert discussion leaders say that just that little bit of Wait Time gives them a good idea for what to say next: "Hmmm … can you say more about that?" "What do the rest of you think about that idea?" "Can anyone put into their own words what Hugo just said?" "Let me see if I've got your idea right. Are you saying that …?" (with space for the student to follow up) or "Hmm …" with a thoughtful nod of the head, a glance up at the ceiling, and more waiting. After a while, invariably, someone else speaks up!

The set of all-purpose follow-up moves, provided above, will help open up the conversation, rather than close it down. But be prepared: It is going to feel strange at first to be nonjudgmental, not telegraphing your evaluation of correctness either verbally or nonverbally. It feels strange whether the student contribution is brilliant or wildly incorrect. If it's brilliant, it seems cruel not to jump up and down and celebrate to boost this student's self-esteem. If it's incorrect, it seems like malpractice not to set the students straight. But this is where the leap of faith comes in. When students are expected to do the "heavy lifting," to listen hard and critically to their peers, they rise to the challenge and do it! Typically, when someone makes a mistake, if you treat the comment as interesting and important, other students will raise a question or an objection. And if they don't, you can say, "Can you say more about that?" and help the student explain his or her reasoning further. (This entails another leap of faith, the belief that students actually *do* have reasons behind wrong answers, and these can be very productive to examine as a group.)

FOCUS ON TALK MOVES AS TOOLS

These talk moves are *tools*—tools that you can get very good at using and that can help you take up the challenge of promoting productive talk. Like all tools, these talk moves take practice, ongoing experimentation, and the patience to try again after making mistakes. There's no such thing as perfection. These moves are relatively easy to pick up and try out, and the process can be exhilarating for both students and teachers alike. Many teachers have said things like the following: "These talk moves are not quite as simple as I first thought, but they totally changed my view of my students—what they can do."

Together, in the context of a rich task, talk moves help build a classroom culture of equity, risk-taking, intellectual effort, and respect. Teachers who use these moves strategically and successfully find that students, from all cultural and linguistic backgrounds—even those who have struggled in the past—make significant gains in learning and conceptual understanding, gains that show up in student writing as well as on standardized tests.

How and Why Do These Talk Moves Work?

Notice that each of the so-called productive talk moves listed above opens up a space for student reasoning, and positions the student as a thinker, a holder of a position, a reasoner, or an explainer. Moreover, these talk moves are ideally suited for classroom contexts—highly complex social arenas with large numbers of speakers. Classrooms are among the most challenging talk environments that exist in society, and most of the work that is accomplished in classrooms is carried primarily through talk. Classrooms are noisy in both a literal and figurative sense. Interruptions are shockingly frequent, and environmental noise (sirens, loudspeakers, hall noise) is unpredictable and invasive. In fact, the cultural, linguistic, and experiential diversity common in most classrooms in this country is another form of complexity, often making it hard to understand what students mean when they attempt to communicate complex or abstract academic ideas.

So, in orchestrating classroom talk so that it is academically productive for all students, these dimensions of the situation (e.g., noise, motivation, differential preparation) create obstacles. The talk tools introduced above can help in this moment-to-moment work. Because teachers need (at one and the same time) to manage multiple dimensions of the basic interaction, the tools can help. Consider that no matter what the instructional activity or what practice or content is being focused on, if it relies on group talk, the teacher has to pay attention to all of the following:

- **Managing intelligibility of the talk:** All students must be able to hear and understand the contributions of others if they are to benefit from being a part of the conversation. Several of these moves (e.g., Who Can Restate That? or Verifying and Clarifying by Revoicing) help ensure that everyone is hearing and following other students' contributions.

- **Supporting conceptual coherence and rigor:** The talk is improvisational, but it has to lead productively to conceptual understanding. This is not just "anything goes" talk, in which one student expresses his or her opinion, followed by another, followed by another. Students have to attend to and build on each other's ideas and provide evidence for their positions. Several of the talk moves press students for evidence (e.g., Say More, Ask for Evidence or Reasoning, or Wait Time). Others ask them to apply their reasoning to the reasoning of others, such as Agree or Disagree and Why? The Revoicing move can be used to juxtapose two different students' ideas (which may have occurred at different times) so that everyone can focus on them and engage with them ("So, let's see, Johan, you're saying …, and Selina, you're saying …? Is that right? So we have two different ideas here. What do the rest of you think?")

- **Encouraging motivation to participate:** Students have to feel as if they have a stake in the conversation and want to go public with their ideas. Several of the moves solicit additional viewpoints and encourage students to engage with the ideas of others. The Agree or Disagree and Why? move motivates students to work hard at explicating their ideas so that others can understand them. This move helps students feel as if they have a stake in the outcome of the discussion and want to hear and understand what others think.

- **Monitoring equitable participation:** This kind of talk is not just for the "good talkers." Some of the talk moves (e.g., Who Can Add On?) help the teacher promote equity, holding students accountable to the norm that it is everyone's responsibility to participate and contribute.

The talk moves on the list above are a set of "all-purpose" or general talk moves that can be used in any content domain, at any time of a lesson, at any grade level, to work on these obstacles. Some of the moves help you manage several of these at once. Moreover, there's a relatively small number of them.

Are Some Talk Tools Better Than Others?

Once introduced to the list of "productive" talk moves, people often ask if these are the *only* useful talk moves. The answer is a definite *no*. There are many productive and powerful talk moves! But many are very context specific, tailored to the particular content, the moment in the conversation, or the place in the lesson, such as a well-timed recap of what students have learned.

At the end of this chapter is an annex (pp. 332–333) with a table showing the productive talk tools discussed above. These can be printed out and kept on a clipboard in front of you. They can also be used as a tool for self-reflection or by colleagues who observe you during a discussion, who can check off each time they hear a talk move used to provide you some nonjudgmental feedback about how you're doing with them.

Talk Tools Are Not Enough

Talk moves and tools will not, in and of themselves, carry the day. Just as spoons, forks, and cutlery are crucial to a chef's work but are not the whole story, so a science teacher needs something great to talk about—rich, challenging tasks, texts, or problem sets. In addition to talk moves in support of the four goals for productive discussion, teachers need to have the following:

- **Clear academic purposes for the discussion (and deep understanding of the academic content itself):** While some teachers occasionally "luck into" a great discussion, teachers who reliably orchestrate academically productive talk take the time to plan and prepare for great discussions. They think in advance about the task their students will engage in—whether this is a specific problem, a text, or a hands-on investigation—and what the purpose of their discussion will be. They take the time to make sure that they truly understand the key concepts in play and how they relate to other concepts (that students have learned or will learn later). But most important, they take the time to get clear on the specific academic purposes of this particular discussion.
  Part of the planning process for a good discussion involves teachers getting clear about what they hope will emerge. (What practices or cluster of practices will the students likely be engaging in? What ideas exactly are you hoping the students will consolidate? What understandings should emerge from student generated data?)

In short, it's helpful to be able to articulate to yourself what key ideas you are hoping the students will come out with. What preconceptions or difficulties are students likely to have? What are some of the likely understandings students will explicate? What questions might prompt them to see an angle that they're not considering? It helps to think through the academic content at hand, the core concepts the task is supporting students to engage with, and the likely challenges the students will have with the ideas.

This kind of planning for academic purposes often leads back to other kinds of nuts and bolts questions about the talk itself. If the students are in a circle, will there have to be a way to make at least some of the science materials available and public? If students want to present their own data, how will everyone be able to see? Should key ideas that emerge be scribed? How will that work? And it helps for teachers to think specifically about their particular students. Who has been quiet lately that might be brought into this discussion? How should the students be seated or grouped? Might there be an opportunity for partner talk? If so, do students need to identify their talk partner in advance? What kind of partner talk question will help you achieve the goals of your discussion?

- **A well-thought-out basic or framing question to launch the discussion and a set of follow-up or cluster questions:** On the basis of these considerations around academic purposes or learning goals, the teacher will then think hard about a way to start the discussion, with an open, but clear, framing question. In order for the framing question to support rich and productive reasoning talk, there should not be one simple right answer that the teacher is looking for. (This would result in the launching of an IRE recitation session.) Rather, the question should be designed to spark multiple positions or perspectives or solution paths that can be taken, explicated, and argued for with evidence. Sometimes, this launching question is suggested in the curriculum materials. Other times, the teacher has to invent it or adapt it from the curriculum guide. Honing or cultivating a good framing question is a major piece of intellectual work that successful teachers engage in.

Do Different Practices Call for Different Kinds of Talk?

Do teachers need to plan different kinds of talk for the different science and engineering practices? Students' talk may look different in some ways when they engage in different practices. For example, when a student is explicating a model and explaining how his or her model differs from someone else's (science practice 2), we may see individual students presenting ideas they have worked through at length, so these may be longer,

Figure 14.1
The science and engineering practices support each other organically

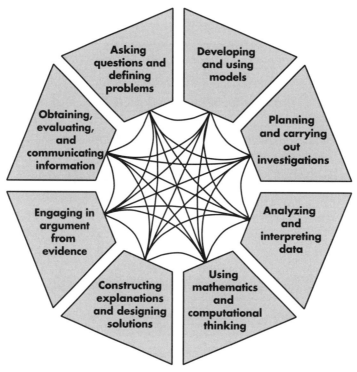

more planned turns at talk. In contrast, when students are Asking Questions and Defining Problems (practice 1), their talk is likely to be more exploratory and tentative, perhaps with more frequent back and forth. This in turn will differ in some ways from talk involved in Analyzing and Interpreting Data (practice 4).

But this does not mean that we need a different framework for using talk productively with each different practice. As we begin to look closely at the actual talk that transpires in classrooms that are supporting students to engage in the practices, we will see a *fluid shifting* among practices from moment to moment. Within one lesson, we may observe several different practices supporting one another in an organic fashion—discussing a model in service of explanation, then discussing data in light of a particular question about developing a model, and so on (Figure 14.1).

This point has been made repeatedly throughout the book, but we'll make it again here: It's important to remember that the practices are not synonymous with different classroom "activities." Rather, they are intellectual practices, and they interrelate and feed one another, so that students will be interpreting and using data (practice 4) to further develop a model (practice 2), to provide an explanation (practice 6) or to critique someone else's argument with evidence (practice 7). In one single student turn, we might find evidence of multiple practices in play.

It's important to note that practices are not equivalent to discrete parts of a lesson (e.g., "On Mondays, we generate questions. On Tuesdays, we develop models. On Wednesdays, we plan and carry out investigations"). They're not simply a different set of terms for what we used to call the scientific method. Instead, these are fluid thinking practices used in service of making sense, building knowledge, developing causal explanations for complex phenomena. All of the practices float on a sea of talk (a phrase first used by James Britten when he was writing about developing student writers), and for talk to support learning, there has to be a classroom culture of public reasoning.

Conclusion

At the outset, we suggested that a focus on talk brings together critical issues relevant to good teaching: a focus on specific academic content and a focus on students as thinkers and what they bring to the conversation in terms of interests, ways with words, and cultural knowledge. Skillfully facilitated discussions—in which students do more of the actual work of explicating and arguing and reasoning—have to become the "new normal" if we expect all students to participate in the intellectual practices called for in the *NGSS*. And while the intellectual practices differ across the domains, at the core of all of these reforms is a focus on reasoning, evidence-based argument, and thinking productively with others. While the shift from "recitation to reasoning" will be complex and challenging, talk moves and strategies are powerful tools for teachers to try out and explore with colleagues in the service of making thinking visible and available, and supporting robust engagement in the *NGSS* practices for all students.

Acknowledgments

Funding for the authors' research came from the National Science Foundation under Grant No. REC-02131893 to Boston University and Grant No. DRL-1251611 to Clark University. Sarah Michaels's research was also supported by a Math Science Partnership grant to the Connecticut Department of Education and grants from the Vermont Science Initiative and the Michigan Department of Education. The opinions expressed herein are those of the authors and not necessarily those of these foundations and other agencies that helped fund this work.

ANNEX

This annex shows some basic productive talk tools and examples of questions to ask.

Encourage individual students to share, expand, and clarify their own thinking.

Partner Talk
• Talk to the person next to you for one minute.
Say More
• Can you say more about that?
• What do you mean by that?
• Can you give an example?
Verifying and Clarifying by Revoicing
• So, let me see if I've got what you're saying. Are you saying …?
• Always leave space for the original student to agree or disagree and say more.

Encourage students to listen carefully to one another.

Who Can Restate That?
• Who can restate what Javon just said?
• Who thinks they understand what Jenny said and can restate it for us?

Press for deeper reasoning.

Ask for Evidence or Reasoning
• Why do you think that?
• What's your evidence?
• How did you arrive at that conclusion?
• How does your evidence relate to your claim?
Challenge or Counterexample
• Does it always work that way?
• But how does that idea square with Sonia's example?
• That's a good question. What do *you* think?
• Where in your model do you see that part of the phenomenon?

Press students to work with the reasoning of others.

Agree or Disagree and Why?
• Do you agree or disagree? And why?
• Are you saying the same thing as Jeyla or something different, and if different, how is it different?
Who Can Add On?
• Who can add on to the idea that Jamal is building?
• Do others have things to add?
• Do some people see it a different way?

Use all-purpose talk moves.

Wait Time
• Wait 3–5 seconds after asking a question and 3–5 seconds after a student provides a response.
Poker Face/Evaluation Avoidance
• Avoid telegraphing positive or negative feedback about a correct or incorrect response.

Source: Adapted from Chapin, O'Connor, and Anderson 2011 and Michaels and O'Connor 2012.

References

Adey, P., and M. Shayer. 2001. *Thinking science*. London: Nelson Thornes.

Bellack, A., H. Kliebard, R. Hyannis, and F. Smith. 1966. *The language of the classroom*. New York: Teachers College Press.

Chapin, S. H., C. O'Connor, and N. C. Anderson. 2011. *Classroom discussions: Seeing math discourse in action, grades K–6. DVDs, facilitator's guide and CD of reproducibles*. New York: Math Solutions and Scholastic Publications.

Michaels, S., and C. O'Connor. 2012. Talk science primer. Cambridge, MA: TERC. *http://inquiryproject.terc.edu/shared/pd/TalkScience_Primer.PDF*.

O'Connor, C., S. Michaels, and S. Chapin. 2015. "Scaling down" to explore the role of talk in learning: From district intervention to controlled classroom study. In *Socializing intelligence through academic talk and dialogue,* ed. L. Resnick, C. Asterhan, and S. Clarke, 111–126. Washington, DC: American Educational Research Association.

Resnick, L., C. Asterhan, and S. Clarke, eds. 2015. *Socializing intelligence through academic talk and dialogue*. Washington, DC: American Educational Research Association.

Reznitskaya, A., R. C. Anderson, B. McNurlen, K. Nguyen-Jahiel, A. Archodidou, and S. Kim. 2001. Influence of oral discussion on written argument. *Discourse Processes* 32 (2–3): 155–157.

Rowe, M. 1986. Slowing down may be a way of speeding up. *Journal of Teacher Education* 37 (1): 43–50.

Sinclair, J., and M. Coulthard. 1975. *Towards an analysis of discourse: The English used by teachers and pupils.* Oxford: Oxford University Press.

Additional Resources

Alexander, R. 2004. Talk for learning: The second year. Evaluation report for the North Yorkshire County Council. *www.robinalexander.org.uk/wp-content/uploads/2015/12/North-Yorks-report-04.pdf.*

Applebee, A. N., J. A. Langer, M. Nystrand, and A. Gamoran. 2003. Discussion-based approaches to developing understanding: Classroom instruction and student performance in middle and high school English. *American Educational Research Journal* 40 (3): 685–730.

Ball, D. L., and H. Bass. 2000. Making believe: The collective construction of public mathematical knowledge in the elementary classroom. In *Yearbook of the national society for the study of education: Constructivism in education,* ed. D. Phillips, 193–224. Chicago: University of Chicago Press.

Beck, I. L., and M. G. McKeown. 2006. *Improving comprehension with questioning the author: A fresh and expanded view of a powerful approach.* New York: Scholastic.

Bill, V. L., M. N. Leer, L. E. Reams, and L. B. Resnick. 1992. From cupcakes to equations: The structure of discourse in a primary mathematics classroom. *Verbum* 15 (1): 63–85.

Boaler, J., and M. Staples. 2008. Creating mathematical futures through an equitable teaching approach: The case of Railside School. *Teachers College Record* 110 (3): 608–645.

Brown, A. L., and A. S. Palincsar. 1989. Guided, cooperative learning and individual knowledge acquisition. In *Knowing, learning, and instruction: Essays in honor of Robert Glaser*, ed. L. B. Resnick, 393–451. Hillsdale, NJ: Erlbaum.

Cazden, C. 2001. *Classroom discourse: The language of teaching and learning.* Portsmouth, NH: Heinemann.

Chinn, C. A., and R. C. Anderson. 1998. The structure of discussions that promote reasoning. *Teachers College Record* 100 (2): 315–368.

Cobb, P., T. Wood, E. Yackel, J. Nicholls, G. Wheatley, B. Trigatti, and M. Perlwitz. 1991. Assessment of a problem-centered second-grade mathematics project. *Journal for Research in Mathematics Education* 22 (1): 3–29.

Driver, R., P. Newton, and J. Osborne. 2000. Establishing the norms of scientific argumentation in classrooms. *Science Education* 84 (3): 287–312.

Duschl, R. A., and J. Osborne. 2002. Supporting and promoting argumentation discourse in science education. *Studies in Science Education* 38 (1): 39–72.

Dweck, C. 2006. *Mindset: The new psychology of success.* New York: Ballantine Books.

Engle, R. A., and F. C. Conant. 2002. Guiding principles for fostering productive disciplinary engagement: Explaining an emergent argument in a community of learners classroom. *Cognition and Instruction* 20 (4): 399–483.

Ford, M. J., and E. A. Forman. 2006. Redefining disciplinary learning in classroom contexts. In *Review of Research in Education*. Vol. 30, ed. J. Green and A. Luke, 1–32. Washington, DC: American Educational Research Association.

Goldman, S. R., and D. M. Bloome. 2005. Learning to construct and integrate. In *Experimental cognitive psychology and its applications*, ed. A. F. Healy, 169–182. Washington, DC: American Psychological Association.

Greeno, J. 1998. The situativity of knowing, learning and research. *American Psychologist* 53 (1): 5–26.

Kuhn, D., V. Shaw, and M. Felton. 1997. Effects of dyadic interaction on argumentative reasoning. *Cognition and Instruction* 15 (3): 287–315.

Kuhn, D., and W. Udell. 2003. The development of argument skills. *Child Development* 74 (5): 1245–1260.

Lampert, M. 1990. When the problem is not the question and the solution is not the answer: Mathematical knowing and teaching. *American Educational Research Journal* 27 (1): 29–63.

Lefstein, A., and J. Snell. 2011. Classroom discourse: The promise and complexity of dialogic practice. In *Insight and impact: Applied linguistics and the primary school*, ed. S. Ellis, E. McCartney, and J. Bourne, 165–185. Cambridge, UK: Cambridge University Press.

McKeown, M. G., I. Beck, and R. G. K. Blake. 2009. Rethinking reading comprehension instruction: A comparison of instruction for strategies and content approaches. *Reading Research Quarterly* 44 (3): 218–253.

Mercer, N., L. Dawes, R. Wegerif, and C. Sams. 2004. Reasoning as a scientist: Ways of helping children to use language to learn science. *British Educational Research Journal* 30 (3): 359–377.

Mercer, N., R. Wegerif, and L. Dawes. 1999. Children's talk and the development of reasoning in the classroom. *British Educational Research Journal* 25 (1): 95–111.

Murphy, P. K., I. A. G. Wilkinson, A. O. Soter, M. N. Henessey, and J. F. Alexander. 2009. Examining the effects of classroom discussion on students' comprehension of text: A meta-analysis. *Journal of Educational Psychology* 101 (3): 740–764.

Nussbaum, E. M., and G. M. Sinatra. 2003. Argument and conceptual engagement. *Contemporary Educational Psychology* 28 (3): 384–395.

Nystrand, M., and A. Gamoran. 1991. Instructional discourse, student engagement, and literature achievement. *Research in the Teaching of English* 25 (3): 261–290.

Osborne, J. F., S. Erduran, and S. Simon. 2004. Enhancing the quality of argument in school science. *Journal of Research in Science Teaching* 41 (10): 994–1020.

Palincsar, A.-M., and A. L. Brown. 1984. Reciprocal teaching of comprehension-fostering and comprehension-monitoring activities. *Cognition and Instruction* 1 (2): 117–175.

Pontecorvo, C., and H. Girardet. 1993. Arguing and reasoning in understanding historical topics. *Cognition and Instruction* 11 (3–4): 365–395.

Resnick, L. B., S. Michaels, and C. O'Connor. 2010. How (well structured) talk builds the mind. In *From genes to context: New discoveries about learning from educational research and their applications*, ed. R. Sternberg and D. Preiss, 163–194. New York: Springer.

Resnick, L. B., and S. Nelson-Le Gall. 1997. Socializing intelligence. In *Piaget, Vygotsky and beyond: Future issues for developmental psychology and education*, ed. L. Smith, J. Dockrell, and P. Tomlinson, 145–158. New York: Routledge.

Scardamalia, M., and C. Bereiter. 2006. Knowledge building: Theory, pedagogy, and technology. In *Cambridge handbook of the learning sciences*, ed. R. K. Sawyer, 97–118. New York: Cambridge University Press.

Sfard, A. 2008. *Thinking as communicating: Human development, the growth of discourses, and mathematizing.* Cambridge, UK: Cambridge University Press.

Shayer, M. 1999. Cognitive acceleration through science education II: Its effects and scope. *International Journal of Science Education* 21 (8): 883–902.

Simon, S., and K. Richardson. 2009. Argumentation in school science: Breaking the tradition of authoritative exposition through a pedagogy that promotes discussion and reasoning. *Argumentation* 23 (4): 469–493.

Slavin, R. E. 2010. Cooperative learning: What makes group work work? In *Innovative learning environments*, ed. D. Istance, F. Benavides, and H. Dumont, 163–178. Paris: Organisation for Economic Co-operation and Development.

Stein, M. K., R. A. Engle, M. S. Smith, and E. K. Hughes. 2008. Orchestrating productive mathematical discussions: Five practices for helping teachers move beyond show and tell. *Mathematical Thinking and Learning* 10 (4): 313–340.

Topping, K. J., and S. Trickey. 2007a. Collaborative philosophical enquiry for school children: Cognitive effects at 10–12 years. *British Journal of Educational Psychology* 77 (2): 271–288.

Topping, K. J., and S. Trickey. 2007b. Collaborative philosophical inquiry for schoolchildren: Cognitive gains at 2-year follow-up. *British Journal of Educational Psychology* 77 (4): 787–796.

Walshaw, M., and G. Anthony. 2008. The teacher's role in classroom discourse: A review of recent research into mathematics classrooms. *Review of Educational Research* 78 (3): 516–551.

Webb, N. M. 2009. The teacher's role in promoting collaborative dialogue in the classroom. *British Journal of Educational Psychology* 79 (1): 1–28.

Wells, G. 2007. Semiotic mediation, dialogue and the construction of knowledge. *Human Development* 50 (5): 244–274.

15

PUTTING IT ALL TOGETHER

Two Examples of Teaching With the *NGSS*

MARK WINDSCHITL, CAROLYN COLLEY, AND BETHANY SJOBERG

In this book, we have provided many vivid images of students who are learning science in meaningful ways. As you read about the different practices, you were probably asking questions such as "How could I design a unit of instruction in which my students have rich opportunities to engage in science practices?" "How could I shape instruction so that the connections between practices make sense to students?" and "How can my students use the practices to develop deep and flexible understandings of important science ideas?"

In this chapter, we provide guidance about how these goals can be accomplished, using two examples. One of these features a fourth-grade teacher developing a unit about sound, and the other tells the story of a teacher developing a unit on ecosystems for high school sophomores. We'll use these authentic scenarios to make visible the thinking of teachers who are implementing the *Next Generation Science Standards* (*NGSS*; NGSS Lead States 2013). To do this, we'll first describe a planning sequence that can help you sort out the important science ideas from the *NGSS* and your own curriculum, and then we'll help you select an anchoring event or phenomenon that will become the object of students' investigations throughout the unit. Finally, we will show you how the science practices can be used together during the unit, as an integrated set of activities, to help students understand content and how the discipline works.

How Do I Plan for a Unit Based on the *NGSS*?

UNPACKING THE CURRICULUM AND THE STANDARDS

Our fourth-grade teacher, Carolyn, and a high school teacher, Bethany, work with very different groups of students, but they used the same strategies to prepare their units. We'll start with the elementary example and the topic of sound.

The first planning move that Carolyn and her teacher colleagues made was to put two resources on the table—their curriculum and the *NGSS*. As they read through their curriculum, they took note of terms and phrases that seemed to represent important science ideas; these often appeared in bold type. Some of the ideas they identified were frequency; pitch; waves; energy; sound traveling through solids, liquids, and gases;

vibrations; and air as a medium. They wrote each of these on an index card so the team could lay them out and prioritize them as a group. But before sorting the cards, they turned to the *NGSS*.

In the *NGSS*, they looked for the kinds of science practices and ideas about sound that were appropriate for their grade level. Figure 15.1 shows two relevant performance expectations. What the teachers focused on at this point were not the science practices but rather conceptual ideas about sound in the *NGSS*. They wanted to see what overlaps there were between ideas in their curriculum materials and the disciplinary core ideas in the *NGSS*. After looking through the *NGSS*, they decided to add more ideas to their index card collection. These were transfer of energy, collisions, producing sound from electricity, and waves as patterns of motion. They felt that these ideas should be given priority when they were compared with ideas drawn from the curriculum. The brief descriptions in the *NGSS* of the disciplinary core ideas (listed below the performance expectations) clarified for the teachers what the performance expectations meant. It is also very useful to go directly to the expanded description of each disciplinary core idea in *A Framework for K–12 Science Education* (*Framework*; NRC 2012) to get a more complete understanding of each science idea.

The teachers tried to unpack all the ideas they had encountered and decided to do some background reading before meeting again. Here we want to emphasize an important point. The teachers we work with have developed the habit of questioning their own understandings of the science. We are talking about high school, middle school, and elementary school teachers. If you try this, it will be uncomfortable at first to admit to colleagues that you are unsure about fundamental aspects of the ideas you'll be teaching. But if you make it a group norm to ask yourselves questions such as "Why does this happen?" and "What exactly does this mean?" then you will begin to feel more comfortable deepening your own content understandings, and your planning will be much easier.

Let's return now to our fourth-grade teachers. When they came together again a week later, they sorted the cards out. This process helped them move from an all-inclusive assortment of ideas to focusing on two or three that they identified as most important. These were the ideas students were going to spend the most time on during the unit. To get to this point, Carolyn and her colleagues arranged the cards on a table and negotiated with one another as to which ideas had the greatest explanatory power, moving them to the center. The key question they asked themselves was "Which of these ideas, if our students could understand them deeply, would help explain a number of other ideas on the cards in front of us?" One helpful aid they used was this sentence frame: If our students understood [our primary idea] they would really be able to reason about these ideas [name at least two or three other ideas] because [describe how our primary idea can explain other ideas].

Figure 15.1
Two performance expectations relevant to sound

4-PS3-2. Make observations to provide evidence that energy can be transferred from place to place by sound, light, heat, and electric currents.

Disciplinary core ideas: PS3.B: Conservation of Energy and Energy Transfer
Energy is present whenever there are moving objects, sound, light, or heat. When objects collide, energy can be transferred from one object to another, thereby changing their motion. In such collisions, some energy is typically also transferred to the surrounding air; as a result, the air gets heated and sound is produced. Light also transfers energy from place to place. Energy can also be transferred from place to place by electric currents, which can then be used locally to produce motion, sound, heat, or light. The currents may have been produced to begin with by transforming the energy of motion into electrical energy.

4-PS4-1. Develop a model of waves to describe patterns in terms of amplitude and wavelength and that waves can cause objects to move.
[Clarification Statement: Examples of models could include diagrams, analogies, and physical models using wire to illustrate wavelength and amplitude of waves.]

Disciplinary core ideas: PS4.A: Wave Properties
Waves, which are regular patterns of motion, can be made in water by disturbing the surface. When waves move across the surface of deep water, the water goes up and down in place; it does not move in the direction of the wave except when the water meets the beach. Waves of the same type can differ in amplitude (height of the wave) and wavelength (spacing between wave peaks).

Two ideas ended up at the center of the table. These were not copied directly from the curriculum or the *NGSS*, but they were combinations of ideas found in one or the other source.

- Sound is energy, in the form of waves, that moves from one place to another, through matter.

- Sound waves are created by the "bumping" of molecules into one another, but the molecules themselves don't move from one place to another.

As the teachers were identifying these central ideas, they were also creating connections between those ideas and several other concepts they had identified. These additional ideas were arranged in a circle that surrounded the two biggest ideas. Other ideas appeared more peripheral, meaning they did not explain very much about sound, and were moved to the edge of the table. For example, the teachers felt that trying to address light waves would spread their instructional time too thin and could cause their students to lose their focus on sound. In summary, the ideas that were moved to the center shaped the unit, and teachers then unpacked these in preparation for the next phase of planning.

This process of identifying and prioritizing science ideas was also used by Bethany and her high school teacher colleagues as they planned for their ecosystem unit. They looked through their curriculum materials and found dozens of seemingly important ideas. They then looked through the *NGSS* and found several expectations that could apply to ecosystems. Similarly to the fourth-grade example, there was a lot of important content embedded in the disciplinary core ideas as described in the orange foundation box and the *Framework*—not just one concept, but many interrelated ideas.

When Bethany and her colleagues recorded all the potential topics from both their curriculum and the *NGSS*, they realized that there was no way to address all the standards in a single unit. They decided to select a set of standards that seemed to be related to one another (Figure 15.2) and to teach those within the context of an ecosystem example. The other performance expectations were going to become part of a follow-up unit. After Bethany's colleagues made this choice, they completed their card sort for the first unit. Two ideas migrated to the center of the table:

- A population of organisms in an ecosystem is always in flux because it is interdependent with other populations in different ways and because populations regularly exceed the carrying capacity of that ecosystem.

- Ecosystem activity is shaped by how energy is made available to different populations, and that energy is constantly being transferred and transformed but never lost.

As with the elementary example, the teachers felt they owned these ideas because they combined concepts from the curriculum and the *NGSS*, but more so because the ideas reflected how the teachers had come to make sense of what was important to know about ecosystems.

DEVELOPING AN ANCHORING EVENT

At this point, both Carolyn and Bethany were ready to select an event, process, or situation that could anchor the unit. An anchoring event is something that happens in the world (a phenomenon) that can become the focus of students' science investigations over the course of a unit. We have found that anchoring events work best if they are context rich, meaning that they are about a *specific* event that happens in a *specific* place and time under *specific* conditions. These specifics are precisely what make the situation interesting to students. Explaining how all these contextual features affect the event

Figure 15.2
Standards related to teaching about ecosystems

HS-LS2-6. Evaluate the claims, evidence, and reasoning that the complex interactions in ecosystems maintain relatively consistent numbers and types of organisms in stable conditions, but changing conditions may result in a new ecosystem. [Clarification Statement: Examples of changes in ecosystem conditions could include modest biological or physical changes.]

Disciplinary core ideas: LS2.A: Interdependent Relationships in Ecosystems
Ecosystems have carrying capacities, which are limits to the numbers of organisms and populations they can support. These limits result from such factors as the availability of living and nonliving resources and from such challenges as predation, competition, and disease. Organisms would have the capacity to produce populations of great size were it not for the fact that environments and resources are finite. This fundamental tension affects the abundance of species in any given ecosystem.

HS-LS2-1. Use mathematical and/or computational representations to support explanations of factors that affect carrying capacity of ecosystems at different scales. [Clarification Statement: Examples of mathematical comparisons could include graphs, charts, histograms, and population changes gathered from simulations or historical data sets.]

Disciplinary core ideas: LS2.B: Cycles of Matter and Energy Transfer in Ecosystems
Photosynthesis and cellular respiration provide most of the energy for life processes. At each link upward in a food web, only a small fraction of the matter consumed at the lower level is transferred upward, to produce growth and release energy in cellular respiration at the higher level. Given this inefficiency, there are generally fewer organisms at higher levels of a food web. Some matter reacts to release energy for life functions, some matter is stored in newly made structures, and much is discarded. The chemical elements that make up the molecules of organisms pass through food webs and into and out of the atmosphere and soil, and they are combined and recombined in different ways. At each link in an ecosystem, matter and energy are conserved.

HS-LS4-5. Evaluate the evidence supporting claims that changes in environmental conditions may result in: (1) increases in the number of individuals of some species, (2) the emergence of new species over time, and (3) the extinction of other species. [Clarification Statement: Emphasis is on determining cause and effect relationships for how changes to the environment such as deforestation, fishing, application of fertilizers, drought, flood, and the rate of change of the environment affect distribution or disappearance of traits in species.]

Disciplinary core ideas: LS2.C: Ecosystem Dynamics, Functioning, and Resilience
A complex set of interactions within an ecosystem can keep its numbers and types of organisms relatively constant over long periods of time under stable conditions. If a modest biological or physical disturbance to an ecosystem occurs, it may return to its more or less original status (i.e., the ecosystem is resilient), as opposed to becoming a very different ecosystem. Extreme fluctuations in conditions or the size of any population, however, can challenge the functioning of ecosystems in terms of resources and habitat availability. Moreover, anthropogenic changes (induced by human activity) in the environment including habitat destruction, pollution, introduction of invasive species, overexploitation, and climate change can disrupt an ecosystem and threaten the survival of some species.

is also what makes the explanations more rigorous (again, not something that can be copied from a textbook). This is not a "basics first" approach, in which students learn disconnected facts, vocabulary, and formulas first. The research literature on learning is clear on the point that students learn best from being engaged with complex problems. It is within the quest to understand these problems that facts, concepts, and mathematical equations become useful to students.

To maximize student engagement, teachers can connect all activities in a unit to an essential question, one that is written to relate to students' lives, previous experiences, or interests. Often, students come up with their own intriguing puzzles that are worth pursuing over the unit. No matter who develops it, an essential question should not be answerable with a yes/no response; rather, it should require students to integrate different concepts they learn with one another. Each activity students do in a unit of instruction is in service of answering this question, and students constantly revisit this question throughout the unit. By coming back to a relevant essential question, teachers are able to do more than just "hook" students at the beginning of a unit. Here are a few sample essential questions: "What makes wounds heal in different ways?" (cell biology); "Why is asthma so prevalent in poor urban communities?" (respiratory system); "What keeps things from rusting and why?" (oxidation in chemistry); "How does a pulley help me lift something heavier than I am?" (forces in physical science). The anchoring event can be the inspiration or starting point for these questions.

We want to make clear that anchoring events cannot be the basis for all learning in a unit of instruction. No event or process can embody every single science idea around a topic in the *NGSS*. There will be days when you have to teach an idea that may only be tangentially related to the anchoring event you've chosen, but these days are the exception rather than the rule. An anchoring event and its essential question, then, are not the only things students study during a unit, but they do represent the focus of students' ongoing attempts to explain something complex, and this adds coherence to the unit of study. Picking one event to focus on over the long term is a different approach to teaching than having students do one separate lesson after another, for which they often don't see a larger purpose.

Selecting Anchoring Events for the Sound Unit and the Ecosystem Unit

Carolyn and her colleagues considered three big questions in thinking of an anchoring event:

- What kind of event, situation, or process will require students to integrate a range of important science ideas (found in the curriculum and the *NGSS*) to explain it?

- How can we add some contextual features to the anchoring event so that it becomes more compelling to explain but also more challenging?

- How can we describe the event or situation to make sure students will construct an evidence-based explanation that is not just reproduced from some textbook?

Many events or situations were nominated by the elementary teachers. They discussed the importance of some event or situation in which sound is clearly "energetic," travels from one place to another, has different qualities depending on how it is produced, and has some evident transformations of energy. The teachers eventually chose the situation of a singer breaking a glass with the sound energy from his voice. Carolyn argued that, as students were developing an explanatory model for this phenomenon, they would have to wrestle with the ideas of sound as energy, air as a medium of transmission, and the characteristics of sound waves at the unobservable level (wavelength, amplitude, frequency) and at the observable level (pitch, volume, the propagation of sound in all directions at once). Her fourth graders would not only have to know about each of these ideas but would also have to coordinate each of these ideas in an explanatory model that described why the glass broke—broke in a particular way, at a particular moment, and under particular conditions.

To prepare for the unit, Carolyn and her teaching partners spent time constructing their own causal models and wrote out their own explanations for the glass shattering. During this process, they found where the gaps were in their own understanding and sought out resources to help them create more coherent and accurate models before the unit started. This groundwork was critical in that it deepened their own content knowledge and understanding of the phenomenon. It gave them confidence to use this event with students. This preplanning also helped them see what parts of their curriculum activities would be relevant to students' final explanations and which would be set aside.

In the high school example, Bethany engaged in the same planning processes with her colleagues. They decided to ask students a question that was simple to express but challenging to fully explain: "Why, in a local ecosystem, was the population of hares oscillating up and down every 12 years?" Bethany and her colleagues knew their students would have to coordinate the ideas of energy moving through an ecosystem in various forms; direct and indirect effects that populations of organisms have on each other; and the concept of niches, competition for resources, and organisms' responses to changes in the environment.

Once Carolyn and Bethany had developed full explanations for their anchoring events, they used these explanations to select readings and activities and determine the sequencing of ideas. For each part of the explanation, these teachers knew that they would have to provide students with learning experiences that would help them understand that component. Much of their standard curriculum ended up being used, but some lessons were rearranged, others were repurposed, and several were thrown out entirely because they contributed little to the final explanation. Once this was done, both groups of teachers could then look at the performance expectations of the *NGSS* and plan for how students would participate in these during the unit.

TEACHING A UNIT: USING AN ENSEMBLE OF SCIENCE PRACTICES FOR SENSE-MAKING

We'll start this section with a cautionary note. The performance expectations in the *NGSS* are not meant to be separate learning events that get dropped into a unit of instruction and "checked off" as students complete them. As you have seen in the other chapters in this book, the practices are interrelated with one another and with content ideas. We use the word "ensemble" to express that each of the practices plays a specific role in knowledge building and that the practices must be used together to create, test, and revise ideas. In our work, we put the practices of modeling and explanation at the core and organize the other practices around these two.

We present basic overviews of these units to show that modeling and explanation are not some exotic processes that teachers might find unfamiliar; rather, these two practices link the types of activity that most teachers already do (experimentation, readings, class discussions, other science practices) in more purposeful ways with the objective of supporting students as they refine ideas.

Carolyn's Unit and the Use of Science Practices to Make Sense of Shattering Glass

Carolyn started her unit by showing students a video of a young man grasping a long-stemmed glass with a plastic straw in it. He appeared to be concentrating on the glass and then began to produce a loud tone with his voice. In a few moments, the straw started dancing wildly, and within seconds, the glass shattered. Students excitedly offered observations without prompting: "He yelled right at the glass," "I saw the glass shaking," and "Only the top of the glass broke!" After some conversation about what they could see and hear in the video, Carolyn shifted their attention to what they thought was going on that they could not directly observe. Students offered ideas about air moving, invisible forces, and the possibility of magic. Following this discussion, students drew their initial models using a before-during-after template supplied by the teacher. Later that afternoon, Carolyn examined their drawings and noted both what students seemed to know already (their partial understandings) and what gaps they seemed to have in their thinking.

The next day, Carolyn had her students do a gallery walk, looking at each other's initial models. She then called them back to the whole-class setting and asked what hypotheses were described in some of the models they saw. The teacher, with students' assistance, decided on five hypotheses (or partial theories) and how they could be stated. They recorded these on poster paper. This served as a way to make the thinking of more of the class visible, but it also organized and consolidated a range of ideas in one place. This resource remained on the classroom wall throughout the unit. The space under each of the hypotheses was eventually filled with note cards, written by students, describing whether an activity, experiment, or reading supported or disconfirmed that particular idea. This is part of the explanation-building process.

Let's pause in our description here to recap how different science practices have reinforced one another so far. The students have drawn a model of what they observed, and some of them included the unobservable, like waves coming from the singer's mouth or particles that make up the glass. This modeling process begins with these drawings. However, they are meant to be revised in upcoming days as students learn more. Carolyn is also asking students to look at these models and offer possible hypotheses for the glass breaking. She uses a low-pressure approach, telling students that even brief statements or guesses are useful at this point. These hypotheses are the beginnings of fuller explanations to be developed as the unit progresses. You may notice this is not like the common (but misnamed) scientific method. Teachers are using practices to "work on students' ideas," but first they have to know what those idea are.

Following the first day of the unit, Carolyn engaged students in a series of lessons. These involved combinations of introducing new ideas (such as air being made out of molecules), activities (using tuning forks to understand what frequency means), discussions (about why the students think sound is energy), and debates (about whether sound travels equally fast in all directions from the source). All these decisions about instructional activities were based on two considerations: (1) What ideas and experiences were necessary for the final explanatory models? (2) What were students thinking currently?

One particular episode on the third day of the unit started a cycle of investigation that later included practices such as Asking Questions, Planning and Carrying Out Investigations, Analyzing and Interpreting Data, Developing and Using Models, and Engaging in Argument From Evidence. The episode began with students' own curiosity about sound from their everyday experience and compelled the teacher to do an unplanned experiment with them. On this day, students came in from recess and reported that when they bounced a soccer ball on the pavement, people in different places around the playground could hear it. Some students asked if sound might travel in all directions from the source. Other students said that if this were true, it would be different from what they drew in their initial models, in which they portrayed sound as moving from the singer's mouth in a straight line toward the glass. This is a good example of how students' questions about a phenomenon can be motivated by a model. Carolyn asked how they could phrase that hypothesis in the form of a testable question and prompted them to consider what a fair test might be of the hypothesis that sound travels in all directions from the source. Students decided to go back out to the playground, arrange themselves in a large circle about 50 yards in diameter, and then bounce the soccer ball. They did this and then signaled with a raised hand when each of them heard the bounce. After returning to the classroom, the teacher asked them to draw out the results of the soccer ball experiment (see Figure 7.1, p. 146).

We refer to this as an experiment even though students were not doing the familiar school science routine of comparing the outcomes of two groups using a dependent variable. Students were, however, being systematic about collecting data to test the question "Does sound travel in all directions at the same speed?" Everyone stood the same distance away from the soccer ball, and they indicated they heard the sound in the same way. Students found out that, indeed, the sound appeared to be traveling outward in all directions at once and with equal speed. Some students, using this analogy as another kind of model to help them make sense of the anchoring event, later claimed that sound waves might be like waves created when a pebble is thrown into a pond.

Carolyn asked, "Why do you think that?" and "What might the water wave hypothesis tell us about the singer's voice?" The students thought that sound energy might fade out as the "ripples" moved farther from the source. They were then given a chance to evaluate their initial models and revise them if they desired. Carolyn prompted them by asking, "Based on what we learned, what should we add? Revise? What still puzzles us?"

Let's pause again to recap the interrelated science practices. The students' question came from a genuine interest in sound, and it was considered useful by some students because their initial models had shown sound only moving in one direction. The question made sense then, because of its relationship to the model. The students had planned and carried out an investigation on the playground, interpreted their data, and made adjustments to their models based on their new information. Whenever an activity is done in Carolyn's classrooms, she presses students to make sense of it, and then she asks if and how it helps them understand the anchoring event.

This two-day period was one of several cycles of reading, discussion, and activity. In this "soccer ball" cycle, students engaged six of the science practices listed in the *NGSS*. All of these practices, used together, served a big goal, which was to continue to refine students' explanations and models for the anchoring event. The students, for example, began to realize that more than one of their original pieces of explanation would be useful in determining why the glass broke. Midway through the unit, they revised explanations by incorporating two or more of the original ideas together—modifying them in the process—and discarding other ideas because they did not fit with new data or information they had gathered.

All of these various science practices were important for their understanding of the concept of sound as energy in a deep and connected way. Near the end of the unit, Carolyn prepared the students to construct final written explanations and provided them with sentence frames as a way to talk about evidence.

After constructing their explanations, Carolyn asked students to share their thinking with the class. In this excerpt, Emma, Tessa, and Krisna explain to their peers what sound waves are. In the process, they claim that sound waves travel across a distance and through matter using evidence from school activities and everyday experiences. Referring to their drawn model, they tap into two key pieces of an explanation: that the singer must be a short distance away from the glass (because the force of the sound energy would "build off" over distance, as Tessa explains later) and that the sound wave can travel from the singer to the glass and *through/into the glass itself.*

Tessa: "We thought that the particles—that the glass is made of particles that are vibrating … um … because the sound waves are vibrating, and when the sound waves hit the particles they … wait … "

Emma: (reading their poster) "They start … they start … they travel through the glass and make it vibrate!"

Tessa: "They make it vibrate and um … "

Emma: "When the glass vibrates—and then when the particles vibrate the glass shatters!"

Krisna: "And what we figured out is that I put my, um, ear to a table, and then I just gently, we just gently knocked on it, and then we, and then I pulled my ear back, and I knocked with the same force, and it was actually quieter. So we figured out that sound travels through wood."

Emma: "That it can travel through wood, and also, you can still hear each other in the water, and there's not that much other things underwater than water, so."

Tessa: "Like in the swimming pool."

Emma: "Uh, well the water, if you've ever tried to talk to someone who's underwater, that the water would be vibrating, and then the air's gonna vibrate, so it matters what matter you're talking in."

Tessa: "And that's what we think sound waves are."

Emma: "Vibrating anything."

Their accompanying model was an annotated drawing that expressed how the glass broke in ways that made sense to them on the basis of what they had learned. The final model from another of the student groups included a "blow up" of the air molecules bumping into one another to show the transfer of energy across space (Figure 15.3, p. 348). It also included new elements—the diaphragm of the singer and

Figure 15.3
Final model of singer shattering glass

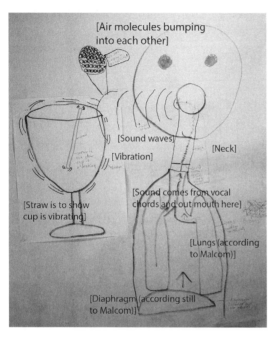

his vibrating vocal cords. Both of these additions were a result of students obtaining and evaluating written information (another science practice) they felt they needed to complete the model. They wanted to know "What's happening in the air?" and "Where did the energy come from in the first place?"

Bethany's Unit and the Use of Science Practices to Make Sense of Ecosystems

Bethany's story is a helpful contrast with Carolyn's, not because her students are older but because understanding of how an ecosystem works requires students to create different kinds of models than in the sound unit and to use different kinds of data and ideas to develop a full explanation. Bethany, for example, cannot take her students into an ecosystem to run an experiment with populations of plants and animals.

Bethany opened her unit with the puzzle of why the hare population in a boreal forest (a northern ecosystem dominated by coniferous forests interspersed with wetlands) rose and fell with predictable regularity in 12-year cycles. Her students started by working in small groups to develop hypotheses that focused on the hare population and what might have been responsible for the fluctuations. These hypotheses were just "trial balloons" for their later explanations and included statements about the possible influence of climate change, new predators, the availability of plants for food, the birthrates of hares and predators like the lynx, poachers, and the role of wildfires. Bethany then asked her students to draw out initial models that were like concept maps but still included pictorial representations of all the factors that they thought would influence the hare population. Because these separate hypotheses and models were made public, students could then reason about the ideas of their peers and how these might be resources for their own final explanations.

For example, a group of students drew a human figure in their model and suggested that once every 12 years a person went into the forest with a cigarette and started a fire. This, they argued, killed most of the hares, and it then took more than a decade for the population to recover. This became known in the class as the arsonist hypothesis. Another group of students who heard about this hypothesis offered a friendly amendment: The fire killed grasses and undergrowth that the hares depended on, and for a few years the hares starved. A third group of students had a good-natured laugh at the arsonist in the model, but one student remarked, "This is not so crazy—what about wildfires that happen naturally every few years?" They asked the teacher to use one of the classroom computers to seek out information about the frequency and consequences of wildfires. Indeed, there were data to show that, as dead plant material accumulates over the years on the forest floor, it provides fuel for small fires to become widespread in an ecosystem, and that this happens in regular cycles. After obtaining and interpreting this information, the students in all three groups agreed that the arsonist hypothesis was not absurd or unlikely when combined with ideas about the natural accumulation of combustible biomass.

Figure 15.4
Data on the changing population of lynx and hares

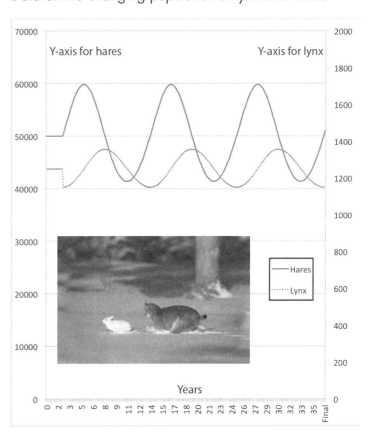

A few days later, Bethany noticed that her students' models included pictures of organisms but did not reflect how many of these organisms were in a particular population. She knew that several of the *NGSS* performance expectations included the idea of carrying capacity and how shifting environmental conditions could affect the populations of plants and animals. She decided to present new data on the changing population of one of the hare's predators—the lynx (Figure 15.4). Students noticed several things. First, the populations of both species went up and down, and in regular cycles. Second, the high point of the lynx population did not coincide with that of the hare population; the cycles were off by a couple years. And third, students saw that the lynx population was always far smaller than the hare population.

These observations produced a flurry of new questions: Why were the population fluctuations not "in sync" with each other? Why were there so few lynx when they had no natural predators? These questions arose from students using one of the science practices: Analyzing and Interpreting Data. The students had not collected any firsthand data, but they were using the secondhand data from the graphs to "identify patterns and explore relationships between variables" as described in the *NGSS*.

In addition to the new information about the lynx population, some students believed that the plants that the hares feed on also had to be at least partially responsible for how the ecosystem worked. Bethany recognized that it was time to introduce some new information on plants, so that students would not be tempted to develop explanations that were too simplistic about one animal eating another. She gave students research reports from a science journal on a shrub-like plant in the boreal forest that hares preferred as food. The data showed that as the shrubs became overgrazed by hares, they started to regenerate leaves that had fewer nutrients and fewer calories. There was even evidence that the plants began to produce chemicals that made the hares less fertile. This sparked a new line of hypothesizing by students. Some students included in their model that plants could actually control the populations of animals that fed on them!

Bethany was careful to keep the idea of food energy at the forefront of class conversations because it was so important for understanding carrying capacity (the ability of an ecosystem to support a particular population of organisms). The students asserted that "rabbit food" always had little energy value, meaning few calories. This was why hares had to forage constantly. But other students wondered what foods contained a lot of energy, and would this matter to other populations in the ecosystem? They speculated that if the hares were food for predators like lynx and coyotes, their bodies might have more energy value than the grasses and leaves they fed on. Bethany introduced to students the idea of food energy being measured in calories and also did a brief demonstration with a calorimeter and a slice of apple (calorimeters are devices that burn small samples of food to show how much heat energy they produce). Students were interested in trying out different types of food themselves, so Bethany asked them to create some testable questions about different categories of foods and the calories they might contain. She asked students to develop a way to be systematic about testing which types of food contained more energy value, using calorimeters as a measuring device. Students designed an investigation to compare the amounts of energy produced by equal masses of vegetable matter (lettuce, carrots), protein (lean meat, fish), and fats (butter, bacon fat). Students analyzed and graphed the data; they were surprised to see how much energy per gram fat produced compared with lean meat, and how little energy was produced by the kinds of vegetation that hares eat.

With this information, students returned to the population graphs and argued that each hare the lynx caught contained a lot of food energy (fats, proteins), so the lynx would not have to hunt constantly—a process that some students speculated would use up a lot of energy. But still, each lynx would need to eat many hares over the course of the year, and competition among lynx and other predators, like coyotes, for this food supply would keep both predator populations from growing out of control. Students were beginning to piece together one of the "energy" parts of the explanation—that is, why a prey population generally outnumbers the population of its predators. This argument used data from the calorimeter experiments and the population graphs. It helped students eventually incorporate the idea of energy transfers and carrying capacity into their final explanations for the rise and fall of the hare population.

Students realized that their final models would integrate *several* of the classes' initial

Figure 15.5

Students' detailed explanation of the changing hare population at the end of the unit

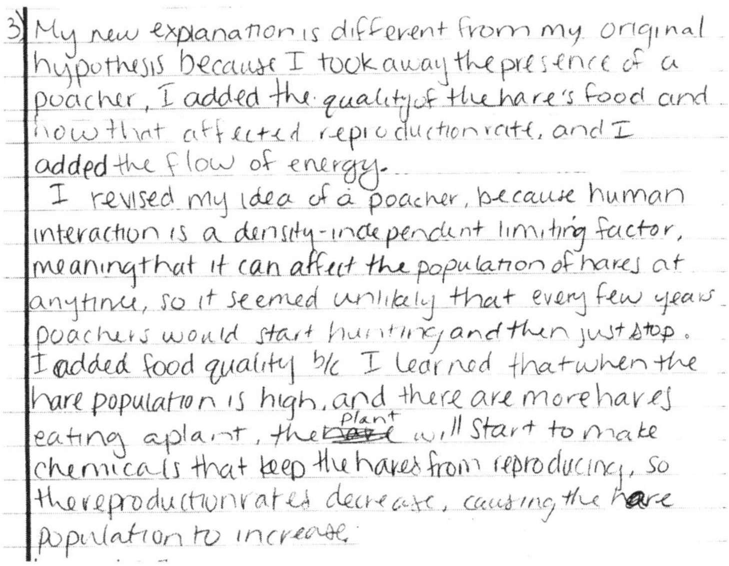

3) My new explanation is different from my original hypothesis because I took away the presence of a poacher, I added the quality of the hare's food and how that affected reproduction rate, and I added the flow of energy.

I revised my idea of a poacher, because human interaction is a density-independent limiting factor, meaning that it can affect the population of hares at anytime, so it seemed unlikely that every few years poachers would start hunting and then just stop. I added food quality b/c I learned that when the hare population is high, and there are more hares eating a plant, the plant will start to make chemicals that keep the hares from reproducing, so the reproduction rates decrease, causing the hare population to increase.

hypotheses: The introduction of new predator species, changes in climate, and the availability of food were among the ideas interwoven into the final explanations. Figure 15.5 shows one part of a detailed written explanation by a student at the end of the unit. Bethany asked students to use new ideas (such as the "density-independent limiting factor" in Figure 15.5) in their explanation as part of the logic for why the relationships portrayed in their models were convincing. This is a form of logic that supports scientific argumentation. The students' explanations also included specific ideas from the scientific journal article they had read about plants. Students additionally offered these ideas as arguments to support their explanations. Bethany asked her students to create explanatory stories for multiple parts of their models; she also asked them to structure their explanations as a reflection on how their thinking had changed from the beginning of the unit to the end of the unit. Students had done this before and knew they should talk about what they had added, what they removed, and what they revised.

Students could see that they, like scientists, were not seeking "right answers" but models that could best predict and explain what would happen in the ecosystem over time. In Figure 15.6 (p. 352), you can see one final model, which shows reciprocal relationships among all the organisms in the ecosystem that were studied. Students included many processes that were not part of their original model, such as photosynthesis as a driving process for the whole ecosystem, the idea that matter as well as energy cycles

Figure 15.6
Students' final model showing the relationships among animals in the boreal forest ecosystem

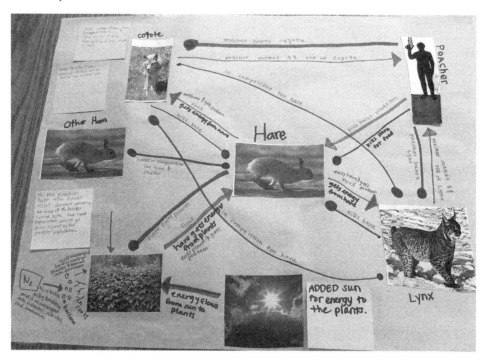

through the ecosystem, and the fact that the hares are in competition with one another for limited food and shelter.

In our work with teachers, we urge them to have their students develop both written explanations and models. As you can see in these examples, some students can express far more detailed rationales for claims in their written explanations than they can through the brief labels and diagram conventions in the models. On the other hand, students can more easily express relationships among a number of variables or factors in a model. In addition, some students are better at one form of expression than the other, and teachers can help students use their strengths in drawing relationships in models, for example, to support their written explanations.

Bethany and Carolyn engaged their students in cycles of activity, gathering and evaluating information, experimentation, and the reconstruction of models. Each cycle allowed students to make their explanations more complete, to see where their gaps in understanding were, and to use the thinking of other students as resources to advance their own understanding. Bethany, for example, pressed her students to use scientific argumentation in their talk, asking them, "What is the evidence for that part of your explanation?" "Why are you convinced by it?" "What alternative explanations are there?" As the school year progressed, students were asking each other these same questions, often without Bethany's prompting.

Conclusions: The Role of Science Practices in Knowledge Building

We've used the word *ensemble* to describe how the science practices can be used together to support meaningful learning. In Bethany's and Carolyn's classrooms, you can see how students used a range of science practices to gradually make sense of complex phenomena. In our work, we've found that it helps to coordinate the use of science practices around the understanding of an anchoring event. In this way, a connected set of ideas can be tested, revised, and added to over time. This reflects something we know from learning research—simply, that knowledge is easier to build when it is integrated with existing ideas.

It is also beneficial to organize much of the students' work around modeling and explanation. Why? Because models show relationships, but they can also show gaps in students' thinking. This is informative for both the students and the teacher. In this way, models can serve as motivation to ask new questions and propose new hypotheses. The experiments students carry out, then, are not arbitrary. They have a clear purpose—not just to answer a textbook question but also to improve their own explanatory models. This helps them decide what kind of evidence to collect and helps them argue for or against different parts of their current models with the evidence they have assembled.

Sometimes students do not need to do experiments. Occasionally, they need to obtain and evaluate new information to improve their models and explanations. This is where common methods such as brief presentations by the teacher, looking up information on the web, or using the textbook as a resource come in. Yes, there is a time for telling by the teacher and a time for the basic learning of new concepts, theories, facts, and principles. These ideas are what students *reason with* as they engage in the practices, and a classroom episode that introduces new ideas in a more didactic way should be undertaken *in service of* advancing understanding more broadly, not as an end in itself.

From the two units we've described, you can see that our teachers were not using "discovery" learning, in which students are left unguided and without direction. The teachers used strategic forms of guidance for all the science practices and for classroom discourse in general. The end result is that students were able to make sense of complex phenomena rather than just parrot back new vocabulary or reproduce textbook explanations.

If you want to make these activities part of your classroom repertoire, it is helpful to note how Carolyn and Bethany framed their units. *Framing* is how you reinforce to students what they are doing in your science classroom, and in particular, what they are "doing with ideas" over time. Framing is like establishing expectations and norms. Many of the teachers we've worked with on the *NGSS* tell their students that they expect them to share partial understandings and puzzlements with one another. The teachers then create tools to help students organize and show their thinking publicly. Teachers provide support for students on how to critique the ideas of their peers in productive ways. Students come to expect that they have to revise explanations over time rather than collect right answers.

These are norms and habits of mind that have to be worked on constantly because, in many ways, they go against the grain of common school behavior. For example, both of our teachers in this chapter cultivated expectations that "knowing" or "explaining" the sound and ecosystem phenomena would require that students integrate ideas across lessons, and that they would not move on to some new topic simply because "content had to be covered." Students who ask, "Can't you just tell me the answer?" are instead pressed further about their understanding. This takes getting used to for both teachers and students.

The *NGSS* offer teachers a chance to work together for a common purpose and toward a clearer vision of learning than ever before. Over the past few years, we have worked with dozens of science teachers at all grade levels on using science practices to support learning. We have seen these teachers succeed in dramatic ways with students, especially those who were previously hard to engage in science. Of course, there were challenges, tensions, and breakdowns along the way, but these too we learned from together so that we made adjustments and moved forward. We promised each other as professionals that we would make our own thinking visible during planning and make our teaching open to observation by peers. This way, we could continue to learn from our collective experience about ambitious forms of teaching.

References

National Research Council (NRC). 2012. *A framework for K–12 science education: Practices, crosscutting concepts, and core ideas.* Washington, DC: National Academies Press.

NGSS Lead States. 2013. *Next Generation Science Standards: For states, by states.* Washington, DC: National Academies Press. *www.nextgenscience.org/next-generation-science-standards.*

16

SUMMARY AND CONCLUSIONS

CHRISTINA V. SCHWARZ, CYNTHIA PASSMORE, AND BRIAN J. REISER

W e began this book with thoughts from Sarah and Carlos—teachers who felt satisfied and frustrated by teaching science. They wondered, "How should my class look different if I am 'doing' the *NGSS* [*Next Generation Science Standards*]? What is this focus on practices all about? I've been mostly happy with what I have been doing, so why would I want to take this on?" Their thoughts and questions are important as educators interpret and respond to new science education standards throughout the country. The goal of this book is to help educators like you, Sarah, and Carlos better understand what science and engineering practices mean, why they are worth taking on, and how to engage students in the science and engineering practices as called for in *A Framework for K–12 Science Education: Practices, Crosscutting Concepts, and Core Ideas* (National Research Council 2012).

This chapter concludes our discussion of the science and engineering practices with a summary of the big ideas from the book and a few strategies. To get a big-picture idea for how you might answer some of the questions like those from Sarah and Carlos, we revisit some important ideas about science and engineering practices we hope you have developed from reading the book, weaving in some of the main messages about bringing particular science and engineering practices into our K–12 classrooms. We finish by considering some productive ways that we can get started or continue incorporating practices into our classrooms.

Revisiting Big Ideas About Science and Engineering Practices

Some of you might wonder, "What is new about the practices in the *Framework* and the *NGSS*? What is the goal?" The most critical part of science and engineering practices as emphasized in the *Framework* and the *NGSS* is that they be used for sense-making. Compared to the way that science and engineering are typically taught and learned, *science and engineering practices move us away from just knowing information toward making sense of the world*. In other words, the goal for teaching using *NGSS* practices is to move away from sharing information and facts with students so that they merely recall that information.

The goal is to move toward helping students do science and engineering practices like asking questions, designing, investigating, and analyzing—all of which involve working through ideas from evidence and information to make sense of the world.

You might also wonder, "Wasn't learning information good enough? Why practices for sense-making?" As you might know, people don't make sense of the world just by learning facts and information. To make sense of the world, be able to use the information, and make decisions, people have to do a number of things. They have to learn what information means—where it came from, how to apply it, how to put it together, and how to test it—usually around problems that are related and relevant to their lives. Some of the facts and information emphasized in the past ways of teaching may be valuable, but only if that information does some work in helping analyze, predict, and explain the world. The emphasis on practices for sense-making provides something of a roadmap for making this transition in our science classrooms. Working with students by engaging them in the practices helps make clear what meaningful engagement in science and engineering actually looks like rather than "doing school to do school."

We see this emphasis on making sense of the world in every chapter of the book. For example, one critical piece of this sense-making process is the importance of having a phenomenon that is an event, circumstance, or experience that can be observed by one's senses to make sense of! Observation of the phenomenon raises questions about how and why the phenomenon happened the way it did. Those questions lead to other practices such as investigating and testing ideas about how the phenomenon happened. In Chapter 5, "Asking Questions" (p. 87), for example, we saw students asking how the human body gets energy. In Chapter 6, "Developing and Using Models" (p. 109), we saw students trying to make sense of what happened to the liquid in the solar still. Those students were not memorizing information about body systems or information about molecules to define them on a test. Students were asking questions, investigating, gathering information, developing and revising models, and arguing to make sense of and explain these phenomena.

To build on this point, we also emphasize that engaging students in scientific and engineering practices may be helpful for students in developing a broader sense of the scientific enterprise. This point is emphasized in Chapters 2 and 4 (pp. 23 and 59), which help situate the practices in our community's larger goals for science education: engaging students in the disciplinary ways of doing science and engineering by teaching how to engage in science and engineering practices that have been useful to others, may be useful in students' own lives, and may be useful in their future careers.

Another question that educators often ask is "Aren't science and engineering practices just new names for the same science and engineering skills that we have always been teaching students?" The *NGSS* science and engineering practices are not the same as the procedures and process skills you may know from the past. Process skills like observation, classification, and measurement focus on teaching skills without a context to understand them or a reason to apply them. For example, a common lesson at the beginning of a unit is one that teaches students to practice measuring weight using a triple beam balance to develop measurement skills. Although learning how to measure is very important and students need to learn how to do it, measuring needs to be used to figure something out, such as whether a growing plant gets heavier over time. The measurement should have a purpose related to making sense of phenomena. Teaching process skills out of context makes them rote and difficult to apply to things that matter in science and engineering.

Working with students in deep and sustained ways on developing disciplinary knowledge by engaging in the practices may allow us to incorporate this kind of skill development into meaningful work in the classroom. For example, rather than teaching students measurement or data analysis techniques in isolation, the chapters on practices show how to engage students in investigating and analyzing to figure out the answer to questions about phenomena. In Mr. Kay's class in Chapter 8, "Analyzing and Interpreting Data" (p. 159), students designed and enacted investigations using dried pasta to measure and analyze the energy of a moving object. This is a much different experience than providing students a data analysis exercise that involves giving students a force equation and data table to run the numbers through. In the same way, asking students to fill out a "claim, evidence, reasoning" table for every conclusion or with three pieces of evidence regardless of the context makes little sense when the goals are about meaningful sense-making. *When classroom communities are actively engaged in sense-making, everyone is aware of the overall goal of explaining phenomena or solving problems, and they engage in the practices to achieve these goals.* The practices not only include the intellectual work but also integrate attention to the skills, the specialized use of language or talk, and the representational tools to accomplish the work.

A related question that you might have is "Aren't the practices just the new version of the scientific method?" The scientific method typically tells students to follow a sequence of asking a question, making a hypothesis, conducting an experiment, analyzing data, and forming a conclusion. While the steps of the scientific method have some similarities with practices, *practices are not just the new version of the scientific method. Practices are used in a purposeful way to build and revise knowledge about how and why the world works (sense-making).* Do you remember how sound was investigated in Chapter 7, "Planning and Carrying Out Investigations" (p. 135)? Children were wondering why they could hear the soccer ball being bounced on pavement all over the playground and whether sound traveled out in all directions like waves on a lake. That led them to develop investigations to test their theories about how this happened. This is a very different experience than giving students a controlled, experimental lab exercise to record their results for the direction or speed of sound.

The cases in this book show how the practices are different from the commonly taught scientific method. As our introduction stated, a big difference between practices and the scientific method is that practices are purposely used to address how and why a particular phenomenon or class of phenomena occurs, not as a rigid set of steps to be followed in sequence. Addressing how and why a phenomenon occurs is critical for sense-making, because without a phenomenon to make sense of, our students cannot meaningfully learn how or why to apply scientific methods. Without the purpose of building and revising knowledge about the world (sense-making), students are simply learning to do school and fill out worksheets.

Another important point about how the science and engineering practices are different from the scientific method is that our students need to understand when and how to apply practices as they engage in sense-making and move back and forth between practices as needed, rather than following the linear steps of the scientific method. Each practices chapter shows examples of the ways in which learners are involved in deciding what needs to happen to accomplish their goals. For example, in Chapter 5, we saw students realizing the need to reframe questions about how the body gets energy to make them suitable for investigation, returning to the questioning practice, even though the class was no longer at the beginning of the unit. In another example from Chapter 5, students also returned to the questioning practice when they articulated new questions about how smell travels after realizing that their models couldn't explain how they smelled the same odor at different times in the same classroom. In Chapter 12, "Obtaining, Evaluating, and Communicating Information" (p. 259), we saw students engaged in a personal health unit making decisions about what information to share from their hand-washing investigations and culturing of microorganisms found in their schools to use in creating a public service announcement. The diagram in Figure 16.1 and the four sense-making questions (What are we trying to figure out? How will we figure it out? How can we keep track of ideas? How does it all fit together?) can help to determine which practices make sense and when to use them.

Another important question is "How are practices different from scientific inquiry?" In many ways, *science and engineering practices are the next generation of scientific inquiry.* The cases in the book show how the practices expand and build on our earlier ideas about scientific inquiry. In other words, we can think about the science and engineering practices as the 21st-century version of scientific inquiry. The practices not only involve testing hypothesis against evidence and evaluating that evidence (which was typically emphasized in scientific inquiry), but also emphasize the knowledge-building work of sense-making. In other words, the goals of the practices are to synthesize the interpretations of evidence to develop powerful explanatory ideas, such as how plants grow or the impact of collisions as described in Chapter 10, "Constructing Explanations" (p. 205), and developing and revising models that account for changes in populations or the

Figure 16.1
Science and engineering practices working together to achieve four parts of sense-making

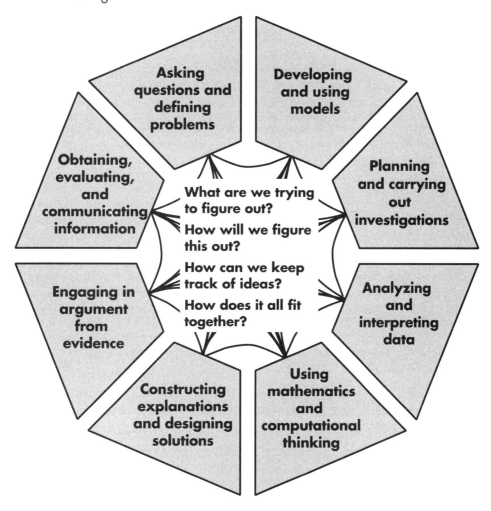

movement of matter, as in Chapter 6. This sense-making requires principled evaluation and comparison, and synthesis of ideas—leading to the critical role of argumentation—throughout all other practices. We have seen in many chapters how students consider competing ideas—competing questions, alternative interpretations of data, competing models, alternative designs, and so on.

You might wonder, "Can I teach the practices separately or in sequence?" *The science and engineering practices are interdependent, but each makes a unique contribution that is important for making sense of our world.* In other words, each practice plays a critical role, but it is incomplete unless used in combination with the others. So rather than thinking about eight independent science and engineering practices, we should think about a system of practices in which different aspects may be foregrounded at particular times that are used in a coherent way for the purposes of sense-making. In Chapter 5, we saw how questions about how smell travels and how we see light could motivate investigations that led to modeling, and how work on models could raise new questions. In Chapters 7 and 8, we saw how planning investigations and collecting and analyzing data are critical for evaluating and arguing for or against competing models and explanations. In Chapter 12, we saw how compiling and interpreting information is important throughout for helping formulate better questions, informing models, and analyzing and interpreting data.

You might also be wondering, "Can I teach the practices separately from the disciplinary core ideas (DCIs) and crosscutting concepts?" Just as it doesn't make sense to separate the practices from one another in teaching, *the science and engineering practices are inextricably linked to the DCIs and the crosscutting concepts. They cannot be meaningfully separated from one another.* The cases in the book have shown how the practices are essential in developing the DCIs and providing a context in which these ideas can be applied and extended. We have also seen how the practices provide a better "definition" for what it means to have understood a scientific idea. Rather than saying that students should learn about energy and motion, the practices enable us to specify exactly what ideas about energy and motion students should be able to use as tools to explain their world. In Chapter 8, we saw students operationalizing their ideas about energy and motion and how to measure them. They did this in service of a larger aim to investigate the phenomenon of a broken arm as a result of a bike accident.

In the same way, the crosscutting concepts are only meaningful within the context of the practices and DCIs. Crosscutting concepts can highlight and provide considerations about practices and DCIs in a manner that can only be done when students engage in the practices around the DCIs. For example, telling students that patterns exist in the world and that patterns highlight relationships in systems is a lot less powerful than asking students to look for patterns in their data, graph or plot the patterns, and then think about what a set of patterns might mean about the nature of the phenomena. We saw this in several examples, including looking at air quality in Chapter 9, "Using Mathematics and Computational Thinking" (p. 181), and looking at patterns in weather in Chapter 8 to decide whether or not it will rain tomorrow. Knowing and using science and engineering practices draw out the crosscutting concepts by helping learners better understand such aspects as cause and effect and conservation of matter within systems—and crosscutting concepts can highlight crucial aspects of the practices (goals, constraints, and rules of thumb) that move beyond the procedures of doing the practices.

Getting Started and Keeping Going

You now know that an emphasis on practices is about sense-making and how it is different from what has come before. You also have some ideas about why you might want to take this on. You might be thinking, "When should I start? What can I do next?" Here are a few answers and some basic steps for incorporating practices into classrooms.

If you haven't already started, why wait? There are many reasons that bringing *NGSS* science practices into your classroom is challenging. And finding excuses to wait may be easy. But really, there's no time like the present. Let's look at some common concerns teachers raise.

"My state didn't adopt (or may not adopt) the *NGSS*." Okay. But nobody will complain if you start to teach science more effectively and if it becomes more meaningful for your students. Even if your state has not adopted the *NGSS*, the strategies we have described in this book for engaging students in science and engineering practices have been shown to help students learn scientific ideas more effectively. Bringing practices into your classroom is likely to help your students meet your current state standards more effectively.

"We don't have the new assessments yet." Again, practices help science learning. That's the message of decades of research. *Ready, Set, Science!* (Michaels, Shouse, and Schweingruber 2007) has a nice summary of this research. For the more conceptual items on your current state test, students should do better when learning with science practices. And for the factual or definitional items, such as naming the parts of a cell, they are unlikely to do worse.

"We don't have *NGSS*-aligned curriculum materials yet." This is definitely a serious problem in making extensive changes. Most teachers will need curriculum resources to change the way they teach science year-round. But it's not a deal breaker. We don't have to change our whole year's worth of teaching at once. In the next section we'll talk about how to get started by trying to infuse practices and the discourse tools in this book by reworking a single unit.

STRATEGIES FOR GETTING STARTED

Chapter 15, "Putting It All Together" (p. 337), describes in some detail one approach to getting started in modifying curriculum and creating a context for the *NGSS* practices to occur in your classroom. A similar endeavor is to write a practice-infused storyline of your unit or lesson plans that addresses the sense-making questions "What are we trying to figure out about how or why a phenomenon occurs? How?" Figure out an anchoring phenomenon that will raise questions and an explanatory model to target. Use the DCIs for guidance. Identify phenomena that could be investigated and explained with the practices, and put together some student supports to help students understand how to engage in the practices. Develop a mini-unit—in other words, two to three weeks of instruction that transforms something you teach now into an investigation that brings in science and engineering practices. Start with one piece of something and then incorporate and revise more during the next semester or the next year.

Ideally, work with a group of teachers to develop the unit together. Share ideas as you play around with the storyline. Try out the storyline in your class and talk about it with your colleagues and even your students. It will give you valuable experience in shifting your classroom toward a practice-based classroom.

As a step toward that goal, work on creating a talk-based learning community in your classroom, in which argumentation plays a more central role. Revisit the guidelines from Chapter 14, "From Recitation to Reasoning" (p. 311), on talk moves. You will find that if your students are like typical students, who expect to get answers from teachers, learn them, and restate them, it will take time to shift that culture. Some students might not like these changes at first. Some of those students might be satisfied with the status quo because it is more predictable and in line with what they are used to doing in school. However, they do not benefit long term from this old way of learning, as they cannot build or extend this understanding over time because it is not deep or meaningful. To change your culture, begin by focusing not only on the expected definitions but also on *how we know. Ask students for their reasoning and experiences that support the ideas they are developing.* Create a culture where everyone listens and builds on ideas from one another. If students do not understand the relative strength or weaknesses of the ideas they bring up and learn about in science class, then they have not gotten the chance to truly make sense of and understand those scientific ideas, practices, and crosscutting concepts.

STRATEGIES FOR KEEPING GOING

One very important decision to make when further engaging in the *NGSS* and the scientific and engineering practices is deciding *how to choose or modify curriculum materials.* We have some recommendations for this process. First, if you are able to choose curriculum materials, do not trust that they are *NGSS* aligned even if they say they are. Many companies will repackage older curricula in an effort to continue selling them. Instead, look for those that align with the EQuIP (Educators Evaluating the Quality of Instructional Products) rubric—designed for this purpose. (You can find this at *www.nextgenscience. org/resources/equip-rubric-lessons-units-science.*)

If you have materials that are not NGSS aligned, what can you do? Our suggestion is to revise the materials in the method we outlined above in the "Strategies for Getting Started" section. In other words, find an anchoring phenomenon linked to a DCI that the curriculum might be trying to address and create a storyline that infuses practices. You may be able to use some components of the current curriculum materials—including the classroom materials themselves. Some of the same advice as in the "Strategies for Getting Started" section is helpful. Work with other teachers and professionals around you to modify the materials by forming or joining a study group, a professional learning group, or an online forum for teachers. In addition, if nothing else, you can still work on changing the culture of your classroom to make it oriented around sense-making by asking students to talk to you and each other and provide their rationales and experiences for their ideas using talk strategies from Chapter 14.

Another question you might have is *how to think about assessments with these new practices*. The current and future state assessments may be limited in how they assess rich practices. However, you can develop and use richer assessments to help you and your students develop stronger practices and sense-making. Some ways to foster richer practice-based assessments include using performance assessments, asking students to provide strong rationales for their reasoning and decisions based on knowledge and evidence, asking students to apply their knowledge in new contexts, and providing students alternative contexts to share the sense-making in one-on-one recordings as well as whole-class discussions and arguments. No one type of assessment can provide a complete view of students' learning, and the best assessments are also ones that provide richer learning and application experiences for students.

PROFESSIONAL DEVELOPMENT THAT CAN SUPPORT PRACTICES

If you are a professional development provider, you might want to coordinate support for your district to help teachers navigate scientific and engineering practices. How might you do that? First, we want to steer you away from planning a day or session on each of the practices for the reasons we mentioned earlier in this chapter. While it is useful to unpack each of the practices, and we hope this book can help provide some guidance for each, the practices only make sense in the context of integrated use in sense-making around phenomena. One of the most difficult things in editing this volume has been to manage a decision we made early on to have a separate chapter on each practice. While we still believe that this approach was fruitful—because deep understanding of each practice is essential—it may have inadvertently sent the wrong message that these practices can be disentangled and separated out. This was not our intention!

The following are some ideas to consider for professional development that mirror some of the suggestions we made to teachers: Start with one or two substantive performance expectations at a grade band or level. Think about a strong anchoring phenomenon that can form the context and purpose for the learning performance(s). To do this, find phenomenon that match the level of complexity of the learning performance, but are not so complicated that they bring in much more difficulty and other scientific ideas. The phenomena should be something of interest to students. As mentioned earlier, sketch out a storyline that addresses the sense-making questions that will guide the inquiry through the unit or subunit: "What are we trying to figure out?" "How will we try to figure it out?" As the unit or subunit evolves, fold in opportunities to determine the answer to "What are we finding out and how does this all fit together?"

The sense-making storylines around phenomena will help you figure out how to fold in practices, the DCIs, and the crosscutting concepts. Occasionally, some curriculum materials can be fairly easily modified to use this approach. For example, the BSCS (Biological Sciences Curriculum Study) 5E model (Engage, Explore, Explain, Elaborate, Evaluate; see Bybee et al. 2006), has an overall storyline that lends itself to revising the curriculum to focus on practices. For example, modify the Engage phase by determining some kinds of questions to ask, and ask your students "What are some ways to investigate them?" Be prepared for following other lines of inquiry that students may also want to pursue. The Explore phase can be enhanced to address some of the Planning and Carrying Out Investigations and Analyzing and Interpreting Data practices. Argumentation, modeling, and obtaining and communicating information can also be folded in.

If you do not have strong curriculum materials that have coherent storylines around making sense of core phenomena, a good place to start is by focusing on a few practices and folding in others over time. Developing questions, analyzing data, and developing scientific explanations, for example, might be a core place to begin. Alternatively, develop a model-based argumentation unit or subunit that asks students to develop, evaluate, and revise several mini-theories about phenomena, and compare those against data. Work on one unit or subunit at a time, and revise others as the year progresses.

Finally, there are several excellent resources that have been developed and continue to be developed to help support engagement in scientific and engineering practices. Some of those can be accessed through the National Science Teachers Association and your state science teachers association. There are others, including rich websites and programs, that can support educators as well. Several of those have been mentioned in the chapters of this book. We encourage you to continue exploring and asking for meaningful resources to help in addressing this very different kind way of teaching. It is potentially challenging, but with the right tools and support, it can be very satisfying for you and your students.

Final Thoughts

We hope that this book has helped develop a stronger argument and vision for engaging students in scientific and engineering practices, along with the beginning tools for teaching using practices. As you can see, the *Framework* and the *NGSS* can support us in bringing powerful science and engineering practices into our classrooms to help students make sense of the world. We hope the ideas in the chapters can help move this process productively forward.

We opened our book with Sarah and Carlos, teachers considering practices, who were both curious and concerned about *NGSS* practices. We think that educators can be inspired by these new ideas and strategies, and then advance, develop, and foster the next generation of learners engaged in science and engineering for our future world.

Acknowledgments

We wish to acknowledge the contributions of many teachers, students, and colleagues with whom we collaborated and thank them for opening their classrooms to us. This material is based, in part, on work supported by the National Science Foundation under Grant No. DRL-1020316 to the Scientific Practices Project at Northwestern University, Grant No. ESI-0628199 to the MoDeLS Project at Northwestern University, Grant No. DRL-0554652 and Grant No. DRL-13489900 to the University of California at Davis, grants from the Gordon and Betty Moore Foundation and the Michigan Department of Education to Northwestern University, and with support from a Math Science Partnership grant to the Connecticut Department of Education. The opinions expressed herein are those of the authors and not necessarily those of the foundations and other agencies that helped fund this work.

References

Bybee, R. W., J. A. Taylor, A. Gardner, P. Van Scotter, J. C. Powell, A. Westbrook, and N. Landes. 2006. *The BSCS 5E instructional model: Origins and effectiveness*. Colorado Springs, CO: BSCS.

Michaels, S., A. W. Shouse, and H. A. Schweingruber. 2007. *Ready, set, science! Putting research to work in K–8 science classrooms*. Washington, DC: National Academies Press.

National Research Council (NRC). 2012. *A framework for K–12 science education: Practices, crosscutting concepts, and core ideas*. Washington, DC: National Academies Press.

INDEX

Page numbers in **boldface** type refer to figures or tables.

A

Adey, P., 312

Algebra, 190

A Framework for K–12 Science Education, 3, 4, 5, 19, 38, 87, 98, 112, 118, 132, 134, 140, 156, 209, 213, 214, 218, 232, 233, 234, 236, 260, 261, 262, 263, 270, 271, 279, 283, 284, 286, 289, 338–354, 355
    agreement on the big picture, 23
    committee assumptions, 25
    committee background, 23–25
    crosscutting concepts, 23, 24
    disciplinary core ideas, 23
    goals, 17
    inquiry, defining, 24
    practices, 6
    science and engineering practices, 23
    standards, developing, 23
    three-dimensional learning, 23

A Long Way Down: Designing Parachutes, 291
    NGSS disciplinary core ideas consistent with, **292**

America's Climate Choices, 78

Analyzing and Interpreting Data, 6, 7, 13, **18**, 25, 159–180, 193, 217, 330. *See also* Data
    abstract and concrete, 161
    analysis and interpretation not a solo act, 163
    answering decontextualized questions, 162
    approaches, 161
    asking how and why, 175
    assessing student analysis and interpretation of data, 177–178
    build over multiple experiences, 179
    in the classroom, 164–175
    climate change example, 74
    common challenges, 175–178
    comparing data sources, 174
    defined, 161
    diet example, 72
    elementary school, 166–167
    engage with multiple practices, 163
    equity, 178–179
    errors and limits in data, 177
    and fast and slow thinking, **64**
    focus, 179
    GIS vignette, 159
    graphs or representations without connecting, 162
    high school, 174
    key features, 162–163
    literacy support and discourse strategies, 178–179
    local context for learning, 178
    measurements, making and recording, 162
    middle school, 170–171
    Mr. Kay's Sixth-Grade Science Class example, 167–169
    Ms. Green's Ninth-Grade Life Science Class, 171–174
    Ms. Stevens's Second-Grade Science Class example, 164–166
    observation, 175
    observation for a purpose, 175
    quantitative investigations, 170
    statistical techniques, 171
    temporal analyses, 174
    tools, 161, 162, 163, 170, 174, 179
    tracking what is being figured out, 16–17
    underanalysis or overanalysis, 176
    variety of analysis tools and procedures, 176
    Venn diagram, 166–167
    what is not meant, 162

Argumentation
    around issues that have a right answer, 240
    example, 247
    norms and expectations, 252
    perceptions about knowledge in, 253
    scientific, 232
    what it is not, 250–251

Arithmetic, 190

Asking Questions and Defining Problems, 6, 13, 16, **18**, 25, 284, 330, 356. *See also* Questioning
    "But What Would Granny Say?" vignette, 47–50

creating a safe space, 106
diet example, 71
engineering practices, 29
examples, **101**
and fast and slow thinking, **64**
getting questions started, 93
key aspects, 93
key features, 94
nature and role of questioning, 93
and phenomena, 16
problem being solved, 16
role of students and teacher, 93
student engagement in, 87–107
"There Was a Bullfrog!" vignette, 41–45
Assessment
    assessing supported claims, 256
    Engaging in Argument From Evidence,
        253–256
    of evaluation and critique, 256
    lack of, 361
    Obtaining, Evaluating, and
        Communicating Information, 263–268
    thinking about, 363
Association of College and Research
    Libraries, 265

B
Baek, H., 123
Bates, Marston, 25
Behavior policing, 107
Bell, P., 216, 273n
Bellack, A., 318
Benchmarks for Science Literacy, 27
Berkowitz, Bob, 265
Big Six, 265
Biodiversity and humans, 40, 41
Boston Public Schools (BPS), 218
Brainstorming, 294
Bransford, J. D., 60
BSCS (Biological Sciences Curriculum Study),
    364
"But What Would Granny Say? The Skylight
    Investigation" vignette, 46–50

C
Calculus, 184
Carolyn's unit and the use of science
    practices to make sense of shattering glass
    example, 344–353, **348, 349, 351, 352**
Cause and effect, simple, **64**

Cellular Respiration example, 137, 146–148,
    148, 152
Choosemyplate.gov, **70**
Christakis, Nicholas, 259
Claim, evidence, and reasoning (CER)
    framework, 212
Claim of the argument, 233
Claims
    arguing about with little concerns, 251
    assessing supported claims, 256
    and canonical accuracy, 254, 255
    defined, 233
    evaluating, 74
    evaluating and critique of, 233, 234, 236,
        237, 238, **238,** 239, 247
    evaluating and critique of, possible
        ways, **238**
    evaluating and critique of claims,
        possible ways, **238**
    evaluation and critique, 233, 234, 236,
        237, 238, **238,** 239, 247
    reason and evidence as support, 235
    reconciliation, 233, 234, 238–239
    reconciliation of claims assessment, 256
    supported, 233, 234–236, 239
    supported with reason and evidence, 235
    support for, 233, 234–236, 239
    and supports for sample performance
        expectations, **237**
    tentative, working with, 254
Classroom talk, 311–336
Climate change example, 72–78, 205–207
    analyzing and interpreting data, 75
    building scientific knowledge to design
        solutions, 76
    and fast thinking, 72
    future scenarios for global temperature, **78**
    gap in science literacy example, 74
    helpfulness of science practices, 72–73
    interpreting and analyzing data, 76, 78
    iterative risk management, 78
    mathematical reasoning, 76
    and models, 75
    news articles, **73**
    patterns in data, global climate change, **74**
    slowing down and critically evaluating
        sources of information, 73–74
    and slow thinking, 72, 76
    stabilization wedges, 76, **77**
    uncertainties, 77–78

Committee on the Objectives of a General Education in a Free Society (COGEFS), 25

Common Core State Standards
    English Language Arts, 262
    Mathematics, 204

Computational thinking, 190–192, **191**
    computational models, **191**
    processes, 190
    simulations, **191**
    tools, building, 191

Computer-based visualization models, 161, 186–187
    freedom from repetition, 187
    what if scenarios, 187

Conant, F. R., 79

Concord Consortium simulations, 125, 203

Confirmation bias, **64**

Constructing Explanations, 205–227
    argumentation, 207, 208
    assessing student explanations, 226–227
    benefits for students, 208
    in the classroom, 218–222
    classroom culture, 224
    connecting students' everyday practices with scientific practices, 222
    and construction of scientific knowledge, 208
    descriptions of processes of data, 213
    developing good questions, **223**, 223–224
    equity, 222
    evidence, based on, 210, 212
    explanations, characteristics of, 223
    explanations, defined, 207
    explanations answer question about phenomena, 211
    explanations based on evidence, 214–216
    facts or definition, 212
    how or why account of phenomena, 207, **210**
    how or why account of phenomena in an explanation, 213–214
    importance of, 208–209
    ineffective questions, **223**
    key elements, **210**
    making implicit rules or characteristics of the practices explicit, 222
    Ms. Garcia's 11th-Grade class vignette, 205–206
    Ninth-Grade Explanation About Force and Motion, 220–222
    and other practices, 216–218
    question about phenomena, **210**
    questions about specific phenomena, 207
    rusty nail example, 213–216
    scaffolding student writing, 225–226
    scientific explanation defined, 209
    scientific explanation *vs.* scientific model, 217
    Second-Grade Explanation About Seeds, 218–219, **219**
    Seventh-Grade Explanation About Seeds, 219–220
    students with disabilities, 222
    support and assess, 223–227
    talk moves, 224–225, **225**
    use of DCIs, 214
    what is not an explanation, 212–213

Constructing Explanations and Designing Solutions, 6, 7, **18**, 284, 303
    "But What Would Granny Say?" vignette, 46–50
    climate change example, 76
    engineering practices, 29
    and fast and slow thinking, **64**
    fitting it all together and meaning, 17
    scientific practice, 26
    "There Was a Bullfrog!" vignette, 41–45
    tracking what is being figured out, 17

Coulthard, M., 318

Critically evaluating sources of information, 69, 73–74, 79–80

Crosscutting concepts, 360

Culture, 35
    building classroom culture of public reasoning, 312
    changing, 362
    classroom culture, developing, 224
    establishing classroom culture, 203
    and modeling, 131
    and school, 35–36
    and talk moves, 224–225. **225**

D

Data, 65, **65**, 66, **66**, 74
    analyzing, 160
    assessing student analysis and interpretation of data, 177–178
    collected for a purpose, 143
    collecting, 142, 143
    collecting for a purpose, 143

comparing data sources, 174
descriptions of processes of data, 213
forms, 160
interpreting, 160
interpreting and analyzing, 71–72
and inventiveness, 143
predominance of, 159
problem-solving approaches, 160
selecting procedures and tools to
    measure and collect data, 143–144
strategies for gathering data to be used
    as evidence, **152**
table, 144
tools, 161
types, 80
Defining Problems, 293
Designing Solutions, 293, **293**
Developing and Using Models, 6, 13, **18,** 109–
134, 356. *See also* Modeling, models
    "But What Would Granny Say?"
        vignette, 50
    in the classroom, 122–130
    climate change example, 74, 75, 76
    diet example, 71
    essence of, 113
    explanations, 119–121
    and fast and slow thinking, **64**
    Fifth-Grade Evaporation and
        Condensation case, **123,** 123–127, **124,**
        125, 126
    fitting it all together and meaning, 17
    High School Evolution Case, 127–130, **129**
    making informed judgments, 69
    model development and revision, 111
    practices and crosscutting concepts, 30
    scientific practice, 26
    support and assess in classroom, 131–132
    tracking what is being figured out, 17
    water evaporation example, 109–110, **110**
Developing Models, 293, **293**
Diet example, 67–72
    building scientific knowledge to build
        solutions, 68
    building scientific knowledge to design
        solutions, 70–72
    changing diets, 71–72
    Choose My Plate, 70, **70**
    and evidence, 69
    how science practices can help, 68
    interpreting and analyzing data, 71–72

media messages, **68**
models, 69
nutrition label, 70, **70**
planning diets, 70–71
slow down and critically evaluate
    sources of information, 68, 69
Disabilities, students with, 222
Discussions with students, 28–29
DiSessa, A.A., 202
Diversity of sense-making, 36
Driving Question Board (DQB), 90, 91, **91, 92,**
    96, 97, 102

E
Ecosystems Dynamics, Functioning, and
    Resilience, 40
EiE engineering design process, 293, **293,**
    298–299
Eisenberg, Mike, 265
Elementary Children Design a Parachute
    example, 291–303, **292, 293, 294, 295, 298,**
    300, 301, 302, 303
Elementary school, 263–264
    Elementary Children Design a Parachute
        example, 291–303, **292, 293, 294, 295,**
        298, 300, 301, 302, 303
    Ms. Smith's second/third grade class
        vignette, 229–231
    Obtaining, Evaluating, and
        Communicating Information as Part
        of a Fifth-Grade Personal Health
        Exploration example, 273–275, **274**
    Second-Grade Explanation About Seeds,
        218–219, **219**
    Upper-Elementary Students Arguing
        About Their Models vignette, 243–245
Energy balance, **75**
Engagement of students, 87–107, 356
    multiple ways to engage, 252
Engaging in Argument From Evidence, **18,**
216, 217, 229–257, 303
    arguing about claims with little
        concerns, 251
    argumentation and constructing an
        answer, 240
    arguments and disagreement, 240
    arguments and the process through
        which explanations are made, 240
    arguments unrelated to disciplinary core
        ideas, 250

assessment, 256
claim of the argument, 233
claims and canonical accuracy, 254
claims and supports for sample
    performance expectations, **237**
claims supported with reason and
    evidence, 235
in the classroom, 243–249, 241
climate change example, 74
collaborative building of scientific
    knowledge, 321
critically evaluating sources of
    information, 69
diet example, 71
disrespect and disagreement, 251
encourage questioning, 255
equity, 251–252
evaluating and critique of claims, 233,
    234, 236, **237**, 238, **238**, 239, 247
and fast and slow thinking, **64**
focal question clarity, 252
High School Students Arguing for an
    Engineering Design Decision vignette,
    248, **249**
ideas treated as tentative, 233
importance of, 231–232
Middle School Students Arguing About
    Their Explanations vignette, 245–247
Ms. Smith's second/third grade class
    vignette, 229–231
multiple activities and group sizes, 254,
    255
multiple ways to engage, 252
and other practices, 241–242
practice explained, 232–240
producing and critiquing knowledge *vs.*
    receiving ideas, 232
reconciliation of claims, 233, 234, 238–239
reconciliation of claims assessment, 256
scientific argumentation, 232
scientific argumentation, norms and
    expectations, 252
scientific argumentation, perceptions
    about knowledge in, 253
scientific argumentation, what it is not,
    250–251
scientific argumentation around issues
    that have a right answer, 240
scientific argumentation example, 247

scientific practice, 26
strategies for teachers, 254
student presentations with little
    discussion, 251
support and assess, 253–256
supported claims, 233, 234–236, 239
tentative claims, working with, 254
"There Was a Bullfrog!" vignette, 41–45
Upper-Elementary Students Arguing
    About Their Models vignette, 243–245
verbal exchange, 241
vs. constructing an explanation, 242
why questions, 254
written argument, 233, 241, 242
Engineering is Elementary, 293, 295, 296, 297,
    298, 298–299
Engineering Practices, 29, 283–307
    asking questions, 299
    Asking Questions and Defining
        Problems example, 285–288
    carrying out the investigation, 301, 302
    connect with science or mathematics, 305
    Constructing Explanations and
        Designing Solutions example, 288–290
    defining the problem, 299
    designing and using models, 302
    determining the nature of the problem,
        287
    Developing and Using Models, 300
    EiE engineering design process, 293, **293,**
        295, 296
    Elementary Children Design a Parachute
        example, 291–303, **292, 293, 294, 295,**
        298, 300, 301, 302, 303
    engaging in argument from evidence, 300
    engineering and science goals, 283–284
    engineering design process, 305
    equity, 290–291
    fostered by engineering design, 291–304
    to frame science units, 306
    High School Students Design a
        Parachute example, 303–304
    imagine solutions, 299
    investigation, 295, 296–297
    iterative nature, 303
    planning, 300
    planning of investigations, 297, 299, 301
    real-world problems, 290
    as a sense-making tool, 290–291

Using Mathematics and Computational Thinking, 301

what an engineering activity should include, 305

what engineering practices are not, 306

why questions, 297

Engle, R. A., 79

EQuIP (Educators Evaluating the Quality of Instructional Products), 362

Equitable learning, 33–58

creating with questioning supported, 106–107

Equity

Analyzing and Interpreting Data, 178–179

Constructing Explanations (science practice), 222

in designing investigations, 154–155

Engaging in Argument From Evidence, 251–252

Engineering Practices, 290–291

equitable learning, 33

modeling, 131

Obtaining, Evaluating, and Communicating Information, 270

talk in the classroom, 316

Evans, Sara, 61*n*

Evaporation and condensation example, 194–197, **195, 196**

Evidence, **210**

to be explained, **210**

diet example, 69

empirical, 100

engaging in argument from, 300

to provide support, **210**

Experiments, 353

Explanations

answer question about phenomena, 211

arguments and the process through which explanations are made, 240

based on evidence, 214–216

characteristics of, 223

defined, 207

developing, 139

developing with investigations, 139

goal, 213

how or why account of phenomena in an explanation, 213–214

models, 119–121

and models, 119–121

students constructing their own, 51

and time, 216

what does not count, 212–213

F

False certainty, **64**

Federal Trade Commission, 69

Fourier, 72

Fox News, 74

Front-Page Science: Engaging Teens in Science Literacy, 265

G

Geographic information system (GIS), 159

Geometry, 190

GET City, 46, 47

Giere, R., 115

GIS vignette, 159

Goldsmith, Tony, 135

Google Spreadsheets, 203

Gouvea, J. S., 115

Graphs, 161

Gravity example, 138

Great Lakes City Youth Club, 46

H

Herd immunity example, 259–260

Higgs boson, 27

High school, 174, 264

High School Evolution Case, 127–130, **129**

High School Students Arguing for an Engineering Design Decision vignette, 248, **249**

High School Students Design a Parachute example, 303–304

Ms. Garcia's 11th-Grade class vignette, 205–206

Ms. Green's Ninth-Grade Life Science Class, 171–174

Ninth-Grade Explanation About Force and Motion, 220–222

High School Students Arguing for an Engineering Design Decision vignette, 248, **249**

High School Students Design a Parachute example, 303–304

Hook, 342

Hypothesis testing, 7

I

Inquiry, defining, 24

Inquiry-based science learning, 27–28

Interdependent Relationships in Ecosystems, 40

Intergovernmental Panel on Climate Change (IPCC), 74, 76, **78**

Investigations, 136, 295, 296–297
 and arbitrary questions, 140–141
 big ideas (BI) person, 154
 clarifier, 154
 conducting, 187
 and controlled experiments, 142
 conversations about why and how, 140
 cookbook exercises, 140
 coordination, 139
 data collecting, 142
 data collecting for a purpose, 143
 equity in designing, 154–155
 explanations, developing, 139
 lab activities, 140
 multiple, 139
 path to truth, 140
 planning of, 297, 299, 301
 progress monitor, 155
 questioner, 155
 roles, 154–155
 skeptic, 155
 what to investigate, 139

J

Judgments, making informed, 69

K

Kahneman, D., 61, **64**

Kirkpatrick, Doug, 275

Knowledge goals in classroom, 114

Krist, C., 106

L

Lab activities, 140

Learning Design Group at the Lawrence Hall of Science and Amplify Learning, 245

Lee, O., 278

Lehrer, R, 202

Less is more, 156

Life cycles of plants and pollinators example, 285–288

Life experiences, 131

Literacy

gap in science literacy example, 74
 goals, 265
 literacy-related skills, 262
 support and discourse strategies, 178–179

Literacy and practices, 59–81

Literacy for Science: Exploring the Intersection of the Next Generation Science Standards and Common Core for ELA Standards (NRC), 262, 277

Local Ground, 181

M

Macrander, C. A., 197

Marcarelli, K., 265

Mathematical reasoning, climate change example, 76

Mathematics, 161, 174
 describing relationships, 190
 patterns and trends, 189
 quantitative description of a system, 189
 relationship between mathematics and computational reasoning and modeling, 193
 universal language, 185

Mather, M., 59

Medin, D. L., 35, 270

Meltzoff, A. N., 134

Memorization, 269

Middle school, 170–171, 263–264
 Middle School Students Arguing About Their Explanations vignette, 245–247
 Mr. Kay's Sixth-Grade Science Class example, 167–169
 Obtaining, Evaluating, and Communicating Information as Part of an Eighth-Grade Classroom Debate example, 275–277, **276, 277**
 Seventh-Grade Explanation About Seeds, 219–220

Middle School Students Arguing About Their Explanations vignette, 245–247

Modeling
 computer modeling, **186,** 186–187
 connecting to phenomena, 130
 contextualized, 130
 and equity, 131
 getting started with, 132
 importance of, 111–112
 making sense of the world, 112
 mathematical modeling, 185–186

and mathematics and computational reasoning, relationship, 122
multiday endeavor, 130
and other *NGSS* practices, **120**
and other practices, 118–122
practice, 192
practice, what is not intended, 116
practice defined, 112–113
in science *vs.* in school, 112
and scientific reasoning, 133
and sense-making, 131–133
social practice, 130
teacher modeling, examples, 104
Models, 65, **65,** 66, **66,** 74
applying, 117
building testable, predictive representations of, 185
climate change example, 75
criteria, 118
defined, 113–116, **115**
defined, distinct from representational forms, 114
defined, how they are used, 114
developing, 117
diet example, 69
evaluating, 117
and explanations, 119–121
explanatory model, 119
goal of science education to think with, 117
model-based explanation, 119
model-based reasoning, 117
models for *vs.* models of, **115,** 115–116
parsimony, 65
revise through questioning, 104
students engaged in thinking about, 118
support for using, 76
think about, 117
tools for reasoning, 114
as underlying rules and description of a system, 121
using in science, 117–118
Using Mathematics and Computational Thinking, 192
Molecular Workbench, 125, **126, 191**
Moon phases cases
agreement, disagreement and consensus, 14–15
explanation, getting to, 14
investigating the question, 13–14

modeling, 112–113
questions for, 13
Moon phases examples, 8–13
Mr. Kay's Sixth-Grade Science Class example, 167–169
Ms. Garcia's 11th-Grade class vignette, 205–207
Ms. Green's Ninth-Grade Life Science Class, 171–174
Ms. Smith's second/third grade class vignette, 229–231
Ms. Stevens's Second-Grade Science Class example, 164–166
Mural and Music Arts Project (MMAP), 52

N
National Research Council (NRC), 23, 78, 209, 232, 260. *See A Framework for K–12 Science Education*
National Science Foundation (NSF), 34
National Science Teachers Association, 364
National Science Education Standards (NSES), 24
NetLogo, 203
NetLogo simulation of Maxwell-Boltzmann distribution, **191,** 192
Newton, Isaac, 189, 304
Next Generation Science Standards (NGSS), 3, 4, 5, 15, 18, 19, 38, 87, 98, 118, 132, 134, 138, 145, 147, 150, 151, 156, 167, 171, 192, 197, 200, 208, 214, 218, 223, 232, 233, 236, 241, 250, 253, 260, 261, 262, 263, 271, 279, 283, 284, 287, 288, 290–291, 303, 305, 311, 312, 318, 319, 337–354, 355, 362
emphasis on science practices, 59
goals, 17
lack of curriculum-designed materials, 361
not adopted in your state, 361
practices, 6
writing of, 23
Ninth-Grade Explanation About Force and Motion, 220–222
Nutrition labels, **70**

O
Observation, 175
Obtaining, Evaluating, and Communicating Information, 6, **18,** 193, 217, 259–280
communicate scientific and engineering-related information, **268**

decontextualized vocabulary work, 269
defined, 260–261
disciplinary literacy-related skills, 262
early grades, 263
English language learners (ELLs), 277, 278–279
equity, 270
evaluate scientific and engineering-related information, **267**
expository multimodal texts, reading, comprehending and interpreting, 277–278
and fast and slow thinking, **64**
figuring it out, 16
focus on final form, 270
getting started, 277–279
herd immunity example, 259–260
high school, 264
importance of, 261–263
interaction with scientific information as an add-on, 269
literacy goals, 265
and memorization, 269
misinterpretations, 268–269
Obtaining, Evaluating, and Communicating Information as Part of an Eighth-Grade Classroom Debate example, 275–277, **276, 277**
Obtaining, Evaluating, and Communicating Information as Part of a Fifth-Grade Personal Health Exploration example, 273–275, **274**
Obtaining, Evaluating, and Communicating Information as Part of a PreK Research Activity example, 271–273, **272**
obtain scientific and engineering-related information, **266**
overlap with *CCSS ELA*, 262
preK, 263
repeated communication, 270
resources, 265
science-specific resources, 265
scientific practice, 26, 27
and scientists' and engineers' time, 261
stand-alone reports of science facts, 269
support and assess, 263–268
and symbols, 262
technical vocabulary, 269
text, variety of, 269

tracking what is being figured out, 17
upper-elementary and middle schools, 263–264
what is not intended, 269
what is science, 270
and working with text, 262
Ocean Acidification example, 151–152, **152**
Ocean example, 138
Opportunities to learn in science, expanding
    engage diverse sense-making, 39
    notice sense-making repertoires, 39
    support sense-making, 39
Osborne, Jonathan, 23–31
Oxbow, 40

P
Pattern finding, **74**
Patterns in evidence, 65, **65,** 66, **66,** 74
Paulo's Parachute Mission, 292
"Pause: Without Me Nothing Matters ... : Lyricism and Science Explanation" vignette, 51–54
Performance expectations, claims and supports for sample, **237**
Phenomena, 15–16
    explanation as goal of science, 51
    explanations answer question about phenomena, 211
    how or why account of phenomena, 207, **210**
    modeling connected to, 130
    observation of, 356
    question about, **210**
    and questioning, 98
    questions about specific phenomena, 207
PhET
Phase Change Simulator, **191**
Simulations, 203
Planning and Carrying Out Investigations, 6–7, **18,** 25, **64,** 135–157, 161, 216, 293. *See also* Investigations
    Cellular Respiration example, 137, 146–148, **148, 152**
    in a classroom, 144–154
    different from current classroom, 138–139
    figuring it out, 16
    getting starting, 155–156
    Gravity example, 138
    initial conversation about goals for data collection, 143

integrated with other practices, 136
Ocean Acidification example, 151–152, **152**
Ocean example, 138
results and observations, 144
The Role of Gravity in Our Universe example, **149,** 149–150, **152**
Sound as Waves example, 145–146, **146, 152**
Sound Energy example, 137
starting, 136–138
supporting in the classroom, 142–144
testable questions, 142
"There Was a Bullfrog!" vignette, 41–45
what is not included, 141
What kinds of data or observations help answer our question, 142
Planning for a unit based on *NGSS,* 337–354
anchoring event, developing, 340, 342
anchoring events, sound and ecosystem unites, 342–344
Carolyn's unit and the use of science practices to make sense of shattering glass example, 344–353, **348, 349, 351, 352**
ensemble practices, 353
essential question, 342
experiments, 353
framing, 354
hook, 342
modeling and explanation, organize student work around, 353
norms and habits of mind, 354
performance expectations relevant to sound, **339**
questioning your own understanding, 338
standards related to ecosystems, **341**
teaching a unit, 344
unpacking curriculum and standards, 337–340
Poker face/evaluation avoidance, 324–326, 333
Practices
assessments, thinking about, 363
continuing, 361, 362–363
coordinating, 15–18, 17
and crosscutting concepts, 30
and crosscutting concepts, connections, 30
in culturally expansive learning, 39–54

curriculum, choosing and modifying, 362
and disciplinary core ideas (DCIs), 360
equitable learning, 33
to evaluate a claim, 74
and fast *vs.* slow thinking, **64**
getting started, 361–362
how people can use science practices, 61–64, 65–66
intertwined knowledge and practice, 65
materials not aligned with *NGSS,* 362
practice-infused storyline, 361
and scientific inquiry, 358–359
and scientific knowledge, key relationships between, **66**
as a step forward, 27–29
strategies for continuing, 362–363
teaching order, 359–360
when and how to apply, 358
why people need science practices, 61
working together for sense-making, **359**
Practices, focus on, 5–7
PreK
Obtaining, Evaluating, and Communicating Information as Part of a PreK Research Activity example, 271–273, **272**
Princeton University, 76
Principled reason, 74
Problem
defining, 299
determining the nature of the problem, 287
Productive disciplinary engagement, 79
Professional development, 363–364
Project BudBurst, 80

Q
Question
decontextualized, 162
sense-making, 6, 16, 99
substituting easier, **64**
testable, 142
well-thought-out or framing question, 329
why, 254
Questioning
about specific phenomena, 207
arising throughout sense-making, 99
bellwork, 103
beyond yes/no, 100

building culture, 107
building explanations and models, 101
celebrate questions, 106–107
in the classroom, 88–97
collaborative work with students and
    teachers, 87, 100
discussion reflection sheets, 107
Driving Question Board (DQB), 90, 91,
    91, 92, 96, 97, 102
empirical evidence, 100
encourage participation, 107
encouraging, 255
explanatory questions, 98, **101,** 104
good questions, 100–101
How and Why Does Odor Travel
    scenario, 88–92, **91, 92**
how and why questions, 95
importance of, 87–88, 98–99
leading into other practices, 99
moving investigation forward, 104
naming or categorizing, 100
nature and role of questioning, 93
phenomena, 98
and phenomena, 98
piggybacking, 100
policing behavior, not ideas, 107
and prior knowledge, 99
problematic questions, **101**
returning to questions, 102–103
revise models, 104
revising questions, 105
scaffolding questioning, 103–104, **153**
in science and engineering practices,
    98–101
sparked by other practices, 99
as starting point, 99
supporting in the classroom, 102–105
taking stock of progress by answering,
    105
What Is Going On in My Body So I Get
    the Energy to Do Things scenario,
    94–97, **96, 97**
what it is not, 102
why, 297
your own understanding, 338
Quinn, H., 278

R
Ready, Set, Science!, 361
Reconciliation

of claims, 233, 234, 238–239
of claims assessment, 256
Repertoires
    noticing, 39, 50
    using to support engagement, 55
Resnick, L., 312
Resources, 265
Risk management, iterative, 78
The Role of Gravity in Our Universe
    example, **149,** 149–150, **152**
Rowe, M., 323
Rusty nail example, 213–216

S
Scaffolding
    questioning, 103–104, **153**
    student writing, 225–226
Schauble, L, 202
Schwartz, D. L., 60
Science and engineering practices, 23–24
    spheres of activity, **26**
Science education
    build scientific understanding, 67
    design solutions to problems, 67
    goal to think with models, 117
    prepare students to slow down
        and critically evaluate sources of
        information, 67
    reform goals, 4
Science for All Americans, 27
Science goal to connect information, 160
Science literacy and practices, 59–81
Science practices
    sense-making, **18**
Science practices and science literacy
    examples
        climate change, 72–78
        diet, 67–72
Scientific explanation
    defined, 209, 214
    vs. scientific model, 217
Scientific inquiry, 25
    and practices, 5–7, 358
Scientific knowledge
    building through argumentation, 231
    building to design solutions, 70–72
    building to design solutions, strategies,
        79, 80–81
    collaborative building of, 321
    construction of, 208

not static, 231
Scientific literacy
    data, 65, **65,** 66, **66**
    defined, 59
    defining the work of, 60–61
    evaluate and connect data, patterns, and
        models, 66
    gap, and climate change, 74
    how, 60–61
    how people use science practices, 61,
        65–66
    how scientifically literate people use
        science practices, 61–66
    importance of, 59
    key strands, 65, **65**
    models, 65, **65,** 66, **66**
    patterns in evidence, 65, **65,** 66, **66**
    as preparation for sense-making, 60
    in the science classroom, 79
    when, 60
    why people need, 61
    why people need science practices, 61–64
Scientific method
    myth, 25
    new version, 357–358
    when and how to apply practices, 358
Scientific practice, 26, 27
Scientific practice
    Developing and Using Models, 26
Scientific reasoning
    modeling, 133
ScratchEd, 203
Scratch simulation of water, **191, 192**
Second-Grade Explanation About Seeds,
    218–219, **219**
Seeing is believing, **64**
SenseMaker, 277
Sense-making, 6, 132
    analyzing and interpreting data, 6
    cases, 8–13
    constructing explanations and designing
        solutions, 6
    coordinating practices, 15–18
    developing and using models, 6
    engage diverse sense-making, 39
    fitting it all together and meaning, 17–18
    four parts, **359**
    how to figure it out, 16
    incremental process, 16

keeping track of what is being figured
    out, 16–17
modeling, 131–133
and *NGSS* and *Framework,* 355
notice sense-making repertoires, 39
observation of phenomena, 356
obtaining, evaluating and
    communicating information, 6
planning and carrying out
    investigations, 6
problem being figured out, 15–16
questions, asking, 6, 99
questions, key, 16
repertoires, noticing, 39, 50
repertoires, using to support
    engagement, 55
and science practices, **18**
shifting to equability, 36–38
supporting, 39
support sense-making, 39
using mathematics and computational
    thinking, 6
using sources, 66
Seventh-Grade Explanation About Seeds,
    219–220
Simple cause and effect, **64**
SiMSAM (Simulation, Measurement, and
    Stop Action Moviemaking), 195
Sinclair, J., 318
Skills, new *vs.* old, 356–357
Sound
    Energy example, 137
    as Waves example, 145–146, **146, 152**
Sources
    amnesia, **64**
    using, 66
Stabilization wedges, 76, **77**
Stagecast Creator simulation of diffusion,
    191, 192
Statistical analysis tools and techniques, 161
STEM careers and underserved communities,
    34
Stories, not statistics, **64**
Students doing work themselves, 31
Students with disabilities, 222

T
Tables, 16
Talk in the classroom
    academically productive talk, 314–315

additional tools, 328–329

ask for evidence or reasoning tool, 321–322, 332

belief in possibility and efficacy of, 315–316

benefits, 312

challenge or counterexample tool, 322, 332

and classroom activities, 330–331

clear academic purposes, 328–329

different practices, different talk, 329–331

divergence, 324

do you agree or disagree and why tool, 322, 333

encouraging motivation to participate, 327

equitable, 316

evaluation as detrimental, 325

goals for productive discussion, 317–318

ground rules, 316–317

how and why the tools work, 326–328

improvisational, 315

IRE drawbacks, 314

IRE pattern, 313–314

key components of academically successful, 315–318

managing intelligibility of the talk, 327

monitoring equitable participation, 327

nonevaluative responses, 325

as participation, 312

partner talk tool, 319, 332

poker face/evaluation avoidance, 324–326, 333

and professional practices, 312

recitation, 313

respectful, 316

say more tool, 319–320, 332

science and engineering practices support each other organically, **330**

some tools better than others, 328

supporting conceptual coherence and rigor, 327

talk-based learning community, 362

teacher lecture, 314

that apply to all four goals, 323–326

that help individuals, 319–320

that help students dig deeper into reasoning, 321–322

that help students orient to and listen to each other, 320–321

that help students think with or apply reasoning to ideas of others, 322–323

tools, 318–329

vehicle for student relationship with science, 311

verifying and clarifying by revoicing tool, 320, 332

wait time, 323, 333

well-established norms, 316–317

well-thought-out or framing question, 329

who can add on tool, 323, 333

who can restate that tool, 320, 332

Talk moves, 224–225, **225**

Text

variety of, 269

working with, 262

"The Modeling Toolkit" (Windschitl and Thompson), 132

"There Was a Bullfrog! Investigating the Oxbow" vignette, 41–45

Thinking, 62–64

fast *vs.* slow, **62,** 62–63

fast *vs.* slow, and science practices, **64**

fast *vs.* slow, climate change example, 72–73, 76

fast *vs.* slow, features of, **63**

problems inherent in, 62

Three-dimensional learning, 23

Tools, 161, 162, 170, 174, 187

ask for evidence or reasoning tool, 321–322, 332

challenge or counterexample tool, 322, 332

computational thinking, 191

do you agree or disagree and why tool, 322, 333

how and why the tools work, 326–328

partner talk tool, 319, 332

say more tool, 319–320, 332

some tools better than others, 328

use a range of, for analysis and interpretation, 163

variety of analysis tools and procedures, 176

who can add on tool, 323, 333

who can restate that tool, 320, 332

U

Underserved communities

creating meaningful learning opportunities for, 46
European American cultural practice, 34, 41
misreading of repertoires, 37–38
resources in schools, 34
and science education, 33–34
science instruction in, 34–36
and STEM careers, 34
and teacher role, 34
vignettes, 39–55
Universal Design for Learning (Rose and Meyer), 252
Upper-Elementary Students Arguing About Their Models vignette, 243–245
Using Mathematics and Computational Thinking, 6, **18,** 25, 161, 181–204, 217, 301
    air quality vignette, 181–184, **182, 183**
    in the classroom, 194–197
    classroom culture, establishing, 201
    climate change example, 74
    computational thinking, 190–192, **191**
    computational tools, 189
    computer modeling, **186,** 186–187
    connect to students' observations and questions, 199
    creating formulas, 185
    defined, 184
    diet example, 71
    elementary school example, 194–197, **195, 196**
    engage in argument with evidence, 192
    equity, 198
    and fast and slow thinking, **64**
    features or properties that influence the system, 189
    find out what works best for your classroom and curriculum, 203
    flashcards, quizzes, wikis, or videos to introduce concepts, 194
    focus away from vocabulary, 198
    formula application, 185
    getting started, 200–204, **201**
    introducing in your classroom, 202–204
    investigations, conducting, 187
    key components of a system, 188
    mathematical modeling, 185–186
    mathematical or computational descriptions, 189
    mathematics, 189–190

    models, 185, 192
    motivating students, 203
    over K–12, 197
    ownership over science ideas and explorations, giving to students, 198
    practice defined, 188–189
    practices and crosscutting concepts, 30
    predator–prey system simulation, **186**
    quantitative specification, 199
    recognizing student interest, 203
    relationship between mathematics and computational reasoning and modeling, 193
    relationships between parts and properties, 189
    relationships to other practices, 192–193
    scientific practice, 26
    spreadsheets without reasoning, 194
    support and assess, 198–200
    toolkit, 189
    tools, 187
    tracking what is being figured out, 17
    Using Science Stories to Make Mathematical Connections example, 200–202, **201**
    using simulations or data to illustrate target, 194
    ways to organize and formalize observations, 199
    what is not included, 194
    what to check for, 199–200
    word problems or data tables to reinforce formulas, 194
    working in partnership, 204
Using Science Stories to Make Mathematical Connections example, 200–202, **201**

V

Valdés, G., 278
Varun's Quest: Into a Bee Tree and Other Adventures (Goldsmith), 135
Vensim, **186,** 203
Vocabulary
    decontextualized, 269
    technical, 269

W

Waves and Their Applications in Technologies for Information Transfer, 104
Wilkerson-Jerde, M.H., 197

Wind turbine example, 288–290
Wolfram Demonstrations model of Maxwell-
    Boltzmann speed distribution, **191**
Workforce, scientists and engineers, 59

World Book Encyclopedia, 269
World Meteorological Organization, 75
Written argument, 233, 241, 242